Masterpieces of Contemporary Jurisprudents in China

Gathering the best Chinese legal scholars in different legal fields, this series collects the most representative academic monographs selected and renewed by authors themselves, showing the world updates and development of legal research in China for a more active academic controversy. Through a living publication, this series can provide a full view of legal theoretical research in China to all English readers, and also could be a reliable and effective reference for foreign jurists that specialise in different fields to search answers about China.

More information about this series at http://www.springer.com/series/15924

Jiahong He

Methodology of Judicial Proof and Presumption

法律出版社
LAW PRESS · CHINA

Springer

Jiahong He
School of Law
Renmin University of China
Beijing, Haidian District
China

Sponsored by Chinese Fund for Humanities and Social Sciences.

ISSN 2523-3025 ISSN 2523-3033 (electronic)
Masterpieces of Contemporary Jurisprudents in China
ISBN 978-981-10-8024-1 ISBN 978-981-10-8025-8 (eBook)
https://doi.org/10.1007/978-981-10-8025-8

Jointly Published with Law Press China

The printed edition is not for sale in China Mainland. Customers from China Mainland please order the print book from Law Press China.

Library of Congress Control Number: 2017963862

中华社会科学基金 (Chinese Fund for Humanities and Social Sciences) 资助

Printed on acid-free paper

This Springer imprint is published by the registered company Springer Nature Singapore Pte Ltd. part of Springer Nature
The registered company address is: 152 Beach Road, #21-01/04 Gateway East, Singapore 189721, Singapore

We cannot see history, and some truths might be lost forever. We can only try to recover them with pieces of evidence. How to obtain and use the evidence constitutes procedural justice, without which the people will lose confidence in social justice.

Jiahong He, *China Daily*, 30/04/2015

To my lovely granddaughter,
Luo Yiran

Preface

The basic function of judicial proof is to revisit the past, and hopefully to reconstruct the past event with the materials of evidence. It is just like to see something through a glass darkly, as said by Saint Paul. In my life, I have had some opportunities to revisit the past, in one way or the other.

I was born in Beijing more than 60 years ago. During the Culture Revolution, in 1969, I went to a farm in Heilongjiang Province, the very northeastern part of China. In November 1977, after working on the farm for 8 years, I returned to Beijing, became a law student 2 years later, and then a law professor. For many years, I tried to forget the hard life on the farm, but my effort could only push the memory deeper and deeper. When I passed the age of 50, the desire to revisit the farm became stronger and stronger, even in my dreams.

...As I stand between the two tall, familiar mud buildings, the Great Barracks and the Great Mess, I feel a rare excitement. But it is shaded with anxiety and unease.

The old company commander seems happy to see me. He calls his company of young people together to listen to me give a talk in the Great Barracks. This is unexpected, but I have given many lectures during my years in education so I am never troubled by nerves. I stand by the door of the barracks building and tell them of my life in the company, of the struggles and triumphs of those years. I watch the young people who are sitting on heated kang beds that line the room. As I grow more animated, their strange faces remain stony. I find it hard to stifle my alarm and, flustered, struggle to find the right words. I start to gibber. When I finally finish speaking there is a smattering of applause. The commander seems unhappy too: he barely speaks to me before leaving. I am so used to enthusiastic acclaim from my audiences that I don't know what to make of this cold reception.

Disheartened, I leave the barracks and wander aimlessly along the muddy paths. Before I know it, the sky has turned dark. Hungry, I head for the Great Mess to buy something to eat, but I have no mess tin and the staff will not lend me a bowl and chopsticks. Everyone stares at me coldly. Their smiles seem to mock me. I have to escape.

I go looking for the commander but he is nowhere to be found. The faint yellow light from the windows of the mud buildings makes me realize how lonely and wild this mountain is. A shiver runs up my spine. I stumble towards the dark-tiled building where I had once lived and push open the door. In the dim light I can make out that the two kang beds are covered with sleeping people. The spot I had once slept in is free, but there is no bedding. I ask my roommates if I can sleep here, and where I might find bedding. They are lying on their stomachs, wrapped in their bedrolls, and look at me without speaking, a strange smile on their faces. Embarrassed, I have no choice but to lie down fully clothed on the cold, hard kang, and suffer until dawn...

This was a dream. More precisely, it was a recurring dream I had. Although the details differed each time, the basic content and tone were the same. I don't know why I had this dream so often, nor did I know how to interpret it psychologically or psychoanalytically, but it had indeed long been a part of my life—something I could neither end nor forget. Eventually I really did revisit the farm. This time, it was no dream.

On the morning of June 10, 2005, straight after giving a lecture at the Law School of Heilongjiang University in Harbin, the capital of the province, I went on a "trip of remembrance", accompanied by some professors of the university. We drove through many towns—Anda, Mingshui, Baiquan, Kedong, and Bei'an—before reaching the famous dormant volcano range of Wudalianchi at 4 o'clock in the afternoon. After we checked in to our hotel, a female guide drove us to see Old Black, the most well-known volcano in the whole range. We passed the meandering Stone River and the magnificent Stone Lake, and then abandoned the car and continued on foot, climbing to the peak of Old Black. I was filled with both terror and joy. Terror at the majesty of nature: the summit and the gigantic, awe-inspiring crater at my feet. And joy at its beauty: the blue skies, the towering volcanoes spread across open countryside, and the interconnected lakes.

The farm where I had once been an educated youth was not far away, but during all my years here I had only heard talk of the five lakes of Wudalianchi, and had never been able to visit them. Tourism was an incredibly decadent concept in those years of the Cultural Revolution when, as our generation like to say, our "passion first burned bright then died away".

Back in Wudalianchi after dark, the town's streets were still lively and it was not until after midnight that the noise dwindled to just the occasional bark of a dog. I lay on my bed, physically exhausted but unable to sleep. The events of 30 years ago replayed in my mind like a film.

...At 1 o'clock in the morning of 7th October, 1969, we pull into Zhaoguang railway station after more than thirty hours of travel. We push our way noisily through the dimly lit station square, bags on our backs and in our hands, like crowds fleeing calamity. Eventually we are divided up into military trucks. My truck leaves the station, leaves Zhaoguang, and heads into the pitch-black wilderness. The headlights illuminate a small patch of road ahead; each frequent jolt of the vehicle shoots beams of light deep into the night sky. By the light of the stars we can make out the contours of the dark mountains that surround us. If we pass the lights

of a house, there is a clamor from the back of the truck. After bumping along the uneven road for around an hour, we finally come to a stop next to two mud buildings. The company commander comes to meet us and tells us we will spend the rest of the night in the storeroom next to the mess hall. There is a kang *bed in the storeroom. The jars by the wall stink of old pickled vegetables. Nineteen of us, boys and girls, squeeze together in this tiny building to spend the first night of our new lives as educated youths. I can clearly hear stifled sobs after the lights are extinguished...*

I finally drifted off to sleep as the sky was turning hazy. When I woke up, a trickle of sunlight had made its way through a gap in the curtains. I looked at my watch: not yet 6 o'clock. After a quick wash, I went downstairs and into the square outside the hotel. It was the day of the Dragon Boat Festival and also of Wudalianchi's annual Water Festival, so the early morning streets were already bustling with pedestrians and cars. I went around the back of the hotel and stood near a small tree. It was calm here. I gazed at the distant volcanoes. Breathing the clean air in deeply, I took in the scenery around me, but my mind had already flown to my second hometown, the place I had been parted from for 28 years. I had offered up 8 years of my youth in the Eighteenth Company of the Seventh Regiment, First Division, Heilongjiang Production and Construction Corps for the Shenyang Military Region.

After breakfast, we bypassed the city of Bei'an and took a smooth, broad, asphalt highway to Zhaoguang, where Zhaoguang Farm was headquartered. As soon as we drove into town, my heart started to beat more quickly, and I felt a nameless anxiety. I scanned both sides of the road, but not a single home or shop was like the Zhaoguang of my memory. Finally, I recognized the now somewhat rundown old building of the regimental hospital, the familiar train station next to a large chimney, and a few buildings and streets that I thought I had seen before. We paused briefly at the intersection with the "Second Battalion" railroad, where we were joined by comrades from the local law court and Procuratorate, and then headed straight for our old Battalion Headquarters.

The roads around here were all made of sand. Because it had recently rained heavily, the surface was covered in deep ruts, and many sections were still muddy. The road brought back strong memories. Back then, I had traveled along this road countless times, sometimes on foot, sometimes in a cart or tractor—occasionally I even drove the tractor myself. We jokingly called these basic tracks our asphalt-lined freeways, though in fact as soon as the wind blew, they became a sea of dust and the slightest drop of rain turned them into a mud pit. The landscape surrounding us was also very familiar. Fields stretched out to the horizon; long unbroken stretches of forest covered the land in an enchanting green, buildings dotted the hillsides, and the clear rippling valley pools added vitality to the panorama. It made me realize for the first time how beautiful the Great Northern Wilderness was—especially the distant blue skies with their white clouds. Perhaps, this proves the truth of the saying that "distance creates beauty"—distance is not merely a scientific measure but also a psychological one. My life now was far removed from my past life here.

I was still in a reverie as car drew to a halt. A stocky, gray-haired old man was stood next to the lead car of our group, talking to the people inside. He came toward our car and I stared at him. It was Chen Wang, the man who used to drive the tractor years ago. I jumped out of the car and went to greet him. We embraced tightly, both excited. It turned out that one of my hosts here had told Chen Wang that I was coming back, so he had been waiting at the roadside since early that morning. I visited his home (he had long since been transferred from the company to the battalion), then I went to the Battalion Headquarters to meet the current leader. After that Chen Wang and I drove to the last stop of my trip: the Eighteenth Company farm where I had once lived and worked.

The farmland was as large as ever, the road as muddy, the sun-baked buildings, and the stick fence had not changed. But the storeroom where we had spent our first night and the great canteen where we ate every day no longer existed, and neither did the Model Theater and Great Hall where we had so often sung and held meetings. The well-house where we learned to draw water by pulley had gone. The field where our tractor and our tools were kept had changed beyond all recognition. Only the maintenance room still stood there forlornly. The Great Hall that we had built from stone and tile ourselves to use as a social club had long since been divided into offices. The dark-tiled building used by the educated youths and the small school behind it had both become homes for workers. What had originally been the basketball court was now divided into vegetable plots for each household. However, the rows of small poplars we had planted, running along the road by the fields, had grown into large trees, testimony to the sweat and ideals of a generation of educated youths.

As soon as the old workers heard that one of the educated youths had come back, they rushed out of their homes. They surrounded me in the yard, pulling at my hands in excitement, telling me simply how much it meant that one of us had come back, and gushing with excitement and pride at having seen me on the television. They showed me around, discussing people and events of the past. It was a real wrench to learn that so many people with whom I had worked back then had died. Then, a middle-aged woman came over and asked me if I recognized her. When I couldn't, everyone laughed and told me she was the daughter of the former canteen team leader, Old Zhang. I had spent 2 years as Mess Officer, responsible for the canteen work. Eventually, I recognized the little girl from all those years ago and sighed with regret. That's when it hit me: we had been young people in the prime of life back then, and now we were all over fifty.

Reluctant to say goodbye again so soon, all the old workers from the Eighteenth came back with us to the Battalion Headquarters. I had always believed that the Company and Battalion Headquarters were a long way apart. But in a four-wheel drive Toyota, the distance was nothing. Back at headquarters, we ate a typical northeastern meal at the restaurant run by Chen Wang's son. Chen Wang very seldom drank alcohol. He was 65 years old now and still barely touched a drop, but today he was so happy he drank until he was red in the face. During the course of the lavish meal, he would often take my hand to tell me of things that had happened back then, and of more recent events. After the meal, we had to hurry back to Harbin. Chen Wang stood next to the car, his eyes moist, and held my hand. My eyes also brimmed with tears. I saw the vague past.

In the summer of 2006, I went back to Heilongjiang again. I was invited to give a lecture to the judges, prosecutors, and police officials in Harbin. Serving as Deputy Director-General of Department of Dereliction of Duties and Infringements of Human Rights, the Supreme People's Procuratorate, I lead a group of researchers to the City of Yichun for empirical study of wrongful convictions. We wanted to revisit the original scene of the wrongful conviction case of Shi Dongyu and to learn more details about it. Shi Dongyu was sentenced to death with 2-year suspension in a murder case in Heilongjiang in 1989 and exonerated in 1995. I will discuss the case in details in Chap. 6.

Criminal cases are events of the past, so judicial personnel cannot see the facts directly and must use the indirect means of reviewing a range of evidence to do so. In other words, they must reconstruct the case with evidence. Consequently, to judicial personnel, the facts of a case are like a flower seen in a mirror. The flower may, indeed, objectively exist, but what the judges see is the image formed by reflection or refraction in the mirror. And that mirror has been broken and shattered during the course of the case, so if they wish to establish the facts of the case, they must first collect all these shattered, scattered fragments and put the mirror together again before they can attempt to understand the flower. In many cases, however, the fragments collected are incomplete or eroded, and the judges can see only the image of the flower, which in some instances is so opaque as to be distorted. That is to say, if there is no evidence, there is no way to know the facts of the case, and a fact established through evidence did not necessarily happen in reality.

Theoretically speaking, in judicial proof of a criminal case, people may see three "facts" through evidence. Fact I is the fact originally happened in the reality. Fact II is the fact basically established by the prosecution with the evidence. Fact III is the fact finally found by the court with the evidence. We may put the three facts into two categories. Fact I is an objective fact, while Fact II and III are subjective facts. Since Fact III has the legal effect on the parties of the case, it may also be named as a "legal fact".

In a given case, the three facts may be same or similar and may be dissimilar or even very different. For example, in the case of Shi Dongyu, Fact II established by the People's Procuratorate, as well as Fact III found by the Intermediate People's Court in 1991, was that Shi Dongyu was the murderer. However, with some new evidence appeared in 1994, the fact was reconstructed as that the true perpetrator in the case was not Shi Dongyu. This should be the objective fact in the case, i.e., Fact I. So, Fact II and III in the original trial of the case were very different from Fact I.

In criminal trials, the judicial personnel should try their best to make Fact III as identical to Fact I. However, the evidence may not always be sufficient, and the facts may not always be clear. With the shortage of evidence in a case, the judicial personnel could only see the case "through a glass darkly". This is by no means an easy job. This is a challenge to all judges in judicial proof. And this is the main theme for this book.

This book was originally published in Chinese by Law Press China in 2012. In 2015, it was awarded a fund for translation (Chinese Fund for the Humanities and Social Science) by National Planning Office of Philosophy and Social Science, China. I would hereby express my heartfelt thanks to the Office, as well as to Miss Wu Fang, the editor of Law Press China. Meanwhile, I would like to acknowledge my debts to those who have assisted me in the preparation of this book. They are Chi Xiaofei, Gong Mingyu, Jiao Li, Meng Sui, Tian Huiwen, Wu Lingli, Yuan Hui, and Zheng Xueying. I am also greatly indebted to Emily Jones and Jesse Field who helped with the writing of some parts of this book in English.

Beijing, China Jiahong He
May 2017

The original version of the book was revised: Section numbering has been updated. The erratum to the book is available at https://doi.org/10.1007/978-981-10-8025-8_13

Contents

About the Author

Jiahong He, S.J.D. Northwestern University, USA (1993); Professor of law, Director of the Center for Anti-Corruption and Rule of Law, Director of the Center for Common Law, and Director of the Institute of Evidence, the Law School of Renmin University of China; Specially Invited Adviser of the Supreme People's Court, Expert Adviser of the Supreme People's Procuratorate, Deputy Director-General of Department of Dereliction of Duties and Infringements of Human Rights of the Supreme People's Procuratorate, PRC (2006–2008); member of the editorial boards of *the Journal of Financial Crime* and *the Journal of Money Laundering Control*, UK; and *International Journal of Criminology and Sociology*, Canada; Member of the Ethics Committee, Federation International of Football Association.

Prof. He has published dozens of law books and five crime novels in Chinese. His monograph, *Back from the Dead: Wrongful Convictions and Criminal Justice in China*, has been published in English by the University of Hawaii Press. It has also been published in French and German. His series of novels featuring lawyer Hong Jun tackle unsolved crimes, the righting of injustices, rape, murder, and corruption. The first two books in the series, *Hanging Devils* and *Black Holes*, have been published in English by Penguin. His novels have also been published in French, Italian, and Spanish.

In recent years, Prof. He has been invited to give lectures on the issues of criminal evidence, wrongful convictions, judicial reform, and anti-corruption to judges, prosecutors, lawyers, and police officers all over China. He has also been invited to give lectures around the world, in places such as New York University, Columbia University, and Cincinnati University in USA; University of Sussex, University of London (SOAS), Kingston University, Leeds University, and Chatham House in UK; the Seventh University of Paris, Aix-Marseille University, and the Third University of Montpellier in France; Max-Planck Institute for Foreign and International Criminal Law, and Korber Forum in Germany; Australian National University, La Trobe University, and Curtin University in Australia; Nagoya University in Japan; the University of Bergen in Norway; and the National University of Mexico and University of Chiwawa in Mexico.

Abbreviations

APL	Administrative Procedure Law
CiPL	Civil Procedure Law
CPC	Communist Party of China
CPCL	Common Provisions of Civil Law
CPL	Criminal Procedure Law
DIC	Discipline Inspection Commission (CPC)
GPCL	General Provisions of Civil Law
IICPL	Interpretation of the Supreme People's Court concerning the Implementation of the Criminal Procedure Law of People's Republic of China
MOJ	Ministry of Justice
MPS	Ministry of Public Security
NPC	National People's Congress
PEAP	Provisions on Several Issues Concerning Evidence in Administrative Procedure
PECP	Provisions on Several Issues Concerning Evidence in Civil Procedure
PEDPC	Provisions on Several Issues Concerning Assessment and Judgment of Evidence in Death Penalty Cases
PEIE	Provisions on Several Issues Concerning Exclusion of Illegal Evidence in Criminal Cases
PRC	People's Republic of China
PSB	Public Security Bureau
SPC	Supreme People's Court
SPP	Supreme People's Procuratorate

Chapter 1
The Dilemma of Judicial Proof

Contents

1.1 Case Illustrations

1.1.1 The Case of Peng Yu, Nanjing

On 20th November 2006, a 64 year-old retired woman surnamed Xu was waiting for a bus at Nanjing's Shuiximen Square station when two buses arrived at the same time. Xu rushed towards the second bus, which had fewer passengers. As she passed the back of the first bus, a 26 year-old man, Peng Yu, was the first passenger to

J. He, *Methodology of Judicial Proof and Presumption*,
Masterpieces of Contemporary Jurisprudents in China,
https://doi.org/10.1007/978-981-10-8025-8_1

alight by the rear door. Peng, anxious to catch his connection, happened to glance backwards and found Xu lying on the ground. He immediately helped her up and, together with her family who were soon on the scene, took her to hospital. While there, he paid over 200RMB in medical fees on Xu's behalf. The diagnosis found that Xu had sustained a fracture of the left femoral neck in the fall, and had to be hospitalized for hip replacement surgery, necessitating fees in the tens of thousands.

Xu filed an action against Peng in Nanjing's Gulou District Court on 12th January 2007, accusing him of having caused injury to her through a collision, and claiming compensation for medical and nursing expenses, disability, and emotional distress totaling 136,000RMB.

The main evidence in the case included:

1. The statements of the two parties. The plaintiff Xu alleged that, on the morning of 20th November 2006, she was waiting for a number 83 bus at Nanjing's Shuiximen bus station. At approximately 9.30 am, two number 83 buses pulled into the station. Just as the plaintiff was preparing to get on board the second of the two vehicles, the defendant alighted at speed from the back door of the first bus, knocking down the plaintiff and causing a fracture to the neck of her left femur, resulting in hospitalization and surgical treatment. The defendant Peng argued that at the time of the incident he was the first passenger to alight from the bus. Before he did so, other passengers still on board were pushing him. However, after alighting there was no collision between him and the plaintiff. The defendant in no way harmed the plaintiff, in fact, after discovering that she had fallen to the ground, he helped her out of a desire to do a good deed.
2. The testimony of an eyewitness from the scene, Chen Erchun. The witness stated that he did not see how the plaintiff fell; he first became aware of her when she was already on the ground, at which time the defendant was already helping her.
3. Transcripts of conversations at the local police station. After the incident, the City Center police station in the Transport Security Division of Nanjing's Public Security Bureau processed the incident according to the law, and produced transcripts of all conversations. The date of the electronic files of these transcripts and file notes was 21st November 2006, that is, the day after the incident. Their contents demonstrated that Peng claimed that he had not collided with Xu, but that she had run into him. During the trial, the officer in charge of the investigation appeared in court and described the process of the investigation, and testified that Peng Yu had admitted that there had been contact between the two parties.

On 3rd September 2007, Gulou District Court issued its verdict. The judgment ruled that there had been a collision between the two parties, but the key facts of the case were unclear (i.e. whether the defendant had run into the plaintiff, or vice versa) and, therefore, the defendant should pay only 40% of the plaintiff's costs. Neither of the two parties was satisfied with the ruling and appealed to the higher courts. A second trial in the Nanjing Intermediate Court was about to start when Peng and Xu reached a settlement: Peng agreed to make a single payment of 10,000RMB in compensation to Xu; both parties agreed that neither would publish any discussions or material relating to the case in the media (including but not limited to television, radio, newspapers, magazines, and online publications); and, both parties agreed that, once charges were withdrawn, neither would seek enforcement of the ruling from the civil case heard in Gulou District Court.[1]

1.1.2 The Case of Xu Yunhe, Tianjin

On 21st October 2009, at around 11 am, Xu Yunhe was driving a car with the local registration plate HAK206 north along Huiqu Road in the Hongqiao area of Tianjin. He was approaching the Red Star Macalline furniture retail store when an elderly woman surnamed Wang climbed over the safety barrier running west-east and fell to the floor injured. Xu Yunhe took her to the People's Hospital for treatment. The case later came to court when there was a dispute between the parties over whether or not there had been a collision, and over financial compensation.

The main evidence in the case included:

1. The statements of the two parties. The plaintiff Wang claimed that the front of the car driven by the defendant hit her leg and, after she was hit, she lay across the bonnet before falling to the ground. The defendant Xu alleged that the plaintiff leapt over the safety barriers on Hongqi Road and in the process of doing so fell onto the first lane of cars running north along the Hongqi Road. He immediately applied the brakes and steered to the left and, when his car stopped in front of the plaintiff, neither of them came into contact with the other.
2. The evidence provided by the plaintiff. Including: photographs taken by the plaintiff of the car with the registration plate HAK206, proving that paint had come off the vehicle in certain places; medical bills, prescriptions and statement of expenses, medical certificate showing lost working time, the expert testimony classifying the plaintiff's injuries as a level eight disability, and the receipt for the costs of the expert examination.
3. The expert opinion. The *Expert Opinion on Road Traffic Accident Evidence Traces* submitted by the Tiantong Forensic Science Center in Tianjin, stated: "It has not been possible to ascertain the place where the passenger vehicle with the license plate HAK206 came into contact with a human body". Later a supplementary statement from the same body explained that the meaning behind that statement was that they could not be sure that the vehicle had come into contact with Ms. Wang, but neither could they eliminate that possibility.

On 16th June 2011, the People's Court in the Hongqiao District of Tianjin found Xu Yunhe 40% responsible, and ordered him to pay Wang compensation of 108,606.34RMB, which included 87,454.80RMB in disability damages. The defendant did not accept the verdict and lodged an appeal. On 22nd August 2011, the

[1] For written judgment see: Xu v. Peng Yu for Personal Injury Compensation, *Peking University Law Database* www.pkulaw.cn, Reference CLI.C.85983; and also Xu Jiling, Nanjing Government Announces: Peng Yu Admits Knocking over the Old Lady Xu, *Liaowang News Weekly*, from *Phoenix News website* http://news.ifeng.com/society/1/detail_2012_01/16/12003299_1.shtml.

Tianjin Number 1 Intermediate People's Court opened its hearing of the case. Having obtained the consent of both parties, the court appointed the Forensic Expert Center at the Institute of Forensic Science under the Ministry of Justice to assess Wang's injuries. On 28th December 2011, the Center published *Expert Opinion Number 157 (2011)*, which found that "the damage to Wang's right knee is consistent with an injury resulting from contact with a large, blunt, external force. This injury would be difficult to sustain from a simple fall, and it is possible that they were caused by contact with a car." On 19th January 2012, the Tianjin Number 1 Intermediate People's Court rejected Xu Yunhe's appeal and upheld the initial ruling.[2]

1.1.3 Case of Wu Weiqing, Guangdong

At around 1 pm on 31st December 2013, Wu Weiqing (male, 45) from Zhangxi town in Dongyuan County, Guangdong Province, was riding his motorbike from Zhonglian village towards Zhangxijiezhen. When he reached a section of road called Zhonglian Street (a tarmacked road, 3.6 m wide), he came up behind Zhou (male, 79) walking with the support of a stick in the middle of the road. After Wu Weiqing overtook Zhou from the right, he realized that the man had fallen to the floor, so he immediately stopped the motorbike by the roadside and went back to help him. Zhou claimed that Wu had knocked him down. Wu denied this, but still took Zhou to hospital and paid his medical bill. The following day, Zhou's relatives demanded over 100,000RMB in compensation from Wu. The two parties asked the police to mediate in this dispute. According to the records kept by Zhangxi police station, Wu acknowledged that he had sounded his horn when he was on that section of road, but denied colliding with Zhou. Zhou insisted that he had been knocked down by Wu and also denied hearing the horn of a motorbike. Mr. Zhou's daughter said she believed that, if Wu had not knocked her father down, he would not have been so kind as to take him to hospital and pay his medical fees. On the third day following the incident, Wu called his family to list his grievances, and then committed suicide by drowning himself in a pond.[3]

Dongyuan County police station set up an investigation team to look into the incident. They questioned the parties involved, their family and other connected people and collected evidence, but were unable to ascertain if the old man fell down, or was run over by Wu Weiqing. Both parties stuck to their own version of events. Although Zhou contradicted himself in his original statement about whether he fell or was run over, when questioned formally by police he insisted he was knocked

[2]For written judgments see: Wang Xiuzhi v. Xu Yunhe for Road Traffic Accident Personal Injury Compensation, Reference CLI.C.515512 *and* Xu Yunhe and Wang Xiuzhi Road Traffic Accident Personal Injury Compensation Appeal Case, Reference CLI.C.1339057, both *Peking University Law Database*, www.pkulaw.cn. See also *360Baike Encyclopaedia* entry for Xu Yunhe, http://baike.so.com/doc/3136413.html.

[3]See *People Website*, ['I Helped Him, I Didn't Hit Him', Man Drowns Himself to Prove Innocence], http://edu.people.com.cn/n/2014/0107/c1053-24041290.html.

down by Wu and said, "If he didn't knock me down, how could I have got such bad injuries?" Wu's decision to commit suicide to prove his innocence attracted public sympathy, but the investigators could not use his suicide as proof that Zhou's fall was accidental. There were no direct eyewitnesses in the case. A villager who lived near the scene, also called Zhou, overheard the initial argument between the two parties but did not see the incident personally. Lan Xiaodong, who worked with Wu at a building company, said that before he died, Wu had called him to ask if he was responsible if his horn had scared someone. Mr. Lan asked if Wu had hit the old man, and Wu replied that he had not.[4] A week later, the investigation team published its conclusion: "There is no surveillance footage from the scene and, despite lengthy investigations and interviewing many witnesses, the police have not been able to identify any direct eyewitnesses. From the investigation of the scene, the examination of the location of the wounds and of the injured party's skin, an inspection of the vehicle concerned and testimony from other interested parties, we have reached the conclusion that there is currently no direct evidence to prove whether or not the two parties were involved in a collision or scrape, however neither can we eliminate other reasons that might have caused Zhou Huoqian to fall to the ground and sustain injuries." Neither side was satisfied with the conclusions published by the police.[5] At the time of writing, Wu Weiqing was already deceased and Zhou was still recuperating, but the truth behind the incident was still uncertain.[6]

In all three cases above, there were shortages in the evidence presented for judgment. Because neither eyewitness testimony nor surveillance footage existed, the only evidence to prove what had happened were the statements from the parties concerned. It is difficult to avoid selfish subjectivity and bias in statements of this nature, because of individuals' vested interest in the outcome. Moreover, it is very easy for perception and memory to be influenced and distorted by both subjective and objective factors. In incidents such as these, the perceptions and memories formed instantly by the parties concerned may not necessarily be a precise reflection of objective fact. In other words, even if someone is truthful, the content of their statement may not match what actually happened. For instance, when an old person falls they may claim they were knocked over, but they may have made a cognitive error. Therefore, in a situation where both parties adhere to conflicting versions of events, judges must rely on other evidence to establish the facts of the case. In the three case illustrations above, however, neither side was able to put forward sufficient evidence to support their position, which therefore slightly obscures the disputed facts. Take the written judgment in Xu Yunhe's first trial where, despite the plaintiff's testimony, the investigation records and the expert opinion issued by the forensic science centers,

[4]See *China News Network*, Man Who Helped Old Man Then Accused of Knocking Him Over Kills Himself to Prove Innocence; Before Death Tells Daughter He Doesn't Want to Die, http://www.chinanews.com/sh/2014/01-07/5708453.shtml.

[5]Zheng Tianhong and Wu Tao, Briefing on the Dongyuan, Guangdong Case 'Man Who Helps Old Man Falsely Accused, Commits Suicide': No Evidence to Prove 'Man Knocked Down Old Man', *Xinhua News*, http://news.xinhuanet.com/legal/2014-01/14/c_118964733.htm. Zeng (2014).

[6]The information on the three case studies above was collated by Zhang Xiaomin, Ph.D. student at Renmin University of China from 2012 to 2016.

the court was unable to establish that the defendant's vehicle had come into contact with the plaintiff, but also unable to eliminate that possibility.[7] When establishing the facts of a case, judges must have sufficient evidence, but in reality, there are frequently shortages of evidence. This is particularly prominent in disputed criminal cases—that is, cases of evidence shortage.

1.2 Empirical Analysis of the Standard of Evidence in Criminal Cases

As mentioned in the Preface, criminal cases are events of the past, so judges cannot establish the facts directly and must use the indirect means of reviewing a range of evidence to do so. There are two types of evidence in criminal cases: the first, that which objectively exists when a case happens—for example, traces of physical evidence on the body and in the surrounding environment during a homicide, or the impressions created in the minds of the people involved in the case. Because this kind of evidence lies in the real, objective world, it is possible for it to be discovered by the people handling the case, and also possible for it to remain undiscovered. This is called "potential evidence". The second kind is evidence collated and used by either those handling the case or the parties involved in the case; in a murder, for example, this includes all the different types of evidence collected by the investigators, such as confessions, bloodstained clothes, or the murder weapon. This kind of evidence can be discovered and used by the people handling the case, therefore it is called "real evidence". In the criminal justice system, real evidence is the only resource which truly has the ability to develop into proof.

In criminal justice, there is always less "real evidence" than "potential evidence"; that is, the evidence that the investigators or parties involved gather and use is less than the evidence which objectively exists. In most cases, it is not possible for these people to discover and use all of the evidence related to the case which objectively exists. To put it another way, the evidence which objectively exists is of a large quantity, and it is hard to avoid a situation where some of the potential evidence is not converted into real evidence—no matter whether that is because the people involved have not discovered the evidence or, having discovered it, have not used it. This situation, therefore, results in a shortage of evidence in the judicial process.

In order to study and further understand the phenomenon of the shortage of evidence and the patterns at play within it, we have selected a sample of 45 wrongful convictions whose verdicts have now been corrected, and against this sample have conducted an empirical comparison with another 20 criminal cases where the evidence was reliable and sufficient for conviction. To ensure that both groups were

[7] Wang Xiuzhi v. Xu Yunhe CLI.C.515512, *Peking University Law Database*, www.pkulaw.cn.

analyzed to the same standard, the charge in all of the cases selected[8] was intentional homicide.[9]

1.2.1 *The Quality and Quantity of Evidence*

"Standard of proof" is the level that judicial proof must reach and is the criterion for the evaluation of the outcomes of judicial proof. "Standard of evidence" refers to the specific requirements of the standard of proof in a case that enable a verdict to be reached. Generally, the standard of proof includes the standard of evidence, but it places emphasis on the degree to which all the evidence in a case proves the facts of a case, or on the degree to which a judge has understood and used the evidence to determine the facts of a case. Therefore, in some countries' legal codes, the description of the standard of proof focuses only on the standard of subjective knowledge that a judge should have, and contains no description of objective standards of evidence—for example, the standards of "beyond reasonable doubt" and "inner conviction". The standard of proof stipulated in China's Criminal Procedure Law (CPL, without special indication, which refers to CPL of 2012) clearly describes the intention of the standard of evidence. Article 195 therein states that the standard of proof required for a court to find a defendant guilty is that "the facts of the case are clear [and] the evidence is reliable and sufficient". Here, the phrase "evidence is reliable and sufficient" is the standard of evidence.

The standard of proof directs the facts of the case, and the standard of evidence directs the evidence that can be used to reach a verdict. From the point of view of judges, the latter has more operability. To ensure the facts of a case are correctly established, both the quality and quantity of evidence in the judgment must reach a certain standard. What we call the "quality of evidence" refers to whether the substance of the evidence can correctly corroborate the facts of a case—including both the relevance and legitimacy of the evidence and, crucially, its true reliability. What we call the "quantity of evidence" refers to the amount of evidence used to prove the facts of a case—including both the type and quantity of evidence as well as the number of factual elements in a case that it supports. The standard of evidence referred to above ("the evidence is reliable and sufficient") includes requirements around both the quality and quantity of evidence. "The authenticity of evidence used for deciding the case has all been confirmed in accordance with statutory procedures" is the quality requirement, and "There is evidence for each fact that serves as the basis for conviction and sentencing" is the quantity requirement. Some scholars argue that "sufficient" is the quantity requirement and "reliable" the quality requirement.[10]

[8]In wrongful conviction cases where the judgments have subsequently been corrected, "guilty" refers to the charge and conviction in the original trial.

[9]The case studies were conducted by Xu Yuedi, Ph.D. student at Renmin University of China from 2014 to 2017.

[10]Li (2013).

Although such division is a little simplistic, it does fundamentally communicate the spirit of the standard of evidence. Of course, in terms of standards of evidence in individual cases, the totality of the evidence in a case must be enough to form a complete, harmonious system of proof sufficient to obtain a single, definite verdict to the exclusion of all other possibilities.[11]

When studying the phenomenon of "shortage of evidence", we must first make clear the standard of evidence sufficient for conviction, and from this develop our discussion around both the quantity and quality of evidence.[12] To this end, we have selected 20 criminal cases which resulted in a secure conviction and which can be defined as having reliable and sufficient evidence. The criteria for selection of these cases were: (1), there was no dispute over how the law was applied (2), the party/ies concerned had no reason for objecting to the guilty verdict and made no appeal; (3), the written judgment was fairly complete and detailed in its description of the evidence of guilt.[13]

The written judgments in these cases do not always all retain the "original flavor" in their descriptions of evidence and there is evidence of "modification and reworking", especially in the wording of the evidence. For instance, witness interrogations, victim statements and defendant interrogations are usually conducted multiple times by investigators yet written judgments will usually cite them only once, or record the content in general terms. Also, in written judgments judges typically adopt reportage style when citing witness testimonies, victim statements, defendant confessions, using forms of expression such as "that same day", "it can be seen", and so on. As long as none of the parties involved disputes the verdict, phrases of this nature present no major problem, however in the event of a dispute, they can conceal differences of understanding. Consequently, our knowledge of the substance of the evidence in these case studies is also, to a certain extent, relative.

---

[11]Ma and Wang (2014).

[12]The object of our discussion is evidence proving facts of substantive law, and does not include evidence proving sentencing specifics or extra-legal hindering causes.

[13]The 20 cases are all taken from *Peking University Law Database*, and the case numbers are 177 (2014) Liuzhou Intermediate Court Criminal One Final, 00165 (2014) Shaanxi High Court Criminal One Final, 63 (2011) Heilongjiang High Court Criminal Three Final, 92 (2015) Yongzhou Intermediate Court Criminal One Final, 17 (2014) Shandong High Court Criminal Four Review, 103 (2014) Shandong High Court Criminal One Final, 40 (2014) Shandong High Court Criminal One Review, 299 (2014) Hunan High Court Criminal Three Final, 00354 (2014) Anhui High Court Criminal One Final, 00184 (2014) Shaanxi High Court Criminal One Final, 3689 (2014) Beijing Number One Intermediate Court Criminal One Final, 96 (2014) Tianjin High Court Criminal One Final, 412 (2014) Beijing High Court Criminal One Final, 118 (2014) Jilin High Court Criminal One Final, 16 (2014) Shandong High Court Criminal Two Review, 163 (2014) Guilin Intermediate Court Criminal One Final, 35 (2014) Shandong High Court Criminal One Review, 36 (2014) Shandong High Court Criminal One Review, 2-1 (2010), Shandong High Court Criminal Four Final, 304 (2014) Guangdong High Court Criminal One Final.

1.2.2 The Quantity of Evidence in the Standard of Conviction

In order to meet the standard of evidence in terms of quantity of evidence, judges must have sufficient evidence to believe that a defendant carried out the criminal activity with which they have been charged. Key to this is that the substance of the evidence should cover all the important facts constituting the entirety of the crime. Traditionally, China's theory of criminal law summarizes the constituent elements of a crime as: the criminal subject (the person who performed the criminal act), the subjective aspect of a crime (similar to *actus reus*), the criminal object (the interest protected by law and harmed by the crime), and the objective aspect of a crime (similar to *mens rea*). Some scholars, however, maintain that "There is a binary system, namely, the act of the crime and the responsibility for the crime. The act constitutes the objective element of the crime, and responsibility constitutes the subjective element. Together, the two bring objective and subjective unity." In this, the act of the crime is the objective basis for conviction, corresponding to what is known in traditional terms as the objective aspect of a crime, and includes such factors as the time, place, manner, consequences and causes of the crime.[14]

The task of judicial proof is to use the evidence to prove the facts of a case. The act of the crime is the core element in the facts of a case, and therefore is also the main focus of judicial proof. We can also separate out the facts of a case into the "Seven Ws", i.e. what (matter), when, where, how, why, what (thing), who.[15] In cases of intentional homicide, the facts of the case can be abstractly expressed as "why did person A at a certain time and place and by certain means (including any object) kill person B". In criminal trials, these elements are proved by the use of evidence, and of these elements, the two most important are "who" and "what matter". In short, the main point of judicial proof is "who did what?".

According to Article 64 of the "Interpretation of the Supreme People's Court concerning the Implementation of the Criminal Procedure Law of People's Republic of China" (IICPL, without special indication, all laws and judicial interpretations are those of PRC),[16] in cases of intentional homicide, the basic facts of a case that must be evidenced and proved include: (1) the defendant's identity and capacity for

[14]Chen (2001).

[15]He and Liu (2013, p. 204).

[16]Article 64 of the "Interpretation of the Supreme People's Court concerning the Implementation of the Criminal Procedure Law of People's Republic of China": Case facts that must be proven by the application of evidence include: (1) the identity of the defendant and victim; (2) whether the alleged crime in fact occurred; (3) whether the alleged crime was in fact committed by the defendant; (4) whether the defendant has the capacity for criminal responsibility, whether there is a culpable mens rea, or a motive or objective for the commission of the crime; (5) the time, place, manner, consequences and causes of the commission of the crime, etc.; (6) the defendant's status and role in a jointly committed crime; (7) whether the defendant possesses circumstances permitting or requiring heavier or lighter punishment, mitigated (below-minimum) punishment, or exemption from punishment; (8) facts concerning the handling of property related to the case, where there is a collateral civil action; (9) procedural facts related to jurisdiction, recusal, postponement of adjudication, etc.; (10) Other facts related to conviction or sentencing (Liu et al. 2013, p. 90).

criminal responsibility; (2) the victim's identity; (3) that the defendant carried out the alleged homicide; (4) the defendant's motive for the homicide, that there existed the direct or indirect intention of committing a crime; (5) the time, place, manner, consequences and causes of the intentional homicide.

From the form of the evidence,[17] evidence usually used to prove "the defendant's identity and capacity for criminal responsibility" includes: documents such as proof of their registered address, identity papers, outpatient records etc.; witness statements; and appraisal opinions on topics such as bone-age identification and forensic psychological assessments. Evidence used to prove "the victim's identity and extent of injury" include: documents such as proof of their registered address, identity papers, identification notes; witness statements; and appraisal opinions on topics such as autopsy reports, physical injury assessments, and DNA reports. Evidence used to prove "that the defendant carried out the alleged homicide" includes audio-visual material such as eyewitness testimony of having directly seen the crime happen, victim statements and surveillance footage; documents such as search records which act as circumstantial evidence, physical evidence and connected appraisal opinions,[18] witness statements, documents including audio-visual material[19] and identification notes. Evidence used to prove "the time, place, manner, consequences and causes for intentional homicide" include: documents such as criminal case files, records of cases reported to the authorities and crime scene investigation reports; the murder weapon and other physical evidence; witness statements; victim statements; surveillance and other audio-visual material; and appraisal opinions such as autopsy reports. When it comes to subjective intent, cases often demonstrate evidence of motive, for example proof that there was a dispute between the defendant and victim, or that the defendant had once said they wanted to hurt the victim, statements from witnesses as to the psychological state and living conditions of the defendant before the crime, the victim's statement and so on. And if a judge wishes to prove intent rather than negligence, they often use evidence which is able to prove the position and extent of the victim's injuries, how the defendant inflicted the injury and how the crime came to be discovered etc. For example, if the autopsy report demonstrates that the victim was injured repeatedly and severely, or that the injuries were sustained in fatal locations such as the head or chest, then it can be believed that the defendant had intent. Therefore, evidence used to prove responsibility for a crime includes witness statements, victim statements, and appraisal opinions such as physical injury statements and autopsy reports.

---

[17]Putting the veracity of the defendant's confession to one side, its content can generally be used to prove the basic facts of a case, consequently here we have not discussed defendant confessions.

[18]Using the two-sided nature of physical evidence to connect the defendant to a case, for example biological evidence from the defendant found at the scene of the crime or biological evidence gathered from the defendant's body or clothing.

[19]Here we mean audio-visual material which acts as circumstantial evidence such as a crime which is not observed by an eyewitness nor recorded during its commission, which is only just enough to prove that the defendant was on the scene when the crime was committed, which contains the time of the crime, the movements of the defendant before and after the crime.

In all of our 20 correctly resolved cases, the prosecution provided the above-mentioned evidence, proving either the material facts that constituted the crime or the "Seven Ws" of the facts of the case—and, as a result of this quantity of evidence, a guilty verdict was reached. Take, for instance, the charge of intentional homicide against the defendant surnamed Deng.[20] Here, the evidence used by the judge as the basis for the guilty verdict included:

1. Police documents including police registration forms, case receipt forms, the arrest process, and process of solving the crime.
2. Victim statement proving both the process of the crime and the defendant's motive.
3. Six witness statements proving the process of the crime, whose contents were fundamentally identical.
4. One CD ROM of audio-visual material proving how the crime came into the open.
5. One witness statement proving there had been an emotional dispute between the defendant and the victim.
6. Notes and photographs proving the identity of defendant and victim as well as the murder weapon.
7. Crime scene investigation notes and photographs.
8. Notes and list of evidence gathered and received, proving the defendant's motive and thought processes in the run up to the crime.
9. Department store receipts proving the origin of the murder weapon.
10. Crime scene investigation reports and photographs, proving the condition of the crime scene.
11. The receipt and statement of items detained for the kitchen knife and rucksack.
12. Basic population information table.
13. Appraisal opinions proving the bloodstains found at the crime scene and on the defendant's clothes were an exact match for the victim's DNA.
14. Forensic assessment of the extent of damage done to the body and statement of injuries.
15. The confession of the defendant, Deng.

From the list above, points (12), (6) and (15) are able to prove the defendant's identity, responsibility for and capacity to commit the crime; (2), (12) and (14) are able to prove the victim's identity and extent of injuries sustained; (5), (8) and (14) are able to prove the defendant had a motive for murder and the existence of intent; (1), (7), (10), (2), (3), (4), (9), (11), and (15) are able to prove the defendant carried out the alleged murder and the time, place, manner, consequences and causes for intentional homicide. To summarize, there was evidence to prove the basic facts of the case, and every item of proof had many supporting pieces of evidence, therefore the quantity of evidence in this case reached the standard of conviction.

[20]For details of the case see: Liuzhou Intermediate People's Court, Guangxi Zhuang Autonomous Region, 2014, Written Judgment on 177 Criminal Two Final.

1.2.3 The Quality of Evidence in the Standard of Conviction

The quality of evidence is the essential component when a judge decides the facts of a case, and is also the basic substance of a judicial review of evidence. Even if the quantity of evidence in a case meets the required standard, if its quality falls short, judges have no way of confirming the facts of the case. Article 48 of CPL clearly states that "the authenticity of evidence shall be confirmed before it can be admitted as the basis for making a decision on a verdict". Here, "authenticity" indicates the true reliability of the evidence. In the "Opinions on Strengthening the Handling of Cases According to the Law and Guaranteeing the Quality of Handling of Death Penalty Cases", jointly issued in 2007 by the Supreme People's Court (SPC), Supreme People's Procuratorate (SPP), the Ministry of Public Security (MPS) and the Ministry of Justice (MOJ), there was an analysis of the term "insufficient evidence":

> (1) There are doubts about the evidence on which the conviction is based, and there is no way of verifying it; (2) There is a shortage of the evidence necessary to prove the essential facts of the case; (3) It is not possible to reasonably remove all contradictions in the evidence on which the conviction is based; (4) Other possible conclusions can be drawn from the evidence.[21]

Of this, points (1), (3) and (4) touch upon a deficiency in the quality of evidence.

The standard of conviction for the quality of evidence is that evidence used as the basis for a conviction must be credible and reliable. In our 20 cases, the judicial personnel had verified all the evidence and confirmed the legitimacy, relevance and true reliability of the evidence in securing a conviction. The quality of evidence had, therefore, reached the standard of conviction. Take, for instance, the charge of homicide by poisoning against the defendant surnamed Shi.[22] Here, the evidence used by the court to confirm the verdict of intentional homicide included:

1. The defendant's statement.
2. The victim statement.
3. Four witness statements, proving both the relationship and the dispute between defendant and victim, as well as how the victim was transferred to hospital.
4. A witness statement proving the defendant first purchased a bottle of cola, returned it, then asked for it to be given back.
5. A witness statement (medical) proving the diagnosis for which the victim underwent treatment.
6. Hospital examination report and statements proving the victim received treatment for poisoning and the severity of the Colchicine poisoning.

---

[21] Clause 25 of the original text of this opinion states "If one of the following circumstances exist, it shall not be possible to determine that the criminal suspect has committed a crime and the responsibility for the crime must be investigated, if evidence is insufficient it shall not satisfy the conditions for prosecution…" Although this clause is guidance for prosecuting bodies issuing indictments, it can also be used as a reference for the standard of judicial judgments.

[22] For details of the case see: Beijing Number 1 Intermediate People's Court, 2014, Written Judgment on 3689 Criminal Final.

7. The crime scene investigation report, interrogation records, case handling report and video screen-shots, proving the defendant had purchased Colchicine.
8. Case receipt form, case handling report, identity documents, student files etc., proving the defendant's identity and how the case was handled.

All of the evidence presented was relevant to the case and, in addition: the substance of points (1), (2) and (4) were fundamentally identical, and showed that the defendant bought a bottle of cola for the victim then, after the victim complained that it was bitter, went with the victim to return it to the shop and later returned to the shop alone to ask for that bottle of cola back; the substance of points (1), (2), (3) and (5) showed that the victim was admitted to hospital for treatment the evening after having drunk the cola; point (7) shows that the investigating team determined that the records of the defendant's online transactions were sufficient to prove that the victim had bought Colchicine before the crime took place.

Once all the evidence had been checked and verified there were no contradictions between individual points that could not be explained, the substance of the evidence was verified and found to be of true reliability, and the only conclusion to be drawn was that the defendant was guilty of poisoning.

Judges often face the difficulty of how to be sure of the true reliability of the evidence they review. Evidence reviews can be both individual and comparative. Individual reviews check the origin, content and form of each piece of evidence, and assesses whether or not is has true reliability. Comparative reviews compare and contrast two or more pieces of evidence that together support the proof of the same fact in a case, and ascertain whether they reflect the situation identically, and whether they can be used together to reasonably prove the facts of a case. Generally speaking, when the content of different pieces of evidence is identical it tends to be reliable, and when evidence contains contradictions, its truth can be questioned. Of course, one cannot blindly accept mutually consistent evidence as true, because a false consistency can be created through collusion in statements, perjury, and the extortion of confessions through torture etc. Moreover, one must also not automatically rule out the validity of mutually contradictory or differing evidence, and must take pains to examine the form, cause and nature of the contradictions and differences, as discrepancies can arise which in no way affect the true reliability of the evidence. For instance, it is very difficult for different witnesses to describe the same fact identically, because their perception, memory and ability to express themselves are by no means alike, and the subjective and objective ways in which they perceive a fact also differ. Consequently, the key to comparing investigations does not lie in identifying the points of unanimity and divergence in differing pieces of evidence, but rather in analyzing these points to see whether or not they are reasonable, and whether or not they conform to a pattern.

China's courts often use the "corroboration" method to make a ruling on evidence. If the content of many pieces of evidence can be mutually corroborated, this raises the level of confidence afforded the evidence. For example, in the charge of intentional homicide against the defendant surnamed Li,[23] the criminal forensic report clearly

[23]For details of the case see: Heilongjiang High People's Court, 2011, Written Judgment on 63 Criminal Three Final.

showed that the victim had been hit on the head repeatedly with a blunt instrument leading to craniocerebral trauma and death; both the flat-head hammer and round-head hammer recovered from the scene by the police were found to contain traces of the victim's blood; the defendant confessed to using first the round-head and then the flat-head hammer during the crime and also identified that the two hammers recovered from the scene were of the same type as that used to commit the crime; and a witness testified that the two hammers were ordinarily to be found in the victim's residence. Taken together, the defendant's confession, the authentication findings, the witness statement, and the official appraisal documents were all substantively identical and mutually corroborative. The judge could, therefore, be certain of the true reliability of the evidence. In other words, the evidence reached the standard of conviction for quality of evidence.

1.3 Case Study of Evidence Shortage in Wrongful Convictions

Wrongful convictions or misjudged criminal cases are, in essence, mysteries. In cases where there are both a shortage of evidence and an ambiguity of facts, erroneous verdicts are reached when the people handling a case do not correctly identify this situation during the initial trial. It can therefore be said that there is always a shortage of evidence in misjudged cases.

There are two types of shortage of evidence in wrongful convictions: the first is a shortage of quantity, and the second is a shortage of quality. The former indicates that the evidence in the case was not sufficient to prove all the elements of the crime or facts of the case, and therefore it was not possible to establish a complete chain of evidence. The latter indicates that certain pieces of evidence in the case possessed neither the capacity to act as evidence nor true reliability, and could not form the basis of a verdict or prove certain facts beyond reasonable doubt. In many cases of wrongful conviction, both these situations exist at the same time. In order to examine these types of shortage of evidence and explore the points of law therein, we have selected 45 cases of wrongful convictions in criminal homicide cases as the object of study.

1.3.1 A Summary of the 45 Wrongful Convictions

All 45 cases of wrongful convictions found the defendant guilty of intentional homicide in a first trial; later, for differing reasons, each verdict was overturned. Within this sample, there are three cases where the verdict was corrected because the victim "came back from the dead" (those of Teng Xingshan, She Xianglin, and Zhao Zuohai) and sixteen cases where "the true murderer came to light later" (those of

Shi Dongyu, Du Peiwu, Li Jiuming, Sun Wangang, Zhang Gaoping and Zhang Hui, Huugjilt, Yang Yunzhong, Yang Liming and three others, Ding Zhiquan, Li Huawei, Tan Junhu and two others, Chen Jinchang and one other, Li Ritai, Qin Yanhong, Zhao Xinjian, and Li Jie and four others). In the remaining 26 cases, "the benefit of doubt went to the defendant" because of a shortage of evidence. In twelve of these "benefit of the doubt" cases, including that of Wang Xueyi, the defendant was acquitted by appeal at the high court after initially being found guilty at an intermediate court. In seven cases including that of Li Huailiang, the high court ordered a retrial which then overturned the original guilty verdict, issued by an intermediate court. In the two cases of Tan Fuyi and Fan Jiali and one other, the high court ordered a retrial after the intermediate court found the defendant/s guilty, and the procuratorate then withdrew charges. In the two cases of Huang Aibin and Li Zhiping, the defendant was found guilty by the intermediate court; when the high court later ordered a retrial, the defendant was released, despite the judicial bodies not legally declaring them innocent. In the three cases of Ai Xiaodong, Chen Shijiang and Yu Yingsheng, the verdict was overturned in a second retrial, after two initial trials found the defendant guilty.[24]

Although the "defendants" in each of these 45 cases were found guilty of intentional homicide, there were differences in the specifics of the crimes considered by the courts. Ten of the cases (22.2%) involved rape or necrophilia; three (6.6%) involved robbery; two involved the destruction of property; and one involved insurance fraud. All of these acts were found to be the motive for the homicide in the original trial. Analysis of the *modus operandi*[25] reveals seven cases (15.6%) of strangulation causing death by suffocation; four cases (8.8%) of poisoning; one case each (each equating to 2.2%) of death by arson, gas poisoning and drowning; 31 cases (68.9%) of using firearms, blades, sticks or other lethal weapons to commit murder. In the seven cases of death by strangulation, six also involved instances of rape or necrophilia.

[24]The source of the 45 cases is as follows. Those of Ma Yanxin, Sun Xueshuang, Li Jie and four others and Yu Yingsheng came from the internet; and the others can be found in: Guo (2011) and He (2014a).

[25]Statistics around *modus operandi* are collected from "cause of death" details. For instance, in Gao Hongliang's misjudged criminal case, the original verdict found that the defendant burnt the victim to death after hitting them with a wooden stick, consequently this case has been classified as arson.

1.3.2 Shortages in the Quantity of Evidence in Wrongful Convictions[26]

Compared with the 20 correctly resolved criminal cases "where the evidence was sufficient and concrete", these 45 wrongful convictions generally show a shortage of evidence. Looking at the act of the crime, a shortage in the quantity of evidence in the cases is concentrated in the proof "that the defendant carried out the alleged homicide". There are in the main two types of shortage. The first, insufficient evidence to connect the defendant with the act of murder. And the second, ambiguities or contradictions in the proof of the time, place, manner, consequences and causes of the intentional homicide.

Generally speaking, proof that a defendant has committed a particular crime, relies either on direct evidence sufficient to prove the whole course of the crime (such as a confession by the defendant, witness statements, victim statements, surveillance footage etc.) or on circumstantial evidence linking the defendant to the act of murder (such as biological evidence or trace physical evidence of the defendant found on the scene or on the body or clothing of the victim, witness statements proving the defendant was on the scene before or during the crime etc.). In the cases described above, there was not only no direct evidence[27] capable of proving the defendant had in fact killed a person other than the defendant's confession, there was also insufficient circumstantial evidence. Consider the murder weapon. Usually, it is highly likely that the suspect's fingerprints, palm prints or other biological traces will be found on the scene or on the murder weapon itself. Moreover, splashes of blood will often be found on the scene or on the suspect's body if the victim has been attacked with a weapon such as a stick, blade or ax. Biological evidence or traces of physical evidence are fairly powerful indicators to help fix upon a suspect or eliminate a suspect from suspicion. But from our count of 33 cases involving use of a lethal weapon, in 13 there was no physical or biological evidence linking the suspect to the scene; in seven the physical evidence which could have linked the suspect to the scene was either not collected, or not examined, or no appraisal opinion was completed, and there was also no biological evidence linking the defendant to the case; in another seven although blood was found on the defendant, no physical evidence linking the suspect to the scene was gathered; and in a further four, relevant physical evidence was found at the scene and blood was found on the defendant, but there was no way to match the two. Although relevant evidence existed in the latter two examples, it was of insufficient strength to act as proof. We will come back to this point about the quality

[26]This section discusses shortages in the quantity of evidence separately from shortages in the quality of evidence. When analysing shortages in *quantity* of evidence, we have not considered the impact of a shortage of *quality* on the evidence. Take two cases for example. In one, the necessary appraisal opinions are missing. When compared to the second case which does have appraisal opinions, we do not consider whether the quality of the second case's appraisal opinion meets the standard of evidence.

[27]In the case of Chen Jinchang, there was a victim statement which acted as direct evidence, but the time of the statement was found to contain errors, and it has been classified as a shortage of quality of evidence. See Guo (2011, p. 311 onwards).

of evidence later. As a whole, of the 33 cases, 20 (more than 60%) contained no evidence to prove a link between the defendant and the act of intentional homicide. There is a similar picture when it comes to circumstantial evidence. For example, of our 45 cases, there are 16 (35.5% of the total number) where the evidence is unable to prove that the defendant had time to do the killing. It can be seen that, in the majority of wrongful convictions assessed, there is insufficient indicative evidence to link the defendant to the act of homicide.

Direct evidence aside, judges often rely on a large quantity of circumstantial evidence (for instance crime scene investigation reports and autopsy reports[28]) when identifying such facts as the time, place, method, consequences and reasons for intentional homicide. These pieces of circumstantial evidence which exist in almost every homicide case are provided by the investigators and take a fixed written format, which we call "evidence format" and which can both prove that a crime took place, and partially restore the process of a crime. Other circumstantial evidence includes physical evidence of the murder weapon, witness statements etc.[29] The content of these pieces of evidence must be overlapped and linked together in order to be able to prove the facts, therefore, the more circumstantial evidence there is, the easier it is for a judge to establish the facts of a case. Conversely, insufficient circumstantial evidence will lead to a shortage of linking proof and a collapse of the chain of evidence. A shortage in the quantity of evidence to prove a crime is on most prominent display when it comes to the murder weapon. Of the 17 correctly resolved cases involving a lethal weapon, 15 (88.2%) were able to identify both the weapon used and its origin. Compared with this, in 11 (33.3%) of the 33 wrongful convictions where a lethal weapon was used, the murder weapon could not be found, in three (9.1%) cases the origin of the weapon was not clear, and in 10 (30.3%) there was no way of identifying it.

In terms of responsibility for an offense, the evidence used to prove the defendant's motive in our sample of wrongful convictions is often weak. Generally, investigating bodies will use knowledge of the interpersonal relationships of the victim to search for and arrest a suspect for reasons including disputes over relationships or property etc. The "evidence of motive" collected during this process will, during the fact-finding stage, be turned into evidence that proves the defendant's motive. Take for example the case of Li Huawei. The victim was his wife and so, after the killing, Mr. Li was treated as the prime suspect. But the only evidence provided by the prosecution of his motive was his confession that "after they were married he had suspected the victim of having had sexual relations with another man. Having always felt hatred and envy over this, he killed the victim after an altercation about family money.[30]" This "motive" was later found to be pure speculation. In our sample of wrongful convictions, there are 16 (35.5%) where, apart from confessions, there is no other

[28]The results of a forensic appraisal opinion in a poisoning case play a similar role of proof to those of an autopsy report, and can be used to prove the cause of a victim's death or injury.

[29]For example, in a case of causing death by explosion, a witness confirms that when the crime took place they first heard the sound of a quarrel, and later heard the noise of an explosion.

[30]See Guo (2011, p. 243).

evidence proving the defendant's motive, or the defendant's direct or indirect intent. In truth, "motive" is only able to act as evidence to prove the defendant's subjective intent, provided that the defendant did in fact commit the crime; in situations where it is not clear whether or not the defendant is guilty, evidence of "motive" does not have the value of proof.

It should be noted that, although the two basic facts "the defendant's identity and capacity for criminal responsibility" and "the victim's identity" are fairly easy to prove compared with other facts which must be proved, in our sample of wrongful convictions there are also situations where there is a shortage of evidence around or no means of verifying the victim's identity. Clearly, the strongest and most direct evidence in establishing the identity of the victim is DNA identification, but there are four instances in our 45 cases where no DNA analysis of the victim was undertaken, or where the DNA analysis produced no matches. We find the phenomenon of the victim "coming back from the dead" in these sorts of wrongful convictions precisely because the identity of the victim was not established.

We have used case study to demonstrate the shortage of quantity of evidence in criminal misjudged cases.

In Li Chunxing's first trial,[31] the proof of the crime provided by the public prosecutors included:

1. The defendant's confession proving he had a property dispute with the victim over the felling of a tree.
2. The crime scene investigation report.
3. The first witness statement proving how the victim was discovered and how the crime was reported.
4. The second witness statement proving the defendant had, before the crime took place, expressed his desire to kill the victim.
5. The autopsy report proving that the victim had been struck on the head by a blunt instrument and had died from an internal brain haemorrhage.
6. The bloodstains on the physical evidence (wooden stick) found at the scene, which were a match with the victim's blood group, proving that it was the murder weapon.
7. An appraisal opinion proving that the paper found at the place of the tree-felling dispute had been written by the defendant.

Apart from the defendant's confession, there was no direct evidence in this case, and there was also an insufficient quantity of circumstantial evidence. First, the crime scene was destroyed before the investigators had conducted their investigation, which resulted in an inability to recover clues of any worth (such as biological or trace evidence), and there was therefore no circumstantial evidence which could prove "the defendant had in fact committed homicide". Second, the crime scene investigation report, autopsy report, wooden stick and appraisal opinion on the bloodstains could only prove the victim had received a blow from the stick and were not able to prove that the person who had used the stick was the defendant, Li Chunxing. Last, although

[31] See Guo (2011, pp. 113–121).

the witness statements and the piece of paper found at the scene of the tree-felling proved the defendant had a motive for the crime, they were not sufficient to prove he had in fact committed murder.

Having no means to determine or being unable to definitively determine that the defendant and perpetrator are one and the same is a direct cause of wrongful convictions. And being unable to definitively identify the perpetrator can confuse the understanding of the process of the crime. In our example cases, where the only direct evidence is a confession, there are often questions over its veracity, because of the possibility that a confession was obtained through use of torture. And, when the quantity of circumstantial evidence is insufficient, there is no means by which to strengthen the validity of the confession or to create a complete chain of evidence. In cases such as Li Chunxing's, the majority of circumstantial evidence (e.g. crime scene investigation reports and appraisal opinions) can only prove that "a crime took place" and cannot prove "the defendant carried out this particular crime". That is, the evidence fails to build an adequate bridge linking "a crime took place", "the defendant carried out a crime" and "the defendant carried out this particular crime". From this we can see that our examples of wrongful conviction contain a shortage in the quantity of evidence used to prove "the defendant carried out the act of killing someone" and "specifics of the course of this incident" and, therefore, fail to reach the standard of evidence for conviction.

1.3.3 Shortages in the Quality of Evidence in Wrongful Convictions

Just as there can be an insufficiency in the *quantity* of evidence, the *quality* of evidence in wrongful convictions can also fail to reach the standard of "authenticity" and be insufficient to prove elements of a crime. This is mainly expressed as a shortage in the capacity of evidence and an insufficiency of true reliability. Deficiencies in the capacity of evidence commonly result from the source, content and form of the evidence being illegal, or a weakness in the relevance of the evidence. And insufficiencies of true reliability commonly result from contradictions inherent in the content of the evidence or a misreading of its value.

Rules surrounding the exclusion of illegal evidence in China's CPL state that evidence which is unlawful in its origin, content or form must be excluded according to the law. However, in the original trials of our 45 wrongful convictions, it was quite common for the legitimacy of the evidence to be suspect. Take, for instance, the case of Li Jiuming. During the first trial the lawyers raised the fact that "the DNA identification results have not been linked to any checks on the source material's origins, acquisition, testing or appraisal process" and, moreover, that there were no records confirming the extraction, storage and examination of the defendant's hair.[32] To ensure the legitimacy of appraisal opinions (including the collection of evidence

[32]See He (2014a, p. 109).

by the investigators and the examinations conducted by the appraisers), both the collection of evidence and the examinations must be legal. Since, in this case, there was no way to prove the legitimacy of either the origin of the physical evidence or of the content of the DNA appraisal opinion, the opinion in question should have either been subject to verification or excluded. Other wrongful convictions were found to contain "man-made" or "fabricated" evidence. In the case of Li Zhiping,[33] investigators found bloodstains, footprints and palm prints on the scene. As previously discussed, biological and traces of physical evidence are fairly powerful indicators to help fix upon a suspect in a crime and, if lawful and regular processes are followed in the production of appraisal opinions, the evidence therein is able to basically "speak" the facts of a case. However here, the investigators did not make good use of the evidence and, when the palm prints were found to not be a match, went to great lengths to use the appraisal to fabricate evidence that could incriminate Li Zhiping. Evidence with zero legitimacy of this nature is, once submitted to court, not only useless in helping a judge determine the facts of a case, but can also become the precursor to an error of judgment.

Another issue around evidence which lacks capacity found in our sample of wrongful convictions is a weakness in the relevance of the evidence. "Relevance" demands that every individual piece of evidence must have substantive significance in proving the facts of a case. In other words, a piece of evidence must be of real use in proving the facts of a case or other disputed facts.[34] Empirical analysis shows that certain pieces of evidence in the cases analyzed did not necessarily have a connection with the unproven facts of the case, or the content of the evidence was not able to effectively prove them. In Li Chunxing's case, one of the pieces of evidence supplied by the prosecution was the piece of paper discovered at the scene of the tree felling. After analysis, the paper was found to have been written by the defendant, so the prosecution accordingly believed the defendant had murdered the victim because of the dispute over the tree. However careful analysis showed that the scene of the tree felling was not the crime scene, so the piece of paper was only able to prove the defendant had once been to the tree-felling scene, and was not able to prove any connection between the defendant and the murder case. Three other similar cases exist. As another example, consider the use of a criminal record as in establishing a motive, and on the basis of this finding someone guilty. A criminal record is merely a judgment of past behavior. In the investigation stage it can be used to decide the direction of the investigation, and it can also be used during a trial to decide the severity of a sentence, but it cannot be used as the basis of conviction. Just as once having committed a theft is not the same as always being a thief, so too once having committed a crime is not the same as repeatedly committing that same crime. In the absence of adequate investigation, it is arbitrary and blind to use assessments of character and morals as the basis for motive in a case. In our sample of 45 wrongful convictions, there are six which draw on evidence of character and morals to prove criminal intent.

[33]See Guo (2011, pp. 162–172).

[34]See He and Liu (2013, p. 114).

Comparative analysis is used to establish whether two or more pieces of evidence, when taken together, may reasonably prove the facts of a case—and this can help decide the true reliability of the evidence. If there are irrational and unexplainable contradictions between the evidence and the facts and between individual pieces of evidence, then the true reliability of the evidence is weak and a judge must be cautious when deciding the facts of a case. In our sample of cases, the most common contradictions seen are in: the defendant's confession of guilt or innocence, including confessions in cases involving multiple defendants; confessions of guilt determined by judicial personnel; and witness statements, crime scene investigation reports, appraisal opinions and other evidence. There are many such situations over 23 cases in total, constituting over half of the total sample of wrongful convictions. We have also found cases where there are contradictions between witness statements, in appraisal opinions and in other evidence, as well as other problems which are more difficult to confirm. These also constitute a definite proportion of the cases analyzed.

Another manifestation of the insufficiency of the true reliability of evidence is the misreading of the value of evidence. Here we mean the judge in the original trial mistaking evidence of lesser value for evidence of greater value and, as a result, making an error when ruling on the facts of a case. In the case of Teng Xingshan,[35] the investigating body identified the murder weapon on two grounds: first, that hair and blood of a group identical to that of the victim were found on the ax and, second, that the shape of the ax was identical to the shape of the wound on the victim. But the characteristics of blood groups and wound marks[36] are not unique; they may match many objects or type of object, so one cannot on these grounds be certain that any particular ax is the murder weapon. In the case of Xu Dongchen, the defendant was identified as the key suspect by the police because his blood was of the same group as that found in the victim's vagina. Police DNA identification could "not rule out that the fine spots found on the toilet paper and on the gauze used to wipe clean the victim's vagina were left by Xu Dongchen". It is clear that this appraisal opinion was not conclusive, and provided neither unique not exclusive evidence. However this very appraisal opinion became the major evidence which determined Xu Dongchen's guilt.[37] Of our 45 wrongful convictions, there are ten where there is no proof that the defendant was the perpetrator because the evidence was neither exclusive nor unique. In addition, whilst there is a certain science behind the use of polygraph tests or identifications based on matching the gait of a person to the indentations on the soles of a shoe, the practices have failed to gain full verification and peer recognition,[38] therefore their value of proof in personal identification is relatively weak.

---

[35]Teng Xingshan was sentenced to death in a murder case in Hunan and excuted in 1989. He was declared innocent in 2005. See He (2016, pp. 13–77).

[36]We speak here of a typical situation. If the features of a murder weapon such as its shape or wear are distinguishing in any way, such as the existence of uneven gaps, then it can be treated as characteristic for matching and identification.

[37]See *Contemporary Misjudged Criminal Cases*: No. 14, 18 July 2016, http://blog.sina.com.cn/s/blog_784904f50100th8e.html.

[38]He (2014b).

It is worth noting that shortages of quantity and quality of evidence often appear at the same time in our wrongful convictions, creating situations where "not credible" and "not sufficient" evidence fails to create a complete system of proof and leaves the facts of a case confused and not clear. Take as an example the case of Du Peiwu.[39] In this case, the proof of guilt supplied by the prosecution included:

1. The defendant's confession.
2. The crime scene investigation report and photographs from the scene.
3. The autopsy report.
4. The polygraph test report.
5. The ballistics report.
6. Evidence collection records and reports on the investigation of physical evidence, namely, the examination of: footprints found at the scene, dirt found on the clutch of the vehicle at the scene, dirt on the defendant's clothes and traces of gunpowder.
7. Results of police dog sniff tests.
8. Non-eyewitness testimony.

In the first trial, the defense raised certain doubts, including the fact that the firearm used to commit the crime had never been found; that there was no dirt found on the brake pedal or the accelerator but the investigation report still took it as a comparative sample; the existence of inconsistencies between the forensic appraisal and the crime scene investigation report; and the fact that the defendant's confession was gathered repeatedly.

Analysis of the evidence shows that since there were shortages in the *quantity* of evidence in the case, there were also shortages in its *quality*. First, the case lacked any direct evidence apart from the defendant's confession and the critical piece of circumstantial evidence that was the murder weapon; moreover the defendant's confession was gathered repeatedly and there were inconsistencies within it. Second, there are scientific doubts around the use of evidence point (4), so it should only have been used as circumstantial evidence, and should not have been deemed to be conclusive. Third, the examination of bullet traces in point (5) was only able to identify the type and not any specifics, and was also not able to prove that the traces of gunpowder left on the defendant's body had come from the same pistol as that which had killed the victim. Fourth, the appraisal opinion in point (6) contained no blank control samples and, also, the origin of the mud was not clear, so as it was not possible to eliminate the chance that the evidence had been faked or that there had been a mix up during testing, its true reliability was not sufficient to prove the defendant had been on the scene while the crime was taking place. Fifth, there is no way to resolve the contradictions between the two identification conclusions in point (7), moreover as the defendant and victim were husband and wife, the possibility that they smelled alike cannot be ruled out. Consequently, the evidence in this case was not only unable to prove "the defendant carried out the alleged homicide" or "the time, place, method, consequences and reasons for intentional homicide", but

---

[39]Du Peiwu was sentenced to death with two-year suspension in a double murder case in Yunnan in 1998, and exonerated in 2000. See He (2016, pp. 36–38).

the "authenticity" of the evidence was also insufficient, and there were gaps in the chain of evidence. Although there was proof that Du Peiwu had fired a gun, given his history of firearm training, there was no way to be certain that it was he who fired the gun which killed the two victims.

1.4 Regular Patterns of Evidence Shortage in Wrongful Convictions

During our comparison of correctly resolved cases with wrongful convictions, we discovered a pattern surrounding the shortage of evidence in misjudgments, connected to the subjective and objective factors present during the act of the crime. This identification is valuable in being able to be vigilant about and correctly identify shortages of evidence, and in reducing the miscarriages of justice that such shortages can cause.

The indirect, reverse-engineered understanding of the facts of a case that investigators have can only be achieved through evidence, and the "real evidence" that they can use is often less that the "potential evidence" that objectively exists when a crime is committed. It is, in this sense, almost an objective fact that there will be a shortage of evidence. Some scholars say that "a shortage of evidence is a prerequisite of a wrongful conviction. A shortage of evidence does not necessarily result in a misjudged criminal case, but all wrongful convictions undeniably contain a shortage of evidence."[40] Whether or not a shortage of evidence ultimately affects the verdict in a case is determined by the nature of the shortage.

1.4.1 Shortages of Evidence in Critical Links of Judicial Proof

Analysis of our wrongful conviction cases reveals that the shortage of evidence that leads to miscarriages of justice is often a shortage in the critical links of judicial proof, that is, a shortage of evidence to prove the main facts of a case—either a lack of evidence to prove certain facts, or the content of the evidence is unreliable causing uncertainty over whether the facts are true or false.

Analysis has also demonstrated a particularly acute shortage of evidence that is capable of proving the basic facts of a case. For example, lack of proof of the identity of the victim, lack of proof the defendant carried out the alleged crime, the only evidence capable of proving the defendant carried out the alleged crime (i.e. the confession) being unreliable, and so on. If the basic facts of a case are unclear, then the whole framework of facts constructed by the people handling the case falls apart.

[40] See Ma and Wang (2014, p. 105).

Of course, proving the basic facts of a case requires not only reliable evidence, but also the support of logic and experience. In our wrongful convictions, all contained only one item of direct evidence—the defendant's confession—about which there were doubts as to its true reliability, and whose ability to prove critical links in the case was weak. Article 105 of IICPL states:

> If there is no direct evidence, but circumstantial evidence simultaneously satisfies all the conditions below, the defendant may be found guilty: (1) the evidence has been investigated and verified; (2) various items of evidence mutually corroborate one another, and there are no contradictions that cannot be eliminated or doubts that cannot be explained; (3) the totality of the evidence in the case already constitutes a complete set of proof; (4) the determination of the facts in the case by the evidence is sufficient to eliminate reasonable doubt, and there can be only one conclusion; (5) the inferences drawn from the application of evidence satisfy logic and experience.[41]

This shows that proof of the main facts of a case can be refined and deconstructed based on circumstantial evidence. For example, in the intentional homicide case involving a defendant surnamed Wang,[42] although there were no eyewitnesses, the victim's spouse was just outside the crime scene when the killing happened, and confirmed that the defendant had entered the scene during the crime and that no other person had gone in. Where a witness statement of this nature can be verified, logic and experience dictates that we can conclude the defendant killed the victim. It is evident from this that logic and experience are important component parts in proving the essential facts of a crime such as the fact that the defendant was present at the scene, had time to commit the crime and so on. But judicial proof cannot rely on logic and experience alone. In a situation where there is a shortage of facts, logic and experience are no more than "castles in the air" and cannot provide a factual framework. Consequently, a shortage of circumstantial evidence can break the chain of evidence and lead to an inability to prove the basic facts of a case.

1.4.2 Shortages of Quality in Testimonial Evidence

During our analysis of criminal misjudged cases, we discovered that it is easy for there to be a shortage in the *quality* of testimonial evidence and a shortage in the *quantity* of physical evidence. An insufficiency in the true reliability of testimonial evidence is a widespread "chronic disease" in wrongful convictions. In our sample of 45 cases, eight contained fabricated witness statements, and one had a mistake in the defendant's confession. These points of evidence were not subjected to rigorous review during the original trial, and eventually became the evidence that decided guilt, leading to wrongful convictions. Of course, the true reliability of oral evidence is nowhere more questionable than when it comes to a defendant's confession. Looking at only objective circumstances, we find that in wrongful conviction cases there

---

[41] See Liu et al. (2013, p. 111).

[42] For details of the case see Shandong High People's Court, 2014, Written Judgment on 16 Criminal Two Final.

are often no eyewitness statements, and the defendant's confession is almost the only piece of oral evidence capable of proving the essential facts of the case. It is, however, precisely because of this "uniqueness" that it is very easy for a confession to become a "hollow shell" where truth and fiction are inseparable. In the 19 cases where either the victim came "back from the dead" or "the real murderer came to light later", the defendant's "confession of guilt" was found to be false and in the other 26 cases, most of the defendants revealed under questioning in court that the confession had been obtained through torture. There was also one case where the defense submitted proof of evidence handling, but did not succeed in getting the court in the original trial to attach importance to this. These confessions are false instances of the principle of "going from evidence to confession"—"man-made evidence" that provides the corroboration it seeks. Instances in our wrongful conviction cases where a defendant's confession was overturned, where there were contradictions in a confession, or contradictions in witness statements add further question marks as to their true reliability. Questionable witness statements, victim statements, accomplice confessions, and defendant confessions not only make a case complicated and confusing, but also impede the ability of the judge to correctly determine the facts of a case.

1.4.3 Shortages of Quantity in Physical Evidence

In misjudged cases, physical evidence is startling in its scarcity. Physical evidence "speaks the truth" far more readily than testimonial evidence. Although easily destroyed or lost, as long as it can be properly and promptly gathered, stored and used, it can fully develop the value of proof. Physical evidence is, however, generally insufficient in misjudged criminal cases, because of both objective and subjective constraints. In the case of Du Peiwu, because the police were unable to find the firearm used in the killing, they forced Du to falsely confess "the gun was broken up and thrown in passing into Dian Pool…[43]" It is also common for biological evidence to be not collected because of the condition of the crime scene, or to be not gathered even when conditions mean it could have been, or, having been collected, for it to be stored and used improperly. In the case of Huugjilt, there is still no answer to the question surrounding the key piece of physical evidence, the bodily fluids found in the deceased's body—were they never gathered or, once gathered, were they never sent for testing? We can see how biological evidence often becomes the "missing link" in the chain of evidence in wrongful convictions. In contrast, in the 20 correctly resolved cases, if we put to one side the 15 where there two or more pieces of direct evidence or where the defendant gave themselves up, of the remaining five there are three where "biological traces of the victim were found on the defendant's clothes" and two where "traces of the defendant were found at the scene". These kinds of indicative biological evidence, when put together with other evidence, enable the chain of evidence to be completed. It is even more rare to find

[43]See Guo (2011, p. 142).

documents, audio-visual material, etc., used as physical evidence in cases resulting in wrongful convictions. And where they do exist, they are mostly—as has been described previously in this chapter—of weak relevance and insufficient to prove facts. We can therefore say that a shortage in physical evidence is a weakness when determining the facts of a case.

1.5 Judicial Rulings in Instances of Shortages of Evidence

Judges often face dilemmas over how to handle shortages of evidence. And, when shortages of evidence exist, the question of how to ensure the impartiality of judicial rulings becomes exceptionally important. There are two fundamental responsibilities of a judicial ruling: one, to determine the facts of a case and two, to apply the relevant laws and regulations. What we call here laws and regulations includes both substantive and procedural laws and regulations as well as ones governing evidence (known as "the rules of evidence"). In truth, when determining the facts of a case, judges must primarily use the rules of evidence. We can thus see that they are of critical importance in guiding and regulating judges' use of evidence when determining the facts of a case. For thousands of years, those who set society's laws have sought to perfect the rules of evidence so as to make it possible for those administering the law to correctly decide difficult questions of proof, but the results to date are still only passable, and sometimes even the complete opposite of what was intended.

We have already described how it is not possible for judges to reach 100% accuracy in their knowledge of the facts of a case and how the facts can also sometimes remain ambiguous. In other words, the facts of a case as understood by judges are never black and white, but always "grey". However, although a judge's knowledge of the facts may be ambiguous, his or her rulings must be definite. For each charge in a criminal procedure, the judge may either find the defendant guilty or innocent, and may not rule that a defendant is 80% likely to be guilty. For each contested fact in a civil action, the judge may find in favor of either the plaintiff or the defendant, and may not rule that the plaintiff is *likely* to be right. Reaching a reasonable judgment amid these sorts of vagaries requires the application of the rule of the burden of proof and making clear which relevant authentication standards have been applied. Article 73 of *the Provisions on Several Issues Concerning Evidence in Civil Procedure* (PECP), published by SPC on 6th December 2001, and brought into force from 1st April 2002, states:

> Where both parties concerned respectively produce contrary evidence to rebut the same fact, but neither party has sufficient grounds to negate each other's evidence, the people's court shall, in light of the case details, decide whether the probative force of one party's evidence is obviously more powerful than that of evidence from the other party, and confirm the evidence with more powerful probative force.
>
> Where it is unable to judge the probative force of evidence, thus causing the disputed fact difficult to ascertain, the people's court shall make its ruling according to the rule on the distribution of burden of proof.

The body of law which regulates judicial rulings is that the rules of evidence should have the basic characteristics of clarity, operability and predictability. Of these, clarity is critical, for it provides the foundation for operability and predictability. When clarity is strong, the operability and predictability of the rules of evidence is high and, when clarity is weak, it is low. In one sense, clarity indicates the level of legislative technology and the degree of perfection of the system of evidence. Therefore, when rules of evidence are established, we should be as precise as we are capable of being in the language we use to express them. However, because of conceptual ambiguity, the polysemy of words, and the changes and developments of language over time, rules of evidence can be to a degree abstract. That is, the central clarity of a meaning is accompanied by a relative ambiguity around its edges. In other words, rules of evidence are relatively clear on an abstract level yet relatively ambiguous on a specific one.

From this we can see that, in order to satisfy general requirements of application, the rules of evidence must be abstract to a certain degree. If they become too abstract, however, judges will be helpless when confronted by difficult issues of proof. Judges must indeed be allowed a certain amount of discretion to determine the facts of a case, but this by no means implies that they are completely free to rule as they please, for they must also deliver impartial justice within the constraints of the rules of procedure and evidence. Article 64 of PECP states,

> Judges shall verify the evidence comprehensively and objectively, shall follow statutory procedure, shall by observing the professional ethics of a judge and by the use of logical reasoning and life experience make independent judgment concerning the probative force and weight of proof of the evidence in accordance with the provisions of the law, and shall make public the reasons and results of judgments.

However, if the rules are too abstract, it is difficult for them to act as an effective constraint on a judge.

All three case studies at the beginning of this chapter dealt with someone who "caused a collision" taking someone "who was knocked down" to hospital and covering their medical expenses. In other words, there was evidence that medical expenses had been paid by one person on behalf of another. So how should judges assess and use such evidence during a trial? There are no specific provisions in either China's laws or judicial interpretations, therefore the judges were obliged to exercise their judgment according to Article 64 and apply "the use of logical reasoning and life experience".

In the case of Peng Yu, the reasons given for the verdict in the initial trial were set out as follows:

> *One*. Life experience tells us that the plaintiff could have fallen to the ground as a result of being knocked over by an external force or could have fallen through her own agency as the result of a trip or slip. But in court neither party testified that the plaintiff tripped or slipped and the defendant supplied no proof to contradict this. Therefore on the basis of the evidence presented in the case we must conclude the plaintiff was knocked over by an external force. When this happens, if one can first determine the origin of the external force, it is usually possible to identify the person who caused the collision. The first reaction of a person who has been knocked down is to call for help and ask others to stop the assailant.

> This particular incident took place at a relatively crowded commuter bus stop. It was a public place and the incident happened extremely quickly, therefore the person who knocked down the plaintiff would have had no time to escape. The defendant himself admits that he was the first person to alight from the bus so, logically, the probability of him being the person to have knocked down the plaintiff is relatively high. If the defendant were truly brave enough to do 'a good deed' then it would be more practical to have seized the person who knocked over the plaintiff. Furthermore social reason dictates that, after the plaintiff's family arrived, he would have made the situation very clear and allowed the family to take the plaintiff to hospital, going his own way. But the defendant did not make these choices and his behaviour was clearly contrary to common sense... *Four*. On the day of the incident, the defendant paid the plaintiff a sum of money amounting to over 200RMB which up to now he has not asked to be returned. Both plaintiff and defendant have consistently agreed on the fact of the payment of the money, but their statements differ as to the reason for the payment: the plaintiff believes it was an advance payment of compensation, and the defendant believes it was a loan. Again, life experience tells us that as it is plain the two parties did not know each other, it is not usual to lend money so rashly. During a time of high anxiety over assuming liability for an accident, he could and should have asked a disinterested third party at the bus station to prove that it was a loan. Or perhaps, after explaining the situation to the plaintiff's family, he could have requested a written IOU or other note of some description. But as the defendant did no such thing and even accompanied the family to the hospital, the likelihood of him having lent the money to the plaintiff is not high. Moreover if one does injure another person by knocking them down, the most conventional course of action is to advance money for treatment. The defendant's witness proves that both parties went to the police station to deal with the incident. From this fact we can infer that even the plaintiff at the time believed she had been knocked over by the defendant. It thus becomes even more improbable that the defendant should lend the plaintiff money. Taking all the facts above together, we can determine that this money was not a loan and ought to be treated as compensation.[44]

The judge's reasoning here is improper in two places. First, the judge used the fact that the defendant failed to supply evidence that the plaintiff fell over "through her own agency" as the grounds for excluding the possibility that she did so, which is truly rash. And second, the "life experience rule" which the judge applied to the issued of the defendant accompanying the plaintiff to hospital and paying the medical expenses is not without bias. This latter point has of course been widely criticized in China as being one of the reasons why whether or not to be a "Good Samaritan" is now a moral dilemma.

In the case of Xu Yunhe, the ruling in the original trial read:

> The law states that whether or not a vehicle came into physical contact with a pedestrian is of no influence in establishing the occurrence of a road traffic accident. Assuming that the defendant's own account to the traffic police and his statement in court are tenable, even if there was no collision between the two parties and the plaintiff was injured through a fall of her own making, because the defendant was only 4 or 5 meters away from the plaintiff when the incident happened, she must, as a pedestrian, have been panicked by the proximity of a car. Therefore her fall must have been influenced by the moving car.[45]

This is another instance of "the use of logical reasoning and life experience" to determine the facts of a case, and it also attracted public disapproval. The appeal upheld the original verdict and, in its ruling, stated clearly that:

---

[44] Xu v. Peng Yu, CLI.C.85983, *Peking University Law Database*.

[45] Wang Xiuzhi v. Xu Yunhe, CLI.C.515512, *Peking University Law Database*.

> Evidence including identification reports, accident scene drawings, photographs, and contemporaneous notes and statements from the parties involved can form a complete chain of evidence, sufficient to prove that Wang's leg injury was brought about by Xu's driving. There is a causal link between Xu's driving and the injuries caused to Wang.[46]

We must, here, point out that neither of the two appraisal opinions submitted as evidence in this case was definite in its conclusions. *Appraisal Opinion No. 157* issued by the Forensic Expert Center at the Institute of Forensic Science under the Ministry of Justice failed to determine if the injury to Wang's right knee had been caused by a collision with a vehicle driven by Xu Yunhe. Consequently, the conclusion which in this written ruling is termed "a complete chain of evidence" is debatable.

Shortages of evidence and ambiguous facts together with abstract legislation in disputes over whether someone fell over or was knocked down present dilemmas for judges. If they rule that someone was knocked over then there is a possibility of delivering an injustice to someone who was merely acting as a Good Samaritan. If, however, they rule that it was an accidental fall, then there is a possibility of inflicting a second wound on the injured party. It is human nature to feel sympathy for the injured and therefore it is inevitable for the judge to incline more towards favoring the plaintiff which can result in judgments such as those above. Objectively speaking, the judges in the original trials of Peng Yu and Xu Yunhe were fairly circumspect in their rulings, and went to great lengths in very challenging circumstances to award proportionate compensation. If the facts of the case had been clear and the judges had ordered shared responsibility and 40% compensation then the judgments would have been above reproach. For in both cases some of the fault lay with the plaintiffs themselves: in Peng Yu's case, Ms. Xu ignored the passengers getting off the first bus when she rushed towards the second and, in Xu Yunhe's case, Ms. Wang broke the law when she crossed the safety barriers in the road. However, a careful reading of the judgments in both cases reveals the judges' ambiguous understanding of the disputed facts and may well reflect also the judges' default position towards probability. For example, the stated 40% likelihood that Peng Yu knocked over Ms. Xu.

It is not uncommon for judges to make their decisions on the basis of probability when faced with a difficult judgment decision. In his article entitled "*Law, Fact or Justice?*", Oxford University's Professor of Civil Procedure Adrian Zuckerman gives an example: Suppose someone is knocked down on a public road and the relevant evidence can only prove that he was struck by a bus, but not which particular one. The investigation reveals that Bus Company A's vehicles accounted for 80% of the total number of buses on the road at the time. Therefore the likelihood that one of Company A's buses hit the person is 80%. As the standard of proof required by a civil action is "the preponderance of the evidence"—that is, if the proof on one side surpasses 50% then it shall be deemed to have won—the court should, consequently, find that Company A should assume responsibility for compensation.[47]

In this example, it was not possible to say that the vehicle which caused the accident in this case definitely belonged to Company A, and only that it was very

[46]Xu Yunhe Appeal, Reference, CLI.C.1339057, *Peking University Law Database*.

[47]Zuckerman (1986).

likely to be so. In this sort of case, the public often demands that the courts find out "the truth" and even go so far as to make specific suggestions, such as looking for eyewitnesses, examining the scene marks or searching for traces of paint and other physical evidence... But in this case, there was no other evidence. Therefore, the judge faced a thorny dilemma: either reject the plaintiff's complaint on the grounds of insufficient evidence, which would mean that the person knocked over received no compensation at all, or award compensation on the basis of probability, which would mean that Company A might suffer an injustice, and bear the blame for somebody else. One decision would mean the certainty that the plaintiff would receive no compensation, but the other would mean the possibility of creating an injustice—and the probability of being wrong was only 20%. Therefore, the judge chose the legal truth of an 80% probability.

As a cognitive process, judicial proof differs from usual society processes because it is one of the most important knowledge bases for dispute resolution in society. As a method of adjudication which must deal with all sorts of social disputes and conflicts, judicial rulings require the approval or acceptance of the public. And the basis for this approval and acceptance is judicial power. Judicial power can rely superficially on a state's power or authority, but its intrinsic building block must be judicial impartiality. For this reason, laws and regulations must be specific and clear and the public must be aware of them, so that they can predict how they might be applied. In short, judicial impartiality develops at the macro level and is implemented at the micro level, and the only real justice is concrete justice.

References

Chen, Xingliang. 2001. *Criminal Jurisprudence in and of Itself,* 220–221, 226–227. Beijing: The Commercial Press.

Guo, Xinyang. 2011. *Analysis of Misjudged Criminal Cases*. Beijing: China Renmin Public Security University Press.

He, Jiahong, and Pinxin Liu. 2013. *Evidence Law*. Beijing: Law Press China.

He, Jiahong. (ed.). 2014a. *Late Justice—The Ten Wrongful Convictions Impacting China's Judiciary*. Beijing: China Legal Publishing House.

He, Jiahong. 2014b. Ten misleading zones in contemporary Chinese criminal justice. *Tsinghua Law Review* (2).

Jiahong, He. 2016. *Back from the Dead: Wrongful Convictions and Criminal Justice in China*. Honolulu: University of Hawai'I Press.

Li, Huiqun. 2013. The Zheng Futian & Fu Bing robbery case: How to handle the standard of proof that "the evidence is reliable and sufficient" in criminal cases. In *Criminal Trial Reference,* vol. 86, 48–54. Beijing: Law Press China.

Liu, Zhiwei, et al. (ed.). 2013. *One Book on Criminal Procedure Law*. Law Press China.

Ma, Kai, and Zhaofeng Wang. 2014. Paths to the prevention of misjudged cases in shortage of evidence. *Heilongjiang Social Sciences* (3).

Zeng, Huanyang. 2014. No evidence to prove 'man knocked down old man'. *Guangzhou Daily*, 15 Jan 2014, A14.

Zuckerman, Adrian A.S. 1986. Law, fact or justice? *Boston University Law Review* 66: 488.

Chapter 2
The History of Judicial Proof

Contents

2.1 Case Illustration

During the reign of the Tongzhi Emperor (1862–74) of the Qing dynasty, there was a certain mother and daughter who lived together in the southeastern province of Zhejiang, where they worked as seamstresses. The daughter, Bi Xiugu, had always had a very fair complexion, which earned her the nickname Bok Choy, or "little cabbage".[1] Bok Choy's beauty attracted much attention from the local men, living as she did in a small county town. Rumors about love affairs began to circulate. Bok Choy was proud of her own beauty, even conceited, never giving any coarse or low

[1]The Chinese word for this cabbage contains the character for 'white'.

J. He, *Methodology of Judicial Proof and Presumption*,
Masterpieces of Contemporary Jurisprudents in China,
https://doi.org/10.1007/978-981-10-8025-8_2

fellow a chance with her. But she was also handicapped by her own lowly status as a seamstress, for this was enough to keep her from finding a husband among the wealthy and elite families. Obstructed from social advancement and unwilling to settle for less, Bok Choy remained single well into her twenties. But she did fall in love. The young man was named Yang Naiwu. Yang came from a good family, was well educated, handsome, and showed talent in writing. He, too, had gained something of a reputation for having many love affairs. He also became involved in various business schemes of dubious ethical nature, and these along with his own penchant for showing off and insulting others earned him the enmity of several members of the local elite. He was eight years older than Bok Choy, and married. The two had become acquainted, but had not consummated an affair. Yang offered to make Bok Choy his concubine, but as the girl's mother would not allow her only daughter to become anything less than a full wife, the deal never went through. Yang's wife died following an illness, and afterward, Yang hoped to marry Bok Choy at last. But in the face of determined opposition from his father and sister, he at last gave up and accepted another woman as wife. With Bok Choy not getting any younger, and rumors abounding regarding her chastity, her anxious mother, with the help of a matchmaker named Feng Xushi, arranged for a marriage with a tofu maker named Ge Pinlian. Bok Choy thus gained another nickname: "the Tofu Beauty". Ge Pinlian was over thirty, came from a poor family, and wasn't in the least handsome. He wasn't in good health, either. Bok Choy had no feelings for Ge, but faced with the fact of the match, she accepted her fate and went on with life. But to her surprise, Ge died just a year and a half later of a sudden and severe illness.

Meanwhile, Yang Naiwu had passed the second of the national examinations and taken on the rank of *juren* scholar, which gained him great fame among the local elite. Everyone wanted to be friends with Yang. Among these was the son of the county magistrate, a young man named Liu Zihan. The young scion sent an invitation to Yang, but Yang, in his arrogance, snubbed Liu, who formed a grudge against Yang. Moreover, Liu had seen how beautiful Bok Choy was. He tried several times to seduce her, without success. Hearing that Bok Choy was in love with Yang just made Liu jealous. When Liu got word of Ge Pinlian's death, he was delighted, for he saw an opportunity to get back at both Yang Naiwu and Bok Choy. First, he sought out Ge's mother and cajoled her into filing a suit at the county magistrate's office. Then, at a meal with his father, Liu junior told Magistrate Liu of rumors that Bok Choy had had an affair with Yang Naiwu and that the two of them had plotted to kill her husband. The county magistrate told his son he did not believe a word of it. But a seed of suspicion had been planted. The next day, Magistrate Liu received word of the suit filed by Ge's mother, and seeing that the details of her accusation matched with what his son had said, he ordered Ge's body exhumed for examination. The younger Liu bribed *Wuzuo*, the corpse examiner, a man named Shen Xiang. Shen duly falsified the evidence of the autopsy. Finding traces of blood in the corpse's nostrils, he reported "copious bleeding from all orifices;" discovering slight discoloration of finger nails, he reported "finger nails blackened by contaminants;" when a silver needle inserted into the patient's throat revealed some slight discoloration, he ignored the standard procedure of cleaning the needle and re-inserting for confirmation, instead recording "clear signs of poisoning." Another member of the magistrate's office, one Shen Caiquan, was present at the examination as well, recording "no blood in the ears of the corpse," and "fingernails discolored, but not blackened." But despite this evidence that the body had not been poisoned, the final report, by Shen Xiang, ruled that the body showed clear signs of death by poisoning.

On seeing the report, Magistrate Liu ordered Bok Choy detained and brought in for questioning. From the first time Liu saw Bok Choy, he felt that such a beautiful woman, married as she was to such an ugly and coarse man, must have been carrying on some kind of adulterous affair. He thus pressed forward with the case under the presumption that Bok Choy was guilty. Bok Choy, however, denied all the accusations. Magistrate Liu detained and questioned all parties involved in the case, including Ge Pinlian's mother, Bok Choy's mother, the matchmaker, and a neighbor named Wang Xinbei. The testimony given by these people was not sufficient to prove that Bok Choy had plotted with Yang Naiwu to murder her husband, but it did indicate that she was unhappy with her husband and was having an affair with Yang Naiwu. Magistrate Liu then ordered Bok Choy interrogated under torture. Bok Choy confessed under torture. Magistrate Liu showed the confession to Yang Naiwu, but Yang not only did not confess himself, he behaved with arrogance, as if his fame and position would protect him. According to regulations of the times, Magistrate Liu must apply to the Board of Examinations to strip Yang of his status as a *juren* scholar before Yang could be interrogated under torture. But it happened that at around the same time, another jealous enemy of Yang had gathered signatures among the local land-owners for a petition to the effect that Yang regularly engaged in dishonorable behavior, and moreover showed no respect for the law, arousing public indignation. They demanded harsh punishment for Yang. This made Magistrate Liu even more determined. After Yang was stripped of his scholar's status, Liu detained him for questioning again. But even under harsh torture, Yang Naiwu refused to confess.

Magistrate Liu considered the evidence basically sufficient, only lacking a confession from Yang Naiwu. But given the importance of the case, further torture was deemed inappropriate, and Liu decided to send Yang to the Prefecture office in Hangzhou for further interrogation. Prefect Chen Lu listened to the case and agreed there was grounds for suspecting a crime had been committed, but averred that some details of the case still needed clarification. Back at the county magistrate's office, Bok Choy had testified under torture that Yang Naiwu had conspired with her on August 24 to murder her husband, and on October 5 of that year had sent her a supply of arsenic for that purpose. But Yang Naiwu maintained in his defense that on August 24 he had been in the provincial capital taking the examinations, and on October 5 he was in the countryside to the south, handling some family business involving his father-in-law. Moreover, Yang had witnesses to prove he was in these places at these times. Prefect Chen did not believe Yang, and proceeded with harsh torture. The instruments of torture at the prefectural office greatly exceeded those of the county magistrate in their variety and cruelty. Yang Naiwu, unable to take it, confessed to the charges. Prefect Chen asked Yang where he had obtained arsenic, and the tortured Yang made up some story about a pharmacy called 'Master Qian's

Medicines' east of the county town. Satisfied with this answer, Prefect Chen ordered Magistrate Liu to seek out evidence of the arsenic purchase.

Magistrate Liu returned and, with his trusted friend Master Zhang Lunxiang, sought out a pharmacy owner named Qian Baosheng, whom he questioned on the matter of whether he sold arsenic to Yang Naiwu. Qian averred that he had not, that he did not even know Yang Naiwu, and further that he kept careful account of all drug sales, which were available for inspection. Master Zhang requested Qian Baosheng's presence at the magistrate's office. There, he was treated with great courtesy by Magistrate Liu, and Master Zhang came straight out with a request that Qian supply false testimony. Qian at first would not agree, but Magistrate Liu produced a document promising that Qian would not be connected to the case and would never have to confront Yang Naiwu. Pressing further, he persuaded Qian to sign a witness statement. With this new evidence in hand, Prefect Chen interrogated Yang Naiwu again, but still, Yang would not confess, and indeed decried his unjust punishment. Prefect Chen could only draw up the confession and take advantage of Yang's delirium under pain of torture to force his fingerprint onto the document. The case was then reported to the imperial inspector as having determined that Bok Choy had conspired to murder her husband, for which crime she deserved the punishment of slow execution by a thousand cuts; Yang Naiwu had plotted to kill a man and steal his wife, for which he deserved to have his head cut off and be placed on display.

The case of Yang Naiwu and Bok Choy went through several appeals, but all were carried out in the same location, and the relevant interrogating officials were connected with the previous investigation, so of course the verdict was never overturned. Later, though, the story was carried in the just-then established Shanghai newspaper, *Shenbao*, which exerted a major influence on public opinion. So much so, in fact, that officials in Beijing petitioned the power behind the throne, the Empress Dowager Cixi, and received her official permission to re-investigate the case under the auspices of the Ministry of Criminal Justice. The investigation was to include a re-examination of the body in Beijing. The body was now so decomposed that only bones remained, but careful comparison of available data with the standards dictated in the ancient forensics text *Xi yuan ji lu* demonstrated that Ge Pinlian had not died of poisoning. This meant that there was no basis to believe that Yang Naiwu and Bok Choy had committed a crime. Three years into the case, both were cleared of all wrongdoing.[2]

Yang Naiwu and Bok Choy present us with one of the most famous cases of wrongful conviction in all Chinese history. The initial and second trials have much to teach us about the judicial system in imperial China, including the arbitrary and barbaric nature of its methods in judicial proof. The case in question occurred at a time that most histories would call modern, or near modern, and yet it shows us a system that had remained basically unchanged since ancient times. The methods of judicial proof, in particular, remained at an ancient standard.

---

[2]See Zhou (1985).

2.2 Evolution of the Methods of Judicial Proof

In the human history of justice, there were major transformations to methods of judicial proof. The first was to transition from reliance on the gods to yield proof to human methods of proof. The second was to transition from basing a case on human evidence to basing a case on physical evidence. The history of the judicial proof falls into three stages, then, corresponding to these transformations. In the first stage, oaths to the gods and the trial by ordeals serve as the main form of proof. In the second stage, the testimony of litigants and witnesses in a case serve as the main form of proof. In the third stage, physical, or scientific, evidence serves as the main form of proof.

2.2.1 Judicial Proof Mainly with the Evidence of Gods

In general, there are two pathways by which humans can solve problems with cognitive activity: in one, someone else reports and you give answers. In another, you yourself go after the answers. Early humans, with their limited cognitive ability, would often seek help from the gods or past sages when they encountered questions otherwise too difficult to answer. Only later, as human cognitive ability improved, did they begin more and more to seek out for themselves all manner of "truth." Case investigation by law enforcement is one type of cognitive activity, and so develops along corresponding lines. Reviewing the development of methods of using evidence in criminal cases since ancient times, inside and outside of China, we easily discover this evolution from having others reveal the "truth" to discovery of "truth" on one's own.

In ancient societies, the range of human action and interaction was narrower, or in other words, the populations of human communities were smaller. Thus, cases were generally not complex and generally involved two parties in contention with each other. A says B stole his live stock. C says D damaged his property. Conflict between two parties leads to seeking out a judge or other party designated to make a verdict on the truth. In some cases, the judge was unable to come to a verdict based on the testimony of the two parties, so, lacking scientific methods of proof, turned to the power of gods for help. "Proof by gods" was the result.

"Proof by gods" entails some form of asking the gods to judge a case, as well as some form of expressing their will and intentions. The simplest method is to make an oath before the gods, and then give the basic facts of the case in a form strictly regulated by the religion. For example, in the Salic Law in use during the European Middle Ages, the use of sorcery was forbidden. If one party, say party A, accused another, say party B, of sorcery, then Party A was to state their claim in an oath to the gods made in court, making their accusation using forms and gestures that had to be in accordance with every detail of the rules of religious practice. The court then demanded that Party B make their counter-claim, also in accordance with detailed rules. Should any person not dare to swear an oath before God, or if they made any mistake in the forms or gestures of the testimony, or if they should stammer or stumble in the narration of the testimony, then their words would be interpreted as false, and the court would consider their suit to have failed.

However, even in those times there were some who did not believe in the gods, or didn't fear them. Perhaps they believed in the gods but felt that their punishments and rewards were more remote than the punishments established by humans. Thus, they lied to the gods. Moreover, with increased application of the oaths to the gods, they inspired less and less fear, precisely because parties could lie to the gods and get away with it. Those in the know on a particular case realized that the gods, too, made mistakes. In the end, all parties in a conflict would swear their case to the gods, making it very difficult to tell who was telling the truth and who was lying. Judicial officials would just have to find other methods of proof. All manner of religious methods were tried, including trial by water and trial by fire. These religious methods differed greatly from place to place around the world, and even the standards in any single method for judgment could differ greatly. Trial by water, for example, held a different standard in Babylon than among the Germanic peoples. Both tested the accused by dropping him into river water. In the former, the accused was considered guilty if he sank into the water, while in the latter, the accused was considered guilty for floating.[3]

Trial by fire made use of the scorching heat of a fire against a human body to determine the truth of a case. If Party A claimed that Party B stole her cow, for example, but Party B denied it, the judge might not be able to determine the truth, and so order both A and B to touch a red-hot branding iron. The judge would also say a prayer to the gods at this point. Then, according to which party's hand was not injured or else injured lightly or else quick to heal, the judge could determine whose testimony was true. In later times, only one party was tested. The judge only made one party undergo trial by fire, and if the question was resolved, the other party need not be tested. But if the result was inconclusive or else showed that the party tested was telling the truth, then the other party had to be tested as well.[4]

Religious methods supported by these sorts of tests were biased against those who took the test. Hands that touched hot iron were generally burnt by it, and only under extraordinary circumstances would 'the gods' ever intervene to prevent injury. There is a clear difference here from the method of taking oaths. In the latter method, as long as no special circumstances occurred, the person taking the oath could avoid punishment. Hence it can be seen that the selection by the judge of the person to undergo the testing in the former method functionally determined the outcome of the trial. Any judge who suspected a party of lying could demand him to take the test, and not simply take an oath, because the probability of a successful oath was in the party in question's favor, while the probability of a successful test result was not. Thus, more and more often, it was the accused who were first to take the tests of the gods.

---

[3]See Chen (1991, pp. 19–20).

[4]See Bartlett (2007). Also see Chen (1982, p. 17).

Under the system of proof by the gods, it was not the role of the judge to determine the facts of the case and to use those facts as the basis for the action of appropriate laws; rather, it was to play the role of host in the arbitration ceremony. The courts were not in fact law enforcement organs established to determine the facts of a case, but rather locations where the facts of the case were revealed by the gods. Judges able to swiftly and efficiently issue case verdicts did so only with the help of the gods. The judgment of the law was thus thought to be the will of the gods, a "truth" revealed as opposed to "truth" discovered by humans. Litigants need not use evidence and reasons to convince a judge of their claims, but appealed for help from the strength of the gods to demonstrate the legitimacy of their case.

These early methods of proof were more effective than we modern humans commonly think. Criminal litigation was at the time commonly seen as a conflict between two private parties, and what judges needed most was the authority to decide the case. Controlling the state meant preventing any litigants from taking the law into their own hands. Under these circumstances, an authoritative judgment was more important than a fair one.

The involvement of the gods certainly increased the authority of the judges. It also helped preserve the stability of social order. This was partly because people of those times blindly worshiped the gods, but also partly because the method did at times uncover the facts of cases. Oaths and testimony, for example, were delivered in the solemn environment of religious ceremony, which greatly increased their mystery and authority. People generally did not lie to the gods, or if they did they did so under great duress, which might cause them to reveal their lies with their expression or by evincing some reaction from the gods.

There is, moreover, a scientific basis for some of these religious methods, as with the method involving eating bread and cheese, once popular in continental Europe. In court, the accused was required to quickly consume an ounce of wheat bread and the same amount of cheese. If the accused swallowed the cheese easily and without trouble, it demonstrated his innocence. But difficulty swallowing, choking or spitting out the food was proof of guilt. There is some logic in this, since a guilty party under duress will often secrete much less saliva, leaving them dry-mouthed and unable to swallow. Of course, such a method cannot be considered scientific.

Europeans were certainly not the only civilization to develop methods of trial by ordeal. Law records from ancient India indicate eight such methods, including trial by fire, trial by river water, trial by scales, trial by poison, trial by holy water, trial by holy grains, trial by hot oil, and trial by the casting of lots.[5]

In ancient China, 'oaths to the gods' were also once used to determine the facts of cases. The *Zhou li*, or *Book of Changes*, records that litigants who filed suit also had to swear solemn oaths certifying the truth of their testimony. Still, there is insufficient historical evidence to demonstrate that 'oaths to the gods' were ever a major method of judicial proof in ancient China. There were methods similar to 'trial by ordeal,' such as the tale of how Gao Yao conducted trials using a 'sacred ram.' Gao Yao was in charge of law enforcement during the reign of the sage king Shun (about 2100

[5]See Chen (1982, pp. 31–32).

BC). During hearings held for difficult criminal cases, Gao Yao would bring in the 'sacred ram' to face the accused. If the sacred ram butted the accused with its horns, this indicated that the accused was guilty. No attempt to ram the accused indicated that the accused was not guilty. Certainly, methods mentioned above, such as trial by fire, or trial by water, never became popular in China, though they were practiced among some of the non-Han minority peoples. Some of these persisted until the first half of the twentieth century, including the Tibetan method of dredging hot oil, the Jingpo method of dredging boiling water, and the Yi peoples' practice of presenting plowshares.[6]

2.2.2 Judicial Proof Mainly with the Testimonial Evidence

Once judicial authority was no longer seen as purely for dispute arbitration, but also as a tool for political control and suppressing anti-social behavior, people became dissatisfied with unreasonable methods of proof. Especially representative of this process is an 11th century "Old West Frisian Law" of that Germanic tribe. We still see some influence from religion in this law, including oaths to the gods, fights with judicial authority and judgments revealed by the gods. But some parts of the law emphasize the use of witness testimony as evidence. West Frisians lived on the Frisian archipelago adjoining the coastal lowlands of the Netherlands, where they lived under constant threat of soil erosion. All communities participated in the construction of dikes and dams. Should any fail to perform this basic duty, the sea respected no gods, so people of the area began to avoid involving "the will of God" in their system of laws. For example, suppose local government charged a resident with shirking dike duty, but the person denied the charges. Both parties gave oaths before God that their testimony was correct, and both sides had witnesses willing to make similar oaths. In such circumstances, the law did not defer to the gods, but stipulated that the parties could employ "legal representation" to investigate the testimony.[7] This is a clear challenge to the authority of God.

It would be several hundred more years before this rebuttal of the proof of the gods would fully develop, because there were two preconditions necessary for it to develop: first, an increase in the legal authority of national governments, and second, increased awareness among the general population. This was a slow process. Only when legal authorities became formal components of government, when said legal authorities established professional criminal investigators, and when skepticism began to replace religious fervor did people begin gradually to rid themselves of the non-rational methods of religious law.[8]

As the general level of awareness increased, more and more people believed that the judgments of religious law were not reliable. More and more people did not

[6]See Xia (1990).

[7]See Noye (1991).

[8]ibid., p. 10.

wish for their fates to be decided by religious authority, so they began to take back legal authority away from religion and instead institute methods of proof centered on people. Witness testimony became the main element of proof in legal proceedings, and interrogation became the main method of determining the facts in criminal cases. Torture became an important tool for extracting evidence.

China has a long history of interrogation by torture, with the practice already widespread by the time of the Zhou dynasty (about 1100–221 AD), some two thousand years ago. A passage in the ancient text *Li ji*, or the Book of Rites, suggests that in the spring, the state would do well to decrease its application of *si lue*, a term that evidently refers to interrogation by torture.[9] In the spring, the practice had to be limited to guarantee normal rates of agricultural production, but this merely indicates that torture was widely applied during the other three seasons of the year. There are also specific rules regarding the use of torture recorded in the legal code Qin dynasty (221–207 AD). A version of the Qin code discovered in Hubei province in 1975 contains a passage that explains that during a trial, the accused must be fully interrogated, and his testimony recorded in written form. If the accused refuse to tell the truth after fully interrogation, he should be tortured according to law.[10]

During the period when interrogation was the main method for finding facts in a case, the use of torture was a necessary byproduct. It reflected the limited general level of understanding, as well as the barbarity still inherent in the legal system. But such methods of interrogation have been opposed and attacked all along. In the Qin legal code, for instance, there is a passage that says that the superior method is to find the truth through interrogation and cross-examination without the use of beatings, and that the use of beatings is an inferior method.[11] Lu Wenshu of the Western Han dynasty (206 AD–8 BC) wrote in his memorials to the emperor his complaints against the evils of the system of interrogation by torture. He believed that torture often resulted in wrongful punishment of innocent people. "Nothing good comes of a beating", he said. And the law of Tang dynasty (618–907 BC) also notes that because legal officials practicing torture often beat the accused to death, torture should be limited by law. According to the law, magistrates could use tortures for three times in interrogating an accused, and the total number of beatings could not exceed two hundred strikes. Should an accused die as a result of torture conducted within these limits, the magistrate was not culpable; otherwise the magistrate was to be given a two-year prison term.[12]

But in practice, legal regulations could not prevent the abuse of the system. Of course there were corrupt officials who could be bribed to torture or even kill on request, but beyond that, even figures like Judge Bao, famous for his incorruptibility, referred to torture as the "house method" for reaching verdicts. "Without torture", Judge Bao is reputed to have said, "how are we to reach truthful confessions"? The Song dynasty (960–1279) text on interrogation methods, *Wen xian tong kao* (or

---

[9]See Zhang (1985).

[10]ibid., p. 122.

[11]ibid.

[12]ibid., p. 230.

"Comprehensive investigations based on documentary sources"), has a whole chapter on interrogation by torture, recording that throughout China at the time, "rattan was preferred to thorned vine, though some use two thorned vines braided together." On frequency of punishment, the same text records that "feet and buttocks can each be given three to five hundred strikes".[13] Under this system, wrongful convictions such as those recorded in the story of Yang Naiwu and Bok Choy were common.

And yet at the same time, other Chinese officers of the law were exploring more scientific methods of investigation. As early as the Zhou dynasty, some advocated "listening to the two sides of every case," for one should not prejudicially trust "single-sided" interrogations. Eventually a theory of "finding facts in a lawsuit with five hearings" appears. A passage in the *Book of Changes* has it that in legal proceedings, there are five expressions of the litigant that must be heard if the real plight of the people is to be sought. Expression one is the words. Expression two is the outward countenance. Expression three is the breath. Expression four is the response, and expression five is the eyesight. Zheng Xuan, a scholar of the later Han dynasty, elaborates on the text as follows: "hearing the words" means "observing how the words come out, for they sound upset when they are irregular"; "hearing the outward countenance" means "observing the expression of the face, for they are blushed when irregular"; "hearing the breath" means "observing the breath, for it gasps, 'out of breath', when irregular"; "hearing the response" means "observing their hearing ability, for it will appear puzzled when irregular"; and "hearing the eyesight" means "observing the pupils, which will appear muddled and dazed when irregular".[14]

Chinese history is full of excellent judicial officers who were adept at catching the sort of little details that others often missed. They asked probing questions that helped them unlock the true facts. Physical evidence of various and sundry kinds also came into use over the same range of time.

2.2.3 *Judicial Proof Mainly with the Physical Evidence*

The use of physical evidence in judicial trials accompanied advancements in scientific technology. Physical evidence had objective existence, but it could not very well take itself to court to help finding the facts of a case. It needed human activities, such as collection, examination, and explain. Generally speaking, physical evidence requires interpretation, which often draws on scientific knowledge. In most instances, physical evidence without science does not live up to its potential.

In judicial trials throughout human history, the use of physical evidence has tended to undergo scattered development, with occasional major shifts. Only since the end of the 18th century, as the relevant scientific techniques were systematized and regularized, did the use of physical evidence first start to become the main method of judicial proof. The nineteenth century was a period of significant improvements.

[13]ibid., p. 255.

[14]ibid., pp. 48–49.

These occur in two main areas: the rise of forensic science; and the methods of human identification, or, more precisely, individualization.

Chinese forensic science dates back for thousands years. Case records from the Qin dynasty indicate rudimentary forensic examinations of bodies. Song Ci, a well-known magistrate in the Song Dynasty, is now celebrated as the greatest scholar of forensic studies of his era. He is the author of *Xi yuan ji lu* ("Records of washing away injustice"), now thought to be the earliest text on the subject of forensic science. Europeans of the Middle Ages also practiced forensic examinations. Some scholars made contributions to forensic examination technique, and some countries established regulations for the application of forensic science to the law. Still, before the 18th century, developments in this area were slow and scattered.

Human identification, including identification of all parties involved in a case, and especially criminal perpetrators, has long been an important job of criminal justice. In ancient China, criminals were once tattooed on the face to distinguish them. In ancient Babylon, ancient India, and some parts of Europe, criminals were branded. Such methods were, we hasten to say, as unscientific as they were uncivilized, the products of a barbaric age. Of course, before the 18th century, law enforcement officials of some countries had begun to make use of facial features, handwriting, or idiosyncratic movements to make identifications, but no scientific systems had yet taken form.

Scientific techniques improved by leaps and bounds in the 19th century, and so did techniques of identification. Handwriting analysis, for example, had become a science. Not only was it taught in universities, but differing schools of thought had developed around the topic. In 1879, a young employee at the Paris Prefecture of Police, Alphonse Bertillon, invented anthropometry. He used the combined results of medicine, demographics, and statistics to identify criminals by their skeletal structure, and this was later successfully applied in criminal justice proceedings. Some say this was the first time scientific method had been applied in human identification. Around the same time, other criminologists in Europe and the United States systematized the analysis of fingerprints, making it the most effective means of criminal identification. The appearance of fingerprinting was certainly a milestone in the history of criminal justice.

Since the 20th century, scientific advancement useful to criminal justice has continued and even accelerated. New weapons in the criminal investigation arsenal include footprint analysis, dental analysis, voice pattern recognition, and lip pattern recognition. An even more significant leap forward took place in the 1980s with the development of DNA identification. In some developed countries, physical evidence now holds pride of place in criminal investigation and judicial proof. Modern criminal justice relies on scientific methods that give a primary place to physical evidence.

In a word, the method of judicial proof has entered the scientific age. In this complex contemporary world, where new scientific advancements are made every day, the technological capability of criminals is ever improving, as it is in the larger environment, which means that a fair criminal justice system needs scientific techniques and improved scientific standards. Judicial officers must handle cases using science. This is what is needed and appropriate in these times. In terms of specific judicial practices in China, criminal investigators, prosecutors, and judges must first transform their mindset, from taking human evidence as primary to taking physical evidence as primary, in order to improve the methods of judicial proof. Meanwhile, they must also improve the technology applied to human evidence, such as psychological analysis and behavior analysis.

2.3 Development of the System of Judicial Proof

Judicial proof can come in two types, "free proof" and "regulated proof." "Free proof" means that the proof is in no way limited by the law; fact finders in legal proceedings may collect and apply evidence as they see fit. Regulated proof, on the other hand, are regulated according to law; these must be followed by fact finders as they collect and apply evidence. In recent years, some Chinese scholars of criminal evidence have been enthusiastic supporters of free proof in its classic form, the 'proof with intimate conviction.' But they have criticized and even denounced the regulated proof in their classic form, the system of legal proof. This has influenced awareness of the two types of judicial proof among the larger public. There are in fact advantages and disadvantages to both free and regulated proof, and now in most countries, judicial officers apply some of both, with mere differences of degree.

Over the long term, the developments of judicial proof exhibit a pattern of reversing the system last applied, passing from the free proof to the regulated proof, and back again, in an upward-moving spiral. On the surface, each "reversal" appears to be a return to an earlier stage, but in actual substance, each reversal takes us to a higher level of the spiral, with something new for every so-called "return." The situation is clearer in some countries than it is in others. It is worth noting that, were the range of evidence types to be increased to include physical evidence and circumstantial evidence, then supplying specific regulations regarding the strength of each type of evidence would have been extremely difficult.

2.3.1 The Trial by Gods as an Initial Step from Free Proof to Regulated Proof

It is widely acknowledged that both criminal trials and conflict arbitration were, in their earliest forms, modes of free proof. Although there are no historical records that testify directly to this, we may so conclude based on the development of human society and other knowledge related to this. The legal rules of judicial proof evolved into existence, as the product of accumulated experience of legal practice. Notably, in the early stage of human society, no rules of evidence were applied in regard to resolving conflicts between parties. There was an arbitration authority, generally the chiefs or elders of tribes or nations, who gave their verdict, which was based on their own experience and conscience, on the evidence supplied by the parties involved, which generally took the form of testimony from parties and witnesses. Clearly, such action falls within the scope of free proof.

As societies grew larger and more complex, conflicts between parties increased, cases requiring arbitration increased, and the cases themselves grew more complex. The general level of human understanding was still low, and the use of evidence to ascertain the facts in a dispute or a case was still rare, which led to many a wrongful verdict. Parties subject to wrongful verdict began to lose respect for the authority of their chiefs and elders, expressing skepticism or even outright challenges to these. judicial decisions require authority; the judgment without authority is doomed. If human authority was insufficient to hold up the judgment, then the authority of the gods had to be enlisted. Hence, the appearance and application of the 'Proof by gods'.

The proof by gods was, as I mentioned above, the product of superstition, and worship of gods. It is a method of proof that lacks rational, scientific basis. But the proof by gods has its advantages, especially given historical conditions of the times. Under the earliest conditions of free proof, the judgments were chaotic and mistake-ridden. With the litigants' testimonies serving as the primary form of evidence, and with the interpretation of such oral testimonies so easily influenced by individual factors related to the arbitrator, the same evidence could receive two different determinations from two different arbitrators. The proof by gods provided a unified standard for selecting trustworthy evidence and determining the facts. The rules and regulations must be followed, regardless of the arbitrator, and judgment must be issued in accordance with pre-ordained standards. The arbitrator was not free to use evidence or state their determinations of the facts as they saw fit, which resulted in effective control over the disorder generated by individual differences among arbitrators. The proof by gods may seem suspicious, even ridiculous, to our modern eyes, but it may have been more effective than we now realize. In those days, the authority of judgment was evidently more important than its having a rational basis, and in any case people's faith in the gods trumped their understanding of justice and rationality. Thus we may observe that the proof by gods helped standardize and regularize legal proceedings more generally by increasing the authority of judgments and protecting the overall stability of society. It was a first step taken during a benighted age, the first step from free proof to regulated proof.

2.3.2 The Legal Proof as a Second Try to Go from Free Proof to Regulated Proof

Between the 13th and 15th centuries, the system of judicial proof in continental Europe, of which the kings of France may be said to be representative, had one basic feature, which is that judges in legal proceedings enjoyed absolute freedom over the use of evidence. In other words, the law in no way limited how these judges collected and used evidence, and these judges could make their determinations based on their individual knowledge, experience, interests, desires and aversions. The mode of judicial proof had once again returned to the primitive state of free proof.

Free proof lacks consistent principles and standards, making it prone to cause disorder within judicial activities, which in turn increased the general disorder of continental European countries, which were just then in a state of political instability and disunity. It was all too common for the similar facts and similar cases to be given different verdicts by different judges. Thus, as the political authority of European countries became more stable and unified, among the very first orders of business was to reform the disorder in law enforcement, unify local and regional judicial activities, and in particular to regulate the use of evidence and determination of facts in criminal justice. Thus, the judicial proof in European countries once again began to trend from the free proof to the regulated proof. Finally, in the 16th century, they reached a new peak by achieving a mode of "legal proof", establishing an evaluation system of legal evidence. The system of legal evidence dictated that the weight of evidence used in criminal justice varied according to legal rules, and any judge determining a case must adhere strictly to these rules. They did not have freedom and discretion in evaluating evidence in criminal trials.

During the 16th century, countries in mainland Europe, such as France, established specific rules regarding the values of all types of evidence, and on this basis established standards of proof to which all judges were to adhere. Criminal cases, for example, were subject to the following rules: 1. A full proof should have a conviction; no full proof should have no conviction; 2. The best full proof should be two reliable witnesses whose testimonies determined consistently and conclusively the guilt of the accused; 3. No matter how reliable, a single witness only constituted half of a full proof; 4. The other half of the full proof could be comprised of a confession by the accused, an official record or a testimony by another party that corroborated the first half of the proof; 5. Testimony from a witness closely connected to the case only counted for one quarter of full proof, and its value further reduced by half when credible counter evidence existed; 6. The addition of any two halves of a full proof constituted a full proof; the addition of any two quarters or four eighths of a full proof constituted half a proof. In sum, when the evidence added up to a full proof against the accused, the judge must issue a guilty verdict, and if the evidence did not so add up, the verdict must be not guilty. Judges hearing trial must rigorously adhere to the rules, despite any individual feelings regarding any specific element of the evidence. This sort of system denied the judge the authority to freely evaluate the evidence and determine the facts of the case. Rather, the judge must work mechanically, in accordance with the standards.[15]

This system grew in popularity in Europe during the period when human evidence was of primary importance in criminal justice. In trials of this period, witness testimony was the most important and oft-used form of evidence. Further, primary among this sort of evidence was testimony with direct bearing on the major facts of the case. In sum, we note two outstanding characteristics of judicial proof in these

[15] See Chen (1991, pp. 25–26).

times: first, the range of evidence was narrow, consisting mainly of witness testimony and well as testimony from others involved in the case and some documentary evidence; second, the truth and reliability of such evidence was of primary importance, because the value of evidence directly bearing on the case was most easily seen. These two outstanding characteristics supported the possibility for a system of legal proof. Indeed, it would have been very difficult to expand the range of evidence types to include all manner of physical and circumstantial evidence, and to assign to each of these new types a particular weight of proof by rules.

The legal proof system has major advantages. First and foremost, the system introduces the concept of "full proof," which also acts as the standard for establishing a guilty verdict in criminal cases. The particular wording of this standard may not have been satisfactorily clear, but a degree of certainty was achieved in combination with other rules, to be discussed presently. This system was also a basis for assigning weight of proof to each piece of evidence. Second, the rule stipulating that consistent testimonies from two reliable witnesses constituted a full proof. Experience tells us that a case narrative compiled from the direct perceptions of the facts of the case as delivered from two fair and upright witnesses can prove the veracity of this case narrative. Thus, this rule was in accordance with the general principle of judicial proof. Moreover, the system of legal proof also contains a rule stipulating that the testimony of just one reliable witness does not constitute a full proof. This rule captures the essence of the old principle "single evidence in isolation do not prove guilt." This principle may seem a little simplistic and mechanical, but determining guilt based on single evidence increases the possibility of wrongful conviction. During a period when judicial practices were less orderly, such a prudent regulation was understandable. Still another rule stipulates that witnesses with close connection to the case could supply testimony that would be taken at only half the strength of proof otherwise admitted. Should such evidence be effectively impeached in court by the accused, its strength would be halved yet again. Since evidence from one side is often impeached in court by the other side, and it is often crucial, in making a verdict, to judge the strength of proof of such evidence, this rule is perhaps the most important and of the most significance in real trials. This was remarkable, given the historical conditions. Finally, the system of legal proof makes clear the additional rules that assign strength of proof to individual items of evidence, and reaffirms the standard whereby a guilty verdict can be delivered. The above analysis shows us that the regulations in the system of legal proof enjoy a degree of scientific and rational basis, and some of these rules would still be useful to criminal justice today.

Of course, the system also presents disadvantages. First and foremost, the system for assigning strength of proof to items of evidence was too inflexible and not dynamic enough. The judge seemed to apply evidence to determine cases by mechanical application of the rules to assign strength of proof to items of evidence. The verdict is then arrived at simply by summing up the strengths. In this manner, complex problems are simplified, which in certain cases can lead to wrong or inappropriate verdicts. Moreover, the system of legal proof makes it easy to abuse the use of torture to obtain confessions. Under this system, because the confession of the accused accounts for half the proof, and the law does not regulate how such a confession is extracted by law officers, confessions obtained through torture were quite common. In fact, the laws of the times seemed to say to law enforcement officers: if you have half a proof currently in hand, torture can get you the other half in the form of a confession. The system thus gives a "green light" to the use of torture to extract confessions.

The system of legal proof is an extreme form of regulated proof. It is the product of the social and cultural factors then. The theoretical and cultural basis for the system of legal proof was the intellectual current of Europe at the time, where worship of authority was popular. In that society, particularly in the area of academic research, authority was very important. Often, when a view or statement was evaluated, the authority of the speaker or the pedigree of the statement outranked the rational or scientific basis for the statement. Thus it became the fashion for speakers to base all their statements on classical texts from long ago, speaking only when ancient philosophers had first mentioned the topics the speaker wished to mention. It was unavoidable that such a fashion should influence views on criminal justice, ushering in the birth of the system of legal proof, with its strong respect for law and refusal to allow free use of evidence. Moreover, the system was also based in part on the division of social classes. Social class was the foundation of European countries in those times. Both the feudal system of secular class and the system of class within the clergy were basic organizing principles of society, exerting major influence on people's views. Since people came in many classes, so then must the types of evidence used in criminal justice, and the law could prescribe the effective strength of each type of evidence. The laws of some countries also assigned effective strength differently to witnesses of different social classes. The testimony of the aristocracy, for example, was more valuable than the testimony of ordinary persons; the testimony of members of the clergy was also more valuable than the testimony of members of lay society; the testimony of Christians was more valuable than that of Jews; the testimony of men was more valuable than women. These are all reflections, in the law, of the social classes in society.

The various rules within the system of legal proof were the summation of legal experience at the time, and provided a degree of scientific and rational basis. As a mode of judicial proof, this system was in part rational and effective, and in part not. In other words, it came with both advantages and disadvantages. Today people may notice easily those contents of the system which were unscientific and irrational, but this system to analyze evidence was a bold attempt to systematize judicial activities.

2.3.3 The Proof with Intimate Conviction as a Big Step to Go Back to Free Proof

After the 17th century, the Bourgeois revolution and the Enlightenment movement in continental Europe spurred new reforms in criminal justice, including in the use of evidence. The system of legal proof received new challenges from humanism and rationalism, which upheld freedom and rights as well as individual knowledge and understanding. Fierce new attacks against the system that encouraged the use of torture to extract confessions were one of the results. One of the thinkers of the French Enlightenment, Montesquieu, believed that extracting confession through torture was a characteristic of feudal tyrannical states, because in a tyranny, what inspires the most terror is what works best. Italian criminologist Cesare Beccaria suggests that verdicts based on the gut feelings of non-legal specialists were often more correct than verdicts arrived at through the rules of law by legal professionals. In some circumstances, confessions extracted through torture might do just the opposite of solving the case, leading instead to wrongful conviction. These attacks reached their climax around the time of the French Revolution, and in the end led to reform of the entire system.

On 26th December 1790, Adrien Duport, jurist in the post-revolutionary Constituent Assembly, presented a reform proposal before said Assembly. He argued that the application of the system of legal proof was preposterous, a threat to both the accused and to society at large. Only by giving the judge presiding over trial the authority to freely decide on the evidence would ensure the court had the best chance of determining the facts of cases, and from there deliver the correct verdict. On 18th January 1791, the Constituent Assembly passed Duport's proposal, and it passed into law on 29th September of that year, thus establishing the system of proof with intimate conviction. This reform to evidence law was later written into the 1808 French Criminal Code, the *Code d'instruction criminelle.* Other countries in continental Europe soon began to imitate the French reforms.

The term "proof with intimate conviction" means that the value of evidence would no longer be determined according to clear and specific rules. Instead, the judge and members of a jury would evaluate all items of evidence in a case according to their own "universal understanding" to judge the strength of proof. The 1808 *Code d'instruction criminelle* gives specific provisions for the system of proof with intimate conviction. It takes jury as main precedent, and requires that the court issue the following information before the jury meets to deliberate the case: the law did not require the jury to supply the reasoning they had taken to reach their verdict; the law supplied no advance rules by which to decide evidence sufficient; but the law did require the jurors to focus, deep in their own conscience, on the impression formed by the evidence against and in favor of the accused. The law would not say to them they must evaluate some specific number of witnesses to prove the facts beyond any doubt. The law would also not say they needed to present a full proof comprised of some specific combination of evidence, from oral testimony to documents and more. The law, in fact, asked them a question, one which their sole duty consisted of answering: "Are you certain with intimate conviction?" For this reason the system of proof with intimate conviction, of which France was the main representative, became so known. Its basic principle was that only free proof led to convincement.[16]

Proof with intimate conviction had the virtue of flexibility and adaptivity with regard to individual cases. Cases with complex circumstances involving many persons could also involve many different types of evidence. The social environment

[16]ibid., pp. 31–33.

was also changing all the time, so that when judicial authorities were using evidence to determine cases according to the way they saw fit, this helped them stick close to the circumstances of the case, and so uphold justice and fairness in the judiciary. However, proof with intimate conviction lacked a consistent standard for authentication, making it easy for the personal bias of the judicial officer to influence the case, which at times led to judicial misuse of evidence. To large degree, the system of proof with intimate conviction depended on the professionalism and moral rigor of the individual judge, which yielded many opportunities for unscrupulous and arbitrary action on the judge's part. Such a system, in other words, was suited to countries in which the highest elites of legal studies served as judges.

While the system of legal proof had been an extreme mode of regulated proof, the system of proof with intimate conviction was an extreme mode of free proof. The shift from one to the other was a clear case of extremes driving towards their opposites, overcompensating for them in the end. Since the mid-20th century, legal systems of continental European countries like France have changed in several ways. The system of proof with intimate conviction has largely remained intact, but continental European countries began to strengthen the regulation by law of judicial proof once again, including strict new rules for the collection and processing of evidence for criminal legal proceedings, for the exclusion of illegally obtained evidence, and a stronger role for the testimony of the accused. The freedom of the judges under proof with intimate conviction was limited by the principle of open and transparent convincement. From this we can see that as European countries have gone from the one extreme to another, they have attempted compromise. If we say that the US and UK systems today are *relatively* more in the mode of regulated proof, then the continental European systems are also *relatively* more in the mode of free proof. In other words, both sets of systems are actually compromises. This likely also reflects a general route of the historical developments of judicial proof.

2.3.4 The Regulated Proof Meets the Requirement of Judicial Proof

The system of regulated proof is opposed to the system of free proof, which means the researcher must place each in context with the other. The primary function of judicial proceedings is accurate determination of the facts in a case. Which of these two modes of judicial proof accomplishes more accurate fact finding? It is generally believed that free proof is better for finding the facts, because the law does not limit judicial discretion, and so judicial officers can use a greater variety of methods to discover the truth. The system of regulated proof, by contrast, is thought to be in allegiance with the overall direction of social policies and values, which in this instance is obstacles to judicial determination of the truth. The author personally believes that a few of the rules of regulated proof (such as the exclusionary rule against illegal evidence) certainly do not serve to bring to light the truth, and in some cases even obstruct officers of the court from so doing, but most rules of regulated proof are of aid in ascertaining the truth. The exclusionary rule against hearsay is one example. The most substantial difference between these two systems has to do with the division of power between the legislation and the judiciary. The system of free proof gives all authority for the case over to the judge, while under the system of regulated proof, some authority is retained by the legislator. While it is certain that authority for the judiciary is of aid in determining the specific facts of cases, the prerequisite for this is that the judicial authority in question must be someone of great moral rigor, knowledge, skills, and experience. Regulated proof, by contrast, begins with a skeptical stance towards the judiciary, so the legislator must first produce universally applicable rules based on the regulation of judicial proceedings. People may note in passing that the system of regulated proof is harder to construct than the system of free proof, because the universal rules for determining cases have to be made on a scientific and rational basis, which is certainly not easy. Still, ascertaining the facts of a case is only one of the problems to be considered in establishing a system of judicial proof. In other regards, regulated proof has considerable advantage over free proof. There are three major considerations.

1. The regulated proof is good for promoting judicial fairness. One of the basic demands of judicial fairness is that the similar cases be dealt with by the judiciary similarly. To make all equal in the eyes of the law, judicial officials must assess and evaluate their evidence with respect for unified rules, without too much freedom to interpret for themselves. From this it can be seen that the mode of regulated proof is better than the mode of free proof at upholding judicial fairness.
2. The regulated proof is good for promoting the predictability of the judgment. In a society under rule of law, the decision of the judiciary should be predictable. In other words, members of society should be able to predict court decisions and so arrange or constrain their own behavior. To satisfy this need, the rules of using evidence in proceedings must be clear and specific, open to everyone to know, and everyone should be able to predict the results of their application. Under the system of free proof, the discretion of the judges to make interpretations lowers the predictability of the judiciary.
3. The regulated proof is good for promoting the authority of the judiciary. Determining the facts of a case according to prescribed rules and on this basis issuing a verdict makes it easier to obtain the approval and consent of society, which in turn raises the authority of the judiciary. On this question, the system of regulated proof certainly gains the approval of society more easily than free proof. Of course, the rules must be scientific and rational to gain social approval.[17]

The nature of judicial decision making requires a system of regulated proof. First and foremost, finding the truth in judicial proceedings is not equivalent to finding the truth in other social activities. For one thing, it directly involves the rights to life and property of the people in the case. Another thing to consider is that judicial proceedings are one way the government manages society, so it comes with a quality

[17] See Cohen (1997).

of public service. People also regularly work to find the truth in the society. A father, for example, may seek to find out why his children are fighting, and determine who has the more reasonable claim. And a wife may seek to determine whether her husband has been having an affair. These determinations of facts are private, individual matters, so the people involved may freely collect evidence and make a judgment. But judicial proceedings are not the same. Judicial officials may not do as private citizens and casually determine cases according to their desires. They must accept the standards and restrictions of the law. What's more, individuals are easily influenced by individual bias or external factors, and judicial officers are no exception to this rule. In judicial proceedings involving large interests, the law does not watch from one side with folded arms, but must use scientific and rational rules to minimize individual bias and error. For this reason, what judicial proceedings require is the system of regulated proof.

The judiciary is a mechanism of human society by which conflicts are resolved. It is faced with all the different kinds of conflict in society. To act as such a mechanism become a symbol for conflict resolution, its proceedings must carry authority, and this authority must be built on a basis of justice and fairness. In democratic societies ruled by law, authority must be protected by principles of transparency. Justice and fairness must also be upheld by rational principles. The system of regulated proof, then, which apply legal rules to limit the judicial officer's freedom to use evidence, is suited to this mechanism of conflict resolution, satisfying the judiciary's need for authority and fairness. In other areas of society, in the study of history or archaeology, for example, people also need to collect evidence and seek the truth. But these activities do not have the function of solving social conflict, so their investigations and proofs can proceed under the auspices of science, without the necessity of legal rules to protect the fairness of the results.

Within the proceedings of a judicial proof, there exists an internal contradiction: the judiciary must make a clear decision based on unclear knowledge. Owing to the limits of subjective observation, judicial officers often possess an unclear knowledge of the cases they investigate. The facts of the case, we might say, are not clearly determined in the mind of the judicial officer—it's not a case of calling a thing black when it's not white, but rather that everything is a shade of gray. In a criminal case, for example, the court may not gain a full understanding of whether the accused is guilty or not guilty, but rather whether the accused is possibly guilty or possibly not guilty. But the judgment must be clear and certain. The judge cannot rule an accused "possibly guilty," but only "guilty" or "not guilty." To give clear and rational judgments based on unclear facts requires legal principles, such as the principle regarding the burden of proof. Without legal principles and rules, the judges may make bad decisions and lead society into disorder.

Finally, judicial proceedings must always be based on certain social values, and serve some social policies. As we said above, establishing the facts of a case is only one of the aims of the judiciary. Other aims include keeping the peace and protecting people's rights. There may be conflict between the various aims of the judiciary, which means the law must be adjusted by further regulation and reform to balance out the aims of social value. In different countries and in different times, social values themselves change and require adjustment, which must be realized through legal principles. Good examples of this are the banning of torture and the exclusion of illegal evidence from criminal justice proceedings. Seen either in terms of practice or in terms of statistics, illegal practices like torture are of use to determine the facts with most of the evidence. But given the value we place in human rights and judicial fairness, the law must strip judicial officers of the freedom to use such evidence.

We can see, then, that the regulations and characteristics of legal proceedings demand regulated proof. They ought, in other words, to tend towards law-based proof. In terms of the development and direction of judicial proof legal, the system of regulated proof is mainstream, while free proof is supplementary. Once humans can devise scientific and rational rules, they should not endow judges with authority of free interpretation. Such authority is deserved only when such rules are not available.

We see, here, the difference between judicial proof and other, more general types of proof in social activities. We also see two forces pushing the development of the judicial proof, and these forces are in conflict. General proofs tend to be free, but judicial proofs tend to be regulated. General proofs seek scientific bases only, but judicial proofs seek both scientific and rational bases, including judicial fairness and alignment with the principles of social values. The scientific aim drives judicial proof towards the free mode, while the aim of rationality drives judicial proof towards the regulated mode. It is the interaction of these two driving forces that cause the history of judicial proof to exhibit the tendency to 'reverse what was reversed before.' Judicial proof can only proceed from free proof to regulated one step at a time. If we admit that the trial by the gods was a first step, during a benighted age, away from free proof and towards the regulated mode, then the establishment of a great number of evidence rules in the UK and the US, and the establishment of the system of legal proof in continental Europe are both examples of the rational-based drive towards regulated proof. Today, people should keep to the path towards the system of regulated proof, a path that requires judicial proof to be more scientific, and more rational.

2.4 Improvement of the Judicial Proof System in China

In recent years, reform of the system of judicial proof in China has been a major concern for the legal profession, as well as a pressing concern for law enforcement practice. To institute the reform, we first need a direction for such reforms, otherwise it will turn into a blind search for novelty that risks causing disorder in law enforcement. And when it comes to a clear direction for reform, one of the basic issues is the selection of free proof or regulated proof. In answering this question, we must study the lessons of the experience of foreign countries, and the trends in world development. We must also analyze the Chinese historical tradition and the practical needs of China today.

2.4.1 The Basic Mode of Judicial Proof in China Is Free Proof

In the last few thousand years of history, the mode of judicial proof in China has passed through the stages of original free proof, to regulated proof with trial by the gods, and then from absolutely free proof to relatively free proof. In judicial proceedings over the long arc of history, judges in China tend not to accept the limitations of law in assessing evidence and finding facts in litigation. Judges make free judgments based entirely on their own experience and knowledge and the specific circumstances of the case. As experience accumulated, however, the law in some dynasties began to restrict the prerogative of judges. In the laws of the Tang dynasty, for example, we find the principle of *ju zhong zheng ding zui*, or "basing conviction on a crowd." One commentary, the *Tang lü shu yi*, explains that "a crowd is defined as three or more witnesses who testify clearly to the facts. This is required to conviction." This rule requiring the clear testimonies of three or more witnesses resembles the continental European stipulation for a full proof, that the testimonies of two reliable witnesses be required. In addition, during criminal trials, confessions by the accused were considered the best basis by which to determine guilt. Hence, two principles that form in Chinese feudal laws are *duan zui bi qu shu fu gong ci*, "determination of guilt must come from confession of the accused," and *wu gong bu lu an*, "no case record shall be made without confession". Of course, some opposed blind faith in confession by the accused, emphasizing that such confessions must be evaluated carefully. In general, Chinese judges enjoyed a wide prerogative in the assessment and use of evidence. The legalistic tone of the two principles "determination of guilt must come from confession of the accused" and "no case record shall be made without confession" are mere exceptions. Chinese judicial proof, in other words, are of the category of free proof.

Between the end of imperial China and the beginning of the Republican era, China began to study the laws and judicial practices of other countries, including the history of evidence systems. The Republic of China's criminal procedure law and civil procedure law, for example, are based on precedents from the west, including the presumption of innocence, proof with intimate conviction, oral arguments, and restrictions against the use of torture. There were also relatively clear provisions for questions of investigative responsibility towards evidence. But disorder over these years, combined with the tyrannical government of the ruling party (the Kuomintang), the system of evidence put into practice by the judiciary was very far from the system of evidence written in law. Presumption of innocence and the restriction against torture, for example, were just so many empty words on paper. Proof with intimate conviction, since it was very close to the traditional Chinese system, and because it placed no restrictions on abuse of power by judicial officers, was adopted without much opposition. Even though Chinese judicial practices in this period still exhibited considerable differences from the system of proof with intimate conviction as used in continental Europe, China was, in its basis, applying a mode of free proof.

With the establishment of the People's Republic of China in 1949, a new system of evidence was established, one that rid itself of the traces of the Republican system and looked instead to a basis in the revolution. New laws of the 1950s saw new principles for judicial work, including 'seeking truth from facts,' prioritizing investigation, prioritizing evidence and no relying on confessions, strictly forbidding torture, clearing the burden of proof, and requiring that evidence be truthful and sufficient. But from the late 1950s until the end of the Cultural Revolution in 1976, repeated waves of political movements and social disorder left law enforcement and judiciary in China paralyzed. Beginning in the late 1970s, Chinese legal system began to recover and improve. The present system of judicial proof in China is based on the criminal procedure law, the civil procedure law, and the administrative procedure law. In terms of judicial proof, despite the strict ban on torture and a provision that says guilt cannot be determined based on confession alone, the habit of applying the principals of 'seek truth from facts' and 'make specific analysis with specific questions' has made the law extremely vague and lacking in its regulation of evidence. The result is that judges enjoy tremendous prerogative over the use of evidence to determine cases. In a word, the present system falls within the scope of free proof.

2.4.2 China Should Take the Road Towards Regulated Proof

Free proof and regulated proof both have their upsides and downsides, but the latter is both better aligned with the internal requirements of judicial work, and better suited to the needs of current Chinese society. There are many problems with the judicial system and its practice in China today: the judiciary lacks authority and independence; the professional character and behavior of judicial officers are uneven and inconsistent; and some officers have frequently misused their authority and accepted bribes to bend the law. These have all left a severe impact on the fairness and effectiveness of the law, as well as a severe impact on the stability and healthy development of society. A wide range of social factors contributes to this, which means that the system of judiciary alone will not solve the problem. Still, faced as we are with this current state of social affairs, the system of regulated proof far exceeds free proof in realizing fairness and effectiveness in law enforcement, and it advances the stability and healthy development of society, as well.

The basis of regulated proof is a clear and unified set of rules. Judges must assess and apply evidence to find facts in a case according to the rules. They do not have much discretion, and there is little space for them to blow 'the back whistle.' The system of regulated proof, then, can increase public trust in judiciary, and increase the authority of the judgments. It would also reduce the outside interference in judicial work, protecting the independence of the judiciary in no uncertain degree. It can also make up for what judges lack in their professional character and behavior, and reduce the opportunity for judicial corruption. In a society like China's, based as it is on *guanxi*, or personal relationships, when too much discretion is given to judges, litigants will use any means they can to find the 'back doors,' making use of their *guanxi* and even bribery to cause the judge in charge to use her prerogative to favor one side. If the rules of the law were clear and specific, and known to all, the litigants would realize that *guanxi* was not useful. The psychological motives for using *guanxi* and giving bribes would be weaken. Of course, a prerequisite is that the regulated proof system is applied by judges as it was written to be applied by legislators. And there must be mechanisms within society and the judiciary that ensure judgment made according to law.

As we can see, the mode of regulated proof and the mode of free proof reflect, in certain sense, the relation between the rule by law and the rule by man. To be sure, what is meant here by rule by law and rule by man is restricted to the scope of judicial work, and does not extend all the way to the level of the guiding principle for the entire country. As all the systems, rule by law and rule by man also have their merits and demerits. The rules of law are cold and strict, and may at times recommend an action inappropriate to a case, in the interests of preserving consistency. The rule by man is nimbler, but may well result in abuse of power under the banner of 'specific analysis for specific circumstances.' In a certain sense, the system of regulated proof is a realization of the essence of rule by law, while the mode of free proof is a realization of the essence of rule by man. In fact, when the judicial officers combines high moral rigor with high level of professional ability, free proof is absolutely a better mode than regulated proof. However, in the real world, such as in China, the professional ability and moral rigor of the judges are not often as people hope. That is why we should choose the mode of regulated proof. Comparison of the merits and demerits, in other words, shows that China should choose the path towards regulated proof, the crucial point of which is not to endow much prerogative on the judges who handle cases. We may say here, too, that one problem with rule of law in China is that the some legal provisions are not specific, not clear, and leaves too much space for 'rule of man.' For these reasons, China's development towards a modern state based on rule of law also demands a system for regulated proof in the judiciary.

In summary, the direction of reform of the judicial proof system in China is from free proof to regulated proof, but this does not mean judicial proof should be extremely or absolutely based on law, as the system of legal proof. There is a degree most appropriate to regulated proof, because the rules of regulated proof must adhere to the general principles of judicial work, and must align with the current level of social understanding, including the present ability to generate rules for judicial proof. If we look at it from the widest perspective, what we see is that the path to reform must combine scientific methods for fact finding with the experience of judicial practice, standardizing judicial activities to the greatest degree possible, and giving judges the prerogative only when it is not possible, or not possible given current ability, to produce consistent rules. In other words, it's a mixed mode in which regulated proof is dominant, and free proof is secondary. We may call it a relatively regulated proof system, or a quasi system of regulated proof.

2.4.3 *The Quasi-system of Regulated Proof*

There should be two traits inherent to a quasi-system of regulated proof. First, most stages of judicial proof apply regulated proof, but use free proof to supplement in certain individual stages. It is not an absolute and complete reliance on rules to assess and use evidence. In a broader sense, the proceeding of judicial proof covers the following four stages: collecting evidence, producing evidence, impeaching evidence, and assessing evidence. Assessing evidence itself includes two jobs, one is to assess the admissibility of evidence, and one is to assess the value and truthfulness of evidence. In a quasi-system of regulated proof, collecting, producing, and impeaching evidence must all be done in strict accordance to law, as well as the assessing for admission of evidence. Only in evaluating the trustworthiness of evidence is there room to apply free proof. In other words, the law must dictate clear rules for collecting evidence, producing evidence, impeaching evidence, and admitting evidence. Only when it comes to evaluating the reliability and value of evidence should the law give judges a certain degree of prerogative.

Secondly, the main basis for standardized proof is the promulgation of legal rules by legislative bodies, supplemented by judicial interpretations and internal regulations promulgated by related governmental agencies, such as the prosecutor's office and the police department. The binding force of the latter has a quasi-law-based character. For example, there should be clear rules for the procedure related to collecting evidence in criminal cases, such as interrogating a suspect and searching a crime scene, and the rules may be promulgated by the police authority. Although they are secondary rules of law, they should have the binding force generally. That is to say, in ordinary circumstances, law enforcement officers must abide by these rules. If an officer investigating a particular case wants decide an action counter to the rules, he must supply clear and specific reasons. While the standards for evaluating different kinds of evidence may be elaborated in judicial precedents, or the Guiding Cases, the judges should generally adhere to the standards. This is a combination of regularity with flexibility. Given the current state of the system of judicial proof and the practice of law enforcement in China, the regularization of proof standards and the regularization of evidence evaluation is the most pressing task in regularization of law enforcement. It is also the most difficult task.

Regularizing judicial proof practices, or putting them on a legal basis, of course includes regularizing the standards of proof. There are three levels of issues associated with these standards. First, is the standard of proof based on objective truth, or legal truth? Second, how is the standard of proof expressed in the law: is proof with reliable and sufficient evidence, proof beyond a reasonable doubt, preponderance of evidence, or something else? Third, how to make a standard for assessing the evidence in specific cases?[18] These first two layers are not subjects considered in this chapter. My research on the third layer suggests the following line of reasoning: first, clarify the specific needs of the proof in different types of cases, second, clarify the specific standards needed to guarantee trustworthiness of evidence. Doing so is to

[18]See He (2004).

realize two facets of systematization of evidence standards. In what follows, I would provide my own thoughts on how to proceed in this question, mainly in criminal cases.

2.4.3.1 Systematizing the Specific Needs of Cases

Systematizing the specific needs of proof in certain type of criminal cases should include actions in the following two areas: first, clarification of the factual elements that are to be proved by evidence in specific cases. And second, clarification of the necessary quantity and quality of evidence needed to proof each element of fact. The former is generally based on legal regulations regarding the necessary conditions to give a guilty verdict. The crime of larceny, for example, means taking, in secret, and with criminal intent, relatively large amounts of property, public or private. It can also mean repeated acts of burglary of property, public or private. The law stipulates that proof of guilt of this crime entails proving the following factual elements: the identity of the perpetrator and the natural circumstances of said perpetrator, which may at times include their age and psychological state; the time, place and specific manner of perpetration of the crime, as well as the value of the property stolen or the number of occurrences of theft; the circumstances of the violation of property rights; and criminal intent to appropriate the property of another. When it comes to the quality and quantity of evidence needed to establish these factual elements, we may generally affirm these to be: one piece of reliable, direct evidence (however, if the direct evidence in question comes from persons with close connection to the case, such as testimony provided by the accused or the plaintiff in a criminal case, corroborating evidence is necessary; such corroborating evidence may be circumstantial) or two or more pieces of reliable circumstantial evidence that fit together to form a complete set of evidence. On the basis of experience, we may define the types of evidence necessary to prove the relevant factual elements, such as witness testimony, documentary evidence, physical evidence, expert opinion and so on. Were we to develop a set of specific standards on the basis of large-scale empirical research on different types of evidence, it would be of great aid to systematization of the actions of judicial officers in finding facts through evidence.

2.4.3.2 Systematizing Standards for Determining Trustworthiness of Evidence

The foundation of systematization of judicial proof standards is systematization of the standards for determining trustworthiness of different types of evidence. In the discussion above, I emphasized the term "reliable," for both direct and indirect evidence. In fact, when judges assess the evidence in a case, assessing the reliability of the evidence is their main task. Generally speaking, only when evidence can be certified reliable can a judge crack the case, determining the facts and the truth. Thus, we can see that coming up with a consistent standard of evidence trustworthiness is crucial for systematizing judicial proof.

Evidence is generally evaluated first as one of two larger categories: human evidence and physical evidence. The former includes witness testimony, statements by persons involved in the case (including, in criminal cases, statements by the plaintiff and the accused). The latter includes all material items, physical traces, documents, audio-visual media, and electronic or digital data. All physical evidence has one thing in common: it generally must undergo scientific analysis to determine its value as evidence. In other words, physical evidence often must be taken in combination with the report that comes with scientific analysis to actually be used, which is why it is also called "scientific evidence." Presently in China, both human evidence and physical evidence are evaluated for trustworthiness primarily on the basis of individual experience and knowledge, without consistent and regularized standards. Even though scientific evidence is often evaluated in consultation with an expert, the evaluation itself if often lacking in consistent standards, with the result that if conclusions of these evaluations are made under very different conditions—and conditions are often very different—the evaluation of trustworthiness will fall into confusion.

We must confess that measurable standards for the evaluation of human evidence are very hard to develop. But in this case we human have accumulated some valuable experience through judicial practice in thousand years. On the basis of this experience, we can identify a few standards for assessing trustworthy human evidence more systematically. The contents of any such evidence, for example, must come from a reliable or certifiable source of information. Any witnesses (including persons involved in the case) must be provided with the information relevant to the evidence, and they must understand this information. There must be a known possibility or probability of connection between said evidence and persons, events or material related to the case. The evidence must possess sufficient detail and consistency. Of course the application of these standards to a particular case is still relying on the judge's prerogative to certain degree, and this constitute a supplement of regulated proof with free proof.

Along with standards for trustworthy assessment on human evidence, physical evidence, also known as scientific evidence, can come with even more systematic standards for trustworthy assessment. This, then, should be the focus of our research efforts. Because the influence of scientific evidence on the outcome of judicial proof continues to grow, the importance of our research will also continue to grow. As I have suggested before, judicial proof has today entered the scientific evidence age.[19]

I believe that there is much to be accomplished in systemizing the trustworthy assessment on scientific evidence. But doing so means changing some views and mentalities that have formed over the course of many years. Take fingerprinting analysis, for example. Some Chinese experts oppose the use of digital techniques to identify traits and matches. A particularly representative view goes thus:

> All material is a combination of quality and quantity. A certain quantity corresponds to a certain quality, and a certain quality in turn is expressed through a certain quantity. But a certain

[19]See He (2003).

> quality is not the sum of several quantities, because each of the smaller quantities has its own quality, positive or negative. To sustain material dialetics, then, we must prioritize analysis of quality, also advancing research of quality in combination with quantity. Only in this way can the outward phenomena be penetrated and the true, basic quality determined. Bourgeois capitalist scholars have advanced the theory that twelve basic traits of a fingerprint can be combined to make a positive individualization, and further that only this manner of analysis be considered reliable enough for a court of law. Lending such absolute value to numbers alone implies a view in favor of 'mathematical evidence.' This is a mechanical, metaphysical view inconsistent with objective reality. Since the founding of the People's Republic, the practice of fingerprint analysis has supported the dialectical materialist view, managing the relationship between quality and quantity correctly. Specific circumstance calls for specific analysis. Sometimes positive individualization can require very few distinguishing characteristics (3 or 4, or 5 or 6). Once the basic, true quality is determined, a determination is made and the material becomes evidence that is of use.[20]

In fact, I have held this view myself, in the past, and I also believe that the method of individualization based on twelve basic traits is mechanical and unscientific.[21] But now, it seems that our previous view was biased. Because we placed so much emphasis on characteristic quality, and further believed that characteristic quality was not measurable, we thought that fingerprint analysis could never be completed according to a consistent standard. There would always have to be an agent working from their own experience to "give specific circumstance specific analysis." Which method easily leads to some experts who will make the individualization, and some who will not, leaving law enforcement officials not knowing who to trust or what to do. This circumstance is also an open invitation to misuse of privilege and the law. Certainly we must continue to question and study the precise means of systemizing analysis of fingerprints, but it still makes sense to have quantitative standards by which to confirm individualizations. And this standard for assessing trustworthy evidence can serve to systematize individualizations made with fingerprint analysis.

In confirming standards for analyzing digitized fingerprint evidence, we must consider both quality and quantity. In fact, quality is also quantifiable. We can use the method of assigning each characteristic with a weighted index. The qualitative value that formerly could not be simply summed up with other values is converted into a number that can so be summed. This method of indexes comes in both objective and subjective varieties. In fingerprint analysis, both should be used. The numbers necessary for a positive fingerprint individualization apply probabilistic analysis based on statistical data. In specific cases of fingerprint analysis leading to individualizations, we take the data from the matching points and multiply each by its prescribed weight, then take the sum of these. Suppose we place the result into one of three different categories based on the values we are looking for in the case: in category A we will call the value X1, in category B we will call the value X2, and in category C we will call the value X3. The formula of our analysis will be as follows:

$$\text{An} \times \text{X1} + \text{Bn} \times \text{X2} + \text{Cn} \times \text{X3} = \text{Characteristic Value}$$

---

[20] Liu (1984).

[21] See He (1989).

If this value is equal to or greater than the value sought, then the individualization is positive. Otherwise there is no positive individualization made.[22]

The number of necessary detailed traits to make a positive fingerprint individualization is nine.[23] These include ridge beginnings, ridge endings, bifurcations, deltas, small dots, small eyes, spurs, bridges, and independent ridges. The quality of fingerprint characteristics is determined by the probability of a certain characteristic appearing on any given hand; characteristics of high probability are of lower value. We know that among the nine characteristic details, ridge beginnings, ridge endings, bifurcations, and deltas have a high probability of occurring—they do so in about 20% of cases. The latter five characteristics all have lower probabilities of occurring—small dots and independent ridges, for example, occur in approximately 4.5% of cases, while the number is about 2.5% for spurs, 1.4% for small eyes, and some 1% for bridges. If we use these data about the chance of appearing, we can assign a weight of 1 to the sum of the four probable characteristics, a weight of 2 to small dots and independent ridges, and a 3 to spurs, eyes and bridges. We shall set the target number as 12.[24] In a specific fingerprint identification, the common characteristics must add up to 12 to signify a positive individualization. A better number of characteristics to analyze might be 12, or 8, or even 6. In one example, an experienced technician identified common points as follows: 3 line beginnings, 2 line endings, 1 branch, 2 recombinations, 1 small cudgel, and 1 small hook. These sum as follows:

$$(3 + 2 + 1 + 2) \times 1 + 1 \times 2 + 1 \times 3 = 13$$

Even though there are only ten matching characteristics total here, still the sum value, 13, is greater than the target value of 12. Therefore the match is positive.

Often, fingerprint analysis also includes evaluation of the difference between characteristics. Depending on the mechanism and formation conditions of the analysis point, if the point of difference could shown to be of substantial quality, then the prints must not have been made by the same hand, and individualization is not confirmed. But if the points of difference are not substantially different, but rather differences caused by the same hand grasping different material at different angle or with different force, then such non-substantial differences should not affect a confirmed individualization. If the analysis of such contrasting points is inconclusive, then they must be subtracted from the analysis total. The unit to be subtracted can be postulated at the outset as “2.” So, if the initial sum value was 12, but one point was determined inconclusively different, the sum is reduced to 10. The positive individualization is lost. If the original sum had been 15, then a point of doubt would have caused a reduction to 13, and positive individualization is still possible. During trial, as long as the detail characteristics add up to 12 or higher, the court considers the

[22] The author here raises a simplistic example that does not conform to rigorous statistical analysis.

[23] Because such minutiae of fingerprints are indeed evaluated, we need not at this point consider the characteristics of pattern shape.

[24] This number and the values presented below are the author's hypothetical examples only. A real fingerprint analysis involves large amounts of data and many factors.

evidence trustworthy. If they add up to less than 12, the court does not consider them trustworthy.

Above, I use the example of fingerprint analysis to elucidate the basic thinking behind systematized standards for scientific evidence. These quantified standards help in making the assessment of trustworthiness systematic and consistent. They are of practical use in judicial proof, as well. But in certain cases they may influence the odds that the facts will be determined. This is because in certain cases, the judge may give a verdict in favor of the prosecution under the system of free proof, but cannot do so under the system regulated proof. Every system has its merits and demerits. Here I say the advantages of the regulated proof system outweigh its disadvantages. Given the complexity of cases and of evidence, no specific rules can be absolutely guaranteed to be useful in the case. That is to say, not all cases can be determined with perfect accuracy, but rational scientific principles can ensure that justice is realized in the vast majority of cases. As for the cases in which these are of no use, these are the price we pay for fairness and effectiveness in judicial proof overall. Certainly, the production of consistent standards to assess the trustworthiness of all types of scientific evidence is a grand and difficult project for judicial proof.

References

Bartlett, Robert. 2007. *Trial by fire and water: The medieval judicial ordeal*, translated by Xu Xin, et al., 14–17. Hangzhou: Zhejiang Rennin Publishing House.

Chen, Shengqing (ed.). 1982. *Legal History of Foreign Countries*. Beijing: Peking University Press.

Chen, Yiyun (ed.). 1991. *The Study of Evidence*. Beijing: China Renmin University Press.

Cohen, Jonathan. 1997. Freedom of proof, translated by He Jiahong. *Translation and Comment of Foreign Laws* (3): 2–5.

He, Jiaohong. 1989. *Individulization: Mystery in Criminal Investigation Methods*, 261. Beijing: China Renmin University Press.

He, Jiahong. 2003. *Evidence of the Gods, Human Evidence, and Physical Evidence*, 169. Beijing: Dazhong Wenyi Publishing House.

He, Jiahong. 2004. Standards of judicial proof and Utopia. *Chinese Journal of Law* (6).

Liu, Shaocong. 1984. *The New Study of Fingerprinting*, 450–451. Beijing: China Renmin University Press (published for use on campus).

Noye, William Andrew. 1991. The Laws of Old-West Frisians, a typical Germanic people of the eleventh century. In *Evidence: Its History and Policies*, 8. Australia: Butterworths Pty Ltd.

Xia, Zhiqian. 1990. *Trial by the Gods*, 1–7, 44–47. Beijing: SDX Joint Publishing Company.

Zhang, Jinpan. (ed.). 1985. *History of Chinese Laws*, 49. Beijing: Qunzhong Publishing House.

Zhou, Lengjia. 1985. *The Four Strange Cases in the Late Qing Dynasty*, 165–257. Beijing: Qunzhong Publishing House.

Chapter 3
The Methods of Judicial Proof

Contents

3.1 Case Illustration

On 15th March 2002, Gao Yingying, an employee of Baoshi (Diamond) Hotel in Laohekou, Xiangfan City of Hubei Province, fell from the hotel building to death. Public Security Bureau of Laohekou conducted postmortem examination the next day and made the report. It is stated "Gao's mouth, nose and right ear bled which demonstrates she died of skull bone fracture and severe traumatic brain injury; no significant injury was found from her skin; and severe craniocerebral and two-thigh

J. He, *Methodology of Judicial Proof and Presumption*,
Masterpieces of Contemporary Jurisprudents in China,
https://doi.org/10.1007/978-981-10-8025-8_3

injuries was characterized with high falling injury". It concluded that Gao committed a suicide and died of craniocerebral injury caused by fall from the high building.

However, the forensic technician only examined the body surface without autopsy. The forensic report did not contain the test result of Gao's private part and vaginal secretions. Gao's family claimed that Gao's neck was strangled and left with bruise, her wrist and back of hands were allegedly grasped and bruised, several buttons on her coat were missing, her pants were zipped off, and the belt was lost. Gao's father, Gao Tianhu, has an aunt named Jiao Xiuying who was once educated in the nursing school and has been working at local clinic in Zhaogang County since 1962. "I suspect Yingying was murdered by others. If she had committed suicide, her body should have been covered with blood. The fact is that there is no blood found on her body except on her face and that her neck and wrist were marked with purple spots." Jiao told the Journalist from Oriental Outlook.

Gao's family did not agree with the conclusion made by the Public Security Bureau and refused to cremate Gao's body. At 4 am of 18th March, with no permission from Gao's family, the local police moved Gao's body out of Diamond Hotel and cremated it that night.

On 19th June, three months after Gao's death, Gao's parents asked Tongji Medico-legal Expertise Center in Hubei Province to test the stained white underwear that Gao was wearing when found dead. Gao's families kept the underwear when the public security conducted postmortem examination. Tongji Medico-legal Expertise Centre concluded that the underwear was stained with semen and very few sperms was founded in it. Gao Tianhu did not request further examination on whom sperms belongs to. Since then, Gao's parents began petition and the media followed with the case.

In 2003, Sun Chuyan, the Party Leader of Xiangfan City, was convicted of receiving bribery and got sacked, which brought over 70 local officials' crimes into the surface. The turmoil led Gao's case back to the public attention. In early 2006, an article titled Nine Questions to Gao Yingying's Death was published in the Journal of Democracy and Rule of Law, and raised suspects toward Gao's death. The article was quoted by online media and raised the public's attention immediately. The local government set up a special investigation group for reviewing Gao's case. There were many discussions and comments about the case in the social media in the following years.

On 18th June 2006, the group asked Gao Tianhu to submit the underwear to the by the Physical Evidence Center of the Ministry of Public Security for examination. On 23rd June, the Public Security Bureau of Xiangfan City decided to arrest Gao Tianhu and his wife Chen Xuerong for perjury, as the sperm on the underwear was proved to be Gao Tianhu's. On 18th August, the group released the result of the Gao's case review that Gao Yingying died of suicide, and claimed that Gao Tianhu fabricated facts, framed up others, and committed perjury. Gao Tianhu was thus alleged to commit a crime and was investigated by The Public Security Bureau of Xiangfan City.

On 20th March 2007, Gao Tianhu was prosecuted with a charge of false accusation against the police. On 17th April, the Court of Xiangcheng District of Xiangfan

City heard the case and decided that Gao Tianhu was guilty and sentenced one-year imprisonment. Gao Tianhu appealed to the Intermediate Court of Xiangfan City. The Intermediate Court heard the case with an open trial on 14th May. Gao Tianhu and his lawyer argued that the police investigation report did not satisfy the standard of proof, while the court responded that the public security designated professional experts to conduct on-site investigation test to ascertain the cause of Gao's death in accordance of law and regulations, and that the investigation report is coherent with crime scene investigation record, and the conclusion of forensic examination was of standard. The defendant also made other arguments like procedural illegality of the police investigation and the invalidity of the examination report of the Physical Evidence Center of Ministry of Public Security, which were all rejected by the Intermediate Court. On 24th May, the Court ruled that the appeal was rejected and the judgment of the lower court was sustained.[1]

Though Gao's case was concluded, there are still questions being asked by people. Does the semen stain found on the underwear belong to Gao Tianhu? Would he really use his own semen to frame up others? If Gao Tianhu had fabricated the evidence, why he had not destroyed the underwear after it was first identified with the semen? If the semen belonged to Gao Tianhu, why would he submit the underwear to the police for examination? Is it possible that the police made a false report? It seems to be unlikely for Physical Evidence Center of Ministry of Public Security to make a false report at the time when the case garnered huge public attention, but is there any problem with the underwear itself? Was the underwear altered by the police? Until now, there have been no satisfying answers to those questions, and there may be no forever. This case illustrate the difficulty of judicial proof with the insufficient evidence and unclear facts, and the importance of judicial proof methods.

3.2 Characteristics of Judicial Proof Methods

Judicial proof is the establishment of an alleged fact by evidence. The process of judicial proof can be divided into four stages: collecting evidence, producing evidence, impeaching evidence, and assessing evidence. The subjects of judicial proof include judges, prosecutors, defense lawyers, police officers, and litigants, while in modern criminal trials in most countries, the primary subjects of judicial proof are prosecutors and defense lawyers, representing the two parties of the litigation. The objects of judicial proof are alleged facts in the case, which may be or may not be identical with the objective facts of the case.

The methods of judicial proof are the methods of the subjects using evidence to establish alleged facts in judicial proceedings. The methods are classified into different categories, like the recognition methods, the reasoning methods, and the operation methods, etc. The way of thinking plays a very important role in different layers of judicial proof methods. It is exemplified by how judicial personnel process

[1] See He (2009).

evidence. When handling a case, judicial personnel need to process collected evidences by discarding the dross, selecting the essential and sorting out the truth. Their thinking, to very large extent, decides whether their actions are correct or not. It is sure that their thinking relies on practical activities, and the practice to thinking is as the root of trees or the source of water.

Thinking is a fundamental function of human brains and is integrated to human life everywhere and all the time. The ways of thinking regarding judicial proof are mainly abstract thinking with the supplement of image thinking. Abstract thinking, also known as logical thinking, includes abstract concepts, judgments, reasoning etc., and concentrates on nature of matters. It must observe certain logical rules, without limitation, like the rule of non-contradictory, the rule of excluding middle, and the rule of sufficient justifications. The substance of image thinking is features of concrete and direct image. The focus of image thinking is appearance of matters. In the judicial proof process, abstract thinking and image thinking are mutually penetrated and correlated. The characteristics of the thinking in judicial proof demonstrate in the following three aspects: retrograde motion or trace-ability, antagonism or adversary, and time limit.

3.2.1 Retrograde Thinking

In judicial proof, retrograde thinking is defined as the direction of the thinking is opposed to the development direction of the object. Generally speaking, judicial proof thinking is to exploit cause and cause of cause based on outcomes, instead of finding out outcomes and outcomes of outcome based on cause. For example, in criminal investigation, retrograde thinking is the basic model used by investigators. In the initial stage of investigation, investigators usually have access to the outcome of the crime like victims killed or property stolen. The investigative thinking is to analyze the outcome and find out the cause. That is the way of finding out case facts by applying the inference of tracing back to cause. When considering specific aspects of a case, investigators also ordinarily infer the cause from the outcome. For instance, when seeing a safe open, investigators need to find out why and how it is unlocked; when finding phlegm stain left in the crime scene, investigators need to infer how and what it is formulated; when finding some burned stuff, investigators need to reason the cause of burning. To sum up, learning the past through the present is one of essential features of investigative thinking. The thinking of prosecutors when preparing or conducting prosecutions and the thinking of judges when finding facts or making judgment also fall into the scope of retrograde thinking.

Retrograde thinking requires the subject to have comprehensive knowledge and to know ways of inference of tracing back to cause. In the proof process, due to complexity of cases, the judicial personnel who do not master retrograde thinking would have no clue to cope with the case, but qualified prosecutors and judges could swiftly sort out the cause and effectively locate the way of retrograde thinking. Therefore, studying the principle and ways of retrograde thinking is of great significance to judicial proof.

3.2.2 *Adversary Thinking*

In judicial proceedings, the basic job of the two parties is to prove the fact, and the facts they alleged are often antagonistic to each other. Therefore the thinking of the parties in judicial proof is basically adversarial. In some cases, whether the thinking of one party is right relies on that of the other party. Thus, judicial proof thinking is also known as adversarial thinking. This is typical in the investigation stage of criminal cases. To certain degree, the thinking in criminal investigation resembles playing chess in which two parties clash on the chessboard and strike to defeat each other. As each party aims to win, adversary formulates. To win, one party shall accurately figure out what the other party thinks. For that reason, the adversarial feature of thinking is also known as the game, which corresponds with the saying while the priest climbs a post, the devil climbs ten.

On the process of criminal investigation, adversary has two manifestations: the simultaneous and the asynchronous. For the simultaneously adversarial thinking, while investigators were identifying the possible escaping route or direction of the offender, the offender also try to identify the possible chasing route or direction of the investigator. For the asynchronously adversarial thinking, while offenders at the time of committing crimes think over all investigative methods and take counter-investigative actions ahead, investigators when making crime scene investigation must figure out possible anti-investigation methods and determine correspondent investigative strategies. The adversarial feature also exists in the process of trial between prosecutors and defendants.

3.2.3 *Timely Thinking*

The time limit or timeliness of judicial proof thinking implicates that the thinking process and outcomes are limited due to time. Taking criminal investigation as an instance, the footprints on snow field left by the offender will be melt and the traces of the offense in open space may be washed away along the time, so the thinking of the investigators must be done timely. In other words, evidence must be collected timely, otherwise it may disappear.

In criminal proceedings, all stages should have their time limits according to law. Investigation, prosecution, and trial should be done within certain time. The litigant's submitting of evidence to the court, as well as impeaching evidence in the court, also has a time limit. If trials come to an end, evidence submission will be out of validity. If the court has admitted the evidence as the means of judicial proof, it will be too late for the other party to impeach the evidence. In conclusion, judicial proof shall be accomplished in a certain period and only within the period the judicial proof is legally effective.

3.3 Types of the Judicial Proof Methods

There are different ways to classify judicial proof methods. According to the approach of proof, judicial proof methods can be classified into direct and indirect proof methods. According to the form of reasoning, judicial proof methods can be classified into deductive and inductive proof methods. According to the pattern of proof process, judicial proof methods can be classified into elementary and systematic proof methods.

3.3.1 Direct and Indirect Proof Methods

Direct and indirect proof methods distinguish from direct and indirect evidence. Direct evidence is the evidence that, if true, proves a fact without inference or the link with other evidence, and is typically based on personal knowledge or observation. Indirect evidence, or circumstantial evidence, is the evidence that can only prove a fact with inference or the link with other evidence, and is typically as physical evidence. Direct and indirect proof methods are different, which are not divided according to the relation between evidence and facts. Direct proof method is to directly establish a case fact with positive evidence, which is commonly applied in judicial practices and includes deductive and inductive methods. Indirect proof method is to establish a case fact by proving what is presumed contradicting to the alleged case fact, and thus indirectly proving the truth in the case, which includes the method of contradiction and the method of exclusion.

Proof by contradiction is to make a presumption contrary to the alleged fact, and then to deny the truth of the presumption so as to justify the alleged fact. In a hypothetical case of murder, the investigators did not have evidence to directly prove that A had killed B, and thus presumed that B had committed suicide. After examining the gunshot residues surrounding the wound on the victim's head, the expert deduced that the shooting range was above 80 cm and B was not able to shoot himself at such a distance. By proving the fact that B had shot himself to death was not true, the investigators thus concluded that B had been shot by another person, in another word, it was a murder. That is how proof by contradiction is applied.

Proof by exclusion is at first making all factual hypotheses about a case, which contradict with each other, and then excluding these hypotheses one by one until leaving only one hypotheses, which is to be proved as the fact in the case. Also with the hypothetical case of murder, A, B, and a third person were all possible shooters. Based on the testimonies of the witnesses outside of the crime scene when the shooting happened, and the examination of the environments of the crime scene, the possibility that a third person had shot B was excluded. Based on the conclusion of gunshot residue examination, the possibility that B had shot himself was also excluded. Then there was only one possibility that A was the shooter. That is how investigators apply the method of exclusion to prove the fact that A had shot and killed B.

3.3.2 Deductive and Inductive Proof Methods

Deductive and inductive proof methods both fall into the category of direct proof methods but with different reasoning forms. Deductive proof method deduces the case fact directly from the evidence. Deductive proof contains two premises: the major premise which is a common theory or rule, and the minor premise which is the evidence in the case. Deductive proof method is to apply general theories or rules to particular cases hereto prove the case facts. In the above Gao's case, forensic experts applied deductive proof method to prove when the victim was dead. The major premise forensic experts applied is a general forensic theory that corpses dying in different time demonstrate different features. The minor premise is the information of the corpse features, like body temperature, *rigor mortis*, *livor mortis*, etc. The conclusion is the time of the death.

Inductive proof method applies induction method to prove the case facts directly with the evidence. To be clear, induction in this context is not strict in accordance with the inductive reasoning in the context of logic. Inductive reasoning is to induce a general conclusion from facts. Deductive reasoning is from the general to the particular, while the inductive reasoning is opposite, from the particular to the general. On the process of investigation, both reasoning forms are applied. Investigators resorted to general theories on death and applied deductive reasoning to deduce the time of the death. For incorporated investigation, investigators may also apply inductive reasoning, through which investigators find out common features of cases of the same type and decide whether the crime is committed by the same person or group.

Inductive proof method is not the same as inductive reasoning. Inductive proof is to find case facts through a series of evidence. In the above A and B case, investigators collected evidence, such as shot marks left on the gun and bullet, the shot wound and residue left on the victim's head, test reports and debt disputes between A and B, used inductive method, comprehended all elements and finally proved that A was the murderer.

Deductive proof is more accurate and reliable than inductive proof, because deductive proof is easy for fact finders to figure out whether the premises of deductive proof are true or not, while the induction in inductive proof is commonly incomplete. However, inductive proof is more persuasive as inductive proof uses specific facts and deductive premises are comparatively abstract. Therefore, two proof methods are commonly combined to apply in judicial proof.

3.3.3 Elemental and Systematic Proof Methods

Elemental proof method is to prove all case facts by verifying every element composing the case facts. The proof process is from the part to the whole, and therefore is also known as bottom-to-top proof method. Systematic proof method is opposite, which starts proving from the basic structure of case facts to elements. It is a process from the whole to the part, and therefore is known as top-to-bottom proof method.

It appears that processes of two methods are different, but the real difference is the focus, which can be illustrated separately in the following three scenarios: (1) in some cases, proving every element could achieve the purpose of proving the whole facts; (2) in some cases, proving every element fail the purpose; (3) in some case, it is impossible to prove certain element while it is possible to prove case facts as a whole. In the first scenario, use either of the methods is of no difference. In the other two scenarios, it may generate different results by applying different methods. Therefore, elemental and systematic proof methods shall be applied in different cases.

The two methods are not limited to be applied in judicial activities. Diagnosing diseases by doctors is considered as a proof process. Doctors usually diagnose diseases with elemental proof method. Chinese traditional doctors apply four methods of TMC (observing, listening, questioning, and pulse-taking), and may use technological equipment to check and justify symptoms of patients, like pulse, tongue states, body temperature, blood pressure, blood states, etc. The more symptoms doctors find, more clear the nature of diseases is. In other words, as more elements are founds, some diseases patients potentially get will be excluded. When there is only one disease patients may potentially get, symptoms are proved and doctors can make the diagnosis. Some doctors may apply system proof method to make diagnosis. With instinct or first impression, doctors may presume the patient gets pneumonia or has cold and then to justify whether the presumption is right by matching symptoms of certain diseases with the patient's conditions.

Historians usually apply systematic proof method to verify historical events. They generally set up a presumption for a certain historical event or period in compatible with historical and logical principles, and then search for resources from comprehensive historical material to find out details which are necessary to construct a complete system. When building the system, historians usually expressly or implicitly add into their own historian philosophy or interpretation to history.

The objects of elemental and systematic proof methods applied to are different. It is demonstrated in the following: (1) whether the problem can be clarified with a YES/NO answer; (2) whether the problem can reoccur. When making diagnosis, doctors usually ask YES/NO questions, like whether the temperature is above 37 °C, whether the quantity of leucocytes in blood exceeds ten thousand. Then doctors can re-see the same type problems and then make a check. Thus, it is more suitable for doctors to apply elemental proof method.

However, in the proof process, problems that historians identify are complicated and cannot re-occur. Why did the Paris Commune Revolution fail? What role did George Washington play in the American Revolution War? Even if turning the two open questions into Yes/No questions as like whether the failure of the Paris commune revolution was attributed to the incompetency of the proletariat and whether George Washington played a decisive role on American Revolution War, it is still very difficult for historians to give a yes or no answer. Doctors can use re-occurrence approach to diagnose, like rechecking patients' temperature and its association with symptoms, but historians cannot apply the same approach to test whether the Paris Commune Revolution could succeed if the proletariat was powerful enough and whether the American Revolution War would succeed without George Washington.

It is partial to simply equate the judicial proof with medical or historical proof. In practice, proof methods applied usually vary case by case. Product liability cases and medical negligence cases may fit the elemental proof method because questions arising from such types of cases can be answered with Yes or No and do not require cases to happen again. For cases involving actors' subjective states like fraud and murder cases, it is more suitable to apply the systematic proof method because answering such questions require a systematic framework and the testers' explanatory notes.

From the practical aspect, the systematic proof method has been widely applied as every judicial professional usually has a proposition coherent with historical and logic principles when using evidence to find facts. On such circumstance, applying the systematic proof method not only enhances the logic of the proof but also simplifies the process. In addition, it fits the common thinking habits formed in daily life as people naturally tend to simplify their cognitive process. For example, someone may remember that he went to a shop yesterday afternoon but may not be able to remember a series of actions like stepping out of the room, locking the door, going downstairs, taking keys out of pockets, unlocking the bike, getting on the bike, etc. When a car passing by, people with no hesitation presume that the car is composed of a set of parts like the body, tires, the engine, and the lights, without necessary to affirm that it is a car after checking those components. The proof of case facts is not as simple as but share similarities with the above examples. In the application of systematic proof method into case facts, the most important is to accurately recognize the system structure and the rules of systematic proof.

3.4 Method of Individualization

Individualization is a basic approach to understanding judicial proof, of which the main purpose is to prove whether the defendant is the one who committed the accused criminal offense in a criminal case. This is an issue of individualization by nature. In addition, many specific individualizations are involved in the judicial proof. For example, to identify whether a suspect is the one who committed a rape by testing the seminal stains on the body of the victim, to ascertain whether a knife collected in a suspect's house is the murder weapon by testing the bloodstain on the knife, or to find out whether an obliteration is conducted by the defendant via authentication of handwriting. The method of individualization may be used in every stage of judicial proof, assisting the subjects to find the facts of the case. Therefore, it is of vital importance for judges to have a good command of the basic theory and the general method of it.

3.4.1 Concept of Individualization

Individualization is a special term originally used in the field of criminalistics, or forensic science,[2] being defined as the recognitive activity that decides whether an object that appears twice or more times is the same object through comparison of its objective characteristics. For example, a burglary happened, and investigators found the perpetrator's footprints and some tool-marks at the crime scene. Then they collected from the suspect a pair of shoes and a pry bar. By examination and comparison of characteristics of the objects and the traces, the forensic expert concluded that this pair of shoes and the pry bar were those that left traces at the crime scene. This is so-called individualization.

As a theory, individualization is originated and evolved from judicial practice,[3] while as a fundamental method of understanding the material world as human beings, individualization is commonly employed in our daily life. For example, one person is going to the airport to pick up a friend and will then drive back home, during this course, his act of recognizing his friend at the exit of the airport, finding his own car in the parking lot, and driving towards his own home are all individualizations. A considerable amount of individualization could be found in everyone's daily life.

In a sense, individualization is the need for human's life, especially for our social life. In the natural world, if we stay away from this method, it could be hardly for us to obtain the knowledge of particular characteristics of a specific cognitive object, or to distinguish some object out of a certain category, like making a distinction between this peach tree and that one or telling two Mongolian gazelles apart. In the social life, without this kind of cognitive method, people's social contacts all turn to be of a generic kind without individuality, meaning that gender is the only distinctive feature of different people. However, everything is furnished with individuality and generality. In the natural world, if we say generality of an object is much more important than its individuality, it would not bother us too much with which tree the peach comes from or which Mongolian gazelle the lamb comes from when we eat a peach or lamb. In contrast, individuality happens to be of great significance. It is incredible to even think about a social life without individuality in that people are all involved in relationships, marriage, raising children and making social connections with a specific person, not women and men distinct only in gender.

[2] "Individualization is unique to forensic science; it refers to the demonstration that a particular sample is unique, even among members of the same class. It may also refer to the demonstration that a questioned piece of physical evidence and a similar known sample have a common origin." De Forest et al. (1983, p. 7).

[3] See He (1989).

First, in order to understand the concept of individualization, the connotation of the word "individualize" must be accurately defined. From a philosophical perspective, "individualize" refers to the category in which an object or a phenomenon is fully equivalent to itself. To be precise, individualization is different from identification.[4] Although in some context, the latter may be used as the former, or the latter has same meaning with the former, such as "eye witness identification", it is not strictly correct.[5] Generally speaking, identification means to equate two things, or to consider one thing to be identical with another thing. In this sense, identification is just a recognitive method to put an object into a class or a group of objects. In forensic science examination, for example, morphological identification is nothing more than the recognition of a physical pattern. Some forensic scientists said: "Pattern recognition identification is common in everyday life. A shopper in a supermarket unconsciously utilizes the process to identify different items, such as fruits or vegetables. An apple is identified as an apple by comparing the general pattern of its visual image with a pattern stored in the brain. The same process is used by bird watchers in identifying a certain species of bird, or by entomologists in identifying insects, although more detailed criteria may also be involved".[6]

The difference between individualization and identification reflects the difference between sameness and similarity, yet they are closely connected as recognition of sameness tends to begin from similarity. In other words, individualization must be conducted from similarity to sameness, based on the characteristics of the object. Meanwhile, similarity and difference are linked tightly with the characteristics. Even an individual object may show some difference with itself. Therefore, to carry on individualization, one should bear in mind both differences within the object itself and the differences between this object and other objects.

It is universally acknowledged that everything in the objective world share similarities and have differences. The degree of similarity and difference varies from different objects. For instance, the difference between the two of a twin tend to be smaller than those of others, while the similarity of a same kind of cases is more apparent than that of different kinds of cases. Nonetheless, however similar two cases are, they are still two different cases. Twin sisters could resemble to an extent that their relatives cannot even tell them apart, but they are two different people after all. It could be seen from above that the object of individualization must be the object per se, to name a few, Jones could only be individualized with Jones himself, so is a murder case. Admittedly, sameness within anything with itself is not always rigid and unchangeable, and it is the same with inherent differences and variations.

Secondly, the object of individualization must appear twice or more times during the process of recognition. All matters in the world have its own individuallity. This

---

[4]"Identification is a process common to all the sciences and, in fact, to everyday life. It may be regarded as a classification scheme, in which items are assigned to categories containing like items, and given names." De Forest et al. (1983, p. 6).

[5]"The term identification as used here really means 'individualization.' Although in common usage people often say 'identification of a suspect' or 'identification of a fingerprint,' this is not strictly correct." De Forest et al. (1983, p. 30).

[6]De Forest et al. (1983, pp. 285–286).

gun is what it is, different from any other guns. This case is what it is, yet it cannot be deemed as the same as any other cases. However, why would we bother to individualize the inherent sameness of objective matters? Or when shall we face the problem of individualization? The answer is that the object must show up two times or more in the subject's cognition courses. For instance, a theft happens and the perpetrator is an object that appears in the first time, then the investigators find a suspect, and the suspect is the object that shows up in the second time. Individualization is to confirm whether those two objects are the same person. In addition, when the object appears for the first time, its recognizable reflections of characteristics must be left, such as fingerprints, footprints, handwriting, blood stains, hair etc. All those characteristics are reflected in the evidence of the case.

If one object only appears once during the subject's recognition, the question of individualization will not be raised. For example, investigators have found a tool-mark on the spot of a burglary, which indicates they have seen one object, the tool that left the trace on the spot, in their recognition. However, if investigators does not find a suspect tool, which means that the object does not show up for the second time, there is no way to carry on the individualization. Just set another example, one burglary happened, yet neither the victim reported it to the police nor the police discovered the case. Then the case would not enter the judicial proceedings, and no individualization would be needed for it.

3.4.2 The Object of Individualization

During the process of judicial proof, objects of individualization include persons, matters, places and events. The individualization of the first three objects is easily understood. For instance, the suspect who went to the crime scene is individualized through his fingerprints or footprints; a car that hit someone and escaped is individualized through the traces of its tires left in the scene of the accident; the place of a kidnapping is individualized through the victim's testimony where she was kidnapped and confined. When it comes to events, there will be some particularity.

As for the recognitive activity of individualization, an event must happen for more than twice. The first time the event happen is usually in the objective world or the real world, in other words, it was the facts that really happened, such as a murder case occurred at some place in some time. The second time it is seen is in the subjective world or the virtual world, namely the case pleaded by the victim or cases that are proved by evidences, which refers to that murder facts depicted or presented by the prosecutors via producing evidences. To be clear about this point is of great significance to the principles and methods of individualization of the event.

In the view of the judicial professionals, as this author has mentioned before, criminal cases are all events happened in the past. Since time is single-dimensional. Once a case has happened, it belongs to the past and cannot happen again. The same offender may commit another crime of the same kind, but it is not the same case. However, the prosecutor or the defense lawyer may make the case to happen for the second time, that is to reconstruct the case with all kinds of evidence, but this is only reproduced virtually. In this sense, the basic job of judicial proof in a criminal case is an individualization of event, to recognize the reconstructed case as the same as the happened case. As is seen from above, the event to be examined by individualization is timely past, and spatially virtual. The two features determine that the thinking pattern of individualization is not only reverse, but abstract, which amount to its extraordinary difficulty.

In despite of diversities of criminal cases, there are only two fundamental issues in the process of judicial proof: (1) whether the crime accused by prosecutors did happen; (2) whether the person who is presently charged with is the perpetrator. The former is individualization of event, namely to identify whether the charged crime is what really happened. The latter is individualization of person, which is to identify whether the defendant is the one who committed the crime. In view of those two issues, the essence of the proof in criminal proceedings is individualization of person and individualization of event, to put it simply, "individualization of person and event".

In summary, to proof facts of a case with evidence is a process of individualization. During this course, the core of judicial proof is "individualization of person and event." However lasting and complicated the proceeding is, the final objective is to prove whether the defendant is the one who committed the crime. It is true that in different cases, legal professionals achieve this goal through different ways. In short, there are two basic approaches to carry out judicial proof in criminal cases: individualization from event to person and individualization from person to event.

Individualization from event to person refers to a scenario that the legal professionals first get known an "event", namely a case, then find out and identify the "person", namely the perpetrator. In this case, the proof is mainly conducted at the core of who is the perpetrator. For instance, the criminal investigators found a female body at a place, and the medical examiners examined the body and stated that the case is a homicide. The investigations mainly focus on who is the murderer, which is also a basic route for the judicial proof.

For individualization from person to event, the legal professionals first get known a "person", namely a suspect, then find out whether there is a specific "event" as claimed or reported, namely *corpus delicti*. For example, the criminal investigation authority received a report that someone committed embezzlement or bribery, then the investigation mainly focused on whether there were facts of embezzlement or bribery. In such cases, investigation was carried out over the "event". No matter which route is taken, the proof activity must achieve the final objective of "individualization of person and event".

Individualization perpetrates through the proof procedure in every criminal case, of which includes the "big" individualization, a general individualization for a whole case and perpetrators, and the "small" individualization considered as specific individualization to a certain fact in the case. Furthermore, the big individualization is commonly composed of several small individualizations and identifications. Taking a murder case as an example, the investigators have collected footprints, bullet shells, blood stains, hairs, fibers and some other physical traces at the crime scene. Then the forensic examiners carried out individualizations of the footprints with the shoes of the suspect, and of the bullet shells with the suspected gun, as well as identifications of the blood stains, hairs and fibers, reaching conclusions that the blood stain was of the same blood type of the suspect, the hairs were similar to the suspect's hair, and the fibers were of the same kind with the suspect's sweater. Moreover, a witness gave a testimony that he saw a car near the crime scene at the time, and he identified the car of the suspect was the same car he had seen. This is also an individualization. On the basis of above-mentioned small individualizations and identifications, the legal professionals ultimately concluded the big individualization that the suspect was the murderer.

In some cases, the process of the big individualization can be accomplished with certain evidence, which is generally the direct evidence, such as the testimony of the eye-witness and the statement of the defendant. The evidence examined in the process of small individualizations and identifications generally falls within the scope of indirect or circumstantial evidence. Although the direct evidence may be of great value to the big individualization in the case, the reliability of the conclusion cannot be necessarily guaranteed. For example, the confessions of defendants may not be all truthful, so the judicial personnel should assess them carefully, and would often compare them with other evidence in the case. Thereby, the judicial proof of a criminal case is usually completed by multiple individualizations and identifications. These individualizations and identifications interact with each other in the way of either convergence, or juxtaposition, or auxiliary, or confirmation, to constitute jointly the "individualization of a person with an event" in the case.

3.4.3 The Basis of Individualization

Individualization is based on features of the object, including mainly four types: the physical pattern, the material composition, the motion habit, and the odor. On these grounds, we may classify individualization into four categories as: (1) the individualization based on physical pattern, such as the individualization of fingerprints, footprints, tool marks, trajectory marks, or vehicle traces; (2) the individualization based on material composition, for example, the individualization of human's blood stain or semen stain on the basis of DNA testing; (3) the individualization based on motion habits, such as the individualization of hand-writings, or of the voice-prints; (4) the individualization based on human odor, for instance, the odor individualization of a suspect by a police dog. Admittedly, this classification is not absolute, since what is needed to be based on for individualization in a specific case may simultaneously incorporate two, or even three sorts of features. It is specially true in the individualization of a person with an event in a criminal case, which is generally based on the evidence reflecting the factual characteristics of the case.

The fundamental task of the judicial proof in a case is to identify the characteristics and to find the facts. And the factual characteristics of the case are possible to be reflected in the cognitive activities of subjects only by means of various evidence.

The individualization of a person with an events is aimed at examining the evidence to see whether it correctly and accurately reflects the characteristics of the case, and then making a judgment about the value of these characteristics to see if they can reach an individualization. Because the individualization of a person with an event is necessarily based on the factual characteristics of the case, and the medium for identifying the characteristics is a variety of evidence, the basis of the individualization is the evidence in the case.

3.4.4 The Scientific Foundation of Individualization

The individual differences between things are the objective foundation of individualization. Without such differences, the discussion about individualization will be out of the question. Criminal cases are different from each other and there are no two identical cases in the world, hence each case is specific and is only identical to itself. However, in terms of the judicial proof, the particularity of the case could only be revealed through its specific features, and the individualization is possible to be achieved only by means of the individualization of object features. Moreover, what an individualization is actually based on is not the characteristics of the object as a whole, but only a combination of some features. In other words, what the judicial officers would adopt in criminal proceedings is not all but only part of the evidence reflecting the case facts, as some potential evidence is not found or provided, or some evidence is not accepted in the proceedings due to a certain "flaw". Therefore, when studying the issue of individualization, it is necessary to examine whether the legally accepted evidence or feature combination has already satisfied qualifications for individualization, which includes the particularity, stability and reflection of the feature combination.

3.4.4.1 The Particularity of the Feature Combination

Since individualization needs to identify each object individually to distinguish a certain object from all the other objects, the required feature combination can only appear on the given object. In other words, each feature combination required for individualization must be specific. And characteristics of the case are identified and found by evidence, which results in that the combination of evidence could represent the combination of features, thereby in terms of the "individualization of a person with an event" in criminal cases, this kind of particularity is manifested as the uniqueness and exclusivity of the evidence combination. To be specific, the particularity of the feature combination is determined by the following three factors.

(1) The quantity of features

Both theories and practices have already demonstrated that the more the number of features, the stronger the particularity of the feature combination and the less possibility of the feature combinations getting overlapped with each other. When features reach a certain amount, it is impossible for the given feature combination to overlap with the others, consequently, such a combination of features possesses the particularity required for individualization. From this point, the first rule of the particularity is concluded as:

> The quantity of features is proportional to the particularity of the feature combination, or inversely proportional to the possibility of the feature combination overlapping with the others.

In examining the quantity of features, the number of feature types possessed by that kind of objects, as well as the number of features that appear on the specific reflector of characteristics, must be examined. For instance, how many feature types there are on fingerprints, such as the end of ridge, the separation of ridge, the dot, the short ridge, the bridge, the island, etc., and how many feature points are manifested on the given fingerprint as an individualization object.

(2) The quality of features

There is certain prescriptive nature of the quality of any feature. This prescriptive nature is exactly the basis for a given feature to be distinguished from others. For different features, the particularities of their qualities are also different, which means the particularities of some features are prominent, while others not. And this results in the emergence of the distinction between the qualities of features. For instance, the quality of fingerprint features such as "small bridges" and "small islands" is higher than that of "ends of ridge" and "separations of ridge".

For the individualization, the particularity value of features with different qualities also vary in their feature combination. When the specificity of the feature combination is expressed as a constant quantity, the higher the quality of each feature in the combination, the less the quantity of the features required for the combination. And the particularity value of the feature is determined by the occurrence rate of the feature in the object. In general, the higher the rate of occurrence, the lower the value of the feature; the lower the rate of occurrence, the higher the value of the feature. The principle of "less is more" is also applicable here. For instance, the incidence of whorl pattern in the population in China is about 50%, while the appearance of an arch pattern is only 2.5%. As a fingerprint feature, the specificity value of the arch pattern is higher than the whorl pattern. Thus, the second rule of the particularity can be concluded as:

> The quality of the feature is proportional to its particularity value; in the case of the fixed specificity of the feature combination, the quality of the feature is inversely proportional to the quantity of features required for its particularity; the particularity value of the feature is determined by and inversely proportional to its occurrence rate.

(3) The quantity of the objects of the same kind

The so-called quantity of the objects of the same kinds, that is, the scope of the objects which may share the same feature combination. For example, the range of the fingerprint feature combinations which may overlap with each other is the population of the world; the scope of the shoe pattern feature combinations of a certain kind which may repeat is the total production of that kind of shoes; the range of the case feature combination of a certain kind which is possible to be repeated is the total occurrence number of that kind of cases. And the specificity required for individualization is closely related to the size of the range in which the feature combinations may be overlapped. Generally, the greater the scope, the higher the requirements of specificity for individualization, and the higher the requirements of the features' quantity and quality. In other words, the same feature combination can not specify the object in a relatively large scope, but in a relatively small range can it specify the object. Of course, from another perspective, the narrowing of the scope generally means the increase of characteristics, which are nothing but the features apart from those in the given feature combination. Thereby, the third rule of the particularity can be concluded as:

> The size of the scope in which a certain feature combination may repeat is proportional to the required quantity and quality of the features for individualization.

3.4.4.2 The Stability of the Feature Combination

Based on dialectical materialism, motion and matter are inseparable. There has been no matter not in motion, or motion without matter. However, various forms of static state also exist in this ever-changing material world, or we can say, objective things have a certain stability in its process of developing and changing. Certainly, motion and change are absolute, while rest and stability are relative. And where the stability of different objects is different, the stability of different features is consequently different. In the case of criminal proceedings, a variety of evidence will change more or less as time goes by, thereby the stability of the evidence, or the consistency of the evidence content should be examined during the process of judicial proof.

The features' stability required for individualization means the attribute that the object feature remains basically unchanged during the necessary time of individualization. The period of "necessary time" is determined by the time length in a specific case, which starts from the target object leaving a feature reflector and ends with the investigators discovering the suspect object and making expert examination on it. For instance, the period from the time point when a criminal left his shoe prints at the scene of theft to the time point when the investigators founds suspect and took his shoes or shoe prints as samples for comparison was the "necessary time" for individualization in this case. If the features of the shoe that left prints at the theft scene remained basically constant during that period, it then has the stability required for individualization; while if the features of that shoe changed qualitatively out of natural reasons or human action reasons, then it does not meet the requirements for individualization. Therefore, judicial professionals should try to shorten the "necessary time" for proceeding with individualization.

There are two meanings for the attribute "basically unchanged" been required for individualization: first, for a feature combination, it means the main features of such combination remain the same, in other words, although some individual features of the combination has changed, those changes are not to such an extent that will change the basic characteristics of the entire combination. For instance, a certain party had changed the wrong way he used to write for a Chinese character out of learning during the period from the time point when he finished the writing of case-related instruments to the subsequent time point when it was needed for him to take expert examination on handwriting, but from the aspect of his handwriting characteristics as a whole, it still remained its original basic features, then his handwriting feature combination had maintained "basically unchanged". Second, for a specific feature, it means the quality of the feature remains essentially unchanged, or we can say, even though the feature itself has changed, the particular prescriptive nature that makes it distinct from other features remains the same. For example, after a criminal leaving his shoe prints at the crime scene, the pattern characteristics of the shoes have changed to a certain extent out of wearing through his continuous use, but due to the same way to be worn as the previous, the change in each feature did not affect the quality which can distinguish it from other features, hence it still remained "basically unchanged". Certainly, if quantitative accumulation is beyond a certain limit, it will lead to a qualitative transformation.

3.4.4.3 The Reflection of the Feature Combination

The reflection of the object features refers to an attribute that the object's characteristics can be reflected on other objects. We know that the object in the course of motion will frequently contact with other objects in some way, as well as leave its own "trace" or a certain form of "reflection" on others. For the individualization, what is significant is not the possibility of such reflection, but rather the easiness and clarity of it. In the case of evidence, it refers to the reliability of the evidence.

Firstly, individualization requires that the object characteristics can be easily reflected on other objects. For instance, the features of fingerprints after we touching things are reflective. While eye-prints are also particular and stable, they are not suitable for individualization since they lack trace. Furthermore, individualization needs relatively high definition of reflection of object characteristics. Although fingerprints leave trace, they are not qualified for individualization if the trace is not clear enough. The factors that influence the definition of reflection of object characteristics include the definition of the object characteristics, the nature of the reflective material, the method and power of the reflection process, etc.

The reflection of object characteristics is closely related to the recognitive and individualization ability of human. In general, the reflection of object characteristics is objective. While whether this reflection can be used in individualization relies on human being's recognitive ability. For example, as the development of science and advance of recognitive ability, we now can not only use human's appearance and skeletal structure in individualization, but also the characteristics of one's writing habits, fingerprints, palm prints, footprints, teeth marks, tip prints, voice-print, DNA, etc. During the course of development, the object characters did not change much and the human body did not create new features to help us to identify, but thanks to the improvement of science, we can identify characteristics that were not be identified in old days. There is no doubt that people in ancient times have voice and DNA characteristics like modern people, and the only difference is that scientific limits cannot identify these characteristics then. In this sense, recognitive ability of human beings, namely subjective condition, is another premise of individualization.

3.4.5 The General Method of Individualization

Individualization is a recognitive process by continual exclusion of similar objects. Of course, this refers to a positive conclusion. While if the conclusion is negative, the process will suspend. That every selected feature is taken into account of the individualization indicates that the objects without such features will be excluded. One more feature added demonstrates that more objects will be excluded. For instance, when identifying the fingerprints are whorl, we have excluded all non-whorl; while identifying this whorl is a central pocket loop, we have excluded other kinds of whorl; and if finding there is a small eye on the left triangle area of the fingerprint, we have excluded other central pocket loops which do not have such an eye. Owing to these exclusions time and time again, the range of objects are limited until there is only one object left, which means the individualization is finally completed.

As to the proof in a criminal case, the judicial professionals, after checking the criminal scenery, firstly identify the case as an unnatural death, which excludes the natural death; then as the evidence increases, the professionals can identify this is a homicide case, an intentional homicide case, a homicide case owing to the break of a relationship, which excludes suicide case, an unintentional homicide case and a homicide not owing to the break up; finally, when all of the evidence could prove that it is a homicide by a specific person, which excludes any other homicide case, the individualization is finished.

Now that individualization is a kind of elimination, it will need some range, since any elimination needs the range. In the practice of individualization, the range is generally relatively big and vague. The process of individualization is a process of exclusions step by step, and every exclusion is made within the range and creates a new range for next exclusion. For example, in the individualization of fingerprints, the original range for the first time exclusion is all the human beings; when the fingerprints are figured out as whorl, this result from elimination will narrow the range of the individualization. It is meaningful to separate the whole process of continual elimination, since in some kinds of individualization, the specific range in the process can become the key of finding out the result.

The original range of individualization is decided by the nature of the object, or natural range of species. Hence, the range of elimination differs when it comes to different objects. Some ranges are larger, while others are smaller; some ranges are clear while others are vague. For example, the amount of human beings is billions, while the amount of a kind of shoes maybe only hundreds or thousands, which has a narrower range. For individualization, the larger range it is, the number of elimination of specific characteristics is more. So, the size of the range is important for individualization.

There are two elimination methods in individualization: direct elimination method and indirect elimination method. The so-called indirect exclusion method, which is also known as the "probability exclusion method", is based on the combination of the characteristics of the recurrence probability to exclude other similar objects. The so-called direct exclusion method, refers to the process that compares every object in the range with the original one and excludes the different ones until the last object is left.

In most cases of individualization, since the species range of the objects are too wide and the number of the objects is too big, people cannot collect all of these objects, and compare and exclude them all. The practical method is to exclude the objects based on the repeating rate of the feature combinations. For example, when we identify the fingerprints, can we collect all the fingerprints around the world to compare and exclude? Of course not since it is impractical. Under such circumstance, we can only use the repeating rate of the feature combination generated from data and experience. If this rate is so low that this combination cannot be shown on other fingerprints, which means other fingerprints can be excluded, we will reach the individualization.

As the basis of indirect elimination method is the repeating rate of feature combination, we should carefully find out the quantity and quality of this kind of combination when using this method of individualization. Moreover, we should consider the range of the possibilities of this combination and figure out the repeating rate, for judging it whether can be used to exclude all the other unqualified objects.

In judicial practice, sometimes the targeted objects have been limited in a very narrow range, and every object in this area is already known and comparable, so the direct elimination method can be used. Under this circumstance, people can find out the main characteristics of the aimed objects by its reflection object through observation and test, and then compare it with other objects in the range and exclude the unqualified ones. If other objects are excluded after one comparison, it will get the result of individualization; while if there are many objects left after one comparison, other characteristics of the aimed objects is needed to take into account in order exclude the left unsatisfied ones, and this process can only be terminated until finding the identical one.

On 25th June 1980, there was a shocking criminal case happened in Qianjing production brigade of Xu Bao commune in Da Tong county, Shan Xi province, that a one-year-old baby girl died with the head being trodden. After investigation, the police found out that there were only two people in the room, the crime scene. One is the girl's father Mr. Xiao, and the other one is the captain of the production brigade, Mr. Wang. There has been discord between them for a time, and they were quarreling when the murder happens. They claimed that the girl was trodden by the other. Since there was no eye-witness in the room, it was hard to decide who was the murderer. But most people think the murderer was Mr. Wang since there is no possibility of accidental injury in this case, and it is abnormal if Mr. Xian trodden his own daughter intentionally.

To find evidence, the police dried the infant corpse. Then there appeared trace of shoes with a neat edge and some points on the face of the infant. The police compared the shoes of Mr. Wang and Mr. Xiao. The brand of Mr. Wang's was Jie Fang, which had wavy pattern on the bottom, and a smooth surface of the worn middle part and the front of the shoe. Mr. Wang's shoes can be excluded since they were different from the trace on the girl's head. Mr. Xiao had a rubble and cloth shoes and the rubble of the right part of the shoes had almost been worn out, which matched with the trace on the infant's face. As Mr. Wang was excluded, Mr. Xiao was suspected as the murderer. In front of the evidence, Mr. Xiao could do nothing but to admit that he did not like the female baby and wanted to frame Mr. Wang up, so that he killed his own daughter. Mr. Xiao has compromised himself when he planned to kill two birds with one stone. However, the shoe-print told the truth, and he was convicted based on the unusual individualization.[7]

Usually the shoe traces on the face of a baby girl cannot be regarded as evidence of individualization, since the feature of the traces are too vague to be distinguished. Hence, the trace can only be used to identify the category of shoes rather than the particular one. But under the special circumstances like this case, the range is so small and definite that all objects are compared with the original one by direct elimination method. Direct and indirect methods are different, but both are methods of individualization and can identify specific objects.

Direct elimination method relies much on the definite range of objects. On the one hand, the direct elimination method can be used only when the definite range of objects is small and clear; on the other hand, the accuracy of the result is decided by the precision of the range. However, the reliance on the range cannot change the fact that direct elimination method is the cognition method of individualization. If the range is not precise in practice and results in wrong conclusion, it only indicates that individualization lacks scientific foundation and does not challenge the scientific basis of this method.

In a sense, individualization can be seen as the combination of many identifications. Hence, direct elimination method can be regarded as the combination of multi-level features. From the case above, we identify the object not only with the shoe features, but also with the specific time and space conditions. In other words, factors of this individualization have two groups of features: the shape features of the shoe prints, and the time and space condition. The combination of these two feature groups help the investigators to identify the object. In our daily life, we cannot identify a person only with the name "Zhang San", since there are many people have the same name. But if we add into more features, such as a graduate student in 1999 of the Law School of Renmin University of China, we can specify the exact person by direct elimination. Hence features narrowing the range of the objects and the features that the direct elimination method relies on can be combined to form the feature combinations of the object. In the criminal procedure, the individualization of

[7] See He (2008).

a person with an event as the basis of the evidence combination should be exclusive, and the conclusion should be unique. In a word, individualization is the basic method of judicial proof in criminal cases.

3.5 The Method of Logical Inference

Logical inference is an important judicial proof method as well. In the litigious process of criminal cases, from investigation to arrest, prosecution to trial, the personnel handling a case usually use inference methods to discover and prove case facts. When particularly using circumstantial evidence to prove case facts, inference is indispensable, and can be said as the bridge between the evidence and the facts.

3.5.1 The Concept of Inference

Inference is a process by which a conclusion is reached by considering all other known facts and deducting a logical consequence from them. It is based on certain logical principles and rules. It is a commonly used method of thinking in judicial proof, and a significant manifestation of power and wisdom of human being. Inference is closely linked with the fact finding in criminal cases. In criminal proceedings, those who have the responsibility to find out facts shall use inference. In accordance with relevant laws, investigators, prosecutors and judges all have responsibilities to find out case facts, therefore they need to use inference. Besides, defense lawyers may have the responsibility to use inference, too.

A concept closely linked to inference is reasoning, which is the act or process of using one's reason to support his argument. According to Grand Chinese Dictionary, reasoning is the inference expressed in language form, that is, reasoning is based on inference. Generally speaking, inference comes first, then comes reasoning; inference is the prelude to reasoning, while reasoning is the continuation of inference; inference is the essence content of reasoning, while reasoning is the manifestation of inference. Regarding judicial proof, inference belongs to the activity of finding out case facts by oneself, which may be named as "self-oriented proof", while reasoning is an activity of proving case facts to others, which may be named as "other-oriented proof". In other words, you may use inference to find out a case fact first, and then use reasoning to prove the fact to others.

In criminal proceedings, criminal investigators, public prosecutors, defense lawyers and judges may all use inference for self-oriented proof, while the other-oriented proof are mainly carried out by prosecutors and defenders, therefore they are the primary users of reasoning. Though judges do not assume the burden of proof in the litigation, in the court verdict they need to explain, in the form of reasoning, their findings of facts to litigants and even to the public. In fact, the most important part of a court judgment should be the reasoning.

3.5.2 The Methods of Inference

Inference methods can be classified in many ways. First, according to the number of inference premise, it can be divided into direct inference and indirect inference. Direct inference reaches its conclusion with one premise; indirect inference reaches its conclusion with two or more premises. Second, based on the direction of inference process, it can be categorized into deductive inference, inductive inference and analogical inference. Deductive inference goes from the general to the particular; inductive inference goes from particular to general; analogical inference goes from one particular to another particular. Third, by the definite degree of inference conclusion, it can be divided into certainty inference and probability inference. The former means: if premise is true, and the form of inference is correct, then the conclusion must be true. The latter means: if premise is true, and the form of inference is correct, the conclusion may be true.

In judicial proof activities, the most commonly used inference is deductive inference. The deductive inference is to deduce particular knowledge on the basis of general knowledge, in other words, to know specific individual things by applying the general attributes or rules of things. For example, the investigators of a murder case found a blood fingerprint at the crime scene, and a suspect with the name of Zhang San. Based on the match of the blood print with the known print of Zhang, the conclusion was made: Zhang had been to the crime scene and was a major suspect. This cognitive process involves deductive inference, which goes as follows:

Major premise: *All who left blood fingerprints on the crime scene had been to the crime scene and were major suspects.*
Minor premise: *Zhang San left a blood fingerprint at the crime scene.*
Conclusion: *Zhang San had been to the crime scene and was a major suspect.*

Deductive inference is generally composed of major premise, minor premise and conclusion. The correctness of conclusion mainly depends on two elements: whether the premises are true or not; whether the form is correct or not. Whether premises are true depends on whether propositions in premises are in accordance with the objective reality, and the premises mentioned here include both major premise and minor premise. The correctness of form means the form of inference in accordance with the relevant rules of logical inference, for instance, syllogism can't have four different terms; when used in the two premises, the middle term exists in both premises; the two premises cannot both be negative; the two premises cannot both be particular, etc.

In judicial proof practice, the major premise of deductive inference can be mainly divided into two kinds: one is the certainly true major premise; the other is probably true major premise. The first kind of premise refers to objective truth or inevitable things, for example, if someone takes poison over lethal dose and is not timely rescued, he or she will die. Whoever he or she is, as long as meeting the aforesaid conditions, it's certain to cause death. The major premise is certainly true. The second kind of premise refers to what may happen or only happen under some circumstances.

For instance, one will revenge after being infringed on by other people. This is a probably true major premise, because some people may not revenge afterward.

The truth of major premise decides the reliability of conclusion. Since the conclusions based on major premises of certainly true proposition are rather reliable, it is better to use certainly true propositions as major premise in the judicial proof inference. Nonetheless, in judicial practices, with all kinds of constrictions, sometimes people can only use probably true proposition as major premise. Though the conclusions based on major premises of probably true proposition are not as reliable, it does not mean conclusions are false. They could be true or could be false. In other words, major premises are probabilistic, conclusions are also probabilistic. Certainly, these conclusions are not valueless. For example, a man was killed, investigators found out that his wife committed adultery with another man, so they reasoned: wives committing adultery tend to murder husbands in conspiracy with adulterers; this wife committed adultery; she probably murdered her husband in conspiracy with her adulterer. This major premise, beyond doubt, is a probabilistic judgment, and its conclusion is also knowledge of probabilistic truth. Nevertheless, investigators finally tracked down the criminal with the help of this inference.

3.5.3 The Truthfulness of Inference Premises

When using circumstantial evidence to prove case facts, it is very important to define the premises of inference. There are two kinds of premises: one is certainly true premise, the other is probably true premise. The first kind of premise refers to objective truth or inevitable things, for example, gravity makes objects back down to ground after they have been thrown into the air, therefore an empty bottle thrown out of window by Mr. A from his high-floor house will fall to the ground. The second kind of premise is only true in some cases. For instance, the bottle may hurt a passer-by below, therefore, to prove the empty bottle thrown out of window by Mr. A is the cause of passer-by B's head injury, it is necessary to prove that the object injured B is the bottle thrown out by A, or to prove no one else in the high-rise building threw bottles down during that time.

One more example: in a case of robbing a bank with a gun, a witness identifies suspect Zhang is the robber, because she saw him with a gun in hand running out of the bank after the robbery. The witness's testimony is circumstantial evidence. As far as the evidence is concerned, a premise must be set to prove the suspect is the robber, that is, whoever ran out of the bank with a gun after robbery is the robber. Here the premise is the bridge linking the circumstantial evidence to *factum probandum*. Probably many readers doubt the truth of this premise, thinking that after robbery who ran out of the bank with a gun may not all be the robber, and the doubt makes sense in some way.

Admittedly, when analyze the probative force of circumstantial evidence, it's better to use certainly true premise, and the probative force of circumstantial evidence on the basis of certainly true premise is obviously stronger than that based on probably true premise. However, in many situations, people can only use probably true premises, and judicial proof rules cannot forbid that. For instance, Miss Wang was killed by a knife in her house. Investigators found a witness who said that Miss Wang had had a bitter quarrel with her boyfriend Li before her death. Based on this testimony, investigators inferred that young people in relationship would adopt the extreme behavior after bitter quarrels, so Li could be the murderer. The testimony is circumstantial evidence, while the premise of the inference is probably true. If there is no other evidence found at the trial, this circumstantial evidence's probative force is not strong enough to support the claim that Li is the murderer.

Probably true premises are generally based on people's life experiences and knowledge. These experiences and knowledge accumulate in people's mind consciously or unconsciously. When do inference, people then extract them out to work as middle link between the evidence and the case fact. Generally speaking, people may make two mistakes when using this type of premises. One is excessively relying on personal experiences, the other is overvaluing the general pattern of people's behaviors while ignoring the effect of specific situation on people's behaviors. Though analyzing the probative force of circumstantial evidences is only part of evidential evaluation, judicial professionals should try not to make mistakes in inference premises, because a wrong inference will lead judicial proof activities go astray.

3.5.4 The Inference Premise and the Probative Force of Circumstantial Evidence

The probative force of circumstantial evidence using certainly true propositions as premises is stronger than that of using probably true propositions as premises. For example, in a shoot-to-death case, the investigators found two pieces of evidence at the crime scene, which could be used to infer the case nature. One was the shooting pistol that was held in the decedent's hand; the other was the injury on the decedent's head with no gunshot residue. The first evidence was likely to prove that it had been a suicide, with the inference premise: the gun-shot-victim holding a pistol in his hand is likely to have committed a suicide. The second evidence would prove that it had been a homicide, with the inference premise: people who commit suicide with a gun in the hand must shoot within a close distance and leave gunshot residue around the wound. In proving the fact of "suicide or homicide", the two pieces of evidence are both circumstantial, but the probative forces are different, because the inference premises are different. The first premise is a probably true proposition, while the second premise is a certainly true proposition. Therefore, the probative force of the second evidence is stronger than that of the first one.

In terms of circumstantial evidence using probably true propositions as premises, the probative force of evidences is in direct proportion to the probability of premises being true, which means, the higher the probability of premise is true, the stronger is the probative force of evidence; the lower the probability of premise is true, the weaker is the probative force of evidence. Because it is very difficult to calculate accurately the absolute probability of some premises, it is practical to calculate only the relative probability, which is still meaningful for analyzing the probative force of circumstantial evidence. The probability of premises being true can be divided into five levels: very high, high, average, low, very low. Correspondingly, the probative force of the circumstantial evidence can be divided into five levels as well: very big, big, average, small, very small.

Here the difficulty is what the measurement people used to calculate the probability of a premise being true. As previously mentioned, the probably true premise generally forms on the basis of people's life experiences and knowledge, so people naturally calculate the probability based on their own life experiences and knowledge, and different people may reach different conclusions. As I have mentioned, public prosecutors, defense lawyers, and judges all need to persuade others to believe in the facts they have found with the evidence, they should consider not only their own life experiences and knowledge, but also the common life experiences and knowledge, that is, the people's consensus or the common sense. Generally speaking, the easier the premise is commonly accepted, the higher its probability is true.

In order to avoid excessively relying on personal life experiences and knowledge in analyzing the probative force of evidences, judicial professionals can turn to colleagues or friends for help. There are two simple ways: first, tell your colleagues or friends the premise you are going to apply and see whether they can accept it; second, tell your colleagues or friends the premise you are going to apply and then ask them to think out the exceptions of the premise. The easier they can accept the premise, the higher its probability is true; the more exceptions they can find out, the lower its probability is true.

In the previously mentioned case of bank robbery with a gun, after investigation, investigators excluded Zhang as the suspect and confirmed that Zhao was the perpetrator. The prosecution supplied the following evidence to the court: (1) witness A (the bank clerk) believed "Zhao looks very much like the gun robber" after a line-up identification; (2) witness B (a gun dealer) said he sold Zhao a pistol two months ago before the robbery; (3) the investigators found out a pistol in Zhao's house, and witness B confirmed that pistol was the one he had sold to Zhao, and witness A said "it looks very much like the pistol the robber brought with him"; (4) the robber took thirty thousand RMB from the bank, and Zhao paid back one of his friends twenty thousand RMB for his debt three days after the robbery; (5) witness C testified that several months ago before the robbery, Zhao was drank and said he "wants to rob a bank"; (6) the investigators prove that soon after the robbery Zhao left the city and disappeared, until six months later he got back; (7) Zhao confessed once to the police that he was the robber, but with no further details of the robbery.

In the trial, the defendant Zhao revoke his earlier confession to the police, and contended that: (1) he bought the pistol for self-protection; (2) he paid back his debt twenty thousand RMB with the money he earned by doing business; (3) his words of wanting to rob a bank were his pure brag after drinking; (4) after the robbery, he left the city to do business in the south; (5) his confession to the police was extorted by torture.

Among the prosecution evidence, No. 1 and No. 7 are direct evidence, while others are all circumstantial evidence. Since No. 1 is an assertion without certainty and No. 7 is revoked by Zhao, the judges should emphatically analyze those circumstantial ones in this case when analyzing the probative force of the known evidence.

The core mission of the proof in this case is "who", that is, whether Zhao was the robber or not. Thus, analyses of these circumstantial evidence should be around "who", to what degree they can prove Zhao was the robber. For this purpose, it is necessary to define inference premises of each evidence and analyze their probability of being true.

The inference premise of evidence No. 2 is "an illegal gun purchaser will use the gun to rob a bank". Obviously, there are many exceptions of it, for instance, buying guns for self-protection, so the probability of the premise being true is very low.

Evidence No. 3 is in fact composed of three pieces: (1) the pistol obtained by the investigators in Zhao's house; (2) the testimony of witness B to assert that the pistol in Zhao's house was the one he had sold to Zhao; (3) the testimony of witness A to assert that the pistol in Zhao's house looked very much like the one the robber used. The inference premise of (1) is "those who have guns in their houses use their guns to rob banks", its probability of being true is clearly very low; (2) is a supplement to evidence No. 2, so there's no need to analyze its probability separately; the inference premise of (3) is "a person who hide a robber-used gun in his house is probably the robber," though its probability of being true is rather high, this evidence is an assertion without certainty—"look very much like", so its probative force should be reduced into the half at least.

The inference premise of evidence No. 4 is "a person paying back his debt with cash in a similar amount of robbed money after the robbery is the robber." There are also many exceptions of it, for example, the money is earned by making business, so its probability is very low as well.

The inference premise of evidence No. 5 is "a person who after drinking tells the intention of robbing banks to his friends is a robber." Exceptions of this premise can be brag after drinking and so on, therefore its probability is rather low, too.

The inference premise of evidence No. 6 is "a person suddenly left the city and disappeared after s robbery is the robber." Obviously, many exceptions exist in this premise, such as going out to do business, thus its probability is very low.

Through the above analyses, it can be seen that the combination of the known evidence in this case has formed an evidence chain, but it has several weak links, its probative force is not very high. Those evidence seem to prove that the defendant had the intention of robbing a bank, illegally bought a gun, and committed a bank robbery, then paid back his debt with cash, and escaped from the city. All of these put together seemly are competent to prove that he was the robber, but the connection between these links are all probabilistic and occasional, especially the central link of committing the bank robbery, because the probative force of the evidence is very weak. Therefore a conclusion cannot be reached from those evidence. If the prosecution could not provide more evidence to prove that Zhao was the robber, the court should acquit him. Thus it can be seen that when analyzing probative force of circumstantial evidences, it is very important to define their inference premises, because it can help people assess the probability directly and intuitively. If not making clear these concrete things, people tend to assess evidences' value with fuzzy thinking mode and possibly shape subjective and one-sided even paradoxical judgment.

When use circumstantial evidences to prove a case, more than one evidence is needed and these evidence should constitute a complete system. In reviewing the evidence system, judicial professionals should refer to these following standards: (1) Each circumstantial evidence must be ascertained and verified. (2) All circumstantial evidence must have objective relevance with the case facts and have substantive meaning for proving the case facts. (3) The case facts proved by circumstantial evidence should have consistency with each other in the cardinal direction, and no conflict without a reasonable explanation. (4) The circumstantial evidence should link up mutually, forming a complete evidence chain. (5) The evidence system constituted by all the circumstantial evidence should lead to only one exclusive conclusion. This is relating to the standards of judicial proof, which I shall discuss in Chap. 6.

References

De Forest, Peter R., R.E. Gaensslen, and Henry C. Lee. 1983. *Forensic Science: An Introduction to Criminalistics*. New York: McGraw-Hill Book Company.

He, Jiahong. 1989. *Individualization: Myths of Criminal Investigation Methods*, 90–107. Beijing: Renmin University of China Press.

He, Jiahong. 2008. *Study on Criminal Investigation: From Similarity to Individualization*, 216–217. Beijing: China Legal Publishing House.

He, Jiahong. 2009. *The Fictitious Reality: Collection of Evidence Law Lectures*, 69–72. Beijing: China Renmin Public Security University Press.

Chapter 4
The Rules of Judicial Proof

Contents

4.1 Case Illustration

In the summer of 1994, there were two successive car-jack murder cases of taxi drivers in the city of Chengde, Hebei Province. First, on the evening of 30th July, Liu Fujun was attacked in the city center. Second, on the night of 16th August, Zhang Ming was attacked in the suburbs. Both men were stabbed to death. In both cases, only a small amount of property was taken—a few hundred yuan (RMB), a pager, and so on—and the vehicles were abandoned at the scene. When searching for leads, the

J. He, *Methodology of Judicial Proof and Presumption*,
Masterpieces of Contemporary Jurisprudents in China,
https://doi.org/10.1007/978-981-10-8025-8_4

investigation team's suspicion fell on four young people who lived in the countryside near the site of the second case. Local accounts identified the four as a gang of youths who were always up to no good. In October 1994, investigators searched the homes of Chen Guoqing and his three friends. An important piece of evidence was found in Chen's home—a blood-stained knife. The investigators believed that Chen and the other three were guilty of theft and murder.

The trial process dragged on for a long time. It started in 1995 and, by the end, after the overturning of many verdicts, the courts had sentenced the group to death four times in total.

In 1995, Chengde's Intermediate Court sentenced all four to death. In 1996, a second instance trial in Hebei High Court ordered a retrial on the grounds of insufficient evidence. By 1998, death sentences had been issued a further two times by the intermediate court, both of which were subsequently overturned by the high court. On 20th October 2000, Chengde Intermediate Court announced its fourth verdict: two death penalties, one death penalty with two year suspension, and one life sentence. All that was left was the judgment of Hebei High Court, but there was another long wait for this.

In 2003, the case began to gain notoriety. Most media ran the story, which became known as "Four Death Sentences in Nine Years". China Newsweek, Southern Weekly and other periodicals ran special reports.

One of the most importance pieces of evidence for the prosecution was the blood-stained knife obtained by the police at the home of Chen Guoqing. The Forensic Laboratory of Chengde Police conducted a blood group test on both the blood found on the knife and on the blood of the victim Li Fujun. The conclusions showed that both were Group B. In terms of judicial proof, this sort of test merely shows a group match, or an identification, and has relatively low proof value, because it can only prove that both of the bloods tested were Group B—a very common blood group in the population. If the police had used DNA testing to determine that the blood on the knife was that of the victim, that would have been an individualization, and its proof value would have been high. But even if there had been an individualization, it would still not be possible to determine that the defendant was the murderer because this sort of appraisal conclusion can only determine that the knife was the murder weapon. When it comes to determining who actually carried out the killing, it is merely circumstantial evidence.

In addition, the proof value of physical evidence depends on maintaining the integrity of the chain of custody. Physical evidence provided in court should be from the suspect's home, from the crime scene, or from a scene connected to the crime scene. Its condition when recovered should also be preserved. This point is often overlooked in China's current judicial practice. Some media coverage reported specific problems with the knife's chain of custody. The knife was found at the suspect's home, so the first link in the chain of custody for physical evidence should be a search report. Usually, when investigators collect evidence from a scene, they take photographs as well as notes. But in this case there were no photographs of the knife in the suspect's home. The language used in a search report is also very important; descriptions must be as objective and precise as possible. In this case, the report contained simply the words: *One knife with a case found in the home of suspect Chen Guoqing*. This kind of language fails to comply with chain of custody requirements because it is so imprecise. *One knife with a case*. What kind of case? What kind of knife? How long was the blade? There are too many knives that could match that description and there is no way to make the description object-specific, that is, it is impossible to be certain that the knife tested was the same knife found at the suspect's home.

There was also a problem with what happened next. The knife was sent to the Chengde Police Forensic Laboratory for testing. The lab kept a record of receiving a sample which states: on X day, X month, X year, one single-blade dagger received from X for testing. This leads to another question: is this "single-blade dagger" the same as the "knife with a case"? When anyone looks at evidence, no matter what the situation, the same question must be asked initially: was the knife sent to the lab for testing the same knife found at the suspect's home? Because of the failings in China's legal system and imperfections in the rules of evidence, investigators are casual in the collection, examination and use of evidence. Some believe: *I'm handling the case, I found the knife, why would I lie!* Others believe that all samples sent by investigators must be reliable. But in a country governed by the rule of law, the legal requirements around the chain of custody should be strict. It should not be possible to establish the reliability of the supplier of a piece of evidence merely by their identity. There are incidents of investigators forging evidence in our judicial practice. In this case, it is possible to raise reasonable doubt: what was recovered from the suspect's home was a "knife with a case", but by the time it reached the department for tests it had become a "single-blade dagger"—so how can it be proved that the two blades are the same?

The expert appraisal opinion itself contained a suspicion. The conclusion reached on blood group matching by the Chengde Police Forensic Laboratory were dated 22nd August 1994. This is a problem. The police identified Chen as a suspect in October 1994 and only later recovered the knife from his home. A knife found in October, but an appraisal opinion written in August. How is this possible? The police explanation was that the date on the report had been recorded wrongly. The rules around the use of expert opinions as evidence should be clear and strict. Of course, an oversight by the expert witness could in truth have led to a mistake in dates, but it could also be true that the appraisal opinion was edited after the event and the editor was careless with the date.

In this case, the main evidence leading to a guilty verdict was the confession from each of the four defendants. However they all later retracted their confessions in court, saying that they had been made under torture. And there were indeed scars on the defendants' bodies. In defense, the defendants claimed that on the two days when the murders were committed they were working in their village, which was supported by the village labor records. This means there was evidence that the defendants were not at the crime scene. But this evidence was deemed by judges to be unreliable: it would be possible for the defendants to report for work and later slip away, or a third party could put a cross next to their name in the attendance register. A judge can indeed raise doubts around a defendant's case, but should then make the prosecution provide evidence to overturn the claim made that a defendant was not at the scene. A judge should not simply disregard or deny evidence which could prove innocence.

On 24th July 2003, the Hebei High Court held a second instance trial which attracted much media attention, with many reporters observing. The judicial process was open and humane. When the four defendants had raised the issue of torture in the first instance trial, they had been ignored by the judges. This time, however, their statements were taken seriously and they were allowed to remove their clothes in court to show their scars. However the verdict was yet again slow to arrive. It was only in March 2004 that the court finally made a ruling. It upheld the guilty verdicts but granted a suspension of execution to the death sentences.

Around this time, a man named Liu Chengjin reported to the authorities that he knew the true perpetrator in the car-jacking and murder case of the two taxi drivers. Liu said that he was arrested for robbery in December 1995. In April 1996 he wrote a report while in detention, to render meritorious service in atonement for his crime, in which he stated that three murders (that of the airport worker Wang Jiang as well as the two taxi driver car-jacking murders) had been committed by Liu Fuquan, Wang Shuzhong and Zhang XX. Liu and Wang had already been convicted and executed for the airport worker killing, and Zhang sentenced to life imprisonment. But neither Chen Guoqing and his co-defendants' pleas of innocence nor the report by Liu Chengjin could overturn the guilty verdict. In 2009, the Hebei High Court rejected an appeal by the families. In August 2015, Liu Chengjin was released from prison. After meeting the families of the four defendants, he stood by his original report and continued to claim their innocence. On 29th June 2016, a judge of the Hebei High Court met the families and lawyers of the defendants in Chengde Intermediate Court. The judge indicated that a review of the case had found that the original verdict should be upheld, and an appeal would be rejected. They were told orally rather than in writing this time, because a formal rejection had already been issued in 2009. It was suggested that they may appeal to the Supreme Court.[1]

The murder trial against Chen Guoqing and his co-defendants was now over in terms of the litigation process. But were these four men the murderers? We do not know. But the case leaves us with many questions which deserve serious consideration, among which is the question of the rules of judicial proof. As the saying goes, nothing can be done without rules. Certain rules must be followed when establishing proof, or there is no way to ensure that the outcome will be correct and just. Judicial proof directly influences people's right to life and property, so it is even more important that rules are established and followed.

4.2 Introduction to Rules of Judicial Proof

The basic content of judicial proof is to apply evidence to prove facts of a case, so rules of judicial proof (hereinafter referred to as "rules of proof") can also be called as "rules of evidence", namely, "rules of applying evidence" or "rules concerning evidence". "Rules of evidence" is a borrowed word from English. Before 1990s,

[1] See Li (2016).

scholars on evidence in Mainland China were used to using concepts as "principles of evidence" and "system of evidence", and usually, only adopted the expression "rules of evidence" when introducing foreign systems of evidence. Later, the concept "rules of evidence" won popularity gradually and became a popular expression. This is a variation not only in language, but also in legal ideas, showing the conversion of Chinese evidence law from a conceptual one filled with idealism and abstractness to an applied one with realistic quality and concreteness.

4.2.1 Definition of Rules of Judicial Proof

Rules of proof refer to the norms and criteria for collecting and applying evidence during the process of judicial activities. Since rules of judicial proof, in general, are mainly for litigation, excluding rules for applying evidence into arbitration, notarization and administrative enforcement of law, they can, in accordance with the basic steps of judicial proof during litigation, be classified into rules of collecting evidence, rules of producing evidence, rules of impeaching evidence and rules of assessing evidence.

Hence, it can be seen that rules of proof, in the sense of procedural law, shall possess basic characteristics as follows: First, they are normative. Rules of proof are designed to specify the activities of collecting, producing, impeaching and assessing evidence during the process of litigation to ensure the accurate establishment of the facts of a case. Secondly, they are procedural. Since the basic content of rules of proof is norms and criteria concerning how to obtain, produce, impeach and assess evidence during the process of litigation, these rules are procedural. Thirdly, they are specific. Rules of proof, different from abstract and general principles of proof, are norms and criteria which can provide guidance for specific activities of proof, so they shall also be applicable. Fourthly, they are systematic. Rules of proof, instead of being a series of legal norms which are not interrelated to each other, are an integral whole that consists of a series of ones interrelated with each other in internal logic.

Rules of proof, being a kind of legal rules, are criteria that provide specifications for judicial proof in legal form. Since different countries have different legal traditions and systems, the legislative forms and content of rules of proof, in different countries, are also not the same. In some countries, rules of proof are all stipulated in a specialized evidence law; in some countries, they are separately stipulated in procedural laws; and in some other countries, they are stipulated in rules of judicial acts or judicial interpretations. In addition, in many countries, some of the rules of proof are stipulated by substantive criminal or civil laws. Therefore, it can be seen that research on rules of proof must be in conformity with the specific circumstances of a country and on the basis of the country's legal provisions as well as judicial practice. Hence, research shall be conducted on not only the content and requirements of various rules of proof but also their functions, pros and cons and reasonableness in specific social environment. Moreover, not only interpretations and explanatory notes shall be made for the current rules of proof, but also proposals, thoughts as well as theoretical bases shall be brought forward for the modification and perfection of these rules of proof.

4.2.2 Nature of Rules of Judicial Proof

Nature of rules of proof refers to the legal attributes displayed by the content of rules of proof and its role in the whole legal system. Due to the rich content and various legislative forms of rules of proof, it is quite difficult, in accordance with traditional standards, to simply classify them into substantive laws or procedural laws. In respect to the nature of rules of proof, there are mainly three kinds of viewpoints among scholars as follows: (1) Rules of proof shall be a part of procedural laws, for, from the perspective of legislation, they are usually an element of procedural laws; besides, evidence law itself can never be separated from procedural laws in nature. (2) Rules of proof are not only procedural but also substantive. On the one hand, all of the basic content of rules of proof is related to legal proceedings, and is about rules concerning how to apply evidence to prove facts of a case in judicial activities; on the other hand, evidence is the basis for establishing the facts of a case, and, among rules of proof, there are also provisions involving the rights and obligations of the parties concerned and witnesses, which are substantive. In addition, some of the rules of proof concerning presumption and burden of producing evidence are stipulated in substantive laws. (3) Rules of proof shall be an independent legal department parallel to substantive and procedural laws. Since the content of evidence law is, in the traditional sense, different from that of the substantive and procedural laws, it shall be neither a procedural, nor a substantive law, but an independent legal department parallel to them.

We believe rules of proof shall, by and large, be a part of procedural laws. Since substantive laws and procedural laws are the basic classifications of laws, a parallel evidence law will cause confusion to classification standards and logic relations. In addition, Substantive laws and procedural laws are classified on the basis of their different legal content. In brief, substantive laws are always designed to stipulate rights and obligations; while procedural laws, in general, are to provide procedures aiming to ensure the realization of rights and obligations. However, such a classification is not inflexible, and there are overlaps between them. For example, in procedural laws, there are also provisions on the rights and obligations of subjects in litigation. Rules of proof are mainly the norms and criteria for collecting, producing, impeaching and assessing evidence during proceedings. The basic function of these norms and criteria is to provide guarantee for accurate application of evidence and correct establishment of the facts of a case during proceedings. Although there are provisions on rights and obligations in rules of proof, these rights and obligations themselves are procedural. For example, the rights and obligations of witnesses are not substantive rights and obligations, but are designed to ensure the accurate application of the procedural provisions on witnesses' testimonies during proceedings.

Thus, it can be seen that the rules of proof shall be procedural, and they shall be an element of procedural laws in legal system.

4.2.3 Types of Rules of Judicial Proof

On the basis of different standards, rules of proof may be classified into different types:

1. From differences in content, rules of proof can be classified into rules of rights and rules of obligations, of which the former are ones that empower a person to conduct or ask others to conduct certain acts, such as the rule of displaying evidence and the rule of preserving evidence, and the latter refer to ones which requires a person to conduct or not to conduct a certain act in a direct manner, such as the rule of burden of producing evidence, the rule of exclusion of hearsay evidence and the rule of exclusion of illegal evidence.
2. From differences in form, rules of proof can be classified into rules of norm and rules of standard, of which the former are provisions with explicit acts and consequences, such as the rule of burden of producing evidence and the rule of displaying evidence, and the latter refer to ones which are used as measurement and are flexible to a certain extent, such as the rule of standards of proof.
3. From differences in function, rules of proof can be classified into regulatory rules and constitutive rules, of which the former serve as regulating and controlling persons' acts, such as the rule of presumption and the rule of judicial cognition, and the latter function as organizing persons to carry out activities involving evidence in accordance with rules, such as the rule of appraisal and the rule of inquisition.
4. From differences in rigorousness, rules of proof can be classified into inflexible and flexible rules, of which the former are ones with no room for flexibility, such as the rule that evidence cannot be used as the basis for deciding a case without being impeached, and the latter refer to ones with certain room for flexibility, such as the rule that witness must appear in court to make testimonies under general circumstances except being stipulated otherwise under special circumstances.
5. From differences in the basis or reason for formulation, rules of proof can be classified into rules of general truth and rules of special policy. The former are ones formulated on the basis of the natural laws of judicial proof, such as the rule of relevancy and the exclusionary rule against hearsay, while the latter refer to ones formulated in the light of certain social policies or value orientations, such as the rule of testimonial privilege and the exclusionary rule against illegally obtained evidence.

4.2.4 System of Rules of Judicial Proof

Though the rules of proof are of rich and abundant content, each of the rule is interrelated with others in logic. Therefore, as an integral system, each rule of proof shall be coordinated, interconnected and complementary with others, and all the rules shall be of an inherent unity. If there are contradictions or inconsistencies among rules of proof, the validity thereof will inevitably be challenged; and if the rules of proof are not interconnected and complimentary, or if there are vacancies, the validity thereof will be challenged as well, resulting in some rules becoming only an empty title and losing practical significance.

Rules of proof are formulated, fundamentally, to provide norms and guidance for proof in proceedings; therefore, the system of rules of proof shall be built based on the steps of proof and in light of the phases of proceedings. As mentioned above, activities of proof in proceedings shall consist of steps or phases of collecting, producing, impeaching and assessing evidence. Accordingly, system of rules of proof shall consist of these four aspects, namely, rules of collecting evidence, rules of producing evidence, rules of impeaching evidence and rules of assessing evidence.

Assessing evidence is an important phase in proceedings, a central element of judicial activities as well. Among the four basic steps of judicial proof (namely, collection, production, impeachment and assessment of evidence), assessment is undoubtedly the most critical one. Indeed, without collection, production or impeachment of evidence, assessment will be a tree without roots and a castle in the air, but ultimately, they all serve for assessment, since all of the results from collection, production and impeachment of evidence shall be manifested through assessment. In other words, assessment is the end or result of collection, production, and impeachment. Without assessment, judicial proof will become a meaningless term, and it will be unable to realize the tasks thereof. Rules of assessing evidence include general rules of assessment, rules of admissibility, and rules of evaluation.

4.3 General Rules of Assessing Evidence

Assessment of evidence refers to the activities in which a judge conducts review and judgment on the evidence, submitted by the two parties or collected by the judge himself, to confirm the competence and validity of evidence during the trial. No matter in criminal, civil or administrative procedures, the judges shall assess the evidence, and abide by the basic laws thereof. However, what are discussed in this book are mainly issues concerning assessment of evidence in criminal trials.

4.3.1 *The Subjects of Assessing Evidence*

Assessment of evidence is a judge's function when exercising jurisdiction, and a judicial act with certain legal effect. Thus, the subject of assessment of evidence can only be judges, excluding the other parties in proceedings. On this issue, it is necessary to distinguish the assessment of evidence from the review of evidence. Indeed, the review of evidence is an essential part for the assessment of evidence, or in other words, the assessment of evidence must be based on the review of evidence. However, the review of evidence is not the same as the assessment of evidence, with different subject and validity.

In the case of the process of criminal procedures, anyone who uses evidence needs to review the evidence. A criminal investigator shall review the evidence collected by himself or submitted by others; a defense lawyer shall review the evidence collected by himself or submitted by others; a public prosecutor shall review the evidence submitted by the investigators; and, without doubt, a judge shall also review the evidence submitted by the two parties in a lawsuit. However, the results from the review of evidence by the investigators, procurators and lawyers are not the same as that of the assessment of evidence by judges. In the context of this book, the subjects of assessing evidence are judges only, while the subjects of reviewing evidence also include investigators, prosecutors and lawyers.

4.3.2 *The Objects of Assessing Evidence*

The assessment of evidence is to review and affirm evidence rather than to establish facts in a case. In other words, the object of assessment is evidence, not the facts in a case. In litigation, it is necessary not only to establish facts of a case but also to assess various kinds of evidence. Assessment of evidence and establishment of facts in a case are two concepts that are closely interrelated but different. Assessment of evidence is the basis as well as the means for establishment of facts of a case, and establishment of facts is the end and result of assessment of evidence. In litigation, though assessment of evidence serves for establishment of facts of a case, they are not the same concept and shall not be confused.

In judicial practice, sometimes, people do not strictly distinguish assessment of evidence from establishment of facts in a case, and even, in general, regard the two as the same, since as the evidence is assessed and affirmed, the facts of a case are established as well. Nevertheless, in terms of cognitive activities in criminal proceedings, assessment of evidence shall be distinguished from establishment of facts in a case, since there are two interlinked but different phases of cognition during the decision-making process of a judge. On the one hand, assessment of evidence does not mean establishment of facts in a case. Even if all of the evidence in a case are confirmed as valid, it does not mean the facts of a case are established. On the other hand, establishment of facts in a case does not mean assessment of evidence either. Judicial officials cannot generally use activities involving establishment of facts in a case to replace or absorb activities of assessing various kinds of evidence in a case. The latter shall be relatively independent of the former in procedure and approach. In conclusion, it is, in the case of formulating corresponding rules of evidence and providing guidance to judges' assessment of evidence, quite beneficial to specify, in theory, the interrelation and differences between assessment of evidence and establishment of facts in a case.

4.3.3 The Contents of Assessing Evidence

The content of assessing evidence refers to the issues needed to be reviewed and problems to be solved by a judge during the process of assessing evidence. It is believed that a judge's assessment of evidence during a trial, in essence, includes two aspects, or in other words, his assessment mainly focuses on solving problems of two aspects: first, to ensure that certain evidence can be approved to enter into the "gate" of proceedings; secondly, to make sure that certain or a certain group of evidence can be used as the basis for judgment in a case. For the purpose of having an accurate command of the two aspects of evidentiary assessment, it is necessary to specify the following concepts and their interrelation.

4.3.3.1 The Competence of Evidence and the Weight of Evidence

The competence of evidence means whether a piece of evidence can satisfy the basic requirements of litigation for evidence. In the case of trial of criminal cases, it means whether a piece of evidence can be "qualified" as evidence in criminal procedures; therefore, it is also called as qualification of evidence. The weight of evidence refers to the proof effect and force of a piece of evidence on a fact-proposition in a case. In other words, it means whether a piece of evidence can be used to prove a fact-proposition in accordance with legal standards; therefore, it can also be referred to as the value of evidence.

In short, the competence of evidence is mainly about the relevancy and legitimacy of evidence; while the weight of evidence is mainly on the authenticity and the value of evidence. Indeed, this kind of discrimination is flexible. When carrying out activities involving assessment of evidence in a specific case, aspects such as relevancy, legitimacy, authenticity and value of evidence are often inter-crossed and inter-actional.

For example, the value of evidence cannot be completely separated from the relevancy of evidence, since the former is, to a great degree, based on the latter. The more relevant a piece of evidence is to facts of a case, the higher value it has. Obviously, the value of a piece of evidence with direct relevance is higher than that of a piece of evidence with indirect relevance; the value of a piece of evidence inevitably connected with facts of a case is higher than that of a piece of evidence accidentally connected with facts of a case. In fact, when assessing the competence of evidence or the weight thereof, a judge both needs to examine the relevancy of evidence, only in different levels. What is mainly examined by the former is whether a piece of evidence is relevant to the facts of a case; while what is examined by the latter is the nature, form and degree of relevance between a piece of evidence and facts of a case. Materials irrelevant with facts of a case are obviously incompetent evidence, but evidence with relevance is not necessarily of sufficient weight.

For another example, there is certain connection between the authenticity of evidence and the relevancy as well as legitimacy of evidence. False evidence, without doubt, also includes evidence that is falsely relevant to facts of a case. When a type of evidence is excluded or the admissibility of a sort of evidence is restricted in accordance with legal provisions, not only issues concerning value orientation such as protection of human rights and judicial justice but also problems about the authenticity of this sort of evidence shall be taken into consideration. In judicial practice, a piece of evidence that is obviously false certainly cannot be approved to enter into proceedings. In addition, since the value of evidence is based on the premise of the authenticity of evidence, the assessment of proof value cannot be isolated from the assessment of authenticity of evidence. In this sense, authenticity is a concept that runs through the whole process of evidentiary assessment, and even a central element thereof. When assessing each piece of evidence in trial, the main problem a judge needs to solve is whether this piece of evidence is authentic and reliable. However, relevancy cannot be replaced by authenticity, and authenticity cannot be used to replace proof value. It is quite necessary, in theory, to distinguish the competence of evidence from the weight of evidence, and to specify the connotation of concepts such as relevancy, legitimacy, authenticity, proof value of evidence.

4.3.3.2 The Admission of Evidence and the Evaluation of Evidence

The admission of evidence and the evaluation of evidence are two related concepts with differences. The core word of the former is "admission", which means whether a piece of evidence is admissible in the proceedings; while the key word of the latter is "evaluation", which refers to whether a piece of evidence is reliable and sufficient to be used as the basis of judgment in a case. In common words, the issue solved by admission is whether a piece of evidence can be approved to enter into the gate of the court; while the question answered by evaluation is whether the evidence is good enough to support a final decision of the court. The work of admission is mainly about the competence of evidence; while the work of evaluation is mainly focused on the weight of evidence.

No matter for admission of evidence or evaluation of evidence, evidence needs to be reviewed and estimated, being different only in modes and requirements for review. In the case of review mode, the admission of evidence mainly focuses on one piece of evidence; but the evaluation of evidence may include reviewing one piece of evidence and a group or even all of the evidence in a case. In the light of review process, the admission is a preliminary review of the evidence, while the evaluation is an in-depth review of the evidence.

In the assessment process of a judge in a criminal trial, admission is the basis of evaluation, and evaluation is the extension of admission. In the light of the results from assessment, a piece of evidence that is inadmissible will not, without any doubt, be evaluated, but a piece or a group of admissible evidence may not certainly be recognized as sufficient for a fact-finding. In brief, admission is a kind of preliminary recognition of evidence; while evaluation is the final recognition of evidence as the basis for judgment.

Admission of evidence and evaluation of evidence are two concepts that are often confused in the current theoretical research and judicial practice in China. In the trial of a specific case, it is not always necessary for a judge to clearly distinguish admission of evidence from evaluation of evidence. Nevertheless, for the purpose of better understanding the evidentiary assessment in criminal trials, it is quite necessary to clearly distinguish one concept from the other, at least in theory.[2] As to this issue, further discussions will be made in the following passage.

4.3.4 The Modes of Assessing Evidence

4.3.4.1 Assessment in the Courtroom and Assessment Out the Courtroom

Considering the different time and place, assessment of evidence can be classified into assessment of evidence in the courtroom and assessment of evidence out the courtroom. The former refers to assessment of evidence, produced by a party and impeached by the other party, made by the trial judge in court during the process of trial; while the latter means assessment of evidence, produced and impeached by parties concerned, made by the trial judge after the trial rather than in the courtroom.

Assessment of evidence in the courtroom shall be the requirement and development direction for the reform of trial mode in China. Production of evidence, impeachment of evidence and assessment of evidence are the inseparable "trilogy" in trial. Where a judge assess evidence in court, the decision-making process in trial will be more transparent, the "manipulation of results" will be less, the quality of trial will be improved, and the judicial just will be guaranteed, thus preventing judicial corruption and improving the quality of judges. However, lots of judges feel, in actual operations, it extremely difficult to make a ruling of evidentiary assessment in court and worry the evidence previously affirmed may be negated by the subsequent evidence, thus resulting in mistake or inaccurate assessment.

It is fair to say that there are various kinds of evidence and details of a case are usually intricate, so it is always hard to assess evidence comprehensively just according to the production and impeachment of a piece or a group of evidence

[2]See He (2011a).

in court. Especially for issues concerning the authenticity or the proof value of evidence, only when all kinds of relevant evidence or even all of the evidence in a case is assessed comprehensively can a proper decision be made thereon, which usually can only be carried out after the courtroom trial.

In general, a judge shall go to great lengths to assess evidence in the courtroom. However, what issues shall be assessed by a judge in court? Are they issues concerning the admissibility of a piece of evidence or issues concerning the reliability and proof value thereof? It is held that the main problems that shall be solved by a judge during assessment of evidence in court are ones concerning the admissibility of evidence, that is, problems concerning whether a piece of evidence can be approved to enter into proceedings, rather than ones concerning the value of evidence. Specifically, a judge shall, in accordance with the admissibility standards for evidence, make decisions in court on whether to adopt the various kinds of evidence produced and impeached by the parties in trial. As to issues concerning whether the adopted evidence is authentic and reliable, and how high proof value it has, decisions can be made in the discussions after trial. As to the two assessment modes of evidence, assessment of evidence in trial mainly applies to assessment of the competence of evidence; assessment of evidence after trial primarily applies to assessment of the weight of evidence.

In addition, in those cases the "disclosure of evidence" before trial is used and the party has a pretrial motion to exclude certain evidence, the ruling on whether a piece of evidence is admissible shall be made by a judge prior to trial. In other words, assessment of the admissibility of evidence shall include assessment of evidence in trial and assessment of evidence before trial.

4.3.4.2 Individual Assessment and Panel Assessment

Considering the different number of subjects, assessment of evidence can be classified into individual assessment of evidence and panel assessment of evidence. In a sole-judge trial, assessment of evidence is conducted by the judge alone, which is individual assessment of evidence. In a collegiate-bench trial, assessment of evidence shall usually be conducted by the collegiate bench, which is panel assessment of evidence. However, since the problems to be solved, for assessment of evidence in trial, are only ones concerning whether a piece of evidence is admissible, which is usually relatively simple, for the purpose of saving time and smooth trial, assessment of evidence may also be conducted by the presiding judge alone. If the problems concerning evidence are relatively complicated, the presiding judge may exchange views with the other judges in court or even call a temporary recess for discussion and then decide whether the evidence is admissible or not.

In a collegiate-bench trial, panel assessment of evidence shall be adopted for the assessment of the authenticity and the proof value of evidence. Because the issues concerning admission of evidence are relatively complex, it is, if the authenticity and the proof value of evidence is estimated and confirmed by all panel members, beneficial for fully developing collective wisdom and overcoming limitations and bias from personal cognition, thus providing better guarantee for the objectivity and accuracy of the assessment result of evidence. When a panel is evaluating evidence, principle of the minority being subordinate to the majority shall be abide by.

4.3.4.3 Direct Assessment and Indirect Assessment

Considering the different mode of reviewing evidence by the subject, assessment of evidence can be classified into direct assessment of evidence and indirect assessment of evidence. Direct assessment of evidence refers to the assessment of evidence conducted by a judge on the basis of direct review on evidence; while indirect assessment means the assessment of evidence conducted by a judge on the basis of indirect review on evidence. In general, when evaluating a piece of evidence, a judge shall stick to the principle of direct assessment. The presiding judge shall, in person, carry out direct review on evidence produced by the two parties during court investigation, and draw a conclusion on whether the evidence is admissible and can be admitted on this basis. Direct assessment of evidence is not only a basic requirement for justice of judicial procedures and correct ascertainment of facts of a case, but also a manifestation of the "principle of direct and verbal trial" in litigation. However, under some circumstances, indirect assessment of evidence may also be conducted by a judge to save judicial resources. For example, a judge may conduct indirect assessment rather than direct review on evidence notarized by notary organs or confirmed by arbitration offices; a judge of second instance may also conduct indirect assessment of evidence confirmed by court of first instance.

4.3.4.4 Single Assessment and Comprehensive Assessment

Considering the different number of evidence subject to assessment, assessment of evidence can be classified into single evidence assessment and comprehensive evidence assessment. The former refers to the kind of assessment in which a judge assess one piece of evidence each time, namely, "one evidence, one assessment". The latter is the kind of assessment in which a judge assess multiple evidence each time, including comprehensive assessment of a group of evidence and that of all the evidence in a case. Comprehensive assessment of a group of evidence refers to the kind of assessment in which a judge gathers several pieces of evidence that are interrelated and used to prove the same fact of a case and which have been produced and impeached separately, and conduct comprehensive assessment thereof. Comprehensive assessment of all the evidence in a case is a kind of assessment in which a judge, after all the evidence of a case is produced and impeached, conducts an overall and systematic analysis, induction, review and judgment on all the evidence, and makes comprehensive assessment on this basis.

In general, single assessment shall be adopted for the assessment of the competence of evidence; that is to say, in the process of a trial, "once a piece of evidence is produced, it is impeached and assessed alone". As to the assessment of the weight of evidence, if the details of a case are relatively simple and the evidence is relatively independent of each other, it is proper to adopt single assessment; if the details of a case are relatively complicated, and there are relatively many issues to be proved which are relatively independent, it is proper to adopt comprehensive assessment of a group of evidence; and if the details of a case are complicated and the evidence is closely related, it is proper to adopt comprehensive assessment of all the evidence in a case.

4.3.4.5 Oral Assessment and Written Assessment

Considering the different form of the result, assessment of evidence can be classified into oral assessment of evidence and written assessment of evidence. Oral assessment of evidence refers to the kind of assessment ruled by a judge in oral language; while written assessment of evidence is the kind of assessment ruled by a judge in written form. Since oral assessment of evidence is often used for relatively simple issues concerning evidence, usually, it may be adopted for assessment of evidence in trial or assessment of the competence of evidence. Written assessment of evidence is used for relatively complicated problems concerning evidence, so, usually, it shall be adopted for assessment of evidence after trial or assessment of the weight of evidence.

4.3.4.6 One-Step Assessment and Two-Step Assessment

Considering the possibility whether the process of a judge's assessment of evidence can be divided into two phases (namely, admission and evaluation), assessment of evidence can be classified into one-step assessment of evidence and two-step assessment of evidence. One-step assessment of evidence refers to the kind of assessment of which the process isn't divided into admission and evaluation, and in which the competence and the weight of evidence are affirmed at the same time. Two-step assessment of evidence is the kind of assessment of which the process is divided into two phases (namely, admission and evaluation), and in which the competence and the weight of evidence are assessed separately. One-step assessment of evidence is used for cases with relatively simple details and evidence; while two-step assessment of evidence is for ones with relatively complicated details and evidence.

Though this kind of classification is a new proposal in Chinese theories on evidence, two-step assessment of evidence is consciously or unconsciously adopted by lots of judges in judicial practice. For instance, according to a survey report, it is adopted by 48% of judges (71% of criminal trial judges) in practice; it is believed by 69% of judges that the two-step assessment of evidence is more consistent with the laws and requirements for assessment of evidence; it is held by 61% of judges that the two-step assessment of evidence is more beneficial for improving the trial skills of judges.[3]

In the jury trial in the United States, assessment of evidence is a typical two-step mode, because assessment of the competence of evidence is one of the functions of a judge and assessment of the weight of evidence is a function of the jury. During the process of trial, the presiding judge needs to make decisions on whether the controversial evidence is admissible in court. However, whether the evidence adopted by the judge is authentic or reliable, or whether it has sufficient proof value, it shall be discussed and decided by the jury after the courtroom trial. Just like what is pointed out by Professor Waltz, a well-known scholar of evidence in the United States, "Even though evidence has been ruled admissible by the trial judge, it is for the jury to decide what if any weight to give to it. Being the finders of facts, the jurors are entitled to assess the persuasiveness or believability of evidence. They can give it no weight at all if its believability is suspect, or they can give it full weight where it is persuasive and uncontradicted.[4]" It is beneficial not only for enhancing the scientificness of evidentiary assessment but also for improving the assessment skills of judges to adopt two-step assessment of evidence in trials.

With a push of a well-known wrongful conviction case of Zhao Zuohai,[5] the Supreme People's Court, the Supreme People's Procuratorate, the Ministry of Public Security, the Ministry of State Security, and the Ministry of Justice jointly promulgated *the Provisions on Several Issues Concerning Assessment and Judgment of Evidence in Death Penalty Cases* and *the Provisions on Several Issues Concerning Exclusion of Illegal Evidence in Criminal Cases* (the so-called "Two Provisions on Criminal Evidence", and the former is hereafter referred to as PEDPC, and the latter is hereafter referred to as PEIE) on 13th June 2010, which became effective on 1st

[3]See Zhang and Liu (2002).

[4]Jon (1983, p. 15).

[5]On 8 May 1999, a corpse with no head and several missing limbs was found in an abandoned well in a village of Shangqiu City, Henan Province. Public security investigation determined that the body was that of Zhao Zhenshang, a local villager who had been missing for more than a year. They also determined the prime suspect to be Zhao Zuohai, also from the same village. Zhao Zuohai confessed to the murder during interrogation. The public security bureau sent the case to the procuratorate, which found the evidence insufficient and ordered the public security bureau to complete DNA analysis to verify the identity of the deceased. Public security officials ordered four separate DNA analyses, but none were able to certify that the body was actually that of Zhao Zhenshang. At this point the case reached an impasse: public security officials refused to release Zhao Zuohai, and the procuratorate refused to issue an indictment, leaving Zhao in a detention limbo. In 2002 the People's Procuratorate of Henan Province chose Zhao's case as one that required clearing up because of overdue custody. The local political-legal work committee held a joint meeting of the three branches and then made a decision to "issue an indictment within twenty days." On 22 Oct., the Shangqiu Municipal Procuratorate issued the indictment. On Dec. 5, the Shangqiu Intermediate People's Court gave Zhao Zuohai a suspended death sentence. On 13 Feb. 2003, the Hebei High People's Court reviewed and approved the decision of the lower court. However, this was not the end of the case. Seven years later, on 30 Apr. 2010, the victim, Zhao Zhenshang, turned up alive! On May 8, the Henan High Court reversed its decision and gave Zhao Zuohai a verdict of not guilty and released him the following day. See He and He (2012).

July 2010. The Two Provisions on Criminal Evidence stressed the importance of the exclusionary rule against illegally obtained evidence.

PEIE establishes the priority rule of procedural review of illegal evidence. Article 5 of the Provisions states that "Where a defendant or the defender argues before or during court trial proceedings that the defendant's pretrial confession has been obtained by illegal means, the judges shall make a courtroom investigation after the public prosecutor has finished reading the bill of prosecution." That is to say, the issue whether the investigators have obtained the confession illegally, such as using torture, should be reviewed by the court before reviewing the substantial issues in the case, such as whether the evidence is truthful and sufficient. In other words, the issue of illegal evidence belongs to the admissibility of evidence, not the reliability or the value of evidence.

It can be seen the two steps for reviewing and evaluating evidence are clearly distinguished from each other in this provision. The first step is to decide whether the evidence to be reviewed can be approved to "enter into proceedings", which means whether it can be announced and impeached in court. That is to say, where the defendant or the defender presents the idea that the defendant's confession made before the trial is illegal obtained, but produces no or insufficient evidence, failing to make the judge have doubt over the legality of the collection process of evidence, or the evidence produced by the public prosecutor is conclusive and sufficient enough to rule out the possibility that the confession is illegally obtained, this confession can enter into proceedings. The second step is to decide whether the evidence approved to "enter into proceedings" can be used as the basis for deciding a case. In other words, only a piece of evidence reviewed in comparison with other pieces of evidence and confirmed as authentic and reliable can be used as the basis for deciding a case. Evidence approved to "enter into proceedings" does not necessarily become the basis for deciding a case, which is the key point and significance of the mode of "two-step assessment of evidence".

4.4 Admission Rules of Evidence

As mentioned above, the problems that need to be solved for the admissibility of evidence is whether a piece of evidence can be approved to enter into the "gate" of proceedings. Therefore, admissibility rules of evidence are these rules concerning whether a piece evidence can "enter into proceedings". Therefore, it can be stipulated from the two aspects as follows: on the one hand, it can be stipulated positively, that is to say, what attributes or conditions a piece of evidence shall possess for entering into the "gate" of proceedings; on the other hand, it can also be stipulated negatively, namely, what kinds of evidence cannot be approved to enter into the "gate" of proceedings. The former can be expressed as admissibility standards for evidence; the latter includes a series of exclusionary rules of evidence.

4.4.1 *General Rules of Admissibility*

4.4.1.1 The Rule of Relevancy

Among the various kinds of evidence submitted by the two parties to court, only the evidence with actual relevance to the facts in a case can be admitted into the proceedings; while irrelevant evidence is inadmissible. Relevance is the natural quality of evidence, which is an objective connection between evidence and facts in a case. In the eyes of philosophers, connection among objects is universal, and distant or close connection can be found between any two objects in the world. However, this universal connection in philosophy cannot be used as the basis for admitting evidence in trials. In litigation, relevancy, as one of the admissibility standards for evidence, must be the kind of relevance with substantial significance for proving the facts in a case, which means evidence can be used to prove a fact-proposition in logic. In common words, with this piece of evidence, compared to otherwise, it will be more obvious to prove the existence or non-existence of certain fact in a case. Professor Waltz says, "…relevance is a combination of (1) materiality and (2) probativeness. If the offered item of evidence is probative of (tends to establish) a material issue in the case, it is relevant."[6]

4.4.1.2 The Rule of Legitimacy

Evidence submitted by the two parties to court must be in conformity with the legal requirements or provisions in aspects such as subject, procedure as well as means of collecting evidence, and form of evidence; otherwise, it is inadmissible in proceedings. Legitimacy is the social quality of evidence, a quality endowed by a state to evidence on the basis of certain consideration on social values and policies. Though the basic function of evidence is to prove facts of a case, when formulating rules of evidence, not only the need to prove facts of a case but also the need of judicial justice and human right protection shall be taken into consideration. In a modern country under the rule of law, it is of extremely important significance to stipulate the legitimacy of evidence as one of the admissibility standards for evidence in criminal trials.

4.4.2 *Exclusionary Rules of Evidence*

4.4.2.1 The Exclusionary Rule Against Illegally Obtained Evidence

The exclusionary rule against illegally obtained evidence can be referred to as the rule of illegal evidence. The so-called "illegal evidence" means evidence collected or

[6]Jon (1983, p. 47).

obtained in violation of legal provisions. In a broad sense, there are three kinds of illegal evidence as follows: (1) evidence obtained by illegal subjects, namely, evidence collected or obtained by persons who, in accordance with relevant legal provisions, are unqualified subjects for collecting evidence in proceedings. For example, in a corruption case, the confession of a defendant obtained by the Party's discipline inspectors, who are not criminal investigators according to the Criminal Procedure Law in China; (2) evidence in illegal forms, namely, evidence with no statutory form or evidence in a form that is inconsistent with the statutory form in proceedings, for example, an anonymous letter from a person with no clear identity to report a crime, and an appraisal report with no signature of the expert; (3) evidence obtained through illegal procedures or means, namely, evidence obtained through procedures or means in violation of legal provisions, such as confessions extorted by torture, and material or documentary evidence obtained through unlawful search. In a narrow sense, illegal evidence only refers to the third.

As to how to handle illegal evidence, there are different opinions in the legal scholarship which may reflect judicial practice in one way or the other. In summery, there are mainly five propositions as follows: (1) Truthful illegal evidence shall be admitted, while untruthful illegal evidence shall be excluded. (2) All illegal evidence shall be excluded, which means where a piece of evidence is illegal, it is inadmissible. (3) Illegal evidence shall be excluded except being stipulated otherwise, which means illegal evidence, in general, shall be excluded, except, under certain exceptional circumstances, being stipulated otherwise by relevant legal provisions, for example, illegal evidence in serious criminal cases, illegal evidence in *bona fide* violation, and illegal evidence with no great danger. (4) Illegal evidence can be converted into clues, which means evidence obtained unlawfully cannot be directly admitted into proceedings, but it can be used as a clue to evidence and be adopted after the procedures or means are converted into lawful ones. (5) Different kind of illegal evidence shall be handled differently, which means illegal evidence shall be handled in different manners, neither being admitted nor excluded completely. Specifically, there are circumstances as follows: first, different kinds of evidence shall be handled differently, for example, testimonial evidence obtained unlawfully must be excluded, but physical evidence obtained unlawfully may not be excluded; secondly, unlawful acts shall be handled differently according to degree of severity, for example, illegal evidence obtained in serious violation of human rights must be excluded, but illegal evidence obtained in slight violation of procedural provisions may not be excluded; thirdly, evidence in different cases shall be handled differently, for example, illegal evidence in minor criminal cases must be excluded, but illegal evidence in serious criminal cases may not be excluded. Countries that adopt different practices for different kinds of evidence usually divide illegal evidence into two kinds: (a) evidence that must be excluded in accordance with explicit legislative provisions; (b) evidence that may be excluded by a judge with discretion.

In China, there was no exclusionary rule of illegal evidence in the CPL of 1979 and in the revised CPL of 1996, which, instead, only stipulates "judges, procurators and investigators must, in accordance with the legally prescribed process, collect various kinds of evidence. It shall be strictly forbidden to extort confessions with torture and to collect evidence by threat, enticement, deceit or other unlawful means" (Article 43, CPL 1996). However, the highest judicial agencies made some efforts to establish the exclusionary rule against illegal evidence in late 1990s. Article 61 of the *Interpretations on Several Issues Concerning the Implementation of the Criminal Procedure Law of the People's Republic of China* issued by SPC in 1998 stipulates: "Where it is ascertained, through investigation, that a witness's testimony, a victim's statement or a defendant's confession is obtained through torture, threat, enticement, deceit or other unlawful means, it cannot be used as the basis for deciding a case". Article 233 of the *Rules of the People's Procuratorate of Criminal Procedure* issued by SPP in 1999 stipulates: "Where a confession of a criminal suspect, a statement of a victim, a testimony of a witness or an appraisal opinion is collected through torture, it cannot be used as the basis for charging a crime; where the above-mentioned evidence is collected through threat, enticement, deceit or other unlawful means, thus seriously damaging the legitimate rights and interests of a criminal suspect, a victim, a witness or an appraiser, or having a possible impact on the objectiveness and authenticity of evidence, it cannot be used as the basis for charging a crime; where any physical or documentary evidence collected through unlawful means can prove the real circumstances of a case can, after being reviewed and verified, be used as the basis for charging a crime, unless the unlawful means seriously damage the legitimate rights and interests of the criminal suspect or other citizens". With the preceding provisions, Chinese exclusionary rule against illegal evidence is one in which "different kinds of illegal evidence are handled differently". However, these provisions are neither specific nor explicit.

As mentioned above, PEIE further specified the exclusionary rule against illegal evidence. Article 1 thereof stipulates: "Confessions of a criminal suspect or defendant extorted by torture or other illegal means, as well as a witness's testimonies and a victim's statements extorted by violence, threat or other illegal means, are illegal verbal evidence". Article 2 stipulates: "The verbal evidence which has been confirmed as illegal in accordance with the law shall be excluded in the handling of cases, and cannot be used as the basis for deciding a case". **Article 14 stipulates: "Where any physical or documentary evidence is obviously collected in violation of legal provisions, which may affect the impartiality of court trial, a correction or justification shall be made, otherwise the evidence shall not be used as the basis for deciding a case"**. Meanwhile, these provisions make the exclusionary rule more applicable. They not only establish the principle of the priority of procedural review on illegal evidence, but also specify the allocation of burden of proof as well as the standard of proof on the issue of torture. Since they will be discussed in Chaps. 5 and 6, it is unnecessary to go into details here.

After some ten years preparation, the amendment to CPL was passed by NPC in March 2012, and came into effect on 1st January 2013. One priority of the amendment is to deter and restrain torture and other illegal means to obtain evidence by the exclusionary rules. Article 50 of the amended CPL copied basically the original provision in previous laws as that "Extracting confessions by torture, and the use of threat, inducement, deceit and other unlawful methods to collect evidence are strictly prohibited, and no one shall be compelled to prove his or her guilt." The Amendment added some new provisions similar to those in the Provisions on Exclusion of Illegal Evidence. Article 54 of the new CPL states: "The confession of a suspect or defendant obtained by unlawful means such as torture and the statement of a witness or victim obtained by unlawful means such as force or threat shall be excluded. The collection of a physical evidence or documentary evidence is in violation of the legal procedure, and may seriously affect the judicial justice, a supplementary correction or reasonable explanation shall be made, otherwise the evidence shall be excluded."

The exclusionary rule against illegal evidence was added into the revised CPL of 2012. Article 54 thereof stipulates: "Confessions of a criminal suspect or defendant extorted by torture or other illegal means, testimonies of a witness and statements of a victim collected by violence, threat or other illegal methods shall be excluded. Where the material evidence or documentary evidence is obtained against the legally prescribed procedure, which may severely impair the judicial impartiality, supplements and corrections, or reasonable explanations shall be made; if the above-mentioned measures cannot be taken, the said evidence shall be excluded." Article 379 of the *Rules of Criminal Procedure of the People's Procuratorate* issued by SPP on 16th October 2012 stipulates: "Where the department of public prosecution of the people's procuratorate finds out, in review, that evidence such as confessions of a criminal suspect, statements of a victim or testimonies of a witness are collected by investigators through illegal means, such evidence shall be excluded, and opinions on making corrections shall be brought forward. Meanwhile, it can require investigation organs to reappoint investigators for investigation and collection of evidence, and when necessary, it can also carry out investigation and collect evidence by itself."

On 21st February 2017, SPC issued the Implementation Opinions for Overall Promotion of Criminal Procedure System Reform with the Trial-Centeredness, in which the forth part stresses the rules of evidence, including the exclusionary rule against illegal evidence, in order to prevent wrongful convictions.

4.4.2.2 The Exclusionary Rule Against Hearsay Evidence

The exclusionary rule against hearsay is an old rule of evidence in common law countries, and now there are similar provisions in some civil law countries. However, at present, there is no specific provision on such a rule in Chinese laws; instead, there are only introductions and discussions thereon among legal scholars. Since the traditional mode of criminal procedure in China is focusing on the stage of investigation, or "the investigation centeredness", no emphasis was put on appearance of witnesses in court. This can be seen in the difference in defining the concept of hearsay evidence in China and the common law countries.

The common law definition of hearsay evidence is: "An oral or written assertion, or nonverbal conduct that carries with it a conscious or unconscious assertion, made or carried on by someone other than a witness while testifying at a trial or hearing, which is offered in evidence to establish the truth of the matter asserted."[7] In simple

---

[7] Jon (1983, p. 58).

words, hearsay evidence is defined as statements made by a witness outside the courtroom. While the Chinese scholars commonly define hearsay evidence as that the information of the testimony does not come directly from the facts in a case, with no consideration on whether the witness gives the testimony in court or not. So hearsay evidence is in contrast to original evidence. The difference can be illustrated in an example, where A testifies that he heard B saying C had grabbed D's wallet, this testimony, no matter in China or in the United States, is a piece of hearsay evidence; where A saw C grabbing D's wallet in person but doesn't make testimonies in court, and his written testimony or the police's inquiry record is announced by a procurator in court, this testimony is not a piece of hearsay evidence in China, but one in the United States. It can be seen the definition of hearsay evidence by common law countries is a product of the trial-centered mode of criminal procedure, while the one in Chins is a product of the investigation-centered mode of criminal procedure.

Now Chinese criminal procedure system is shifting from investigation centeredness to trial centeredness, it is important to establish the exclusionary rule against hearsay evidence as in common law countries. The main reasons are: First, it is possible that the hearsay evidence is misinformed or inconsistent with facts, which may affect judicial substantive justice. It is well-known that it is extremely easy for errors or misinterpretations to occur during the process of reporting other people's testimony, thus failing to reflect the details of a case truthfully. Moreover, where a witness doesn't make testimonies in court, circumstances such as his perception, memory, ability of expression and character cannot be reviewed directly, which is not beneficial for determining whether his testimony is authentic and reliable, thus easily resulting in occurrence of misjudged cases. Secondly, admission of hearsay evidence actually deprives the other party's right to impeachment, thus affecting judicial procedural justice. In accordance with the provisions of Article 14 of the *International Covenant on Civil and Political Rights*, everyone charged with a criminal offense shall have the right to examine, or have examined, the witnesses against him. Only when a witness who perceives facts of a case in person makes testimonies in court can the other party's right to impeachment be realized and the justice of judicial procedures be guaranteed. In short, the basic requirement of the exclusionary rule against hearsay evidence is to ask witnesses to give testimonies in the courtroom.

With the mode of investigation centeredness, the courtroom trial is justa nominal stage of criminal proceedings, and the appearance rate of witness in court is as low as only 3% in Chinese criminal trials.[8] The CPL of 1996 does not have a provision requiring the witnesses to testify in court. In fact, it was one of the goals for the amendment to CPL in 2012 to enhance the appearance of witnesses in trial.

Article 187 of the CPL stipulates: "Where the prosecutor, the party, the defender or agent ad litem has any objection with the testimony of a witness, which has a major impact on the conviction and imposition of criminal punishment, and the people's court deems it necessary for the witness to make testimonies in court, the witness shall appear in court and make testimonies. The provisions of the preceding paragraph shall apply to the police who is needed to make testimonies in court as a witness about the

[8]See He (2011b).

situations he witnessed when performing his duties. Where the prosecutor, the party, the defender or agent ad litem has any objection with the appraisal opinions, and the people's court deems it necessary for the appraiser to appear in court, the appraiser shall appear in court and make testimonies. If the appraiser refuses to appear in court and make testimonies upon notice of the people's court, the appraisal opinions shall not serve as the basis of deciding the case".

Article 188 thereof stipulates: "If a witness refuses to appear in court and make testimonies upon notice of the people's court without justifiable reasons, the people's court may force him to do so, with the exception of the spouse, parents and children of the defendant. If a witness refuses to appear in court or refuses to make testimonies after appearing in court without justifiable reasons, he shall be admonished; if the circumstances are serious, he shall be imposed a detention of not more than 10 days upon approval of the president of the court. If the punished is dissatisfied with the decision on the detention, he may apply to the people's court at the next higher level for reconsideration. During the reconsideration, the execution of the punishment shall not be stopped." The preceding provisions are not of the exclusionary rule against hearsay, but beneficial for increasing the appearance rate of witnesses in criminal trials, which could be considered as one function of the hearsay rule.

Certainly, considering the costs of the proceedings, it is not necessary to require all witnesses to testify in court, in other words, not all hearsay evidence is unreliable or inadmissible. Under some circumstances where the original evidence has already been destroyed or lost, or where the original evidence cannot be obtained, the hearsay evidence then becomes the necessary access and means to prove facts of a case. Besides, some hearsay evidence is produced under certain reliable situations. Therefore, it is necessary to formulate several exceptional or supplementary rules to the rule of exclusion of hearsay evidence by law. In general, there are provisions exceptional to the rule of exclusion of hearsay evidence in foreign countries. Article 141 of IICPL, Article 56 of PECP, and Article 41 of the *Provisions on Several Issues Concerning Evidence in Administrative Procedure* (PEAP), the latter was issued by SPC in 2002, all make provisions on the exceptional circumstances under which a witness doesn't need to make testimonies in court, which are similar to the exceptions to the exclusionary rule against hearsay evidence in common law countries.

In summery, the exceptions mainly include circumstances as follows: (1) the original narrator is dead; (2) the original narrator, due to physical or mental reasons, has lost abilities of discrimination and expression; (3) the original narrator, due to force majeure such as natural disasters or accidents, cannot appear in court to make testimonies; (4) the original narrator is missing or abroad, being unable to appear in court to make testimonies; (5) the other party has no objection with the written testimonies. Under the above-mentioned circumstances, the hearsay evidence is admissible, or in other words, the witness is entitled to testify out of the courtroom. Nevertheless, the judges shall conduct especially serious review on the authenticity, reliability and proof value of these written testimonies.

4.4.2.3 The Exclusionary Rule Against Opinion Evidence

In common law countries, witnesses include lay witnesses and expert witnesses. An expert witness is entitled to provide opinion testimonies in accordance with scientific principles; but a lay witness, in general, is not allowed to do so, according to the rule against lay opinion testimony. In China, the term of "witness" is used in narrow sense, which does not include litigant and expert. A witness is a lay person who makes statements on facts of a case perceived or understood by him. Therefore, a witness should not making inferences, analyses or comments on facts of a case. In other words, a witness's opinion testimony is inadmissible in trials. This is the basic content of the exclusionary rule against opinion evidence.

Chinese judiciary did not formally recognize the opinion rule for many years. It was the first time to do so when SPC issued PECP in 2002. Article 57 thereof stipulates: "A witness that appears in court to make testimonies shall objectively state the facts that he has perceived in person…When making testimonies, the witness may not use hypothetical, commentary or deductive words". Article 12 of PEDPC, which is mentioned above, stipulates: "No hypothetical, commentary or deductive testimony of a witness can be used as evidence, unless it is consistent with the facts as judged on the basis of ordinary life experiences."

There are mainly two reasons for establishing the exclusionary rule against opinion evidence. First, since a lay witness doesn't possess the specialized knowledge for providing conclusive opinions, his opinions tend to be subjective and partial, thus disturbing a judge or a juror from making correct judgment on facts of a case. Secondly, since no specialized knowledge is needed for establishing the common facts of a case, a judge or a juror is fully capable of making his own judgment, and there is no need for a witness to provide opinions thereon.

Nevertheless, under some situations, it is not easy or proper for excluding opinion testimonies. Therefore, it is necessary to establish exceptions to the opinion rule. On the basis of the principles of judicial proof and the experience from judicial practice, the main exceptions are as follows: (1) opinions that are extremely difficult to be separated from facts of a case, for example, "it smells like Maotai (a well-known wine in China)"; (2) descriptive opinions on issues such as figure, appearance and mental state of the person under observation, for example, "he seems extremely terrified"; (3) opinions concerning common-sense judgment directly based on personal experience, for example, "the speed is about 100 km per hour"; (4) opinions concerning identity and similarity of compared things, for example, "I think the voice in that call is his voice"; (5) opinions concerning climatic conditions such as temperature and wind power, for example, "I think the temperature in this room is quite high"; (6) opinions on the value, quantity, nature, color and other issues of an item, for example, "I think that item must be quite expensive". Though the above-mentioned opinion evidence can be admitted in trials, judicial officers shall carry out serious review and judgment on the basis of the opinion evidence provided by the witness.

4.4.2.4 The Exclusionary Rule Against Character Evidence

Character evidence refers to the evidence which can prove the conducts, personality, behavioral habits and other characteristics of a person. Character evidence includes not only good but also poor character evidence. The character evidence used in litigation are mainly as follows: first, evidence concerning a person's reputation at work or in society; secondly, evidence concerning the special behavioral modes or social communicative modes of a person; thirdly, evidence concerning the former misdeeds or criminal records of a person. In criminal procedures, the objects of character evidence not only include defendants, but also victims and witnesses. Generally speaking, character evidence cannot be used as the basis for proving facts of a case. For example, evidence that proves a defendant's criminal record cannot be admitted into evidence to prove he committed the criminal act charged in the case. It shall not be held by judicial officers that because a defendant once committed a crime or a misconduct, he is more likely to be the perpetrator in the case. "Once a thief, always a thief" is a kind of misconception that must be excluded from judicial proof. All of these are the basic content of the exclusionary rule against character evidence.

However, under some circumstances, it is indeed valuable to adopt character evidence. Therefore, it is necessary to stipulate exceptions to the exclusionary rule of character evidence. In accordance with the principles of judicial proof and the experience from judicial practice, there are mainly two kinds of exceptions as follows: (1) Character evidence concerning the same and special patterns of committing a crime is admissible. For example, where there is evidence to prove the defendant has once used the same special method or tool to crack safe, and the perpetrator of the case also uses this method or tool to crack a safe, then though the evidence is a piece of character evidence concerning a person's criminal records, it is still admissible in the trial of the case to prove the defendant is more likely to be the perpetrator. (2) Character evidence concerning deceit and lying is admissible. For example, evidence that proves the defendant once conducted deceit or is used to lying can be used to impeach the reliability of the defendant's statements on facts of the case. However, this kind of evidence can only be used with limitations, that is to say, it can only be used for impeachment, rather than proving the defendant's guilt directly. In addition, though it can also be used to impeach the reliability of the statements of a victim or a witness on facts of a case, when using character evidence to impeach the witness's testimonies, the evidence shall only be about the witness's character in integrity, and shall not be used to insult or attack the witness's personal dignity. Under some circumstances, a defendant may use the character evidence of a victim to support his claims. For example, for the purpose of supporting his claim of justifiable defense, a defendant may produce evidence concerning the violent tendency of the victim to prove that the victim is the person who attacks first. Certainly, in such a situation, the prosecutors can also, to rebut the defendant's claim, produce evidence that proves the victim is always peaceful.

4.4.3 *The Rule of Limited Admissibility*

4.4.3.1 Definition of Limited Admissibility

The limited admissibility of evidence can also be referred to as "partial admissibility" of evidence, which is a special rule on admissibility of evidence in common law. In accordance with the interpretations by the *Black's Law Dictionary*, this rule is defined as "the principle that testimony or exhibits may be admitted into evidence for a restricted purpose. Common examples are admitting prior contradictory testimony to impeach a witness but not to establish the truth, and admitting evidence against one party but not another[9]".

The limited admissibility rule is a supplement to the relevancy rule of evidence. Evidence with "limited admissibility" is mainly used for impeaching a witness, in the mode of cross-examination in common law countries. But under some circumstances, a judge can also adopt other evidence to impeach a witness, which is aimed at proving the witness's statements are not authentic on the one hand, and the witness has physical disabilities or character problems on the other hand.

Evidence of "limited admissibility" is a means used for the realization of impeachment. Specifically, there are mainly five situations as follows: (1) it can be used to prove that there is sensory impairment of a witness, for example, the testimony of a technician in an optical store which can be used to prove the witness is short-sighted, color-blinded or has other vision problems; (2) it can be used to prove there are problems in a witness's mental state, for example, pathological liars; (3) it can be used to prove a witness has a criminal record of felony, for example, a guilty verdict by court; (4) it can be used to prove that a witness once made contradictory statements to his testimonies in court and he denies this, for example, former written testimonies or inquiry records; (5) it can be used to prove that the bias, interests or other factors of a witness may have an impact on the authenticity of his statements, for example, speeches proving his racial discrimination.

Indeed, in judicial practice, it is not an easy job for judges to strictly distinguish the impeachment function of evidence from the conviction function thereof. In some situations, evidence for impeaching may be, consciously or unconsciously, used by a judge as the basis for conviction of a crime. However, in any case, it is necessary to distinguish evidence for impeaching from that of conviction in trial. Judges shall, through learning and training, be capable of telling one function of evidence from the other and cultivate the mode of limited admissibility of evidence in mind.

4.4.3.2 Objects of the Rule of Limited Admissibility

No matter from theories on evidence or from judicial practice, the rule of limited admissibility" is of significance, for it enables us to understand the validity of evidence more accurately and apply evidence more properly. Nevertheless, the "rule

[9]Garner (1999).

of limited admissibility" cannot apply to all evidence. In fact, the law provides no limitation on the validity of most evidence. In other words, as to the proof value of most evidence, judges are endowed with discretionary power. In reference to foreign practices, together with taking the situations in Chinese judicial practice into consideration, it is held that the "rule of limited admissibility" can apply to the kinds of evidence as follows:

(1) Contradictory statements. Statements, made by a witness (including victims and defendants, "similarly hereinafter") before trial, which are contradictory to his testimonies in court cannot be used to prove facts of a case directly, but can be used to impeach the witness's credibility.
(2) Similar statements. Generally speaking, it is unnecessary for the court to listen to the testimonies, made by a witness before trial, identical with or similar to his testimonies in court, but where the lawyer opposed proposes that the witness's statements are "stories" made up recently, the party with the witness can produce evidence to prove he has made identical or similar statements before, thus proving the reliability of his testimonies.
(3) Character evidence. Usually, character evidence can only be evidence of "limited admissibility". For example, the criminal records or the former immoral behaviors of a defendant can only be used as the basis for impeaching his statements, rather than the basis for convicting him of a crime.
(4) Hearsay evidence. In general, hearsay evidence is inadmissible. However, in some situations, it can be used to prove a person once said something, but cannot be used to prove whether the content of his statements is true or false. For example, A say he once heard B say C had killed a person. As to whether C killed a person or not, A's testimony is a piece of hearsay evidence and is inadmissible, but it can be used by the judge to prove that B once said such words.
(5) Written records and audio-visual materials. Materials such as written records, recordings and videos of inquiry and interrogation are also evidence of "limited admissibility", which means they can only be used to prove the authenticity and legitimacy of the process of inquiry and interrogation, rather than be used to prove the authenticity of the content of the statements.

It can be seen that, the "rule of limited admissibility" is applied widely and of high practical value, but is not emphasized enough in the theory and practice in China. Further study on the "rule of limited admissibility" will help us to solve some tough problems in evidence law. For example, the evidential validity of the conclusions from lie detection is a controversial issue which can be provided with beneficial inspirations from the "rule of limited admissibility".

4.4.3.3 The Limited Admissibility of Polygraph Evidence

Since the appearance of polygraph testing, or lie-detecting technology, scholars of many countries have conducted survey and research on the accuracy rate of conclusions of lie detection, and found out it was relatively high. However, in judicial practice, errors did exist. For example, Du Peiwu, a criminal suspect, was tested on a polygraph for a double-murder case by the Forensic Science Center of the Intermediate People's Court of Kunming, Yunnan in 1998, and was confirmed as telling lies when answering questions related to the homicide. Later, under the "intense" interrogations by investigators, Du Peiwu was forced to admit guilty and confessed the process of the murder. In the first instance trial, he was convicted of intentional homicide and sentenced to death. Afterwards, since the weapon (a gun) in the case had not been found, the original sentence was commuted to suspended death penalty by the High People's Court of Yunnan, as the second instance trial court or the court of appeals. In 2000, when investigating another criminal case, the local public security officers found out the murderer of the above-mentioned case is not Du Peiwu but an extremely large criminal gang of homicide and carjacking. Therefore, after being in prison for 26 months, Du Peiwu was acquitted.[10] Without doubt, in this case, the basis for the court's judgment is not the result of the polygraph testing but some other evidence; however, the conclusion also contribute to the occurrence of this wrongful conviction.

It is because of these misjudged cases that some persons bring forward severe criticisms on the reliability of the polygraph evidence and firmly oppose the result of the polygraph testing to be admitted into evidence. We believe though some conclusions of lie detection may be wrong, not all conclusions therefrom shall be excluded from proceedings accordingly. In fact, no evidence is completely reliable, and errors may occur as well. Even conclusions from scientific evidence such as handwriting, fingerprint and DNA appraisals may also be mistaken. Above all, the reliability of the result of the polygraph testing should be objectively assessed, with neither simple negation nor overestimate.

It must be pointed out here that though polygraph is a scientific psychological detector, it can only provide a scientific basis for recognizing lies in the hand of qualified professionals. Whether a result of the polygraph testing is correct depends, to a large extent, on the quality, technical ability and experience of the persons who carry out the examination. Currently, Chinese polygraph examiners are of various qualifications and different levels of skill, and there is no unified and standardized qualification authentication for or administration over lie-detecting profession. Moreover, since some investigators use polygraph as a tool for investigation and regard it as a "powerful tool for cracking criminals", they tend to, when analyzing, estimating and using the result of the polygraph testing, "choose what they need". For example, in the above-mentioned case of Du Peiwu, the lie detectors, when estimating the polygraph map, just ignored the physiological signs that can prove Du Peiwu's innocence.[11] Just as what was said by Du Peiwu in interviews by reporters after being released from prison, "they intentionally hided the beneficial conclusions but

---

[10] I mentioned this case in Chap. 1. See also Guo (2011).

[11] After Du Peiwu was exonerated in 2000, the polygraph examiners were widely criticized. One of the examiners sent a letter to me, this author, outlining her opinion of what she knew of the case. She averred that Du's answers had been inconsistent. Although he exhibited signs of having told lies, he showed signs of telling the truth when he answered questions directly related to his case.

used unbeneficial ones against me[12]". In brief, it is not only an important guarantee for the reliability of the result of the polygraph testing but also an urgent affair to promote lie-detecting technology, to improve the quality of the polygraph examiner, and enhance the administration over the industry in China.

It is undoubted that lie-detecting technology plays an important role in criminal investigations. However, it is another issue whether the result of the polygraph testing should be admitted into evidence in trials. Though the two aspects are interrelated, they are not the same issue. As to criminal investigations, the fundamental goal is to ascertain facts of a case; while in trials, it is necessary to take not only the need for ascertaining facts of a case but also the need for maintaining judicial justice, protecting defendants' rights and other social values into consideration. In addition, when applying lie-detecting technology into criminal investigations, it is also necessary to strengthen legal awareness and handle cases in strict accordance with the law. Where cases are not handled in accordance with the law, it is possible that lie-detecting technology becomes an "accomplice" for illegal collection of evidence or even torture. Nevertheless, in court trials, the law shall have higher requirements for evidence.

The result of the polygraph testing can be admitted into evidence in proceedings, but they are only of "limited admissibility", which means they can only be used to review the authenticity and reliability of verbal evidence rather than be used directly to prove facts of a case. Specifically, the result of the polygraph testing can only be used to prove whether the statements of a criminal suspect, a defendant, a party or a witness in civil procedures are authentic and reliable, rather than be used directly to prove whether a criminal defendant is guilty or not, or whether a party in civil procedures shall assume the responsibilities resulted from losing the lawsuit. However, as to cases as perjury, if whether a person's statements are authentic or false is a constitutive element of the basic facts of a case, the results of the polygraph testing can also be used as the basis for establishing the facts of a case, but cannot be used as the only evidence for deciding a case. In other words, the facts of case, which are used to confirm the existence of perjury, on the basis of the result of the polygraph testing need to be corroborated by other evidence.

To sum up, the results of the polygraph testing are not infallible, but as to issues concerning the reliability of defendants' statements and witnesses' testimonies, the results of the polygraph testing are definitely more reliable than human's subjective assessment and judgment. Therefore, there is no reason to exclude all polygraph evidence in criminal or civil proceedings. It is better to place them as the evidence of limited admissibility. Simple exclusion is not a scientific attitude towards those evidence, because it would be like "to give up eating for fear of choking".

She says she noted this in the final report of the polygraph testing, but her concerns were overlooked by investigators who simply wanted proof that Du had been telling lies.

[12]Ai (2001).

4.5 Evaluation Rules of Evidence

When discussing issues concerning assessment of evidence, what shall be examined is whether the evidence is reliable and sufficient, or in other words, whether the evidence in a case can be the sufficient basis for deciding a case. Although a judge is endowed with certain discretionary power when evaluating evidence, it is necessary to provide limitations on his discretionary power through evaluation rules. As to the circumstances in Chinese judicial practice, it is of extremely important significance to formulate evaluation rules of evidence.

4.5.1 General Standards for Evaluation of Evidence

4.5.1.1 Authenticity

Authenticity, or reliability, of evidence is one of the basic standards for evaluation of evidence. Review on the authenticity of evidence is a necessary procedure for using it as the basis for deciding a case. Article 48 of CPL stipulates: "Any of the above evidence must be verified before it can be used as the basis for deciding cases." In other words, among the evidence approved to enter into proceedings, if a piece of evidence is found out to be inauthentic through review, then it cannot be admitted by a judge and cannot be used as the basis for deciding a case. Article 195 of CPL also stipulates: "If the facts of a case are clear, the evidence is reliable and sufficient, and the defendant is found guilty in accordance with the law, he shall be pronounced guilty accordingly". "The evidence is reliable" here refers to the authenticity of evidence. In proceedings, judicial officers shall conduct review on the authenticity of each piece of evidence one by one, which means to conduct review to see whether each of them is reliable. Undoubtedly, in the case of review methods, whether a piece of evidence is authentic and reliable shall always be estimated comprehensively through corroboration with other evidence.

4.5.1.2 Sufficiency

Sufficiency of evidence is also one of the standards for evaluation of evidence. When being used as the basis for deciding a case, the evidence shall not only be authentic in content but also of sufficiency in proof, which means the "evidence is not only reliable", but also "sufficient". "Evidence is sufficient" means the weight or value of the evidence is sufficient for proving the to-be-proved facts of a case. In theory, the evidence in "evidence is sufficient" can be used to refer to a piece of evidence as well as a group or all of the evidence in a case. As to one fact or circumstance, a piece or a group of evidence may be "sufficient", that is to say, this piece or group of evidence is of sufficient weight to prove the existence or nonexistence of the fact or the circumstance. As to the whole case, "evidence is sufficient" means all of the evidence in a case is of sufficient weight to prove the truth of a case. Thus, to conduct review to see whether the evidence is sufficient is to conduct analysis and judgment on the proof value of evidence.

Since the evaluation standard for evidence and the proof standard in proceedings are closely interrelated, and they are two concepts expressing interlinked conceptions from different perspectives, they can also be deemed as two aspects of an issue. From the perspective of assessing evidence, it is the evaluation standard for evidence; from the perspective of establishing facts, it is the proof standard for case. For instance, in the current Chinese criminal procedures, the evaluation standard for evidence is "evidence is reliable and sufficient", and the proof standard for case is "facts of a case is clear". In a specific case, where the evidence is reliable and sufficient, the facts of a case is clear; and in order to satisfy the requirement of "the facts of a case is clear", the evidence must be reliable and sufficient. As to issues concerning proof standard, more discussions will be conducted in Chap. 6.

4.5.2 The Rule of Corroborating Evidence

The content of the rule of corroborating evidence is that, in accordance with the explicit provisions in law, certain kinds of evidence, being insufficient to prove facts of a case, cannot be used independently to prove facts of a case, and need to be corroborated by other evidence. Therefore, the rule of corroborating evidence can also be referred to as the rule of corroboration. For example, Article 53 of CPL stipulates: "A defendant cannot be found guilty and sentenced to a criminal punishment if there is only his confession but no other evidence". The rule of corroborating evidence actually means: (1) this kind of evidence needs to be corroborated by other evidence; (2) without corroboration, this kind of evidence cannot be used independently as the basis for establishing the facts of a case.

In accordance with the relevant laws in China, the spirit stipulated in the judicial interpretations (such as Article 69 of PECP and Article 71 of PEAP) as well as the experience from judicial practice, besides a defendant's confessions, the following evidence may not be used independently as the basis for establishing facts of a case, namely, evidence that needs to be corroborated: (1) testimonies of a minor that are not suitable to his age or intelligence; (2) testimonies of a witness who is a relative to or has an interest in a party; (3) photocopies or reproductions that cannot be verified against the original document or original thing; (4) audio-visual materials that cannot be confirmed as original; (5) circumstantial evidence.

4.5.3 The Rule of Weight Priority

The priority rule of proof weight is a rule of prior acceptance that shall be abided by when a judicial officer conducts assessment on the contradictory evidence used to prove the same fact of a case. For example, where both evidence A and B are used to prove whether the defendant accepts bribes or not, but A proves that the defendant accepts bribes while B proves otherwise, since it is unable to confirm one of them is false through analyses just on the two pieces of evidence, it is necessary to determine which piece of evidence shall be accepted prior to the other on the basis of the comparison of their proof weight.

In accordance with the relevant theories on judicial proof and the experience from judicial practice, the following rules shall be abide by when comparing the proof weight of different kinds of evidence: (1) the weight of original evidence is heavier than that of derived evidence; (2) the weight of direct evidence is heavier than that of indirect evidence; (3) the weight of the written evidence that has been notarized is heavier than that of other written evidence; (4) the weight of the written evidence that is preserved in files of state organs in accordance with relevant procedures is heavier than that of other written evidence; (5) the weight of physical evidence with a proper expert opinion is heavier than that of other verbal evidence; (6) the weight of the testimonies of a witness who is not a relative to or has no interest in a party is heavier than that of a witness who is a relative to or has an interest in a party. A judicial officer must, when comparing the weight of two pieces of evidence in a specific case, confirm that they are used to prove the same issue and are of same content. Where the fact propositions of the two pieces of evidence are not the same, or their specific contents are not identical, the weight cannot be compared with each other. The priority rule of proof weight is of significance for the guidance of judicial officers' evaluation of evidence in China now, because of the professional qualities of the judges in general.

4.5.4 The Rule of Publicity of the Intimate Conviction in Free Evaluation

A judge must be endowed with certain discretionary power when deciding whether a piece of evidence shall be accepted as the basis for fact finding, since it is difficult for him to completely follow objective standards when estimating the authenticity and weight of the evidence. In other words, there exists "free evaluation with intimate conviction" when a judge finds facts of a case through evidence. "Intimate conviction" means a judge shall feel certain about his judgment on the authenticity and weight of the evidence and his understanding of the facts of case shall be beyond a reasonable doubt. Nevertheless, a judge's "free evaluation with intimate conviction" is not absolute freedom without any restriction. On the one hand, it shall follow the evidence-based principle and must be built on the basis of evidence; on the other hand, a judge's intimate conviction must be publicized in certain ways, which is the basic requirement for the rule of publicity of intimate conviction.

Publicity of intimate conviction means the conclusions and reasons of a judge's evaluation of evidence shall be open to parties concerned or even to the public. There are two manners for publicity of intimate conviction as follows: (1) publicity in court trial, which refers to the publicity through activities such as the in-court evaluation of evidence by a judge; (2) publicity in written judgments, which means the publicity through a judge's explanations on the reasons for accepting evidence and bases for finding facts in his written judgments. Since judgment on the authenticity and weight of evidence is usually carried out after a courtroom trial, publicity in written judgments is actually the main manner for publicity of intimate conviction. We believe a judge shall make specific explanations on the bases and reasons for his judgment in written judgments, especially specific explanations on the reasons for evaluation of evidence. What needs to be emphasized here is a judge needs to make explanations not only on evidence that is accepted as the basis for deciding a case but also on evidence that has been adopted (namely, evidence which has been approved to enter into proceedings) but ultimately isn't accepted, and he needs to explain the specific reasons why the evidence with relevancy and legitimacy isn't accepted as the basis for deciding a case.

Article 64 of PECP stipulates: "The judges shall examine and verify the evidence in accordance with the legal procedures in an all-round and objective manner, shall observe the provisions of law, follow the professional ethics of judges, use logic reasoning and daily life experience to make independent judgment on the weight and forcefulness of the evidence, and publicize the reasons and result of the judgment." There is also a similar provision in Article 54 of PEAP. These provisions both manifest, to a certain extent, the requirement for the rule of publicity of intimate conviction in free evaluation of evidence. Publicity of intimate conviction is a kind of manifestation of the open trial system during the phase of a judge's evaluation of evidence, as well as a guarantee for the realization of judicial justice. Through publicity of intimate conviction, a judge's evaluation of evidence will be under the supervision of the parties concerned and public, which is beneficial for not only improving the quality of judicial proof, but also enhancing the authority of judicial decisions.

At present, Chinese system of rules of judicial proof is imperfect, which is mainly manifested as follows: Firstly, there is no unified legislative form. The rules of proof are stipulated separately in three procedural laws and other relevant laws, regulations as well as judicial interpretations, which results in inevitable inconsistencies and discrepancies. Secondly, they are of no authority in legal validity. Since most of the current rules of proof are stipulated in the judicial interpretations by SPC and SPP, which are of relatively low level in legal validity, it is hard for them to be implemented in a unified manner, and there are disputes among the public security organs, the people's procuratorates and the people's courts. Thirdly, they are inapplicable in some contents. Most of the rules only provide principles for the validity of evidence, with no specific provisions on admissibility or exclusion. Finally, they are incomplete in system. For example, there are not rules on testimonial privileges, resulting in some vacancies in the system of rules of proof.

In conclusion, Chinese system of rules of proof is roughly formulated within a broad framework, with few articles and careless content, which makes it difficult for the rules of proof to play a proper role in guiding, adjusting and regulating judicial proof. Therefore, further improvement shall be made for Chinese system of judicial proof.

References

Ai, Jun. 2001. Worries on polygraph. *China Youth Daily*, February 16.

Garner, Bryan A. (Ed.). 1999. *Black's Law Dictionary*, 7th ed, 48. St. Paul: West Publishing Co.

Guo, Xinyang. 2011. *Critical Evaluations of Wrongful Convictions*, 140–152. Beijing: China Renmin Public Security University Press.

He, Jiahong. 2011a. Admission and evaluation of evidence: From issues concerning the language of two 'Provisions on Evidence'. *Chinese Journal of Law* 3.

He, Jiahong. 2011b. Empirical studies on nominalization of criminal court trials. *The Jurist* (6).

He, Jiahong, and He, Ran. 2012. Empirical studies of wrongful convictions in Mainland China. *University of Cincinnati Law Review* 80(4): 1278–79.

Jon, Waltz. 1983. *Criminal Evidence*, 2nd ed. Chicago: Nelson-Hall Press.

Li, Xianfeng. 2016. Hebei Supreme Court rejects appeal in 22 year old case of murder by Chen Guoqing. *Beijing Youth Daily*, *Sohu News*, August 29. http://news.sohu.com/20160629/n456903980.shtml. Retrieved on 16 Nov 2016.

Zhang, Sulian, and Yan, Liu. 2002. Practical survey and analysis on assessment of evidence by judges. In *Evidence Forum*, vol. 4, 471–482. Beijing: China Procurator Press.

Chapter 5
The Burden of Judicial Proof

Contents

5.1 Case Illustration

The plaintiff Hu Guangrong has made four term deposits in Changsha Branch of XX Bank in Hunan Province, the total amount of which is USD 48,000. On 31st January 1996, upon expiration of the deposit accounts, he went to the bank with the deposit receipts to withdraw the money, but an employee of the bank told him that his deposits had been withdrawn already. The employee said the four term deposits were taken by "Hu Guangren" who claimed to be Hu Guangrong's younger brother. That person used his and Huang Guangrong's ID cards to report the lost of the deposit receipts on 12th January 1996, and, going through the reporting-for-lost formalities,

J. He, *Methodology of Judicial Proof and Presumption*,
Masterpieces of Contemporary Jurisprudents in China,
https://doi.org/10.1007/978-981-10-8025-8_5

saved those money into another current account on 19th January, then exchanged the money into RMB and withdrew all the money on 25th January.

With the help of the local police, the bank found out that the ID card used by "Hu Guangren" was fake and there was no such person at all. And the ID card of Hu Guangrong used by him had been reported lost two years ago by Hu Guangrong, who had already published a missing notice in the newspaper and received a new ID card from the police department. In addition, Hu Guangrong found some "technical problems" on the Loss Reporting Application Form, e.g. there were five handwriting corrections, the first seven digits were missing for all four accounts, the ID cards' numbers were not inconsistent, and some of the contents were wrote by the bank clerk instead of the person who withdrew the money. Notwithstanding, the bank insisted that they had made the payments according to rules, and there were no faults in their acts, so they refused to pay again. Hu Guangrong had no option but to sue the bank to the court.

In the court, the plaintiff claimed that the employees of the bank had committed gross negligence, and had not performed the duty of care which they should. First, the Loss Reporting Application Form should be annulled because of the handwriting corrections and the omission of the first seven numbers of the accounts. Secondly, although the bank staff did not have the special ability to verify the truthfulness of an ID card, the inconsistency of the ID cards' numbers filled-in by the applicant should have attracted the bank staff's attention.

The defendant claimed that the bank staff had no fault. The duty of care borne by the bank staff regarding the ID card was just form check, not substantive check. The bank staff had no ability to check whether or not an ID card was counterfeited. In short, the bank made its payments according to the rules and it should not bear any liability. So the cheated withdrawal of USD 4, 8000 was mainly due to the negligence of the plaintiff, who did not take necessary measures after the loss of his ID card and keep well of his own account information. At last, the court ruled that the plaintiff lost the case on the ground that he did not provide sufficient evidence to prove that the defendant had acted with gross negligence.[1] This is a judgment based on the allocation of burden of proof.

The burden of proof in litigation is both a complicated theoretical issue and an important practical issue. Though the legal experts started to make research on the issue of burden of proof since the age of Ancient Rome, until now, people still have divergent opinions and cannot reach agreement on some basic questions, such as the concept, the nature, and the allocation of the burden. In judicial practice, the court ruling on burden of proof is very crucial, because it tends to determine the outcome of a trial. Especially in a complicated lawsuit, if the ruling on burden of proof is not correct, it will directly lead to the error of judgment.

[1] See Xiang and Shu (1998).

5.2 Categories of Judicial Proof

I have used and defined the term of judicial proof in previous chapters. However, I need to return to the concept and categories thereof, for the discussion of the burden of judicial proof. Proof in judicial activities means the activities that judicial personnel or participants use evidence to establish or verify a fact proposition in a case. This includes two types of activities: one is that the parties use evidence to establish the alleged facts; the other is that the judges use evidence to verify the facts in the case. The judicial proof in a narrow sense may only refer to the former. In order to have a better understanding of the concept, we should distinguish the following categories.

5.2.1 Self-oriented Proof and Others-Oriented Proof

As one of the cognitive activities of human beings, proof exists universally in people's social lives and works. For example, Zhang San wants to prove that his decision to study abroad is correct; Li Si wants to prove that he is an honest and good man; a mathematician wants to prove that "Goldbach's conjecture" can be founded; and an archaeologist wants to prove that the Great Wall was built even before the time of Qin Shihuang, the First Emperor in China.

All these are proofs, but there is a slight difference among them. In the case of Zhang San or Li Si, the subject has already got the conclusion of the proof, i.e. the decision of Zhang San is correct, or Li Si is an honest and good man. However, in the case of the mathematician or the archaeologist, the subject has got no conclusion yet. It is true that both of the mathematician and the archaeologist have certain expectations, i.e. the Goldbach Conjecture can be founded, and the building of the Great Wall had already began before the time of Qin Shihuang. Nevertheless, before the end of such proving process, they cannot conclude that such expectations are truthful. In other words, in the first type of proof, the subject has already known the fact and the purpose of the proof is to make others known; while in the second type of proof, the subject is not known yet, so the purpose of the proof is mainly or firstly to know the fact himself.

Based on such difference, we can divide proof into two categories, or in other words, proof has two fundamental forms: one is self-oriented proof; and the other is others-oriented proof. Self-oriented proof is proof to oneself. Generally speaking, the subject first puts forward a hypothetical conclusion, and then seeks for evidence and uses such evidence according to certain rules to prove such conclusion is correct or can be established. Others-oriented proof is proof to others. The subject has already known the conclusion, but others don't know or believe, so the subject needs to use evidence to prove it to others.

Both self-oriented proof and others-oriented proof are existing in the litigation activities, however, the subjects of which are different. Generally speaking, the subject of the self-oriented proof is the person who makes certain determination or adjudication with respect to certain factual issues, e.g. the investigator, procurator, and judge; while the subject of others-oriented proof is the person who puts forward certain factual claims, e.g. parties in a lawsuit and their attorneys. Nevertheless, the subjects of self-oriented proof and others-oriented proof can be transferred in the litigation process. In the investigation stage, the investigators are the subjects of self-oriented proof; while in the stage of review for prosecution, the investigators change into the subjects of others-oriented proof, because they have to prove the factual claim to the procurator. As the decision-maker of whether or not file the prosecution, the procurator is the subject of self-oriented proof, while at the stage of courtroom trial, the procurator has to prove the alleged facts to the court, hence, the procurator has changed into the subject of the others-oriented proof. The judge who acts as the umpire of the lawsuit is basically the subject of the self-oriented proof.

In litigation activities, self-oriented proof generally belongs to functional acts of the subject, the purpose of which is to satisfy the requirements of implementing his/her certain powers and functions, e.g. self-oriented proof of a judge is the requirements for him or her to execute his or her judicial powers. While others-oriented proof generally belongs to the obligatory acts of a subject, the aim of which is to satisfy certain cognitive requirements of others, e.g. the others-oriented proof of the parties concerned in a lawsuit is to meet the requirements of the judge to ascertain the facts of a case. Though others-oriented proof of the parties concerned in a case is finally to serve for their litigation purposes or claims, as far as adjudication activities are concerned, others-oriented proof is manifested as certain obligations, e.g. it is the liability of a subject of litigation that should be performed. Therefore, the subject of others-oriented proof shall bear corresponding burden of proof in a lawsuit, and the subject of others-oriented proof will not bear such burden of proof even though such subject has the function of providing proof.

Hence, it can be seen that self-oriented proof is centered with judicial power, and others-oriented proof is centered with parties' activities of a lawsuit. As a result, under different litigation systems, the status and function of both such proofs are different. Under the inquisitorial, or *ex officio*, procedure system, though others-oriented proof by the parties concerned is indispensable, the self-oriented proof by the judicial officials clearly plays a particularly important role. While in the adversary litigation system, though the self-oriented proof still exists, it is rather weakened and the others-oriented proof becomes the basic content of the judicial proof. To clearly distinguish the two categories is a requirement of the allocation of the burden of proof, and good for the judicial reform towards trial-centeredness in China now.

5.2.2 Subjects and Objects of the Judicial Proof

The subjects of the judicial proof are people who carry out proving activities in the judicial proceedings. According to relevant provisions in laws of China, the subjects of proof in criminal procedure include parties concerned, attorneys, investigators, prosecutors and judges, among whom, the parties concerned, attorneys, investigators and prosecutors are subjects of others-oriented proof and can be subjects of self-oriented proof in certain circumstances; and the judges are only subjects of self-oriented subjects.

Although proofs and demonstrations in the trial activities can be deemed in general as judicial proof and the judge play a very important role in the process of judicial proof, the judge is not a person who uses evidence to prove or demonstrate the facts of a case to others, it is a person who ascertain such facts of the case, it is the person who accepts or recognizes the facts of the case explained or demonstrated by evidence. In other words, judges are not persuaders in the proving process; they are persons who should be persuaded. It is true that judges may collect evidence by themselves in necessary circumstances, according to Chinese law, but they do so because they want to ascertain the facts of the case, they do so to make themselves to understand the factual issue, not to make others to understand.

In a lawsuit, the subjects of others-oriented proof shall bear the burden of proof in accordance with certain principles, and under the circumstances of unclear facts of a case and shortage of evidence, such persons who bear burden of proof must bear the consequence of losing the lawsuit or unfavorable legal consequence. If judges belong to the subjects of others-oriented proof, then, they shall bear the burden of proof and even unfavorable legal consequence, which apparently violates the fundamental principles of judicial proceedings.

Different subjects play different roles in the litigation, and the means and angles to prove the facts of a case are different as well. In a criminal case, the parties involved carry out proving activities in order to protect their legal rights and interests; the attorneys carry out proving activities in order to protect the legal rights and interests of their clients; the investigators conduct proving activities from the angle to expose and confirm the crimes; the procurators conduct the proving activities from the perspective of investigation and prosecution; and the judges carry out their proving activities from the perspectives of ruling for guilty or not guilty, as well as sentencing. With respect to adjudication, all activities of the first four subjects belong to others-oriented proof and only the activities of the judges belong to self-oriented proof.

In the judicial activities, the object of a proof mainly refers to the facts of a case which need to be proved with evidence. It is of great importance to make research on the objects of proof, because it is the fundamental contents of proving activities. Generally speaking, the proving activities are always beginning with an object of proof and being carried out with concentration on the object of proof and also deeming the object of proof as destination.

When trying to understand the concept of the object of proof, people should know the basic characteristics of it. First, the object of proof is based on the factual claims of the litigation, and generally, without claimed facts, there will be no object of judicial proof. In civil lawsuits, all plaintiffs' claims include factual claims, and in criminal trials, the charges submitted by the procurators on behalf of the State and People also include factual claims. Secondly, the object of proof is closely related to the burden of proof. All objects of proof have corresponding proof burdens; and all proof burdens are relating to certain objects of proof. Thirdly, the objects of proof refer to facts of a case that must be proved with evidence. If a fact does not need to be proven or is self-evident, then, the fact shall not be the object of proof. Finally, the objects of proof are basically provided in substantial laws. Since the factual claims in litigation should be in accordance with the provisions of substantial laws, therefore, the constitutive requirements of specific facts in a case, provided in the substantial laws, are the fundamental contents of the objects of proof.

Chinese laws do not make direct and clear definition on the object of proof. Article 50 of CPL stipulates: "the judges, procurators and investigators shall collect various evidence in accordance with due process that are able to prove that the criminal suspect and/or the defendant is guilty or not guilty, and the seriousness of the crimes". On the basis of the spirit of this Article, all facts in relation to whether or not the criminal suspect and/or the defendant is guilty and the seriousness of the crimes shall belong to the objects of proof.

Clause 2 of Article 5 of PEDPC provides that, in death penalty cases, the reliable and sufficient evidence is required for proving the facts as follows: (1) the occurrence of the facts of the charged crime; (2) the defendant has committed the crime, and the time, place, means, consequences and other circumstances of the criminal acts committed by the defendant; (3) the identity issues that may affect the conviction of the defendant; (4) the defendant's capability of bearing criminal liabilities; (5) the fault of the defendant, (6) the existence or not of a joint offense, and the status and role of the defendant in such joint offense; and (7) the facts which may demand severe punishment upon the defendant.

The above mentioned legal provisions and judicial interpretations are bases for determining the objects of proof in criminal trials. However, there exist another question that needs to be discussed, i.e. whether or not the procedural facts should be deemed as objects of proof.

The so-called procedural facts refer to the facts that have nothing to do with the offense itself but have important legal significance for resolving some procedural issues, including facts about the challenge to a member of the bench, the deferment of trial, the adoption of certain compulsory measures, the violation of statutory proceedings, and the change of the implementation of court orders, etc. For example, if one litigant challenges a judge or a people's juror in the bench, he or she should provide the factual reasons for the challenge, e.g. the judge is a relative of the other party. Such facts are the so-called procedural facts.

With respect to the issue whether the procedural facts can be deemed as objects of proof, there are different viewpoints in the evidence law scholarship in China. Some scholars hold the opinion that the procedural facts should belong to the objects of proof, because these facts are basis for the judicial organs to make a corresponding rule or decision, and such facts require the claiming party to prove with evidence. Some scholars argue that the procedural facts should not belong to the objects of proof, the main reason for which is that the objects of proof in the litigation shall only be limited to the facts within the meaning of substantial law, i.e. the facts that have direct influence on the judicial consequence or judicial adjudication. I think such debate does not have very much practical significance, because no matter whether or not it is called the object of proof, the party involved need to provide factual bases when they propose a procedural request, and they should prove the request with evidence. Of course, the procedural facts are different from the substantial facts in a case, while the latter are the main objects of proof in judicial activities.

As previously mentioned, the objects of the proof are unknown or controversial facts of a case. If a fact is known or uncontroversial, there is no need to prove. The term "known facts" mentioned here include the commonly known facts, the facts that have been confirmed, and the facts that can be assumed. The term "uncontroversial facts" refer to facts that one party has put forward and the other party has expressly admitted. From the perspective of judicial proof, such facts can be called as "facts exempted from proof".

The facts exempted from proof as provided in Article 334 of *Criminal Procedure Rules of People's Procuratorate* promulgated in 1999 by SPP include: (1) facts regarding commonsense as universally known by general public; (2) facts confirmed by the effective judgment of people's court and were not retried according to trial supervision procedure; (3) contents of laws and regulations and facts used within the scope of performance of duties by the judicial personnel; (4) procedural facts without any objection in the court trial; and (5) the assumed facts provided by laws and regulations.

The facts exempted from proof as provided in Article 75 of *Opinions on Several Issues regarding the Application of the Civil Procedure Law* promulgated in 1992 by SPC include: (1) the facts of a case and the proposed litigation claims of a party that have been clearly recognized by the other party; (2) facts universally known and natural laws and theorem; (3) facts that can be assumed according to the laws and regulation and already known facts; (4) facts that have been confirmed by the judgment of the people's court that have already come into effect; and (5) facts that have been proved by the effective notarization certificate.

5.2.3 Contents of the Object of Proof

The basic contents of the object of the proof are constituted by the facts of a case that need to be proven. In criminal cases, as the object of proof, the facts of a case shall include the facts regarding guilty or not of the defendant, the facts regarding serious or not of the offense, and the facts regarding the criminal liability of the defendant. Though the facts of a case are complicated and diversified, all kinds of cases are constituted of certain basic factual elements and such factual elements are the basic contents of the object of proof. As I mention briefly in Chap. 1, the factual elements of the criminal cases can be called simply as "Seven Ws", i.e. what (matter), when, where, how, why, what (thing), and who.

5.2.3.1 What (Matter)

Any case is a kind of event, so, it must have certain nature. The so-called "what matter" means the nature of event, and there always exist several levels for the nature of event. For example, in case of an accidental death of a person, we should first determine whether it is a normal death or an abnormal death; if it is an non-normal death, we should determine whether it is a suicide or a homicide; if it is a homicide, we should further determine whether it is a crime or not, e.g. self-defense; if it is a criminal homicide, then we should determine whether it is a kill for revenge, or a kill for money, or a kill for love, or a kill in the heat of passion, etc. The nature of a criminal case is mainly decided by the nature of the action and the infringement consequences thereof. Therefore, to prove the nature of a case, you have to prove the nature of such action and its infringement consequences. After the occurrence of a case, though the nature of such event may be very clear to the investigators and adjudicators, as far as litigation concerned, all these things are facts that need to be proven. In short, the nature of a case is one of the key objects of the judicial proof.

5.2.3.2 When

All cases occurred within a certain time, so the time is one of the constituent elements of the facts of the case. The so-called "when" refers to the temporal characteristics of such cases. It has three meanings: first, it is the sequence in the course of time of the objective world, or, it refers to on what time such case occurred, e.g. a theft occurred at 2:30 am on 20th October 2016, or a traffic accident occurred at 9:21 pm on 25th October 2016; second, it refers to the continuity in the course of time of the objective world, or, it refers to how long such case lasts, e.g. the theft lasts for 40 min, or the traffic accident lasts for 20 min; third, it refers to the relevance in the course of time of the objective world, or, it refers to the time relevance between the case and other event, e.g. the theft occurs before the raining of that day, or the traffic accident occurs after the driver drinks. In the judicial proof, in some cases, the times of their occurrences are known; in some cases, the times of occurrence can be inferred; in some cases, the times of occurrence are needed to be investigated. Furthermore, in some cases, we only know the times but do not know the time periods; in some cases, we do not know the exact times but we do know their sequential relations with other events. No matter under which circumstances, the time of a case is an important object of judicial proof.

5.2.3.3 Where

All cases occurred within a certain space, so the space is one of the constituent elements of the facts of a case. The so-called "where" refers to the space feature of a case. Space represents the position of objects in the universe and their interactions with other objects. It has many characteristics such as wide ductility, three-dimensionality, and arrangement etc., which is needless to repeat. In addition, the space feature of a case also includes natural and social morphological characteristics. The natural morphological feature of the space of a case mainly refers to the natural environment and natural element features of the place of the crime scene such as terrain, surface feature and geomorphology and the like. It has great significance to the judicial proof, because it always implies information in relation to the case. For example, if the police officers found a body who has been drowned to death in the river, then, the situations of the river and the surrounding mountains is likely to provide basis for the identification of the death of such person: homicide, suicide or accidental death. If it is determined to be homicide, such situations are likely to provide clues for investigating the offender(s). The social morphological feature of the space of a case mainly refers to the social background features of the crime scene's social nature and its surrounding environment such as political, economic, cultural, religious features etc., which has important meaning for judicial proof. Generally speaking, the occurrence place or scene of a case is relatively clear when the investigation started, hence, the main task of judicial proof is not to find such place or scene, but to dig out all kinds of information that related to the case in such place or scene. Nevertheless, in some cases, "where" such cases occurred can also be the primary task for the judicial proof. Because when accepting such cases, the investigators do not know the places or scenes such cases occurred, or that already known places are not the true places or main places of the cases, murder postmortem case is a typical example of this. In short, "where" is a very important constituent part of the facts of a case, which is an object that must be proven by evidence.

5.2.3.4 How

"How" refers to the situation when a case occurs, or, it means on what circumstances a case occurs, and how did it happen, so, it can be also called "what way". It includes the means and process of the occurrence of a case. First, any case is manifested in certain ways and the manifestation methods of different cases are different. for example, murder cases and injury cases are expressed in different ways, rape cases and robbery cases are committed in different ways, theft cases and fraud cases are shown in different ways, arson cases and explosion cases are manifested in different ways and corruption cases and bribery cases are also committed in different ways. Strictly speaking, each case has different manifestation ways that are not completely identical to that of other cases. For example, for murder cases, the manifestation ways may include kill by poison, kill by gunshot, kill by strangulation, kill by stifling, kill by smothering, kill by drowning, kill by electricity, kill by stabbing and kill by sticks etc. Hence, one of the missions of judicial proof is to prove the manifestation means of a specific case. Second, the occurrence of each case has an independent and complete process, because each case is composed of a series of acts or activities of relevant persons. To prove the occurrence process of a case is also an important task of judicial proof, because only after the proving of the whole process of a case, we can get a clear understanding of such case, and then ensure the accuracy of the results of the judicial proof. For example, in a burglar case, the investigators and public prosecutors should exploit the case information and collect evidence from the whole process that how did the offender prepare to steal, how to enter the scene, how to implement the stealing, how to flee the scene and how to dispose the stolen goods and destroy the evidence, and to grasp the interaction between such elements as a whole, and then carry out a complete proof regarding the facts of the case. Special attention is required to be attached to "how", which acts as the object of proof, which both include the circumstance of guilty and not guilty of the criminal suspect/defendant, and also include the circumstance of heavy crime or light crime of the defendant.

5.2.3.5 Why

"Why" refers to the reason why the case occurred, or why did the case happen, so it can be also called "for what reason". It includes the subjective and objective reasons for the occurrence of a case. The former means the motives and purposes of the parties or the offenders of a case, e.g. the purpose of somebody to make bribery. The latter refers to the exterior elements that procure or cause the parties or the offenders of a case to make certain decisions or carry out certain acts, e.g. the external reasons for somebody to make bribery. In addition, "why" also refers to the reasons that lead to the consequences of a case, e.g. the reason that causes the death of somebody. In litigation activities, the nature to prove the reason of the occurrence of a case or the reason leading to the consequences of a case is to prove the causal relationship of the case. The causal relationship of a case has the features of complexity and polymorphism. First, the form of causality is diversified: there is one reason for one result, multiple reasons for multiple results, one reason for multiple results and also multiple reasons for one result. Second, the nature of causality is diversified: there are direct relations, indirect relations, inevitable relations and also accidental relations. Third, the combination of causality is diversified: there is direct-chain-type, network-based type, parallel type and cross type. To prove the causal relationship in a case has very important significance. On the one hand, the causality of a case is always the key to correctly verify the facts of the case; and on the other hand, the causality of a case can also be deemed as the clues and bridges to prove other facts of the case. For example, in the proof of homicide cases, based on the situations of the crime scenes and the witnesses' statements that prove the motives of killing are revenge, wealth or adultery, such causality can be deemed as proof "bridges" that connect the defendants and their killing acts. In a word, the causal relationship in a case is also one of the important objects of judicial proof.

5.2.3.6 What (Thing)

Any case occurs in the objective physical world, so it always involves certain things. The so-called "what thing" is the thing that involved in a case. Based on the relations between these things and the cases, or the positions of such things in the cases, we can divide such things into three categories: first are the subject matters of cases, e.g. the fraudulent properties in fraud cases; second are things used in cases, e.g. weapons used in murder cases; and third are related things in cases, e.g. cloths of offenders and related traces left on the crime scenes of theft. Since such things recorded relevant information related to the cases in different ways, so they can reflect corresponding facts of cases. Here, we must distinguish such things from the facts of cases they reflect. For example, the fraudulent properties can prove the fact that defendant has committed the fraud; the murder weapon can prove the fact that the defendant has used such weapon to kill people; and the left-behind things can prove the fact that the defendant has left such things on the crime scene. In the litigation proceedings, these things will generally become evidence of such cases, therefore, these things themselves are not objects of proof, and the facts of cases they reflect are the objects of proof.

5.2.3.7 Who

The criminal cases are generally centered with people's acts. Without people and people's acts, the cases may lose their basis and meanings. The so-called "who" refers to the person who has committed criminal act in a specific case, who is the core that constitutes the facts of a case. In a criminal lawsuit, the offender is the most important object of proof. To use various evidence to clarify who is the offender of a case, will complete the core task of judicial proof. Of course, what needs to be proved here not only include the identity of the offender, but also include relevant factual situations that can rule out or reduce the criminal responsibilities of the offender according to law, such as the age and mental status etc. of the offender in the course of committing such crime.

The above-mentioned constitutive elements of the facts of a criminal case have very close relationship with constitutive elements of a crime. The constitutive elements of a crime include the subject of the crime, object of the crime, subjective aspect of the crime and objective aspect of the crime. So, "who" always refers to the subject of the crime; "what matter" reflects the object of the crime; "why" can prove the subjective aspect of the crime in a certain extent; "when", "where", "how" and "what thing" illustrate the objective aspects of the crime from different perspectives. If the constitutive elements of the facts of a case have been proved, then constitutive elements of a crime will be proved. Therefore, all these are facts of the case that needs to be proved by evidence and all of them are objects of the proof. Of course, different cases have different circumstances, and the focus of the object of the proof will be different.

5.3 Definition of the Burden of Proof

The so-called "burden of proof" refers to the liability assumed by the parties of a lawsuit that they provide evidence to the court to prove the facts of the case they claimed in the judicial proceedings. To understand this definition, we should first clarify two points as follows:

First, the burden of proof is an issue for others-oriented proof, while there is no issue of burden of proof for self-oriented proof. So, in litigation, the subjects who assume the burden of proof are only parties concerned in litigation, not including judges. To be specific, with respect to criminal litigation, the subjects who bear burden of proof are mainly procurators who institute public prosecution on behalf of the State, and of course, under certain special circumstances, the subjects may be the defendant and his attorneys.

Secondly, the burden of proof is an issue for judicial adjudication, centering at the stage of trial. There exists no issue of the burden of proof in the stage of criminal investigation. Although all investigation activities and evidence-collection activities and the like before trial serve for the proving at the trial, and although the investigators have to carry out others-oriented proof, these activities, strictly speaking, are not performance of the burden of proof. In other words, the investigators are not the subjects who assume the burden of proof in the lawsuits.

5.3.1 The Burden of Proof and the Burden of Producing Evidence

In China, legal scholars have different understandings of the two concepts, the burden of proof and the burden of producing evidence. Some think the two meanings can be the same; some view that the two concepts shall be strictly distinguished; some prefer to use the unified "the burden of proof"; some like to use "the burden of producing evidence" without exception; some hold that the burden of proof includes the burden of producing evidence while others think the opposite. In short, there are many different opinions in this aspect. But with regard to the habit of using vocabularies, scholars seem to prefer "the burden of proof"; while legal practitioners, including legislators, tend to like "the burden of producing evidence". Among the three procedure laws in China, CPL[2] and CiPL don't have a clear definition, but Article 64 of the CiPL stipulates: "A party shall have the burden to provide evidence for its claims". The *Administrative Procedure Law* (APL) adopts the concept of "the burden of producing evidence". Article 32 stipulates: "The defendant shall have the burden of producing evidence for the administrative action taken, and provide evidence for taking the administrative action and regulatory documents based on which

[2]Here refers to *the Criminal Procedure Law* amended in 1996. The Article 49 of *the Criminal Procedure Law* amended in 2012 uses the concept of "the burden of proof".

the administrative action was taken." In addition, judicial interpretations represented by PECP generally use "the burden of producing evidence" in relevant provisions.

In my opinion, the burden of producing evidence and the burden of proof are two close-related concepts with little differences in Chinese. Literally, one is to provide evidence, and the other is to prove; their meanings have differences. Providing evidence refers to presenting evidence or providing evidence; proving refers to using evidence to show or indicate. Strictly speaking, the burden of producing evidence is just to provide evidence, while the burden of proof is to prove the facts through using evidence; clearly, they have different focuses. However, if analyzing their connotations deeply, we can find that these two concepts actually don't have too much difference, because the aim of providing evidence is similarly to use the evidence to prove facts and proof is also concerned with providing evidence. Without the aim, providing evidence doesn't make any sense; in return, proof also becomes a lip service. Therefore, the two concepts can't separate one from each other. Proof must rely on the basis of providing evidence; and the aim of providing evidence is also to prove the facts. What's more, language is conventional. When legal practitioners use "the burden of producing evidence" in the long term, they have entrusted it the similar meaning with the burden of proof; in other words, the burden of producing evidence mentioned here not only refers to the action of providing evidence but also the meaning of proving facts.

To sum up, the burden of proof and the burden of producing evidence are basically the same. In different language circumstances, people can choose the words according to their habits as long as the connotation and extension of the concept are consistent. Specifically, the burden of proof or the burden of producing evidence refers that parties have the duty to provide evidence to prove the facts before the court and it should involve the three following concepts: (1) the burden of action—parties have the responsibility to provide evidence before the court; (2) the burden of persuasion—parties have the responsibility to use the legal evidence to persuade adjudicators to believe their claims; (3) the burden of results—parties shall bear the unfavorable results when they fail to provide evidence or persuade adjudicators and the facts are not clear.

Many scholars in the field of Chinese evidence law share similar views with me. For example, Professor Bian Jianlin holds that: "the burden of producing evidence is the integration of the responsibilities of providing evidence and persuasion. The responsibility of providing evidence refers that, in the proceedings, two parties should, according to the state of lawsuit, provide evidence to prove their claims and objections; some scholars consider it as 'the responsibility promoting by evidence' or 'the nominal burden of proof'. The persuasion responsibility refers that, the parties who bear the burden of producing evidence shall be responsible for using evidence to indicate and argue the facts so that the judge can believe the facts. Therefore, only providing evidence cannot be equal to perform the burden of proof, parties should, within their abilities, persuade adjudicators to believe whether the facts exist or not."[3] I shall continue this discussion in Chap. 11.

---

[3]Bian (2004).

5.3.2 The Burden of Proof and Factual Claims

When discussing the burden of proof, it is necessary for us to first clarify the relationship between the burden of proof and factual claims. As far as litigation is concerned, there is no the burden of proof if there are no factual claims; and the contents of proof are decided by the factual claims. Because these two elements have a very close relationship, so, there are scholars believe that the burden of proof not only include the responsibility to provide evidence, responsibility to persuade and responsibility to bear consequences, but also include the responsibility to make claims, i.e. the responsibilities to present factual claims.[4] In my opinion, the burden of proof is certainly based on certain factual claims and the persons who bear burden of proof shall first make certain factual claims, otherwise, the burden of proof will like a tree without roots. However, to present the factual claims is the premise of the burden of proof, not the contents of the burden of proof. These two issues cannot be confused with each other.

In the criminal trial, the scope of factual claims presented by a public prosecutor shall include: what kind of crime the defendant has committed; how many crimes such person committed, one or more; and whether there is any circumstances that such crime shall be imposed with heavy punishment, or light punishment or mitigated punishment etc. With respect to burden of proof, there are two meanings: first, since the factual claims are the basis for burden of proof, so, the public prosecutor shall assume the burden of proof for the above-mentioned factual claims; and second, since the innocence of the defendant does not belong to the scope of the factual claims presented by the public prosecutor, so, the public prosecutor shall not bear the liability to prove that the defendant is innocent.

In a civil lawsuit, the factual claims of the plaintiff might be a more complicated question. If the factual claims of a plaintiff are not appropriate, it might lead to the fact that allocation of the burden of proof may have an adverse consequence for the plaintiff. In the previously mentioned case: *Hu Guangrong v. XX Bank*, the factual claim of the plaintiff is: the defraud of Hu's deposit was the Bank's mistake, therefore, the bank should compensate for his loss. Such factual claim with such expression is not conducive to the plaintiff.

Objectively speaking, since this case is short of evidence, the facts of the case are vague to a certain extent. To be specific, there are three possibilities for the facts of the case: first is that Hu Guangrong conspires with another person to cheat the bank to take the money away; second is that somebody colludes with the bank personnel to take the money away; third is that someone who has no collusion relation with Hu Guangrong or the bank took the money away. If the plaintiff's claim is that it is the bank's mistake that causes the loss, then the plaintiff has to bear the burden to prove that the bank has made the mistake. This is obviously not beneficial to the plaintiff. As a matter of fact, the plaintiff can choose another expression of his factual claim, i.e. he deposited his money on the bank and demanded that the bank pay his money back. As for this factual claim, the plaintiff can provide the certificate of fixed-term

[4]See Bian (2000).

deposit as evidence. When facing such factual claims of the plaintiff, if the defendant refuses to pay, it must put forward a factual claim that can confront with the plaintiff's claim. There are two choices: first, the money concerned had been withdrawn by the plaintiff or the person entrusted by the plaintiff; second, the money concerned has been cheated and taken away by another person. However, the second option is not favorable to the defendant. Because if the money deposited by a depositor in a bank has been cheated and taken away by others, the bank cannot let such depositor to bear such loss. Therefore, the defendant can only choose the first factual claim, i.e. the money concerned had been withdrawn by the plaintiff or the person entrusted by the plaintiff. As for this claim, the defendant needs to bear the burden of proof. The defendant may provide evidence such as reporting-for-lost certificate and the later withdrawal slip and the testimony of the bank personnel concerned, etc. However, such evidence cannot sufficiently prove that such person is a person that entrusted by Hu Guangrong. Since the defendant cannot provide sufficient evidence to prove that the money has been taken away by the person entrusted by Hu Guangrong, then, the defendant shall bear the unfavorable adjudication consequence. We can see that the difference of factual claims may lead to difference of allocation of the burden of proof, and then lead to difference in adjudication consequences.

5.3.3 Equality and Partiality of Allocation of the Burden of Proof

The allocation of the burden of proof in a lawsuit is not only an important legal academic issue, but also a significant judicial practical question. The clarification of the allocation rules of the burden of proof must be based on certain litigation theories and must start from certain judicial concepts. Meanwhile, the allocation of the burden of proof is a very practicable and operational question, and currently there exist several chaotic situations in the judicial practices of China. In a word, in civil procedures, the allocation principle of the burden of proof is "who claims, who bears the burden of proof", while in the criminal proceedings, the burden of proof is borne by the public prosecution. Nevertheless, no matter in a civil proceeding or a criminal proceeding, there are always some special cases for the allocation of the burden of proof.

From the perspective of laws and regulations, the allocation rule on the burden of proof seems relatively clear. Article 64 of SiPL as revised in August 2012 stipulates: "the parties concerned shall be responsible for providing evidence for the claims they presented." Article 2 of PECP states: "the parties concerned shall be responsible for providing evidence to prove the facts on which their own claims are based or facts on which they confront with the other parties' claims. In case there is no evidence or the evidence are not sufficient to prove such parties' factual claims, the parties who bear the burden of proof shall assume the unfavorable consequence." In these Regulations, after the special situations such as "inversion of burden of proof" has been listed,

Article 7 prescribes: "in case that law does not provide any specific regulations, and the assumption of burden of proof cannot be determined according to these Regulations and other judicial interpretations, the people's court may determine the assumption of the burden of proof in accordance with principles of equality and good faith and in combination of the parties' proof capabilities and elements like that".

The allocation principle which simplified as "who claims, who bears burden of proof" reflects the justification of natural law, however, when encountering the difficulty of judicial proof for "fell down or knocked down", it seems short of sufficiency. As for the provision of "the parties concerned shall be responsible for providing evidence to prove the facts on which their own claims are based or facts on which they confront with the other parties' claims", if both parties have put forward two opposite claims for one fact, then, who shall bear burden of proof? For example, in the case of *Xu v. Peng Yu*, as illustrated in Chap. 1, the plaintiff Xu claims that she was knocked down by Peng Yu, but the defendant Peng Yu said he did not hit Xu. Then, who should bear the burden of proof in the case? Or, if both parties have not provided sufficient evidence to prove their claims respectively, then, who should bear the consequence of losing the case?

According to principles of evidence law, the party who presents active claim regarding the same disputed fact shall bear the burden of proof, and the party who puts forward the negative claim shall not bear the burden of proof. In Peng Yu's case, Xu's claim is an active factual claim, and Peng Yu's claim is a negative factual claim, so, the plaintiff shall assume the burden of proof and the defendant shall not bear the burden of proof. However, in judicial practices, judges often ask the party who makes a negative claim to bear the burden of proof, and if such proof is not sufficient, the judges will rule that the claim has not been established. This approach is not fair, actually, and it is contrary to the principle of allocation of the burden of proof, and even makes the burden of proof only exiting in name.

The allocation of the burden of proof should be both fair and partial, which means, the allocation of burden of proof is always been partial to one party, but such partiality shall be in conformity with the judicial fairness and justice. If the burden of proof of one disputed fact is borne equally by both parties in a lawsuit, then, the burden of proof will lose its meaning of existence. In the case *Xu V. Peng Yu*, the plaintiff Xu put forward an active factual claim: because she was knocked down by Peng Yu, so the defendant should bear relevant economic compensation liability. When adjudicating this case, the judges first needs to check whether the evidence presented by the plaintiff is sufficient to prove her factual claim. If the evidence is insufficient, the plaintiff shall bear the unfavorable litigation consequence. Of course, the defendant can also introduce his rebuttal evidence with regard to the plaintiff's factual claim, but it is his right to present evidence, not the burden of proof. Therefore, even if he cannot use sufficient evidence to prove his "innocence", he will not bear the unfavorable litigation consequence. Hence, the basic question that a judge should answer in such cases is that whether the evidence presented by the plaintiff has reached the proof standards required with such a litigation.

5.4 Allocation Rules of the Burden of Proof in Criminal Proceedings

5.4.1 General Rules

In criminal proceedings, the primary principle to decide the allocation of burden of proof is presumption of innocence or presumption of guilt. If presumption of innocence is implemented, the burden of proof shall be borne by the public prosecution, because the public prosecutor must prove to the court that the defendant is guilty, otherwise, the court shall find the defendant innocent. If presumption of guilt is implemented, the burden of proof shall be borne by the defendant, because the defendant has to prove to the court that he is innocent, otherwise, the court will find the defendant guilty. Article 12 of CPL stipulates: "No one shall be considered as guilty unless the people's court makes such judgment according to law." Although people have different opinions towards the interpretation of this provision, it does reflect the fundamental spirit of the presumption of innocence. Article 50 of CPL as revised in 2012 added a provision that "No one shall be compelled to prove himself to be guilty". This is also a reflection of the presumption of innocence.

The presumption of innocence includes three meanings: first, any person shall be first presumed as innocent before the people's court makes its judgment as guilty; secondly, in the trial of a criminal case, the public prosecutor shall bear the burden of proof, and the defendant generally does not bear the burden of proof, to be specific, the defendant has no obligation to prove himself to be guilty or innocent; thirdly, in case of the prosecution evidence cannot reach the proof standard as required by law, the court shall pronounce that the defendant is innocent. In other words, the adjudication of the court shall abide by the principle of "*in dubio, pro reo*". The presumption of innocence is a criminal procedure principle established on certain value orientation. The purpose of presumption of innocence is to protect the legitimate right of the defendant and guarantee the justification of judicial practice, and lower the possibility of wrongful conviction to the minimum.

5.4.1.1 The Public Prosecutor Shall Bear the Burden of Proof in Cases of Public Prosecution

Article 49 of CPL provides: "In cases of public prosecution, the burden of proof to prove that the defendant is guilty shall be borne by the people's procuratorate; while in cases of private prosecution, the burden of proof to prove that the defendant is guilty shall be borne by the private prosecutor." According to this provision, the general rule of allocation of burden of proof in a public-prosecuting criminal case is that the public prosecutor shall bear the burden of proof and the defendant shall not bear burden of proof. In the trial, the public prosecution shall provide sufficient evidence to the court to prove the charged criminal facts and such proof shall reach the statutory standard. The defendant has no obligation to prove that he is guilty or not guilty to the court. In other words, the defendant may not provide any evidence to the court, and he can only challenge the evidence provided by the public prosecutor, and then he finishes his/her defense mission. And the defendant can even do not make any defense, and the court shall not make any unfavorable judgment to such defendant thereof.

As mentioned above, the public prosecution's bearing of burden of proof is the requirement of the principle of presumption of innocence. In addition, the allocation of burden of proof like this has other reasons in terms of operation. On the one hand, the public prosecutor is the initiator of a criminal procedure, is the one that requires the court to make judgment, so, the public prosecutor shall provide evidence to the court to support its demand and claims. This is also in conformity with the principle of "who claims, who bears the burden of proof" for allocation of burden of proof in a litigation. On the other hand, since the public prosecutor has already prepared well for prosecution, he or she is naturally in the convenient position to prove, so, it is logical for the public prosecutor to bear burden of proof. There are two reasons for the defendant not bearing burden of proof: first, the defendant is in the passive position in a lawsuit, it is not easy for him to prepare evidence; second, the claim of the defendant is to deny the criminal facts charged by the public prosecutor, and such denial of the existence of such facts is very hard to prove. It is true that the defendant can present evidence in trial to prove that he is innocent or commits light crime, but this belongs to the defense right of the defendant, not burden of proof. The defendant may exercise his defense right according to law, or, he may not exercise his defense right; the defendant shall not deserve the unfavorable factual determination or judgment only because such person has not exercised his defense right.

5.4.1.2 The Private Prosecutor Shall Bear the Burden of Proof in Cases of Private Prosecution

In the criminal cases of private prosecution, the private prosecutor, i.e. the plaintiff, shall bear burden of proof, and the defendant does not assume burden of proof. This is also a reflection of the fundamental principle of "who claims, who bears the burden of proof" in the judicial activities. If the private prosecutor cannot make use of sufficient evidence to prove the criminal facts charged by himself, before the initiation of the trial, the judge will try to persuade such private prosecutor to withdraw his charges, or make judgment to dismiss his prosecution. After the trial, the judge shall sentence the defendant to be innocent. In a word, if the private prosecutor cannot present evidence or the evidence he presented are insufficient, such person shall bear the consequence of losing the case.

5.4.2 *Special Rules*

5.4.2.1 Shifting the Burden of Proof

In the criminal litigation, the burden of proof is borne by the public prosecutor or private prosecutor, which doesn't mean that the defendant under no circumstances shall not bear any verification obligations. The allocation rules of burden of proof established according to the principle of presumption of innocence only defines that the burden of proof for the whole case shall be assumed by the public or private prosecutor who puts forward the criminal charges. While the verification obligation for specific facts or circumstances of a case shall be distributed in conformity with the principle of "who claims, who bears the burden of proof". That is to say, in some cases, the burden of proof may be shifted to the defendant from the public or private prosecutor.

The shifting of the burden of proof is not the denial to the principle of presumption of innocence. The basis for the establishment of the principle of presumption of innocence is the particular value orientation of criminal legislation and judicial practice, i.e. the requirement to protect the rights of the criminal suspects and defendants. However, the stipulation on the transfer of burden of proof prescribed by the law is mainly considering the requirements of verification and convenience of providing evidence in the litigation activities, i.e. which side to first provide evidence can be more beneficial to the smooth progress of the judicial proof. From the perspective of this meaning, the transfer of burden of proof deems the convenience of providing evidence and litigation efficiency as the premise.

For example, in a homicide case, the defendant claims that he could not be at the crime scene when the case occurred, because he was at some other place. In other words, he has an alibi. As for this claim, the defendant has to bear the burden of proof, i.e. to provide evidence to prove that he was in a location other than the scene of the crime at the relevant time. Under this circumstance, the burden of proof was transferred from the public prosecutor to the defendant. Such shifting is in conformity with the rule of judicial proof. Since the defendant puts forward a specific factual claim, he needs to provide corresponding evidence to support his claim, and obviously he is at the convenient position to prove that factual proposition. If the defendant can raise any factual claim and then the public prosecutor has to present evidence to refute and such defendant bear no burden of proof, this apparently violates the principle of judicial fairness and will greatly impact the efficiency of judicial proof.

Nevertheless, based on the strength contrast and offensive and defensive positions of both public prosecutors and defendants, the requirements of law regarding the burden of proof for the defendants can be lower than that to the public prosecutors. In other words, the proof of the defendant is not necessary to reach the standard of "the evidence shall be reliable and sufficient" or "beyond the reasonable doubt". If the defendant can prove that the possibility that the defendant did not appear at the crime scene is bigger than the possibility that the defendant was at the crime scene, the mission of proof is done. Such standard is equal to the "preponderance of evidence" standard used in the civil trials in some common law countries. Once the defendant finishes his proof, the burden of proof is shifted back to the public prosecutor, and the public prosecutor shall use reliable and sufficient evidence to prove that the defendant is thc true perpetrator.

The defendant does not bear all burdens of proof for all of his asserted claims. If the defendant only negatively denies the factual claim of the public prosecutor, e.g. he asserts that he did not kill anyone, then he will not bear the burden of proof for such factual claim, or, there will be no shifting of the burden of proof. Only when the defendant proposes a specific positive factual claim for his defense, the burden of proof will be shifted to the defendant. For example, if the defendant claims not only that he did not kill anyone, but also said the victim was murdered by another person, and use this claim to prove his innocence, then he shall have a burden to introduce evidence to prove this factual claim.

In the judicial practices, there are four categories of defense claims that may lead to shifting of the burden of proof: (1) factual claim regarding the capacity to bear responsibilities of the defendant, e.g. the defendant is insane or is in the state of mental disorder when the case happened; or the defendant has not reached the statutory age for bearing criminal liabilities when the case occurred; (2) factual claim regarding the legitimacy or justification of the defendant's act, e.g. the act of killing or injuring belongs to self-defense; or the acts of destroying properties belongs to necessity; (3) factual claim regarding the illegality of acts of the investigators or law enforcement personnel, e.g. the reason why the defendant committed the charged criminal act is because of the "investigative entrapment" of the public security officers, or the reason why the defendant admits that he is guilty is because of the extorting confession through torture by the interrogators; and (4) factual claim regarding that there is no possibility that the defendant commits the charged criminal act. E.g. the defendant cannot commit the robbery, because he has an alibi; the defendant cannot commit the killing, because the victim was murdered by another person. Whether or not the transfer of burden of proof happens in a criminal lawsuit, we have to make specific analysis on the factual claim of the defendant in the case.

There was a well-known case happened in the United States in 2012. On the night of 26th February, a patrolman, George Zimmerman, shot and killed a black teenager, Trayvon Martin, in Sanford, Florida. Zimmerman was prosecuted, but he was found not guilty by a jury on 12th July.[5] The acquittal of Zimmerman and the following demonstrations in many cities in the USA have been widely reported in medias in many countries, including China.

The acquittal of Zimmerman may be a bad example of the jury trial system. However, the jury should not take all the blames for the verdict. Jurors are lay people, who do not have the knowledge and skills of legal professionals. The jury's mission is to find the facts in a case, but the factual issues are often closely connected with legal issues; therefore, the judge's instructions are crucial.

In Zimmerman's case, there were two factual issues the jury had to answer: first, whether Zimmerman shot and killed Martin; second, whether the shooting was in

[5] See https://en.wikipedia.org/wiki/George_Zimmerman, retrieved on 10 April 2017.

self-defense. The first question was purely a factual issue and well-established by the prosecution's evidence. The second question was not a purely factual issue and the evidence was not sufficient.

According to the reports, the important evidence was Zimmerman's call to the non-emergency police-response line (not 911) on the night of 26th February 2012. He reported seeing a suspicious person and that he was following the guy. His call ended at 7:13 pm. When the first police officer arrived on the scene at 7:17 pm, the person, Trayvon Martin, was already dead. What happened during those four critical minutes? Zimmerman said he had shot the guy in self-defense. In other words, Martin had attacked, or tried to attack him, so Zimmerman shot Martin to prevent the imminent death or great bodily harm to himself.

Are these the facts? There is no other evidence to prove or disprove his claim. There is no eye witness. There is no video footage. Unfortunately, the other participant of the event, Trayvon Martin, cannot give any testimony. With the shortage of evidence, the facts are obscure or fuzzy.

Finding the facts were the most difficult part of this jury's job, and the judge should have given some help with instructions. The judge should give instructions to the jurors not only about the definition of self-defense but also about the allocation of the burden of proof. According to the reports, the judge did give the self-defense instruction based on Florida law, which says a defendant is "justified in using deadly force if he reasonably believes that such force is necessary to prevent imminent death or great bodily harm to himself." The key word here is "reasonably". How to interpret this word? First, a reasonable belief should be based on the common sense of reasonable people. Secondly, there should be facts to support the reasonable belief, and the facts should be proved with evidence. Here comes the critical question: who should provide the evidence, the prosecutor or the defendant?

As stated above, if the defendant establishes the defense on some special claims such as alibi, insanity and self-defense, the burden of proof will shift to the defendant. In legal terms, the defendant shall have the burden of going forward with the evidence. Although the defendant's burden need not meet the standard of proof required for the prosecution, which is proof beyond a reasonable doubt, the defendant's evidence shall be sufficient to persuade the fact finders. The job cannot be done by just telling a story! If the defendant cannot provide evidence, he shall lose the battle on the issue. If the judge in Zimmerman's case had given instructions regarding the burden of proof on the issue of self-defense, the jury might have accepted the charge of manslaughter, and the story would be very different.

In the criminal cases of private prosecution, shifting of the burden of proof is a more common phenomenon. When the defendant presents specific factual claim to rebut the allegations proposed by the private prosecutor, the burden of proof will be transferred to the defendant. After the defendant provides sufficient evidence to back up his factual claim, the burden of proof will be shifted back to the private prosecutor. In addition, in accordance with provisions of laws and regulations, the defendant may propose counterclaim to the private prosecutor in the proceedings. As for the factual claim of such counterclaim, of course, the defendant shall bear corresponding burden of proof.

5.4.2.2 Inverting the Burden of Proof

The burden of proof in a criminal case is generally borne by the public prosecutor or the party who presents specific factual claims. However, under certain circumstances, laws may stipulate that the burden of proof shall be borne by the defendant or the opposing party of the specific factual claim. This is the inversion of the burden of proof, i.e. the unconventional allocation of burden of proof under special circumstances. The inversion of the burden of proof is generally prescribed explicitly by law through the form of presumption. The reasons for legislators to decide to apply the inversion of the burden of proof in certain cases include the requirement of judicial proof, convenience of proof by various parties concerned, and social policy considerations to reflect certain value orientation. The following cases illustrate the circumstances of inverting the burden of proof in criminal proceedings.

(1) Burden of proof for the crime of holding a huge amount of property with unidentified sources

Article 395 of Criminal Law stipulates: "Any State officers whose property or expenditure obviously exceeds his lawful income, if the difference is enormous, may be ordered to explain the sources of his property. If he cannot prove that the sources are legitimate, the part that exceeds his lawful income shall be regarded as illegal gains." This is the inversion of burden of proof. In the cases of this category regarding "the crime of holding a huge amount of property with unidentified sources", due to the requirements of severely cracking down the crime of bribery and corruption, the legislators require the defendant to bear the burden of proof. As long as such defendant cannot use sufficient evidence to prove that the large amount of his/her property has a legal source, then judges may infer such properties are illegal incomes. Of course, such requirement is also considering the convenience of proof. In such cases, even such large amount of property are indeed illegal gains, it would be difficult for the public prosecutors to prove. However, if such properties truly have legal sources, it would be more convenient for the defendant to prove.

Under the circumstance of inversion of burden of proof, the public prosecutors who shall bear burden of proof do not completely bears no burden of proof, they only bear burden of proof at the very beginning to proceed such cases. In cases regarding the crime of holding a huge amount of property with unidentified sources, the public prosecutors may finish their proof obligation only by using evidence to prove that the properties or expenditures of the defendants have obviously exceeded their legal incomes, and the differences are really large, then, they complete their burdens of proof. Then, the burdens of proof shall be borne by the defendants of such cases. If such defendants cannot make use of those truthfully sufficient evidence to prove their factual claims, i.e. those parts of properties belong to legal income, then, they shall bear the adverse consequences, i.e. they will be found guilty.

(2) Burden of proof for crime of illegal possession

In cases regarding crime of illegal possession (including criminal cases of illegally possessing narcotics, illegally possess guns and ammunition, illegally possess confidential and secret documents and data of the State etc.), the allocation of burden of proof is also inverted. For example, in cases of crime of illegally possessing narcotics, as long as the law enforcement officers seized drugs from a person, they can identify that such person holds such drugs illegally, unless such person uses evidence to prove the legality or reasonableness of holding such drugs. To be specific, if the defendant who was seized to carry narcotics asserted that he has a legitimate reason to carry those narcotics, or, in order to set him up, somebody else put the narcotics on him or into his bag and he did not know it, then, he has to bear burden of proof for such factual claim. If he cannot use evidence to prove the legality or reasonableness of carrying such narcotics, then, the court may infer his acts belong to illegal possession and sentence him to be guilty. In other words, when the question that whether the defendant "illegally" holds such narcotics is at an unclear stage, the defendant has to bear the adverse litigation consequence.

In the judicial practices of the common law countries, "possession of recently stolen properties" is a very representative inversion of burden of proof. In the case of *Barnes v. United States* in 1973, the Federal Supreme Court of US accepted the trial judge's instruction to the jury regarding the issue of "possession of recently stolen properties" and affirmed the District Court's sentence of finding the defendant guilty. The District Court instructed the jury that "possession of recently stolen property, if not satisfactorily explained, is ordinarily a circumstance from which you may reasonably draw the inference and find, in the light of the surrounding circumstances shown by the evidence in the case, that the person in possession knew the property had been stolen." In short, the jury may find the defendant guilty based on the fact that the defendant cannot explain why he has the recently stolen properties.[6]

(3) Burden of proof for strict liability crimes

Strict liability mainly applies to the liability fixation doctrine in civil tort cases such as highly dangerous acts and product liability accidents etc. In such cases, laws do not deem the actor's subjective intention or omission to the detrimental consequence as the condition for their bearing of compensation liabilities. For example, Article 123 of the *Common Provisions of Civil Law of the People's Republic of China* (CPCL)[7] prescribes that: "If any person causes any damage to other people by engaging in operations that are greatly hazardous to the surroundings, such as operations conducted high above ground, or those involving high pressure, high voltage, combustibles, explosives, highly toxic or radioactive substances or high-speed means of transport, he shall bear civil liability; however, if it can be proven that the damage was deliberately caused by the victim, he shall not bear civil liability." In addition, to some extent, certain cases involving environmental protection, product quality, medical malpractice, hurting people by domesticated animals and the falling of hangings of building to cause damages to other people, are also be applied with strict liability

[6]See Waltz (1983, p. 277).

[7]CPCL was promulgated by NPC in 1986. On 15th March 2017, NPC passed the General Provisions of Civil Law (GPCL), being effective on 1st October 2017. However, CPCL will still be effective then.

principle to certain extent. In common law countries, when this civil law principle is applied to the criminal cases, the concept of strict liability crime occurred therefrom.

The so-called strict liability crime, that is to say, the law does not require the public prosecutor to prove the defendant has the criminal intent or omission in the adjudication, as long as he proves that the defendant has committed such criminal act and caused damaging consequences therefrom, he has finished the burden of proof, and the court may sentence such defendant to bear corresponding criminal liabilities. According to the explanation in the Black's Law Dictionary, the strict liability crime "does not require a *mens rea* element, like traffic offense or attempting to bring weapons boarding".[8] In common law countries, strict liability generally only apply to minor crimes, and the punishment for such crime is generally fine.

In a strict liability crime, the public prosecutor bears no burden of proof for the defendant's subjective fault or "*mens rea*". Of course, the defendant may list evidence to prove that he has no subjective fault or that he shall not bear the criminal liability, however, as long as the defendant did not make such proof, the court may sentence him to be guilty. As a matter of fact, this deems presumption as the premise, i.e. all people who have committed strict liability crimes shall be presumed to have subjective faults, unless such persons use evidence to prove that they have no subjective faults. This is a presumption that can be contradicted; hence, it can also be applied with the principle of inversion of burden of proof. In other words, in strict liability crimes, the defendants must bear the burden of proof to prove they have no subjective faults; if not, they will have to bear the adverse litigation consequence.

Though the Criminal Law has not provided any explicit provisions on strict liability crimes, the scholars in China have made very deep research on this issue. Some scholars point out that, the strict liability in the criminal law refers to the criminal law system that investigates the criminal liabilities for those special injurious acts that lack subjective faults or the subjective faults are not clear. From the perspective of theory of constitutive elements of a crime in China, it denies strict liability; nevertheless, from the viewpoint of the criminal legislation and judicial practices of China, there are circumstances of investigating strict liability.[9] In my opinion, in the trials of criminal cases involving manufacturing and sale of quack medicines and toxic and harmful foods etc., we can refer to provisions regarding strict liabilities in US and/or UK and apply the principle of inversion of burden of proof.

(4) Burden of proof for extorting confession with torture

The inversion of burden of proof for crimes such as unidentified source for a huge amount of properties belongs to inversion of the burden of proof for the whole case or the main facts in a case. Under certain circumstances, laws may also apply inversion of the burden of proof to certain circumstances of a case. Extorting confession with torture is a good example.

As stated in Chap. 4, Chinese laws explicitly forbid extorting confessions with torture, and have adopted the exclusionary rule against illegally obtained evidence.

[8]Garner (1999).

[9]See Zhang (1997).

Furthermore, extorting confessions with torture is a statutory offense according to Article 247 of Criminal Law in China. However, it is very difficult to collect sufficient evidence to prove tortures in judicial proceedings. The tortured persons would have little ability to collect the evidence against the police officers. Even though the procurators get involved in the investigation of the alleged torture, it would still be difficult to do so, due to the fact that most eye-witnesses of the torture are also policemen. Thus, on the one hand, there are quite many complaints regarding tortures in criminal trials; on the other hand, there are only a few officers convicted for the offense of torture. Inverting the burden of proof in those cases may help to solve the problem, and to restrain the acts of extorting confessions with torture in law enforcement.

Extorting confession with torture is generally presented as a factual issue in the criminal proceedings. For example, a defendant in a murder case accuses the policemen have tortured him. Here, the defendant presents a specific factual claim, i.e. the policemen have conducted extorting confession with torture. As stated above, when the defendant proposes a specific positive factual claim for his defense, the burden of proof will be shifted to the defendant. Under such circumstance, the defendant shall bear the burden to prove the fact of torture. Indeed, it was the way that many judges in China would take, i.e. to ask the defendant to introduce evidence to prove the alleged torture. When the defendant was not able to produce sufficient evidence, the claim of torture would not be sustained, and the confession would be admitted into evidence.

Inverting the burden of proof in those cases meas to ask the prosecution to bear the burden to prove that there has been no torture for obtaining the confession. If the prosecutor cannot provide sufficient evidence to prove that, the prosecution will bear the corresponding consequence, i.e. the confession will be excluded. Of course, the defendant who has put forward such a claim shall bear some initial burden of proof, i.e. the burden of going forward with evidence. The defendant shall introduce some evidence, such as a reasonable statement, wounds, an injury assessment report, and a witness testimony, to prove the alleged torture. Like shifting the burden of proof to the defendant, as mentioned above, the standard of proof here is lower than the standard for prosecution. Then, the burden of proof shall be borne by the prosecution.

In summary, as for the factual dispute of whether or not there exists the extorting confession with torture, the defendant shall bear initial burden of proof and make the judge believe in that there is a substantial likelihood that the police committed a torture. Then, the public prosecutor shall bear the burden of proof for the legality of the evidence, i.e. no torture, and reach the standard of proof with reliable and sufficient evidence. This is inverting the burden of proof. PEIE and CPL have adopted this rule to some extent.

Article 6 of PEIE provides: "Where a defendant or the defender thereof argues that the defendant's pretrial confession has been obtained by illegal means, the court shall ask him to provide clues or evidence with regard to the person(s) involved in the alleged illegal activities, as well as the time, place, way and contents thereof."

Article 7 therein stipulates: "Where, upon investigation, the court has any doubt over the legality of the collection process of the defendant's pretrial confession, the public prosecutor shall provide the interrogation transcripts, the original audio or visual recordings of the interrogation or other evidence to the court…to prove the legality of the collection."

Article 10 therein provides: "Where, during court proceedings, any one of the following circumstances occurs, a defendant's pretrial confession may be introduced and cross-examined in court: (1) Neither the defendant nor the defender thereof has provided any clue or evidence to prove that the confession has been illegally obtained; (2) though the defendant and the defender thereof have provided a clue or evidence to prove that the confession has been illegally obtained, yet the court has no doubt over the legality of the collection process; or (3) the evidence produced by the public prosecutor is reliable and sufficient enough to rule out the possibility that the confession has been illegally obtained."

Article 11 therein provides: "If the prosecutor fails to provide evidence to prove that a defendant's pretrial confession has been legally obtained or the evidence they provided is not reliable or sufficient, the confession shall not be used as the basis for determination in the case."

Article 56 of CPL also stipulates: "the parties concerned and his defender and agent *ad litem* shall have the right to apply to the people's court to exclude those evidence that have been collected through illegal means according to law. If they apply so, they shall provide relevant clues and/or materials."

Article 57 therein provides: "In the process of conducting investigation upon the legality of evidence collection by court, the people's procuratorate shall prove the legality of evidence collection."

Article 58 therein provides: "…after court investigation, as for circumstance that has been confirmed with illegal means of evidence collection or circumstance that the evidence collection through illegal means cannot be excluded according to provisions of Article 54 of this Law, the relevant evidence shall be excluded."

Inverting the burden of proof for the issue of extorting confession with torture is not only beneficial to finding truth in the dispute, but also good for restraining the behaviors of the law enforcement officers. Allocating the burden of proof on the prosecution is in fact putting the burden on the police. Facing the challenge to the legality of evidence and the potential punishment, the law enforcement officers would be more careful in investigation activities, such as an interrogation. In order to avoid the awkward impeachment in the courtroom, they'd better to collect evidence according to law strictly. I will continue the discussion on the issue of torture in Chap. 10.

5.4.3 Exemption of the Burden of Proof

In a criminal trial, the party who bears the burden of proof for the facts of the case shall complete the corresponding mission of proof; otherwise, such party shall bear the adverse consequence. However, under certain circumstances, the laws permit judicial staff to exempt the burden of proof of one party of the litigation according to certain rules. In accordance with theory of judicial proof and experiences of judicial practices, there are mainly several types of situations as follows that can be exempted from the burden of proof in the criminal proceedings:

5.4.3.1 Facts of Self-confession

The term "self-confession" refers to the guilty confession made voluntarily by the defendant at the court. The written confession made by the defendant at the stage of investigation or the interrogation records prepared by the investigators are not sufficient enough to constitute a self-confession. As for the issue that whether or not the self-confession of the defendant may exempt the burden of proof for the public prosecutor, the Chinese laws have not provided any explicit provisions. Therefore, the answer to the question shall be different in judicial practice, depending on specific circumstances. If a self-confession is of only a part of the case facts, the judge may exempt the public prosecutor from the burden of proof for the fact. For example, in a bribery case, if the defendant self-confessed that he had accepted money from a businessman, but disputed on the amount of money, then, the public prosecutor shall be exempted from the burden of proving the bribery act itself, but still bear the corresponding burden of proving the amount of bribery. If a self-confession is of the whole case facts, the public prosecutor shall not be exempted from the burden of proof completely, because Article 53 of CPL stipulates: "A defendant cannot be found guilty and sentenced to a criminal punishment if there is only his statement but no other evidence". In such cases, the prosecution's burden of proof may be reduced depending on actual circumstances. For example, it will be accepted if the prosecutor can provide some evidence, in accordance with the self-confession, to prove the basic elements of the charged offense, such as the subject, the act, and the consequence.

5.4.3.2 Facts of Judicial Notice

The term "judicial notice" refers to one of judge's functions that during the trial of a case, the judge shall affirm some adjudicative facts through the means of direct confirmation. It is a decision, in fact, to exempt the burden of proof for the parties concerned. Professor Waltz states: "The existence of some facts is thought to be to self-evident that no formal proof of them is necessary during a trial. Thus no witnesses need be called and no tangible evidence need be offered to establish these widely accepted facts. A trial court will simply take notice of them and instruct the jurors that they are to be taken, or can be taken, as established without formal proof.[10]" Although Chinese laws have not adopted the concept of judicial notice, there are similar provisions therein. For example, paragraph 2 of Article 75 of the *Opinions on Several Issues regarding the Application of the Civil Procedure Law* issued by SPC stipulates: "the well-known facts and natural laws and theorem" belong to fact

[10]Waltz (1983, p. 282).

that need not be proved by the parties concerned, they can be directly accepted by the judge. The previously mentioned "facts exempted from proof" are the examples.

5.4.3.3 Facts of Predetermination

There are two types of the predetermined facts: one is the fact that has already been determined by the legally effective judgment or verdict made by the court; the other is the fact verified by an effective notarization certificate. Both belong to the case facts that have already been confirmed through legal effective means, and thus the burden of proof for relevant parties concerned can be exempted. However, a legally effective judgment and ruling is not absolutely infallible. In order to avoid repeating an error, laws shall adopt more flexible attitude upon this issue, or provide some conditions for the exemption, i.e. except those that with contrary evidence, the predetermined facts shall exempt the burden of proof for the parties concerned.

With respect to the above-mentioned facts, the court may make rulings directly to exempt the burden of proof from the parties concerned. The ruling may be made at any stage of proceedings, however, it generally gives the opposing party opportunities to make objections and provide rebuttal evidence. As long as the opposing party did not present opposite evidence to such exempted facts, the party who claims the facts shall be exempted from the burden of proof. The significance of exemption of burden of proof can be mainly shown in the following three aspects. First, It may reduce the burden of proof of the parties concerned, which is conducive to the fair and reasonable allocation of burden of proof. Secondly, it may avoid delaying in the trial or incapability of making judgment because of lacking of evidence, in other words, which can promote the efficiency of trial. Thirdly, it may save some manpower, material resources, and financial resources for the judiciary.

5.5 Allocation Rules of Burden of Proof in Civil Proceedings

5.5.1 General Rules

In civil proceedings, the allocation rule of the burden of proof can be simply expressed as "who claims, who bears the burden of proof". Paragraph 1 of Article 2 of PECP stipulates that: "The parties concerned shall be responsible for producing evidence to prove the facts on which their own allegations are based or the facts on which the allegations of the other party are refuted." Nevertheless, in a specific case, the allocation of burden of proof is not so simple. For example, in a case involving loan dispute, the fact that whether or not the defendant has paid back the money may be the focus of such controversy of this case, and whether such fact belongs to the fact that the plaintiff's claims are based on or belongs to the fact that the defendant's claims to rebut the plaintiff's claims are based on may also be the difficulty for the judge. For example:

Party A suits Party B for that Party B has borrowed 10,000RMB from him, but Party B did not write a IOU note at the time of borrowing. In the defense, Party B admitted that he did borrow 10,000RMB from Party A but such money had been returned and Party A did not write a receipt at the time of returning. In this case, there is no other evidence except for the statements of both parties. There are two facts: one is the fact of borrowing money and the other is the fact of returning the money. Since Party B has admitted, so the fact of borrowing the money has been proved. Now the dispute of both parties is the fact of returning of such money, Party B said he has returned such money and Party A said Party B did not pay such money back, and it is really hard to decide whether or not such money has been paid back. Under the circumstance of unclear facts, how does the court make its judgment? This involves the issue of allocation of the burden of proof.

According to general understanding, Party B has presented a positive factual claim in this case, and then burden of proof is transferred to Party B. Hence the court shall make its judgment unfavorable of Party B. However, the judge thinks Party B is an honest man. If he said he has never borrowed any money from Party A at the very beginning, and since there is no IOU note and it is hard to investigate such facts, the judge will make a judgment in favor of him. Now, he honestly and sincerely admitted that he has borrowed some money, but Party A did not admit that Party B has returned such money, if the judge makes a judgment in favor of Party A, is it unfair to Party B? The judge was somewhat in a dilemma. As a matter of fact, we can change another point of view to analyze this problem. What's the factual claim of Party A? Party A brought a lawsuit to the court to make Party B to pay back his money, such factual claim can be understood as: he lent 10,000RMB to Party B and Party B did not pay back. If understand as such, Party A shall not only bear the burden of proof for the fact of borrowing of such money, but he shall also bear the burden of proof for the fact that Party B did not pay back. Then, under the circumstance of unclear facts, the court shall make its judgment not in favor of Party A. We can see that in even seemingly simple case of debt disputes, the allocation of burden of proof may be not so simple.

Of course, the allocation of the burden of proof is not the only path for a judge to make his ruling. A judge may make his decision on the basis of the judgment of the truthfulness and reliability of the statements of both parties. Facing "one to one" evidence, a judge can also make his judgment. We cannot simply say that "one to one" evidence is certainly the probability of 50 to 50%, is certainly that the case has very unclear facts, and the judgment that which party has won the lawsuit shall be decided only depending on the allocation of burden of proof. If the judge believes that Party B's statement is more reliable, then he may make a judgment in favor of Party B.

5.5.2 The Burden of Proof in Cases Involving Contract Disputes

PECP has materialized the general rules regarding allocation of the burden of proof and makes explicit regulations respectively according to several circumstances of contract dispute cases.

1. In a contract dispute, the party that claims the establishment of a contractual relationship and the contract has taken effect shall be responsible for producing evidence to prove that the contract has been concluded and that it has taken effect. According to methods of theory of classification of legal requirements, the establishment of a contractual relationship and the fact of the effectiveness of a contract belong to the fact of creation of rights, thus, the party who advocates the establishment of a contractual relationship and its effectiveness shall bear the burden of proof to prove the fact of such establishment and effectiveness. The party who denies the establishment and effectiveness shall not bear the obligation of burden of proof. Although the party who denies such fact may also present the claim of denying the establishment of such contractual relationship and its effectiveness and provide relevant evidence to prove such fact, if such fact of such establishment and its effectiveness is unclear, the adverse consequence for the claiming of the establishment of such contractual relationship and its effectiveness shall be borne by such party claiming so.

2. In a contract dispute case, the party that claims that the contract has been altered, dissolved, terminated or canceled shall bear the burden of proof for the fact that has led to the change of such contractual relationship. The fact regarding the alteration, dissolution, termination and cancellation of the contractual relationship belongs to the fact to interfering with or extinction of rights, hence, the party who claims that a contract has been altered, dissolved, terminated or canceled shall provide evidence to prove corresponding facts, and if not, the relevant claims of such party cannot be established and such party shall bear corresponding adverse consequences. Similarly, the opposing party who denies the alteration, dissolution, termination and cancellation of such contractual relationship shall not bear burden of proof, that is to say, such party will not bear the adverse consequence of non-demonstration.

3. In a contract dispute, if a dispute over whether a contract is performed occurred, the party under the obligation of performing the contract shall be responsible for burden of proof. According to theory of classification of legal requirements, the performance of the contractual obligations is the reason for the extinction of corresponding contractual rights, hence, the party who claims the performance of the contract shall prove the fact that such contractual obligations have been performed; and if failed to do so, the factual claim of such party that the contract has been formed cannot be established, and therefore, the court may make corresponding unfavorable judgment. According to this article of PECP, in a dispute involving debt contracts, if one party has the obligation to deliver the subject matter according to the agreement, when dispute regarding the performance of such obligation between both parties occurred, the party who has the obligation to deliver such matter shall bear the burden of proof

to prove that he has performed his obligation, if he failed to do so, the court may determine that such party did not perform his obligation.

5.5.3 The Burden of Proof in Cases Involving Tort Disputes

The bearing of burden of proof in cases involving torts disputes shall also apply the general principle of bearing of burden of proof; i.e. the party who claims the right of action for the recovery of damages shall bear burden of proof for the fact of legal requirements generated by such right of action. That is to say, such party has to prove the required facts regarding the damages as prescribed by the civil law: the illegality of the acts of offender, causality between the tort acts and their consequences, such offender is in fault and there is fact of damage. On the contrary, if the offender presents his defense against such factual claims that interferes the occurrence of such rights, such offender shall prove the existence of such facts. For example, Article 4 of PECP stipulates: "In an infringement action resulting from personal damage caused by highly dangerous operations, the infringing person shall be responsible for producing evidence to prove that argument that the victim caused the injury." In the tort dispute lawsuit like these, if there exists the fact that the victim intentionally cause the damage, such victim cannot enjoy the right to require the offender to give damages. The fact that the victim intentionally caused the damage belongs to fact that interferes right, so the party who claims such fact shall bear burden of proof for such fact. Although the victim may voluntarily prove that he did not intentionally cause the damage in order to protect his own interests in a lawsuit, and if he cannot prove that, as long as the opposing party did not prove the fact that such victim intentionally caused the damage, such victim shall win the case.

In addition, Item 5 of Article 4 of PECP stipulates: "In an infringement action of damages caused by a domesticate animal, the person who raises or manages the animal shall be responsible for producing evidence to prove that the victim is at fault or any third party is at fault." Item 6 of Article 4 of PECP prescribes that: "In an infringement action of damages caused by a defective product, the producer of the product shall be responsible for producing evidence to prove that there exist the exemptions of liabilities as provided in laws."

5.5.4 Inverting the Burden of Proof in Civil Proceedings

Article 4 of PECP stipulates several circumstances for inverting the burden of proof. However, this is not inverting the burden of proof for the whole facts in a case.

1. Item 1 of Article 4 of PECP stipulates: "In a patent infringement action resulting from the innovation-creation of ways of producing new products, the entity or individual that produces the same product shall prove that the ways used are different from those of the patent holder." In this stipulation, "the entity or individual that

produces the same product shall prove that the ways used are different from those of the patent holder" is the inversion of burden of proof. Because according to the principle of burden of proof, the right holder shall prove the infringer has committed the act of infringement, and such infringement fact includes that fact that the method used to manufacture the similar product by infringement is the same with the patent method; that is to say, the right holder shall prove the manufacturing method of the infringer is the same with the manufacturing method of the right holder. However, in order to make a fair judgment, this provision makes inversion of the burden of proof for such fact, i.e. the infringer shall prove that his manufacturing method is different from the patent method, if he failed to do so, the patent infringement shall be constituted. Nevertheless, other facts did not apply inversion of burden of proof, for example, the infringing facts are still needed to be proven by the right holder.

2. Item 3 of Article 4 of PECP stipulates: "In a compensation lawsuit for damages caused by environmental pollution, the infringing party shall be responsible for producing evidence to prove the existence of exemptions of liabilities as provided in laws or that there is no causal relationship between the his act and the harmful consequences." In this stipulation, the burden of proof for the fact that there is no causality between the infringer's act and the harmful consequences belong to the inversion of burden of proof. Because according to relevant principles, the fact of such causality shall be proved by the victim, but the above-mentioned stipulation implements the inversion of burden of proof and makes the infringer to prove the non-existence of causality from the point of view of being beneficial to protect the victim and in consideration of the difficulty for a victim of an environmental pollution case to prove such causality. This is because that it is easier for the infringer to prove such fact than the victim. One thing that needs to be noted here is that the proving of the exemptions of liabilities of the infringer does not belong to inversion of burden of proof, because the exemption itself is the fact that interferes the creation of rights, which shall make the infringer to bear burden of proof according to general rules.

3. Item 4 of Article 4 of PECP stipulates: "In an infringement action of damages caused by the collapse, breaking off or falling of a building or other facilities and the thing that is laid or hung on the building, the owner or administrator of the building shall be responsible for burden of proof thereon." In this stipulation, the proving obligation for the fact that the infringer has no fault shall apply inversion of burden of proof. Because according to general principles, the fact that the infringer has no fault shall be proven by the victim as the ultimate fact of his right of claim. Other ultimate facts do not apply inversion of burden of proof, for example, fact of damage, causality fact etc.

4. Item 7 of Article 4 of PECP stipulates: "In an infringement action of damages caused by common danger, the persons who commit the common danger shall be responsible for producing evidence to prove that there is no causal relationship between the act thereof and the harmful consequences." In this provision, the bearing of burden of proof for the causality also belongs to inversion of burden of proof.

5. Item 8 of Article 4 of PECP stipulates: "In an infringement action of damages caused by medical acts, the medical institution shall be responsible for producing evidence to prove that there is no causal relationship between the medical act and

the harmful consequences or it is not at fault." In this provision, the tort lawsuit led to by a medical act has applied inversion of burden of proof for facts of the two legal requirements of the right holder's right of claim for tort damages: one is the fact of causality; the other is the fact that the infringer has no fault. SPC does not provide further provisions on other facts, so burden of proof for such facts shall be borne according to general rules.

The previously illustrated provisions regarding inversion of burden of proof have actually implied rules of presumption. Therefore, I shall make more discussions thereon in later chapters.

References

Bian, Jianlin (ed.). 2000. *Evidence law*, 325–326. Beijing: China University of Political Science and Law Press.

Bian, Jianlin (ed.). 2004. *The theory of criminal proof*, 177. Beijing: Renmin Public Security University Press.

Garner, Bryan A. (ed). 1999. *Black's law dictionary*, 7th ed, 378. West Group: St. Paul.

Waltz, Jon. 1983. *Criminal evidence*, 2nd ed. Chicago: Nelson-Hall Press.

Xiang, Jidong, Shaofu Shu. 1998. Savings account book: how let me believe on you—about a case of 400,000 RMB saving claim. *Law and Life* 1.

Zhang, Wen, et al. 1997. *Essentials of criminal liabilities*, 91–92. Beijing: Peking University Press.

Chapter 6
The Standards of Judicial Proof

Contents

6.1 Case Illustration

Late night on 5th April 1989, on the Youyi Forest Farm of Yichun City in Heilongjiang Province, a forest-fire ranger, Guan Chuansheng, was stabbed to death with a knife. During the crime-scene investigation, it was discovered that the back center of the victim's overcoat had been cut, and that a corresponding cut in the body had corner angles. Investigators concluded that the cut to the coat had been made by a bayonet, and the other cuts by a single-edged cutting tool. The victim died at midnight after leaving the farm office an hour earlier, at which time the electricity of the farm went out.

That same night, the oldest son of a neighboring family, Shi Dongyu, who had been demobilized from the army nine days previously, was out, his whereabouts unaccounted for. Investigators listed him as a suspect and when Dongyu returned home that day, he was taken in for questioning. Dongyu said that in the afternoon of 5th, a friend of his had shot a deer and invited him for a bite and drink. He returned

J. He, *Methodology of Judicial Proof and Presumption*,
Masterpieces of Contemporary Jurisprudents in China,
https://doi.org/10.1007/978-981-10-8025-8_6

about 20:00, and went to his *fiancée*'s house to discuss the preparations for their marriage. He then went home to get some money, and to the boiler plant around 22:00 to drink water, smoke and chat. He went to the railway station after 23:00, and took the 2:00 train down the mountain to the town next morning. He spent the whole morning to go among the local government offices for his demobilization papers.

Investigators found a witness to corroborate Dongyu's statement. According to the owners of the boiler plant, Dongyu had left the plant after the electricity went off. Site-investigation clarified that the plant was located on the roadside between the office and his house, and was not far from the site of the murder. Therefore, investigators believed that Dongyu and the victim had walked along the same road at the same time. Additionally, investigators proved by experiment that it would take only 20 min to walk from the farm to the railway station. In a word, investigators believed Dongyu had time to commit the murder.

In the night of 6th April investigators searched Dongyu's home and found a bloodied military coat and a single-edge fruit knife with a black plastic handle. The front collar of the coat was lacerated and three lost buttons were found in one of the pockets. The coat was stained with both O and A blood types. The victim's blood was type A. The knife was not bloodied, but the blade matched the cut in the corpse.

At the beginning of his subsequent interrogation, Dongyu insisted that he hadn't killed the victim and explained that the blood on the coat was from his father and his brother when he had fought with his brother on the afternoon of 4th April. But after having been questioned for >30 h, Dongyu admitted to the crime.

Almost 10 days later, the People's Procuratorate of Yichun City approved the arrest of Dongyu and filed for the prosecution for murder. In court, Dongyu denied his confession and insisted on his innocence, to no avail: he was convicted of murder and sentenced to death with immediate execution. Dongyu appealed. On 13 May, after reviewing the case, the High People's Court of Heilongjiang Province ruled that some of the facts were unclear and that overall there was a lack of evidence. They sent the case for retrial, and listed several issues needing further investigation, such as the incomplete match of the killing tool and the cut in the body, the existence of two types of blood on the coat, and the reason for the buttons being in the pocket, etc.

On 19th September the Intermediate People's Court of Yichun City reopened the session to discuss the murder prosecution of Dongyu. Although the prosecutor was not able to provide more evidence, the court held that presented evidences, including the testimony of his availability to commit the crime, the murder tool, the expertise testimony, and the crime scene search record, etc., satisfied the "two basic standards" of proof.[1] On 2nd December, the court again convicted Dongyu and sentenced him to death with two years' probation. On 7th January 1992, the Intermediate Court transferred the case to the High Court for review. On 26th February the High Court

[1]According to the provision in CPL, the standard of proof for conviction is that the facts of the case are clear and the evidence is reliable and sufficient. However, the standard of proof in judicial practice was lowered to that the facts of the case were basically clear and the evidence was basically reliable and sufficient in 1980s and 1990s.

confirmed the judgment. On 31st August, Dongyu was sent to Beian Prison. However, this was not the end of the story.

In April, 1994, a burglar, Ma Yunjie, was arrested in the public security bureau of Yichun City, and revealed in his written statements that: "I want to survive by giving evidence. The murder on 5th April 1989 was not committed by Shi Dongyu. The true criminal was Liang Baoyou!"

He told the police what he knew. In the early morning of 6th April 1989, he had been doing morning exercises near the railway tracks when he saw Baoyou running down the mountain with a bloodstained overcoat. He stopped him, and asked what had happened. Baoyou said that nothing had happened, and that the blood was from a pig he had slaughtered. Two days later, Baoyou invited him for a drink, and told him that the night when the farm's electricity went out, he was waiting at the gate of the farm office to pin back Xia Baoxi's ears. At about 11 pm, someone similar in height and shape as Baoxi walked out. Baoyou then followed him and strongly stabbed a dart into his waist. The guy turned around, grabbed the dart and shouted. At that moment, Baoyou saw that this was not Baoxi but Chuansheng. However, because Chuansheng had recognized him, he felt he had to kill him.

The High Court of Heilongjiang, the Intermediate Court of Yichun, and the Public Security Bureau of Yichun paid great attention to the statement and formed a special reinvestigation team of the "89·4·5" case, and quickly found that Baoyou had been stabbed dead in a fight on 26th October 1990. Baoyou's mother told police the true story, which proved the truth of Yunjie statement. They also found some contradictions and gaps in the case file; however, these findings were not enough to overturn the original judgment. But if DNA from the blood in Dongyu's coat were not the victim's, it would be very persuasive. The investigators made great efforts and finally obtained permission from the victim's family to open the grave of Chuansheng to collect the skull and hairs for a DNA sample.

The Forensic Medical Examination Center of Beijing Public Security Bureau revealed that the victim's blood type was AB, and that Dongyu's coat was stained with type A and type O, which were respectively the same as his father's and his brother's. Therefore, Dongyu's coat was not stained by the victim's blood and, further, it was ridiculous that the previous medical examiner had mistakenly identified the victim's blood as type A.

On 12th April 1995, the High Court of Heilongjiang Province acquitted Shi Dongyu and released him ten days later. He received 60,000RMB in state compensation and government assistance.[2]

The standard of judicial proof is a very important theoretical issues in the evidence law, and also a very important practical problems in the judicial judgment. In recent years, the scholars of our country have been carried on the extensive discussion on the judicial proof, and have made some impressive results. These results, not only promoted the development of the evidence law research in China, also, to some extent, lead the development of judicial proof practicing in our country. When discussing this issue, it is necessary to clear the related basic categories.

---

[2]See Guo (2011).

6.2 The Basic Categories of the Standard of Judicial Proof

6.2.1 Objective Facts and Legal Facts

The objective fact and the legal fact are important categories of judicial proof. The objective fact is a fact of objective existence. In terms of judicial proof, it is the case fact which actually happened in the objective world. The legal fact is a fact in the legal sense, which is defined by legal norms and has certain legal consequences. In the judicial activities, legal facts are shown by the evidence and confirmed by the judges.

Generally speaking, legal facts should be based on objective facts, but they are not equivalent to the latter, while the differences between the two may be in quality and quantity. First, the legal facts in a case may not be equal to the objective facts in quality, because the legal facts are proved by evidence with human behavior, and therefore are often mixed with those persons' subjective factors. Secondly, the legal facts may not be equal to the objective facts in quantity. In general, the number of objective facts is more than the number of legal facts in a case, because not all the objective facts relevant to the case can be proved by evidence. For various reasons, some objective facts of the case may not become legal facts, and may even be lost forever in the process of judicial proof.

In summary, the legal fact is the objective fact with some humanistic characters. Clifford Geertz, an American scholar, once pointed out: "Legal fact is not formed naturally, but is man-made. As anthropologists said, they are according to such things and structure from that the rules of evidence, the rules of court, reports tradition, defense skills, court eloquence ability and legal education. In short, it is the product of society.[3]"

Some Chinese scholars have similar viewpoint that, "The fact presented and decided by the court in lawsuits ultimately, is adjusted and remolded by the evidence law, procedural law and substantive law. As this new fact permeated inevitably with human subjective willingness, it may be called subjective fact. Since it is formed in the process of litigation, based on the procedural law, and of significance to the judicial proceedings, it may also be called litigation fact or legal fact.[4]" In short, the legal fact is not equal to the objective fact.

6.2.2 Objective Truth and Legal Truth

The categories of objective truth and legal truth are based on the objective fact and the legal fact, but the concepts of objective truth and legal truth are not the same as

---

[3]Liang (1994).

[4]See Jiang (1999).

the objective fact and the legal fact. The facts established in the judicial proof may not be the truth. And they should not be confused as one.

The so-called objective truth means that the facts found in a case match the objective facts in reality, which is complied with the objective standard. The so-called legal truth means that the facts found in a case meet the legal standard for truth, which may be or may not be the truth in reality, but the truth in legal sense.

Law is man-made, so as the legal standard for truth. Therefore, in different countries and in different historical periods, the connotations and standards for legal truth are different naturally. As discussed in Chap. 2, the tests of the trial by gods or the trial by ordeals in ancient times are standards for legal truth, the "full proof" in the system of legal proof in the medieval European continental countries is a standard for legal truth, and the proof with intimate conviction or beyond a reasonable doubt adopted tn modern countries is also a standard for legal truth. So, what should be the standard for legal truth in my country or in your country? In China, the standard is based on the dialectical materialist epistemology, which has In this has three basic points of view.

First, the legal truth does not belong to the category of subjective truth. The subjective truth is people's understanding or belief about the case facts with the subjective standard, which is separated from the objective reality. In other words, the standard of truth is based on some authoritative recognition, and is subjective test to the specific judicial proof. However, legal truth is not completely out of the objective truth. It is the truth based on objective reality, and consists of the contents of objective truth.

Secondly, although the legal truth contains the contents of objective truth, it is not equal to objective truth. The main difference between the two is that the objective truth is fully and absolutely truthful, while the legal truth implies the possibility of error. According to the requirements of objective truth, the result of judicial proof in a case must be absolutely correct with the objective reality, and there should be no error at all. The legal truth is recognized by law, with the standard of proof lower than that for the objective truth. In most of the cases, the legal truth should meet the objective actual situation, while in some cases it may deviate from the objective truth. As is known to all, the judges cannot not find facts in a case without evidence, and the information stored in the evidence is not always reflecting the objective facts accurately. For example, witness Zhang said that he saw Wang had been killed by Li with a stick. This testimony may not be absolutely correct, even though the witness is an honest man. It may be partly true and partly false. In many instances, testimony is the integration of truth part and false part. Even the testimonies admitted by judges may have some false part. This is the undeniable fact, and is the fact that the law have to accept. The legal truth is just the truth based on this kind of evidence.

Thirdly, in a sense, the legal truth is based on probability, which has the nature of objective reality. Zukerman, a professor at the University of Oxford, cited an example: someone was knocked down by a bus on the road, and the evidence obtained can only prove that it was a bus, but cannot make an individualization. The investigators found out that the number of the buses from Company A accounted for 80% of the total on this road. According to the probabilistic calculation, the probability that a bus from Company A did the crash is 80%. The standard of proof in civil proceedings is 'preponderance of evidence'. If the proof provided by one party is more than 50%, he will win the lawsuit. So the court decided that Company A shall assume the compensation liability.

Then Professor Zukerman said, "As I have pointed out, this view is based on the objective assumption. The assumption is that the only function of judicial process is to seek for the objective reality out of law and independent from law. However, as Hilary Putnam said, the reality is not the underline. Reality is the life that has reasonable standards, moreover, if we want to find out science inherent value, we must face up to the standards. Through investigation, we will find the objective facts about lawsuit could not separate from the rest of legal system completely. As the different form between law and reality, the objective assumption is reflected in the each important stage of judicial process.[5]"

In the above case, the court could not identify the hitting bus, but believed that it was more likely to be a bus of Company A. Faced with a case like this, people may ask the court to find out the "objective truth", with further investigation to collect more evidence, such as looking for a eye-witness, and searching for transfer and trace evidence. However, the reality in this case is that there is no other evidence. So the court faces a dilemma: dismiss the action for lack of evidence, thus the victim will get no compensation; or make a compensation decision according to the probability, with 20% probability that Company A is wronged. If the latter option is accepted by law, it is the legal truth. Of course, it is not equal to the objective truth.

In a sense, this legal truth is 80% objective truth. However, we cannot conclude that there will be 20 misjudged cases in every 100 such cases. The result would not be so simple. The court's recognition of the fact is 80% true, but the court's decision could be completely correct. In theory, the probability of occurrence is only 80%, but it may be actually existence in reality. For example, the weather forecast says the probability of precipitation is 80%, and it rains actually.

In the above case, there is another way to solve the dilemma. Among all the buses on that road, 80% of which belongs to Company A, 15% of which belongs to Company B, and 5% of which belongs to Company C. The victim sues all the three companies as co-defendants. Then according to the analysis of probabilities, the court makes a judgment ordering the three companies to share the compensation in proportion of the probabilities, i.e. 80% of the compensation by Company A, 15% of the compensation by Company B, and 5% of the compensation by Company C. This is also a legal truth based on probability, and seems to be a more reasonable, but is not objective truth. In the judgment of compensation by Company A, the error is just a possibility. In the judgment of compensation by three companies, the error is a sure one, because there must be two companies wronged in reality.

Actually, some judges have used this method of sharing compensations in personal injury cases. For example, a plaintiff suffered some organ damage caused by using of certain drugs for a long time, and the drugs were produced by several pharmaceutical factories. The evidence could not prove which factory's product had caused the

[5] Adrian A.S. Zuckerman: Law, Fact or Justice, Boston University Law Review, Vol. 66, p. 488.

damage. In the case, the court allowed the victim to sue all the manufacturers as co-defendants. Then the judge decided that those manufacturers should share the responsibility of compensation.

In China, there have been some well-known personal tort cases, in which the injuries were caused by falling objects from tall buildings, such as "the ashtray case" in Chongqing in 2000, "the flowerpot case" in Dandong in 2002, and "the glass case" in Beijing in 2006. Since there was no evidence to prove the ownership of the falling object in those cases, the courts decided that all the residents who might own the object should share the compensation liabilities. Let me take the Beijing case as an example.

On 7th April 2006, when Mr. Wang was walking home, a piece of glass fell down from the tall building and injured his head. He was sent to a hospital for medical treatment. His family tried to find out where the glass came from but failed, then they reported the case to the police station. After investigation, the police concluded that Mr. Wang had been injured by a piece of glass fallen down from an apartment of the building above the second floor, but could not identify the apartment. Mr. Wang sued all the 30 families living in the apartments above the second floor. After hearing the case, the court issued a judgment for the plaintiff, in which 28 families were ordered to share the compensation, while the other two families had provided evidence to prove their innocence or no fault.[6]

In those controversial judgments, the facts found by the courts could be put in the category of legal truth, but there were definitely not in the category of objective truth. Here comes another pair of categories of judicial proof, which are absolute truth and relative truth.

6.2.3 Absolute Truth and Relative Truth

Judicial proof is a kind of human cognitive activities. Human cognitive conclusions may not always be correct or true, and are often true to certain extent. Therefore, absolute truth and relative truth are also important categories regarding to judicial proof. The so-called absolute truth is the truth absolutely equal to the objective reality, or 100% truth. The so-called relative truth is the truth tallying with the objective reality to some extent, which is not 100% truth, but 90, 80, or 51% truth.

In the opinion of dialectical materialism,the world is knowable, and human beings have the ability to understand all the objective truth. But, this is not to say that everybody absolutely recognizes the whole things in the world. This is not to say that every individual has this ability. The case truth found by the judiciary belongs to the 'individual recognition', which is realized by putting completely limited personal thinking within limited time. Therefore, in each specific case, the truth recognized by the judiciary is not "absolute truth", but only "relative truth". In other words,

[6]See Zhou (2007).

people's cognition for each specific case is not completely "real", but is the "real" to different degrees.

The human cognitive ability is being of relativity, and the result of judicial proof is being of relativity too. Only in the infinite development cognitive process, the ability of human cognition can get rid of the constraint of relativity, and come into the reality of the absolute truth. In other words, the absolute truth cannot be reached in a specific cognitive activity, but in the infinite development of cognitive process. Thus, in any case, the conclusion of judicial proof is a truth, but it is not the absolute truth. Of course, the relative truth and the absolute truth are not completely opposite or separate. The relative truth contains the content of absolute truth, more or less. In this sense, the result of judicial proof contains the content of absolute truth.

Here we need to go back to the probability again. A good judgment does not require 100% truth of the case facts. For example, in a murder case, even some details of the defendant's action are not fully known according to the evidence, the court's conviction may still be considered as a correct judgment. Although the judges' cognition of the case facts are relatively clear, the judgments should be definitely certain. When answering a criminal charge, the court must issue a verdict for conviction or acquittal. The judge may believe that there is a 90% chance that the defendant is guilty, but he can not make a 90% conviction. A conviction is a conviction. On every dispute of fact in a civil litigation, the judge shall rule either for the plaintiff or for the defendant. The judge cannot rule that the plaintiff has greater possibility to win the case. However, the principles of probability theory should be absorbed into the assessment the probative value of the evidence. This may serve as an enlightenment for judges from the study of the relations between the absolute truth and the relative truth.

Since the judicial proof has the nature of relativity and its conclusion belongs to the category of relative truth, it will be accepted only when the conclusion has rationality and legitimacy. There are two aspects about the rationality and legitimacy of relative truth: first, the result of judicial proof is reasonable, or acceptable according to the general knowledge and experience; secondly, the process of judicial proof is legitimate, or in accordance with the legal provisions. This is also the requirements for judicial just, reflecting another pair of important categories, the substantial just and the procedural just.

6.2.4 Objective Truth Theory and Legal Truth Theory

On the issues of the standards of proof in litigation, Chinese scholars adhered to the "objective truth theory" for a long time. So the judiciary regard it as the guiding principle consciously or unconsciously. In the ideological environment of 1970s and 1980s, any question to this principle was incredible and unacceptable. In 1990s, as the thought liberation, some scholars challenged the "objective truth theory". They proposed "legal truth theory" for the standard of the judicial proof. Then there were fierce arguments between these two scholarships.

The scholars supporting the "legal truth theory" argue that the objective truth cannot be achieved in judicial practice, and the old principle may also cause some negative consequences, such as arbitrary justice, contempt to the laws, and violation of the rule of law.[7] The scholars on the other side argue that the legal truth theory cannot take the place of guiding principle for the standard of judicial proof, because the objective truth is the real truth, while the legal truth cannot be established, no matter in the epistemological theory or the legal theory.[8]

Superficially, the two viewpoints are mutually exclusive, but after careful study of the two, I have found something in common. On the one hand, the scholars of the 'legal truth theory' also acknowledged the value of pursuing objective truth in judicial proof, while this is the basic viewpoint of the scholarship on the other side. For example, Professor Fan Chongy, a leading scholar of the "legal truth theory", pointed out, "Everyone would agree that it would be the best thing if the objective truth could be found in the process of a lawsuit. In other words, it is a perfect theory for judicial proof. Because of this, people have poured much passion and energy to discover the objective truth.[9]" On the other hand, scholars of the "objective truth theory" also acknowledge that the objective truth cannot be reached absolutely in each case, while that is emphasized by scholars of the "legal truth theory". For example, Professor Chen Yiyun, a leading scholar of the "objective truth theory", said, "In judicial practice, not really every proof achieves the objective truth. The reasons are various, such as the failure to collect sufficient evidence, the failure to conduct further investigation, the lack of necessary science and technology, the interference with the judiciary from authority or other persons, and so on.[10]"

The debate between the objective truth scholarship and the legal truth scholarship also reflects the conflict between judicial ideal and judicial reality to a certain extent. As the ideal standard, it is better for the judicial proof to pursue objective truth, which is 100% true. However, when facing reality with all sorts of limited conditions, judges would often have to accept the legal truth in specific cases.

In addition, the stability of society and the dignity of law also require the *res judicata* of judicial decisions. Once a proper trial is ended, the result of the judicial proof shall have certain effects, and the legal facts shall not be altered freely. Even if the facts may not be confirmed with the objective reality, the law recognize its effectiveness. Some countries have adopted the principle of "no double jeopardy" or "*ne bis in idem*" in criminal trials, which is a way to recognize the "legal truth". In short, no matter people agree or not, the legal truth exists in reality. The disputes between the two scholarships reflect the confusion of concepts, such as "aim" and "standard", which is the topic of the next section.

[7] See Fan (2000).

[8] See Zhang (2001).

[9] See Fan (2000), pp. 202–203.

[10] See Chen (2000).

6.3 The Aim and the Standard of Judicial Proof

In Chinese, *the word* "standard" refers to the criterion or the rules of measurement. The standard of proof in judicial activities is the criterion or the rule to measure whether the result of judicial proof is correct or the degree and level the judicial proof must reach. In other words, the standard is to confirm that under what circumstance the judge can decide the evidence submitted by the plaintiff or the defendant has reached the sufficient degree and level. The aim of judicial proof is the goal that the subject of the judicial proof is pursuing, or the aim of judicial proof activities. They are different but related concepts.

The relationship between the aim and the standard is shown in the following aspects. First, the aim of proof is the basis or foundation of the standard of proof, while the standard of proof is the embodiment of the aim of proof. Secondly, the aim of proof is functioning through the whole process of litigation, while the standard of proof is mainly an issue for decision making in judicial proceedings. Thirdly, the aim of proof is not changing in the whole process of litigation, while the standard of proof may change in the proceedings, in other words, the standards may be different at different stages of litigation. For example, the standards of proof are not the same for the decision of arrest, prosecution, and conviction in criminal proceedings. Fourthly, the aim of proof should be the same for all sorts of cases, while the standards of proof may be different for different cases. For example, the standards of proof in criminal cases and civil cases are different in some countries. Fifthly, the nature of the proof result shall not change the aim of proof, but may change the standard of proof. For example, in criminal cases, the standard of proof may be different for guilty verdicts and non-guilty verdicts. In summary, the aim of judicial proof sets the direction of judicial activities with some ideal colors, while the standard of judicial proof sets the criteria for judicial activities with certain realistic values. In specific cases, the aim of proof may not be achieved, but the standard of proof must be satisfied in one way or the other.

6.3.1 The Aim of Judicial Proof is to Pursuit the Objective Truth

Indeed, in specific cases, the aims of each proof are not the same exactly. Someone's proof is in order to make the facts of the case clear for others, or for themselves. Someone's proof is in order to clarify the facts of the case happened objectively, or clarify their own claims even fictional. But, as a proof activity with legal significance, the judicial proof also has the goal of surpassing the individual goal, unity and 'ought to be'. Therefore, the aim is not for individual behavior particularly, but the goal pursued necessarily by the abstract judicial proof activities, the united goals for both self-oriented proof and others-oriented proof.

The aim of judicial proof is to clarify the facts of the case so that the judicial authorities could apply the law correctly. The fact here should be objective fact, or the goal is objective truth. We could not define the goal as identifying legal fact clearly, because legal fact is just the result of judicial proof. In the process of judicial proof, especially at the beginning of collecting evidence, if investigators or others concerned even do not clear the nature of the case, it is inappropriate to request them to identify the legal facts. What the legal facts is even difficult to determine, naturally it could not be said the goal of proof is to identify the legal facts. Moreover, taking the legal truth as the goal for guiding investigation is easy to lead to collecting evidence subjectively and unilaterally. That also violate the principle of objectively comprehensive collecting evidence. In short, the epistemology of dialectical materialism requires us to regard the objective reality as the aim of judicial proof.

The aim of proof could show the direction of the proof behavior, and it also has a driving force of the proof behavior. We should not deny or ignore the guidance function and direct function of the objective truth for judicial proof activities. However, the aim's effect is mainly shown in the process of behavior, but may not always be as the result of behavior in reality. In some cases which are simple and have the evidences completely, the result of proof may be consistent with the actual situation completely. But in most cases, the result of proof has a certain error with the actual situation.

The aim of proof should be unified in all kinds of cases, as well as in every stage of the each case. So, the goal of judicial proof is 'unified'. Whether in the criminal proceedings or in the civil proceedings, whether in the investigation stage or in the trial stage, the aim of judicial proof should identify the objective real situation clearly. We could not say, the aim of the proof standard in the criminal procedure is to pursuit the objective reality, and the aim of the civil procedure is to pursuit legal reality. We could not say either the aim of investigation stage is to pursuit objective reality or the aim of the trial stage is to pursuit legal reality. We could not claim, in serious criminal cases, the aim of proof must be the strictly objective truth, but in minor criminal cases, the aim can be proved to be loose legal truth. The aim is just the aim, whatever any cases, the aim should be unified and continual. Otherwise it will enter the misunderstanding of pragmatism. This is the 'unified' on the aim of judicial certification.

6.3.2 The Standard of Judicial Proof Belongs to the Legal Truth

Although the standard of proof has certain guidance to the proof behavior, but its main function is to regularize the result of proof. Similarly, the legal facts are not the aim of behavior, but the result of action. In other words, the legal truth is not the truth perused by the judicial activities, but the achieved one necessarily in the judicial activities. So, the laws should provide and regulate the realistic standard of proof for the judicial activities.

6.3.3 The Standard of Judicial Proof is Not Equal to the Criterion for Testing the Truth[11]

Dialectical materialism believes the practice is the sole criterion for testing the truth. So, some scholars point out the standard of judicial proof must be tested through the practice. When discussing this question, we need to answer first: is judge's judgment on each evidence a truth? Is judge's decision a truth?

In philosophy, the truth is a belief, principle or theory which is fully accurate or true. It is a recognition which reflects correctly the rules of the objective world and the human society. However, not all correct recognition can be called "the truths". For example, Tom said he saw a magpie when he went out in the morning; Dick said he was a monitor in childhood; Harry said he heard cross-talk of Hou Baolin, a famous Chinese cross-talk master, on radio last evening. These statements are all correct recognition, but we should not put them into the category of the truth. The truth is not only a correct recognition, but also a recognition about principles or rules, a belief or guiding theory for human activities. In this sense, we emphasize the practice is the criterion for testing the truth. For example, the objective truth theory and the legal truth theory are both guiding theories on judicial proof activities, so they belongs to the recognition in the level of the truth. Which one is correct? Which one is good for guiding judicial activities? These questions shall be answered with the test of judicial practice. However, it is difficult to say that the recognition of Tom, Dick or Harry is the truth, and such recognition is difficult to be tested by practice.

The meaning of the word 'practice' in Chinese is to implement and to fulfill a work. It extends to the activities for the humans to reform the nature or the society actively, such as social practice and production practice.[12] According to the points of dialectical materialist, practice is the basis of human recognition and the source of acquiring knowledge. Practice includes people's own direct practice, as well as indirect practice of predecessors or others. When we say that the practice is the criterion for testing truth, we mean that any belief, theory or principle shall be tested by practice.

Practice is the criterion for testing truth, it does not mean that practice is the standard of all people's recognition. Generally speaking, people's recognition about past events cannot be tested by practice. For example, how will Tom's statement be tested by practice? Even if there is other evidence to prove its correctness, we cannot

---

[11]The Chinese word here is *Zhenli*, the fundamental truth in phylosophy. There was a well-known debate about the criterion for testing the truth in China in late 1970s. The conclusion of the debate was that practice should be the only criterion for testing the truth, which cleared the way for the "Reform and Open-up" policy in China.

[12]See Luo (1988), *Cihai* (1979).

say that it is tested by the practice. So, we could not put the practice equated with objective reality. We are convinced that certain judgment is in line with the objective reality, but this is not necessarily the result of practice testing.

Practice is the criterion for testing truth, which is mainly concerned with the outcome of the forward thinking. For reverse thinking, especially for those unable reproduced 'historical events', the practice is unable to test. For example, what is the cause of the 1911 Revolution of China? We may make a judgment that the cause is serious corruption of the government of Qing Dynasty. However, we cannot test this judgment with practice, because we cannot recreate the historical process and get a conclusion whether Qing Dynasty would not collapse if the corrupt was not serious.

Although modern science technology is quite developed, it is still a fantasy for human beings to travel through a 'time tunnel' back to the past. When hearing cases, the judge could not perceive the facts directly that happened in past. The only thing they can do is to find the case facts through a variety of evidence. In fact, the judge's fact finding is the same as Tom's, Dick's and Harry's. It is not the truth, and is difficult to test by practice.

Someone may say that it depends on whether the case facts is consistent with the objective reality. It is a truth if it is in conformity with the objective reality. However, this argument makes people feel a bit far-fetched, and it is hard to be put into practice. In a case, the objective event is hard to replay, and the facts happened in the past cannot be reproduced. Since it cannot be replayed, it cannot be tested by practice certainly.

We should not debase the concept of the truth. If we rose all trifles known by people to the height of the truth, we would desecrating the truth. Litigants' statements about the case and judge's recognition about the case is not in the category of the truth, and there is no way for them to be tested by the practice. Practice is the criterion for testing the truth, but it is not the standard for judicial proof.

6.3.4 The Unified Aim and the Diversified Standard in Judicial Proof

As mentioned earlier, the aim of proof may not be achieved in every cases, but the standard of proof must be satisfied in all cases. The aim of judicial proof may have a certain ideal and abstractness, while the standard must have reality and operability. The aim of judicial proof should be unified in the various cases and in different litigation stages of each case, while the standard of proof could be different according to different cases and different litigation stages. So, the aim of judicial proof has a nature of 'unify', and the standard of judicial proof has the nature of diversity.

The aim of judicial proof is to identify the case facts, so that the judiciary organ apply the law correctly. Author think that case facts should be objective, or, the goal pursued by the judicial activities is objective truth. We could not define the aim of judicial proof as identifying the legal facts, because legal facts are in terms of the result of judicial proof. In the process of judicial proof, especially in the initial stage of collecting evidence, investigators or other relevant people could not clear the nature of the case, it is inappropriate for asking them to identify the legal facts. It is still difficult to determine what the legal facts is in this case, so it's naturally that we could not say the proof aim is to identify the legal fact. Moreover, the evidence investigation with the aim of legal truth can easily lead to subjectivity and unilateralism in collecting evidence, and also offend the principle of comprehensive evidence collection objectively. In all, the dialectical materialism epistemology asked us to take the objective truth as the aim of the judicial proof. And furthermore, whether in the criminal litigation or in the civil litigation, whether in the investigation stage or in the trial stage, the aim of judicial proof should be to clear the objective reality of the case. This is the 'unified' on the aim of judicial certification.

When determining the standard of proof, people should not only consider the needs for proof, but also the value of other goals, such as the realization of judicial fairness, the protection of the human rights, the improvement of judicial efficiency, and the reduction of litigation cost. So, the standard of judicial proof should be practical and feasible. Legal truth exactly expresses the legitimacy and rationality that the standard of proof requires.

6.4 The System of the Standards of Judicial Proof

The standards of proof should be achieved in each case, but there may be some difference in different cases and at different litigation stages. For example, the standards may be different in criminal cases and civil cases; the standards may be different at the stage of investigation and the stage of trial; the standards may be different for conviction and correcting a wrongful conviction.[13] In this regard, the trial of O.J. Simpson, a famous American football player, could provide some beneficial enlightenment.

In October 1995, O.J. Simpson was acquitted in the so-called "trial of the century". There is no doubt that the race problem plays a very important role, or as some experts pointed out that defense lawyers use the "race card" excellently. But many people have misunderstanding that the jury believed O.J. Simpson is not the murderer for the jury's innocent verdict. Actually, among the twelve-member jury, acquitted reasons are not same. Among them, someone think he is the murderer, because the evidence may be fabricated by police, so he was declared not guilty; some people think that the evidence is not reliable, since the evidence is fake, and other evidences are hard to make sure; others believe O.J. Simpson was innocent; someone with race sympathized thought he was innocent. Above all, the innocent verdict in law is: The prosecution's evidence could not prove O.J. Simpson guilty with 'beyond a reasonable doubt', so the jury decides O.J. Simpson may not be the murderer. In other words, although the jury believe O.J. Simpson may be the murderer, but according

[13]See He (2012).

to the common sense of reasonable doubt, they could only announce his innocence as long as they have doubt in their heart.

In the subsequent civil trial, based on the same evidence, another jury decided he is "guilty". Why O.J. Simpson won in criminal procedure but lost in civil one? The main reason is the standard is different between civil trial and criminal trial. The standard of criminal trial is 'beyond a reasonable doubt', while the standard of civil trial is preponderance of evidence. If explained by percentage, the proof standard in criminal cases is >90%, but the other is >51%. In general words, in a criminal trial, the prosecution must prove O.J. Simpson is the murderer undoubtedly. But in a civil trial, the plaintiff should only prove the guilty possibility is more than the innocent possibility.

From current law regulations, there is no difference between the proof standard of criminal and civil lawsuits in China. The same standard is "proof with reliable and sufficient evidences." But in legal theory and judicial practice, people generally think that the proof standard of criminal cases should be higher than the one of civil cases. Even in criminal proceedings, at different stages, such investigation stage, examination prosecution stage and trial stage, the standard also be different. Generally speaking, the standard of examination prosecution stage is higher than the one of investigation stage; the trial stage's is higher than the examination prosecution stage's. In the cases that investigation organ submit for examination and prosecution, it is normal that some of the cases failed the prosecution, because of the evidences meet the standard of investigation stage, may be not meet the prosecution's, *vice versa*.

Different object, different standard of proof. Such as, the proof standard of substantive law is higher than procedural law's; the proof standard of main facts or the facts of the criminal form are higher than the secondary facts. The law in some nations and regions divided the proof standard to strict proof and hermeneutic proof. The former refers to achieve high degree, needs higher proof standard, such as the facts of the case are clear and the evidence is reliable and sufficient" or a proof "beyond a reasonable doubt." The latter refers to lower proof standard, such as the proof with "preponderance of evidence".

As mentioned above, the aim of judicial proof is to identify clearly the objective facts and to explore the objective truth; the standard of judicial proof is using evidence to proof the legal facts that specific cases need to identify, and achieve the truth in a legal sense. According to our nation's current legal provision, the standards of the three kind of litigation seem to be no distinction, are all "proof with reliable and sufficient evidences". But starting from the basic spirit of the law, we could make different explanation about these three kind of standards.

Specially, the proof standard of civil litigation and administrative litigation could be interpreted as "preponderance of evidence," that means on the basis of the evidence examination of reality and proving ability on both sides, evaluating both side's result probability, the probability of dominants would win or would obtain a favorable judgment. There are similar provisions in PECP. For example, Article 73 provides: "Where both parties concerned produces contradicting evidences to prove a same fact but neither has enough evidence to rebut the evidences of the other party, the people's court shall determine which evidences are obviously more forceful than the other evidences by taking the case into consideration, and shall affirm the evidences that are more forceful." The proof standard of criminal litigation could be interpreted as "proof beyond a reasonable doubt".

Article 53 of CPL makes a further explanation about 'unquestionable and sufficient evidences: (1) all facts for convincing and sentencing are supported by evidence; (2) all evidence used to decide a case has been verified under legal procedures; and (3) all facts found are beyond reasonable doubt based on all evidence of the case. That is to say, all evidence of the prosecution able to prove prosecutor accused of criminal facts beyond a reasonable doubt, is the proof standard which have to be achieved in making a guilty verdict in criminal litigation.

In fact, "proof with preponderance of evidence", "proof beyond a reasonable doubt", and "proof with reliable and sufficient evidence" are not contradictory, because they are statements from different angles. The standard of "reliable and sufficient evidence' is in terms of evidence assessment, while the standards of proof with "preponderance of evidence" and proof "beyond a reasonable doubt" are in terms of facts ascertaining. Although the proof standard of "beyond a reasonable doubt" is higher than the proof standard of "preponderance of evidence," both are based on reliable evidence. In civil litigation and administrative litigation, it will be considered by law as sufficient when the proof reaches the level of "preponderance of evidence", while in criminal litigation, it will be so considered when reaching the level of "beyond a reasonable doubt".

In the process of criminal procedure, not only the final verdicts needs to have proof standard, but in the investigation phase, examination and approval detention phase, examination and prosecution and public prosecution phase should have corresponding proof standards. Here, we could draw lessons from foreign practices. For example, in the United States, some scholars divided the proof standard into seven levels: (1) The lowest level is 'on significant proof', which means suspicion without factual support, applying to the investigation not involving restraints upon the person; (2) Reasonable basis, namely there is the possibility of crime, applying to temporary restraint that restricts personal liberty, such as 'stop and frisk'; (3) Probable cause, believe that there is a substantial likelihood that the individual committed a crime, applying to deciding on arresting offenders; (4) Preponderance of evidence, which is based on all of the evidence presented, that it is more likely than not, that the individual committed a crime, applying to preliminary hearing bindover, etc.; (5) *Prima facie* case, based on prosecution evidence only that individual is so clearly guilty and to eliminate any reasonable doubt, used in some jurisdictions for issuance of indictment; (6) Proof beyond a reasonable doubt, considering all of the evidence presented, that individual is so clearly guilty as to eliminate any reasonable doubt, applying to conviction for crime; (7) Absolute proof of guilt, believing so certain that defendant is guilty as to eliminate even unreasoned doubts, is the proof standard that the criminal lawsuit could not reach generally, and is the standard considered by some people which should be achieved in death penalty cases.[14]

[14]See He (1997).

In accordance with the relevant provisions of the current criminal procedure law in china, the standard of investigation is 'If it believes that there are facts of a crime and criminal responsibility should be investigated'; the standard of arrest is 'there is evidence to support the facts of a crime'; concluding investigation to transfer to initiate a prosecution, initiating public prosecution, and pronouncing guilty, the standards of all of which are 'unquestionable and sufficient evidence'. Since these rules are abstract, it is difficult to grasp in practice, and hard to find out the difference between the proof standard of each litigation stage. We suggest dividing the proof standard of criminal litigation to four levels: the standard of investigation is 'reasonable criminal suspect', the arrest's is 'advantage probability proof'; the proof standard of investigation conclusion and initiation of public prosecution is 'clear and convincing evidence proof' (considering the relationship between investigation organ and public prosecution organ, it is suitable that the proof standard of investigation and public prosecution are the same); the proof standard of pronouncing guilty is 'proof beyond a reasonable doubt'. If explained by probability, the four levels are 40, 51, 80, 90%. Admittedly, these numbers just illustrate the difference between the above standards, but are not strict statistics and calculation results. In specific cases, using these standards correctly needs to strengthen and standardize the judicial standard.

In summary, the standard of judicial proof can be described at three levels. The first level is the nature of the standard. Does the standard belong to objective truth or legal truth? This is the most abstract description of the standard. The second level is the legal expression of the proof standards, namely, what language should be used to reach the degree and level of judicial proof. Laws in different countries have various expressions for the standard of proof, such as the evidence is reliable and sufficient, the proof beyond a reasonable doubt, and the proof with preponderance of evidence. The third level is specific, clear, operable proof standard. The standards at this level may include specific standards for different kinds of cases, and specific standards for different types of evidence. This is the proof standard with the most practical value and the most difficult one to set. I shall make more discussions thereon in Chap. 11.

References

Chen, Yiyun (ed.). (2000). *Study of Evidence*, 2nd ed, 117, Beijing: China Renmin University Press.

Cihai. 1979. *Language and Vocabulary*, revised edition. Shanghai: Shanghai Lexicographical Publishing House (5), 1071–1072.

Fan, Chongyi. 2000. *Frontier Study on Criminal Evidence, Evidence Forum*, vol. 1, 206. Beijing: China Procuratorate Press.

Guo, Xinyang. 2011. *Analysis of Misjudged Criminal Cases*, 213–222. Beijing: China Renmin Public Security University Press.

He, Jiahong (ed.). 1997. *Legal English*, 339–340. Beijing: Law Press China.

He, Jiahong. 2012. Analysis of Famous Cases on the Standard of Proof in Wrongful Convictions. *China legal science* (1).

Jiang, Wei (ed.). 1999. *Evidence Law*. Beijing: Law Press China, 117.

Liang, Zhiping (ed.). 1994. *Cultural Explanations of Law*. Beijing: SDX Joint Publishing Company, 80.
Luo, Zhufeng (ed.). 1988. *The Great Chinese Dictionary*. Shanghai: the Great Chinese Dictionary Publishing House, 1988, Vol. 3, p. 1620.
Zhang, Jicheng. 2001. *Logical Introspection of 'Legal Truth' and 'Sole Proof', Evidence Forum*, vol. 2, 416–427. Beijing: China Procuratorate Press.
Zhou, Yongkun. 2007. A Jurisprudence Analysis on the High Building Falling Objects Case. *Legal Science Monthly* (5).

Chapter 7
The Concept of Presumption

Contents

7.1 Case Illustration

In the city Changsha, in the middle of the night, a man riding a bicycle was checked by a policeman, and be found a naked female that has been dead in the sack from the backseat of the bicycle. The man explained that he saw the sack from a dump, and thought that there are some valuable things and wanted to take it home. He knew nothing about the female corpse. The policeman didn't believe his "nonsense", then took the man back to the public security bureau. After a series of "matches", the man confessed that he had raped and killed the female. But, later in the court, the man withdrew his confession and claimed that he had been tortured. After talking to the staff members of the detention house, the judge found that the defendant might have been tortured. In this case, besides the confession and the evidence of that the defendant rode a bicycle with a female corpse at that midnight, the public prosecutor could not provide any other evidence to prove the murder and rape.[1]

[1] See He (2000).

J. He, *Methodology of Judicial Proof and Presumption*,
Masterpieces of Contemporary Jurisprudents in China,
https://doi.org/10.1007/978-981-10-8025-8_7

According to the evidence in this case and the common sense of people, the defendant is probably the murderer. But, anyone who has the normal thinking ability will not deny that it is still possible that the defendant is innocent. In other words, although it feels ridiculous about the statement that the defendant said about 'the sack from the dump', we also dare not say there is no such ridiculous person in the world absolutely. Most importantly, the public prosecutor's evidence could not fully prove that the defendant is the man who raped and killed the woman. Faced with this situation, how should the court make a proper judgment? Could the judge use presumption to find the fact in the case?

During my study at Northwestern University School of Law in the early 1990s, I attended courses in evidence law given by two renowned evidence law professors in the United States and China. One was my SJD supervisor Professor Jon R. Waltz; the other was Professor Ronald J. Allen. I once talked with Professor Waltz on presumptions. Professor Allen mentioned in his class that the rule of presumption was a very important and complex theoretical issue in evidence law. However, Professor Waltz simply used a very short chapter to discuss presumptions in his book *Criminal Evidence.* After hearing my question, Professor Waltz humorously responded, "One basic ability of a professor of law is to complicate simple questions. But, presumptions were not that complex, especially in criminal proceedings". I accepted his view and therefore adopted a "simplistic" attitude towards presumptions.[2] However, this "simplistic" approach did not make the knowledge condensed or understandings clear as I had expected. Then I had to admit presumptions were indeed very complex, although some "man-made" factors contribute to the formation process of this complexity. Later, I learned that Professor John H. Wigmore, a well-known professor in the history of Northwestern University School of Law and a more influential jurist in evidence law, looked upon presumptions as the "bats of law". Therefore, I decided to try to use my way "to complicate the simple issues" to revisit the mysterious "bats of law" and to start with the concept of presumption.

7.2 The Concept of Presumption in English

As a legal term, the concept of presumption in Chinese is introduced from western languages, majorly in English, which gives this concept some trace of translation. On the one hand, we learn, through this concept, the theory of presumptions in evidence law of common law countries; on the other hand, we also have introduced the confusion of presumption theories. As the saying goes, the very English that introduces the concept is what confuses the concept. Therefore, before defining the concept of presumptions in Chinese, we must first and foremost clarify the concept of presumptions in English.

In English, even the authoritative professional literature do not provide a uniform definition of presumptions. Based on the sources of these authoritative literature, we

[2]See He (2001), He and Liu (2004, pp. 271–277).

can, nonetheless, "presume" the validity of these definitions to some extent. This cautious "presumption" is also one of the prerequisites of the presumption problems I discuss in this chapter. In *Oxford Advanced Learner's English-Chinese Dictionary*, a presumption includes the meaning of "supposition", that is, "Presumption: suppose something to be true or the case".[3] Although Bryan A. Garneris the chief editor of both *A Dictionary of Modern Legal Usage* and *Black's Law Dictionary*, the definitions of presumptions given by the two dictionaries differ from one another. In *A Dictionary of Modern Legal Usage* it says "Presumption: a judicially applies prediction of factual or legal probability",[4] and in *Black's Law Dictionary* "Presumption: a legal inference or assumption that a fact exists, based on the known or proven existence of some other fact or group of facts".[5]

In addition, law scholars in common law countries give various interpretations of presumptions. For example, Professor Waltz held that "presumption is an inference of the existence or nonexistence a fact which arises from proof of other basic, underlying facts".[6] Professor Allen believed that "the presumption is the term that courts and commentators use to describe and define a set of rules of inferential process of proof, that is, a specific, created legal relation between a proved fact A, which leads to a presumed fact, and the presumed fact B…There also exist some inferential relations between a presumed fact and the fact that leads to such a presumed fact. For instance, in the case of presumed death, the proved fact A (the whereabouts not heard from for seven years) provides some supporting inferences for the fact B (the death). In some cases, those who can determinate facts rationally could guarantee the fact B based on the fact A even without presumptions".[7] Professor John Smith at the University of Nottingham argued that "presumptions are rules whereby on proof of a certain fact or facts, say A and B, the trier of fact either must, or may, presume the existence a further fact, C".[8]

Stripping away the linguistic embellishment of the above definitions, we can find that the use of keywords include suppose, prediction, inference, assumption, inferential process of proof and so on. Then, what are the similarities and differences between the keywords that define presumptions? When answering this question, we had better temporarily put aside Chinese translation of the words in dictionaries, and understand them in English, for the translation of a word is not necessarily equivalent the original. In English, suppose refers to "accept as true or probable"[9];

---

[3]Presume: suppose something to be true. Presumption: presuming something to be true or the case. See *Oxford Advanced Learner's English-Chinese Dictionary* (Fourth edition), Beijing: The Commercial Press, 1997, p. 1166.

[4]Presumption: a judicially applies prediction of factual or legal probability. Garner (1995).

[5]Presumption: a legal inference or assumption that a fact exists, based on the known or proven existence of some other fact or group of facts. Garner (1999).

[6]Waltz (1983).

[7]Allen et al. (2006).

[8]Smith (1995).

[9]Suppose: accept as true or probable. See *Oxford Advanced Learner's English-Chinese Dictionary*, p. 1536.

prediction, "say in advance that something will happen"[10]; inference, "reach an opinion from facts or reasoning"[11]; assumption, "accept something as true before there is proof".[12] In addition, when explaining presumptions and the above mentioned words in English people often use another two words, namely, "reasoning" and "deduction". Reasoning refers to "act or process of using one's power to think, understand, form opinions; arguments produced when doing this"[13] and deduction means "reasoning from general principles to a particular case".[14]

After clarifying the meanings of these keywords, we are back to the definitions of presumptions with the following understandings. First of all, the word, presumption, in English has a certain degree of fuzziness or ambiguity and people can use it to express an assumption or supposition, an inference or inferential process of proof, or even a prediction. Secondly, presumptions are related to how people perceive facts; therefore, be it a hypothetical assumption or an inferential prediction, it is aimed to know the facts. Finally, the original meaning of presumptions is the presupposition of facts whereas in the legal context people tend to emphasize that the foundation of such a presupposition is the relation between facts or the probabilities of occurrence. Possibly, under such complex context, Professor Wigmore came up with the "bats of law" to refer presumptions. So far, I have vaguely felt that presumption in English do not seem to have exactly the same meaning as *tuiding* (presumption) in Chinese. But this is only my perceptual knowledge waiting to be conceptualized after further verification of the concept of *tuiding* in Chinese.

7.3 The Concept of Presumption in Chinese

It is not easy to find the origin of *tuiding* in Chinese. Yet, the word was used in the early 20th century. For instance, one essay in *Northern and Southern Dialects Mixed*, a prose collection by Lu Xun, is titled "From the feet of Chinese women, it is presumed (*tuiding*) *inferred* that Chinese are not mediocre and that Confuses has stomach diseases". In this case, *tuiding* means "speculative judgment" or "inferred affirmation". In addition, *tuiding* also has the meaning of "recommended decision",[15] but it does not belong to the contents of this discussion.

---

[10]Predict: say in advance that something will happen. See *Oxford Advanced Learner's English-Chinese Dictionary*, p. 1156.

[11]Inference: reach an opinion from facts or reasoning. See *Oxford Advanced Learner's English-Chinese Dictionary*, p. 762.

[12]Assumption: accept something as true before there is proof. See *Oxford Advanced Learner's English-Chinese Dictionary*, p. 74.

[13]Reasoning: act or process of using one's power to think, understand, form opinions; arguments produced when doing this. See *Oxford Advanced Learner's English-Chinese Dictionary*, p. 1241.

[14]Deduction: reasoning from general principles to a particular case. See *Oxford Advanced Learner's English-Chinese Dictionary*, p. 372.

[15]See Luo (1990).

In mainland China, law scholars began introductory study on presumptions in late 1980s. In *Study of Evidence* published in 1983, a tryout textbook for tertiary law education, the editors did not discuss presumptions in particular but only gave a brief introduction to the basic concepts of "presumption of guilt" and "presumption of innocence", categorizing "anyone who recently occupies stolen objects shall be presumed to be the thief" in Anglo-American law into "presumption of guilt".[16]

Study of Evidence, chief-edited by Professor Chen Yiyun was one of the earliest textbooks that introduced the theory of presumptions. With its first edition published in 1991, the textbook dedicated a chapter to issues of presumptions. Regarding the concept of presumptions, editors wrote "in legal contexts, the term 'presumption' refers to assumption and inference…the presumption in law is a term explicitly provided in law, that is, the confirmed existence of a fact guarantees the existence of another presumed fact without proof…Presumptions are 'presumptions' defined in law, which means based on certain facts it is presumed that other facts exist in accordance with the law." This textbook maintained the view in its second edition published in 2000.[17]

Other following textbooks in the field of evidence or evidence law generally discuss presumption in particular and give a similar description of its concept. For instance, Professor Jiang Wei believes that "the so-called presumption is a principle of evidence that the existence of an unknown fact is inferred from a known fact, and parties are allow to rebut the existence of the unknown fact by providing evidence in accordance with provisions of law or practice in courts".[18] Professor Fan Chongyi considers that "presumption means inferences of existence of certain facts in accordance with the law, and such inferences are established based on other foundations or facts".[19] Professor Bian Jianlin argues "presumption refers to a principle of evidence that that in accordance with provisions of law or practice in courts, the existence of an unknown fact is inferred from a known, basic fact, and parties are allow to rebut the existence of an unknown fact by providing contrary evidence".[20] Although we can see vaguely the influence of the concept of "presumption" in English and differences between the above statements, these statements basically maintain the meaning of *tuiding* in Chinese, that is, inference and determination.

However, the definition of concept is abstract and minimalist. Though the definitions of presumption are similar in Chinese scholars' works, some notable differences and inconsistencies occur when it comes to specific usages of the term. For example, Professor Chen Yiyun thinks *tuiding* (presumption) and *nizhi* (legal fiction) are two different concepts, and shall not be confused; such phrases as regarded as and seen as belong to the scope of *nizhi* rather than *tuiding*.[21] Professor Bian Jianlin also

---

[16]Wu (1983).

[17]Chen (1991, 2000).

[18]Wei (1999, pp. 178–181).

[19]Fan (2001, p. 252).

[20]Bian (2000, pp. 370–371).

[21]See Chen (2000, p. 179).

holds that view.[22] However, Professor Jiang Wei believes that there is a connection between *nizhi* and *tuiding*. The phrase of regarded as and other terms are often used in "inferential fictions" in order to determine the declaration of will of parties in accordance with law.[23] Professor Fan Chongyi largely agree with Professor Jiang.[24] In addition, some scholars bring paradoxical concepts when introducing presumption. For example, some scholars define that presumption refers to "inferring unknown facts based upon the basic, known ones" and "involving two kinds of facts". They also define that presumption includes direct presumption, which means assumptions of existence of a fact without any factual premise, that is, without depending on any basic facts, such as "presumption of innocence".[25] If presumptions consist of basic facts and presumed facts, how can a direct presumption be called presumption without the basic fact? In order to get rid of the embarrassment of this paradox, some scholars have to say "direct presumption is not a real presumption".[26]

The above discussion just shows differences between "presumption" in English and *tuiding* in Chinese. We have become accustomed to translate "presumption" in English into *tuiding* in Chinese for years, and have consciously or unconsciously believed that the two words are equivalent to each other. Through careful comparison, we can see that presumption and *tuiding* are not completely identical. In English, the basic meaning of presumption is "pre-assumption", whereas in Chinese, the basic meaning of *tuiding* is "inference and determination". Therefore, the usage of presumption in English is appropriate whereas it is not very precise to transplant it into *tuiding* in Chinese. For example, the presumption of innocence is a logical, precise expression in English, for it refers to "presumed innocent until proved guilty"; however, the translated Chinese counterpart is not that appropriate, because we cannot say that "the charged is innocent after the inference and determination". This is a problem. While we vaguely accept the concept of presumption in English, we cannot help using *tuiding* in Chinese to explain the meaning of presumption in English. Therefore, using "inference and determination" to explain "pre-assumption" inevitably brings linguistic confusions. It seems that Chinese "bats" are not identical with the English "bats".

Some American scholars also believe that presumption of innocence is different from evidentiary presumptions. The presumption of innocence is not what lawyers call an "evidentiary presumption". It does not arise from factual inferences, statistically supported, that accused persons are in fact more likely to be innocent than guilty.[27] Thus, we can translate the presumption of innocence into a better correspondence, "*wuzui jiading* (assumption of innocence)". Chinese scholars once used "*jiading* (assumption)" when introducing the principle of presumption of innocence. For example, Professor Wu used *jiading* when introducing the presumption of inno-

[22]See Bian Jianlin ed., p. 124.

[23]See Jiang Wei ed., pp. 125–126.

[24]See Fan Chongyi ed., pp. 258–259.

[25]See Bian Jianlin ed., p. 374.

[26]See Jiang Wei ed., p. 135.

[27]See He (2008).

cence in *Declaration of the Rights of Man and of the Citizen* of France (*Déclaration des droits de l'homme et du citoyen*) and Article 14 of *International Covenant on Civil and Political Rights* of UN.[28] Indeed, language is established by usage and I do not intend to change the established use of the term "wuzui *tuiding*" in Chinese. However, we must note the semantic differences between presumption and *tuiding*. When translating "presumption of innocence" into "wuzui *tuiding*", we should know that we just borrow its linguistic form of *tuiding*. It is certain that presumption of innocence is an important principle in criminal justice and criminal proceedings; however, presumption of innocence does not matter much in or belong to the issue of presumptions in the field of evidence law and judicial proof.

In Chinese, *tuiding* and *jiading* are two interrelated but different concepts. On the one hand, the similarity they share is that both of them are not factual findings in the strict sense; in other words, presumption of and assumption of facts are not necessarily the objective occurrences or facts, and tend to be "supposititious". On the other hand, there are some difference between *tuiding* and *jiading*. The former belongs to category of proof methods while the latter does not; the former could be the conclusion of argumentation while the latter can only serve as a precondition; the former requires facts as its basis while the latter does not; the former must be concerned with the truthfulness of conclusion while the latter may not or even can deliberately violate objective facts sometimes. Say, assuming (*jiading*) that human beings can live to 500 years, we have a chance to evaluate China's current policy of "reform and open-up" personally in a more objective and comprehensive way centuries later; assuming that human running speed can reach 500 km per hour, we need no cars or other vehicles and better protect the environment. Based on objective principles or common sense, these two assumptions are obviously not truthful, or even absurd; however, in order to illustrate an issue or present a point of view, one can come up with such assumptions without explaining their bases or explanation. However, one cannot make such presumptions (*tuiding*), for if it is made, it must be made on the basis of facts.

In judicial proceedings, the judge can determine facts or disputable facts based on presumptions rather than assumptions. Some Chinese scholars have made insightful remarks regarding the differentiation between presumptions and assumptions. For example, Professor Jiang Wei holds that "presumptions and assumptions are two completely different concepts" and that "contrary evidence can only disprove presumptions whilst only after verification assumptions can be affirmed, that is—there is no need to prove the truthfulness of presumptions or the falseness of assumptions".[29] The above assertions might be a little absolute, but it deserve researchers to explore and unearth its connotations.

In summary, the concept of presumption is confusing in evidence law, and the term may be misleading in theoretical studies as well as in judicial practices and legislative and judicial interpretations.[30] I believe that in order to define the concept

[28]See Wu Yusu ed., p. 98.

[29]See Jiang Wei ed., pp. 124–125.

[30]See Long (2008).

in Chinese, we need to clarify the relationship between *tuiding* and synonyms. In Chinese, the synonyms of *tuiding* include *tuiyan* (inference and discussion), *tuiming* (verifying and ascertaining), *tuizhi* (knowing through presuming), *tuili* (inferring), *tuice* (speculating the unknown based on the known), *tuiduan* (inferring and ascertaining), *tuilun* (reasoning) etc. Among the terms above, we need to clarify relations between *tuili, tuiduan, tuilun* and *tuiding* specially for this discussion. Although these concepts are within the scope of the logical thinking category, that is, deducing unknown facts from known ones, they have different semantic foci. In judicial proof, the focus of *tuili* is the thinking process of finding the facts; *tuiduan* is the thinking result of finding the facts; *tuilun* is the linguistic argumentation of the thinking process of finding the facts; *tuiding* is the inference method of finding the facts. During the thinking process, *tuili* is the foundation of the other concepts whereas *tuiduan*, *tuilun*, and *tuiding* are results or manifestations of *tuili*. Therefore, the comparison of these above concepts should be started from *tuili*.

Tuili, or inference, means that new recognition of facts is deducted from the known facts according to the rules of logic and practice. Inference is one common thinking method of investigating and proving cases in judicial activities, and also the significant magnification of mankind thinking power and intelligence. For example, a man was murdered. Investigators found that the man's wife committed adultery and therefore made the following inference:

Major premise: *The adulterate wife and her adulterer often conspire to murder the husband*;
Minor premise: *This wife committed adultery*;
Conclusion: *She and the adulterer probably conspired and killed her husband*.

Undoubtedly, the major premise belongs to the judgment of probable truth and so does the reasoning conclusion. However, based on such reasoning, investigators eventually identified the facts of the case and captured the criminal. Nonetheless, the court cannot make a judgment based solely on thus a reasoning, for other evidences are also needed.

In some contexts, the meanings of *tuiduan* and *tuili* are basically the same, which mean mental activities that infers unknown facts from known ones. Strictly speaking, however, there are still differences between the two words in semantic focus: the semantic focus of *tuiduan* is the process of thinking and activities; *tuiduan*, the conclusions or results of such thinking activity. In this sense, we can say that *tuiduan* is the judgment made on the basis of *tuili*. In the above case, investigators could make a judgment based on the above inferrence: the wife and the adulterer conspired and murdered the husband. As for the meaning of *tuilun*, we can explain it as argumentation based on the inference. If the investigators need to convince judicial officials to issue an arrest warrant after the wife and the adulterer, they have to use logical argumentation or to explain the inferring process. Thus, *tuiduan* and *tuilun* are both based on *tuili*. As for the thinking process, we must begin with *tui* (thinking process), and then we have *duan* (judgment) and *lun* (argumentation); there exist no *duan* and *lun* without *tui*. *Tui* is the precondition and *duan* and *lun* are the result and continuation. From the perspective of content and formality, *tuili* is the flesh and blood of *tuiduan* and *tuilun; tuiduan* and *tuilun* are manifestations of *tuili.*

Regarding semantic meanings, *tuiding* refers to judgments or determinations that are made on the basis of *tuili*. Here, the morpheme *li* refers to the accompanying relationship or the normal linkage between two facts. Thus, the existence of one fact tells the existence of another fact. In other words, due to the accompanying relationship between the fact A and B, the existence of B could be determined with the existence of B. For example, in many countries it is stipulated that a person who has been missing for a number of years (four years, five years or seven years) can be presumed dead by the court. The reasoning of the presumption is as follows:

Major premise: *Persons that have disappeared for years are generally died*;
Minor premise: *This person has disappeared for years*;
Conclusion: *This person is dead*.

Indeed, in this presumption the major premise is a judgment of probable truth; thus, the presumed fact may not be an objective fact. Yet, the whole presumption is reasonable, because the inferring it depends on is well established. Here we need to note that not every line of inferring can be transferred into a presumption although the inference is the basis of presumption. For instance, in the above case of "she and the adulterer conspired and killed her husband", the inference cannot become a presumption. Why? This is the question I will discuss below.

7.4 Three Progressive Criteria to Define the Concept of Presumption

When using the concept of presumptions, people may have deviations of the denotation of presumptions due to a hazy understanding of its connotation. There are two occasions when the denotation of presumptions is wrongly expanded. On the one hand, the concept is expanded to all reasoning activities that judges take when determining facts in particular cases, which is the case when the reasoning that "the wife and the adulterer conspired and murdered the husband" is treated as a presumption. On another, the concept is expanded to the all the legal provisions that involve probability or suppositional element, say, one may confuse the "presumption of innocence" with presumptions in judicial proof. The above two expansions involves other meanings that does not belong to the concept of presumption, which inevitably leads to confusion. Therefore, to step out of this confusion, it is necessary to define the criteria of the concept, which, I think, are three progressive criteria.

7.4.1 Presumptions as Determinations of Unknown Facts or Disputed Facts

Presumptions belong to the scope of judicial fact-finding, whose basic function is to provide judicial personnel with a convenient way to determine unknown facts or disputed facts. Although judicial personnel make presumptions according to the law, it does not necessarily mean that presumptions are meant to solve legal issues in specific cases. Since provisions on presumptions tell judicial officers how to determine unknown facts or disputed facts, a provision does not belong to the scope of presumptions if it does not involve fact-finding but deals only objects stipulated or how it stipulates objects. And this is the basic criterion to distinguish presumptions and legal fictions.

What we call a legal fiction is that law equals one fact as another different fact and gives them the same legal effect in particular cases. Paragraph 2 of Article 67 of CL provides, "if a criminal suspect or a defendant under compulsory measures or a criminal serving a sentence truthfully confesses his other crimes that the judicial organ does not know, his act shall be regarded as voluntary surrender". In order to encourage truthful confession, this article equals the action of giving a true confession as voluntary surrender. In Paragraph 3, Article 14 of *the Labor Contract Law of the PRC*, it is provided that "in case any employer fails to sign a labor contract in written form with a worker after the extension of one full year as of the date of start to use him, it shall be regarded that the employer and the worker has concluded a labor contract without a fixed period". This article equals failing to sign a labor contract in written form as signing a labor contract without a fixed period, thereby protecting the rights of laborers.

Both fictions and presumptions are used to describe the relation between two facts (A and B), yet with distinctions. The meaning of a fiction is that the law regard A as B, knowing A is not B whereas in a presumption, B with its existence unknown is presumed on the basis of A. In other words, in the case of a fiction, A and B are concrete facts that need no further identification; however, as for a presumption, since A is clear while B is not and in want of verification, the determination of B is established on A. Although "regard…as" might be used in either provision, the two concepts can be distinguished according to the contexts they are used. For example, Article 15 of GPCL stipulates that "if a citizen's habitual residence is not the same as his domicile, his habitual residence shall be regarded as his domicile". This is a legal fiction, for the habitual residence is not the domicile of a citizen but is regarded as the same in law. In addition, Article 66 of GPCL stipulates that "if a principal is aware that a civil act is being executed in his name but fails to repudiate it, his consent shall be deemed to have been given", which belongs to provisions of presumptions. Firstly, the fact A "a principal is aware that a civil act is being executed in his name but fails to repudiate it" is clearly verified; however, the fact B is not verified, that is—the person may or may not consent to the act. Secondly, on the basis of empirical rules, being "aware something but fails to repudiate it" is usually accompanied with consent. Thus, the action is presumed as under consent.

In addition, I do not agree with the notion of "inferential fiction". According to explanations of some scholars, the so-called "inferential fiction" refers to that "when the party does not make a declaration of will or when the declaration of will is ambiguous, it is regarded that the party makes such a declaration of will or that the ambiguous declaration of will has a specific meaning according to what is provided in law." Scholars who hold that view also admit the "notable difference between" the inferential fiction and other fictions and that "the inferential fiction is actually a kind of legal presumption".[31] I think that this kind of provisions belong to the category of presumption not fiction, as is stipulated in Article 66 of GPCL.

7.4.2 Presumptions as Indirect Fact Finding Based on Inference

As for cognitive activities, judicial personnel can adopt both direct and in direct determination approaches to unknown, or disputed facts. Presumptions belong to the indirect approach to find unknown facts; therefore the direct finding of unknown facts does not belong to the scope of presumptions. For instance, the "presumption of death" means that the court indirectly determine a person's death based on the person's disappearance of years; however, if the court directly determine a person's death with the person's body or the death certificate issued by the appropriate authority, the fact finding process does not belong to the scope of presumptions. In addition, the indirect fact finding relies on reasoning as the bridge connecting the facts, that is, the existence of some facts are derived based on certain existing facts according to rules of relations between object things. In this case, the known fact is called the "basic fact" or "given fact" (A); the other is called the "presumed fact" or "resulted fact" (B); the inference process bridges and connects the two facts (A and B) cognitively.

The foundation of presumptions generally manifests as the accompanying relationship or normal linkage between the basic fact (A) and the presumed fact (B). This relationship or linkage does not necessarily exist; therefore, the existence of (A) does not guarantee the existence of (B), that is, the existence of (A) may lead to (B) with a certain degree of probability. However, as for a criterion for establishing presumptions, a high degree of probability is required for such relationship or linkage, which means that (A) may lead to (B) with a high degree of probability. It is also a major criterion to determine whether a piece of reasoning can be transformed into a presumption. In other words, it is the main criterion to evaluate the reasonableness of an established presumption. For instance, as aforementioned, the reasoning that "the wife and the adulterer conspired and murdered the husband" cannot be transformed into a presumption, because the fact "the wife having adulterer" does not have an accompanying relationship of a high probability with "the murder of the husband". Nonetheless, there exists some degree of probability between the fact and the reasoning. In real life, some adulterous wife might murder her husband, say,

[31] See Jiang Wei ed., p. 126.

the wife Pan Jinlian and the adulterer Ximen Qing together murdered the husband Wu Dalang.[32] Yet, life experience also tells us that many other adultery wives will not murder the husband; in other words, the murder of the husband is necessarily committed by the adulterous wife. There is nothing wrong with using a reasoning approach to determine the investigation direction in a criminal case, for the aim is to determine suspects and collect evidence. However, if we add the accompanying relationship of a low probability as the basis for presumptions, determining that "any murdered husband is presumed to be killed by his unfaithful wife", it is prone to create miscarriage of justice as in the case of *Yang Naiwu and Bok Choy,* the case illustration in Chap. 2.

When defining presumptions, some scholars use such expression as the "existence or non-existence"[33] of the presumed fact. An inadvertent expression as it seems, it brings a question worthy of discussion: whether presumptions of alleged facts include negative conclusions. In other words, whether an inference of non-existence of a fact made based on some fact can be included in the scope of presumptions. On this issue, Professor Chen Jierong makes an unusual illustration that is equally inadvertent: "If the alibi of defendant has been checked out in a tort case, it can be regarded as the basic fact and leads to a presumption, i.e. a fact to be proved, that the defendant is not the tortfeasor".[34] It is a presumption when the defendant is regarded as the tortfeasor based on the basic facts; however, is it a presumption when the defendant is not regarded as the tortfeasor based on the basic facts? In criminal proceedings, the "alibi" is also a frequently-used means by the defense to prove the innocence of the defendant. Does such a confirmation also belong to the scope of presumptions? In the trial of civil or criminal cases the judge can be made the decision based on the proven facts of the defendant's alibi that the defendant is not the tortfeasor or the criminal, but this kind of judgments also belongs to the indirect fact finding based on the inference bridge. The inference process is as follows:

Major Premise: *The person who is not at the scene of the infringement is not the tortfeasor*;
Minor premise: *The defendant is not at the scene of the infringement*;
Conclusion: *The defendant is not the tortfeasor*.

The inference could be established; however, the above "presumption" brings me a question. The presumptions we often talk about are the inferences that the existence of a fact deduced from another fact, rather than the non-existence of a fact. Does the inferences with the negative conclusions belong to the scope of presumptions? My answer is no. As is known to all, the main function of presumptions is to reduce unnecessary proof processes and to avoid proof processes that are difficult to complete. It directly results in the exemption or reallocation of the burden of proof. Firstly, the inclusion of the negative concluded inferences into presumptions does not

---

[32]The three are well-known characters in Outlaws of the Marsh, one of the best classical novels in China.

[33]See Jon Waltz, p. 275; See Fan Chongyi (ed.), p. 252.

[34]Chen (2007).

help reduce unnecessary proof processes; secondly, the example inference is clear and simple, and not difficult to accomplish: it is not necessary to regard such an inference that "the person who was not at the scene of act did not commit the act" as a presumption; and finally, such an inference does not influence the exemption or reallocation of the burden of proof, because in such cases, the defendant does not bear the burden of proof. I realize that when answering the question, we are actually discussing into the third criterion of defining the concept—the most important one.

7.4.3 *Presumptions as Legal Rules of Fact Finding*

One important difference between the presumption which is a legal term, and reasoning, inference, argumentation and other concepts is that the concept of presumptions generates from legal provisions. It is worth noting the difference, for it answers the so-called problem of "the source of conceptual chaos of presumptions": whether the inferences of unknown facts made by the judge under empirical rules rather than legal previsions[35] belongs to the scope of presumptions. On this issue, scholars have different views although differences might be blurred due to wording and phrasing. For example, in the textbooks edited by Professor Jiang Wei and by Professor Bian Jianlin the question is not directly answered but it mentions that the inferences "made by the court according to empirical rules" are included in the concept of presumptions.[36] In the textbook edited by Professor Chen Yiyun, although presumptions as legal provisions is not explicitly mentioned, the related discussion apparently excludes those inferences and clearly defines that "presumptions are the presumptions of law".[37] In the textbook edited by Professor Fan Chongyi, it says, on the one hand, "the so-called presumptions refer to the inferences that existence of facts are made in accordance with law"; on the other, "presumptions can be made in accordance with law or empirical rules" and the inferences "that are adopted frequently in judicial practices though not stipulated by law" are also presumptions.[38] In fact, I did not entirely think through this question before. When defining the concept of presumptions I rashly included inferences not made in accordance with law and used ambiguous expressions such as "made by the judge" and "in accordance with certain rules".[39]

After much consideration, I believe it is necessary to define presumptions within the scope of law. Nonetheless, this is a man-made convention and may not be consistent with words used in other areas of social life. Yet, we need to reach the agreement

[35] Among the three concepts, reasoning, inference and argumentation, inference has the closest meaning and usage with presumption; therefore, I will take inference as example to compare it with presumption.

[36] See Jiang Wei ed., p. 124; See Bian Jianlin ed., pp. 370–371.

[37] See Chen Yiyun ed., pp. 178–181.

[38] See Fan Chongyi ed., pp. 252–257.

[39] See He Jiahong and Liu Pinxin, p. 275.

in the legal field. On the one hand, it can effectively avoid the usage confusion of the concept of presumptions, especially compared with concepts of inference and other words. As legal term, presumptions should be distinguished from inferences: inferences are the way of thinking of judicial personnel when determining facts; presumptions are inferences established in legal form. Some inferences can become presumptions while the other inferences, though not presumptions, can still be used independently by judicial personnel in specific cases. On the other hand, it also helps improve the rationality and normality of the establishment and use of presumptions. In judicial proceedings, the judicial personnel often employ presumptions to determine the facts of cases, and therefore the principle, methods and rules of presumptions lie in the core of evidence science. However, the judicial personnel can use various kinds of inferences, some of which can become presumptions while others cannot. Without a clear line between presumptions and inferences, questions of presumptions will tangle and mingle with those of inferences, which undermines further studies of presumptions. We need to exclude the inferences made by judicial personnel in specific cases before having a clearer look of the connotation and denotation of presumptions. It helps people to better focus on the rules of presumptions and the conditions when an inference can become a presumption, thereby contributing a more reasonable and standardized establishment and use of presumptions. Perhaps, as for countries that follow the common law tradition, it is difficult to draw a clear boundary between the two concepts. However, in China, it is possible and necessary to make the distinction. As a side note, the "law" we discuss include not only the laws (acts) and legislative interpretations but also judicial regulations and interpretations.

After clearly defining presumptions as legal rules, we enter into a more meaningful discussion: Why it is provided that some inferences become presumptions. Or, in other words, what kind of inferences can transform into presumptions. From a historical perspective, although we cannot accurately trace the formation of each of presumptions, we find that presumptions are generally growing out of the inferences made by judicial officers in individual cases, and then becoming the case law and even the law with the accumulation of experience and unified understandings. Take "the presumption of holding recently stolen property" for example, initially, a judge made the inference that someone who held recently stolen property and cannot give a reasonable explanation was the theft, which was acknowledged among and cited by other judges. Later, this inference became a rule that judicial personnel generally adopted. Therefore, it is a growing general pattern of formation that presumptions develop from individual experience of judges to a universal rule.

Then, why should individual experience of judges be elevated into a universal rule? I think it is mainly aimed to regulate the use of inferences by judiciary personnel when they determine unknown facts. In judicial activities, judges often face some difficult facts hard to prove. For example, a person who has disappeared for years, and the spouse intends to remarry or the family intend to inherit the property, requiring the judge to announce the person's death. However, there is no evidence to prove that a person's death. Faced with the problem, some judges make the judgment of death declaration; some may not. In addition, judges do not agree on the missing period before the death declaration: some judges insist on the missing period of ten years while others consider sever years or even four years; thus it leads to confusion in judicial decisions. In order to unify judicial decisions, the law must regulate such inferences made by judges and it is stipulated that a person who has disappeared for seven years is presumed dead. Thus, standardizing the behavior of making inferences in judicial process is the major goal of such provisions. However, behind this issue, we can also explore deeper, that is, why the law should regulate these behaviors, and under what circumstances the law may regulate these behaviors. In answering these questions, we have to consider requirements of both epistemology and axiology, for the intertwining of these two requirements perplexes the question of presumptions.

Through establishing presumptions, the law regulates behaviors of making inferences so as to ensure the correctness of judicial decisions. Inferences are cognitive activities, and their correctness remains a basic requirement in judicial adjudication. Since complex facts of various cases as well as the cognitive abilities, psychological tendencies and other subjective factors of judicial personnel may affect the results of inferences in judicial decisions, the inference activities by judicial personnel should be regulated by the law so that the judiciary can rightfully determine cases or disputable facts. To this end, when it comes to establishing some inferences as presumptions in legal form, we need to carefully examine the accompanying relationship between the basic facts and the inferred facts. In general, only when the accompanying relationship occurs with a high probability, can an inference become a presumption in law.

The second goal of regulating inference activities in law is to ensure the fairness of judicial decisions. The acceptance of judicial decisions in any society lies in the judicial justice. Judicial justice has two meanings: on the one hand, results of judicial decisions should reflect the spirit of justice; on the other, the judicial proceedings should follow the principle of justice and fairness in judicial activities. The former is called "substantive justice"; the latter, "procedural justice". Substantive justice should be established on correct understandings of case facts, which is in line with epistemological requirements of justice. Procedural justice, which helps ensure the substantial justice, has a distinctive function from determining case facts, that is, to equally protect the legitimate rights of the parties. Standardizing the inference activities of the judiciary in law manifests such kind of protection. In other words, the parties in the face of the same findings of fact will receive the same judicial determination.

The third goal of regulating inference activities by establishing presumptions in law is to ensure justice economy. As a settlement mechanism of social disputes, the administration of justice also need to consider cost and efficiency issues so as to minimize justice cost and maximize judicial benefits. Developing from individual inferences, the presumptions adopted by judicial personnel can not only reduce unnecessary repetitive proving activities and the cost of the administration of justice but also prevent facts difficult to prove from impeding the progress of the whole case, thereby improving justice efficiency.

In addition to the three goals aforementioned, when examining whether an inference can become a presumption, we also take the universality of a presumption in judicial activities. It means that presumptions are inferences that have the universal significance in judicial activities. Since some types of inferences which, though with a high probability, are only applied in specific cases, there is no need to include them into the scope of presumptions. For example, in my detective novel *Hanging Devels*,[40] Hong Jun, the protagonist, who is a lawyer, made the inference based on glass fragments on an overturned bench that Li Qingshan was murdered. That inference, though subtle and reliable, is lack of universality and thus cannot become a presumption.

In summary, presumptions are inferential findings of fact made by judicial personnel in accordance with legal rules. Clarification of the concept contributes to the making, examining and using of the rules related with presumptions, which is also the reason why we discuss the concept of presumptions. Thus far, Professor Wigmore's vivid description occurs to me once more "presumptions…may be looked on as the bats of the law, flitting in the twilight, but disappearing in the sunshine of actual facts".[41]

References

Allen, Ronald J., et al. 2006. *Evidence: Text, Problems, and Cases*, 3rd ed, 852, trans. Baosheng Zhang et al. Beijing: Higher Education Press.
Bian, Jianlin (ed.). 2000. *Evidence Law*. Beijing: China University of Political Science and Law Press.
Chen, Yiyun (ed.). 1991. *Study of Evidence*, 162–165. Beijing: China Renmin University Press.
Chen, Yiyun (ed.). 2000. *Study of Evidence*, 2nd ed. Beijing: China Renmin University Press.
Chen, Jierong. 2007. *Introduction to Evidence Law*, 242. Beijing: China Renmin University Press.
Fan, Chongyi (ed.). 2001. *Evidence Law*. Beijing: Law Press China.
Garner, Bryan A. (ed.). 1995. *A Dictionary of Modern Legal Usage*, 2nd ed, 689. Beijing: Law Press China.
Garner, Bryan A. (ed.). 1999. *Black's Law Dictionary*, 7th ed, 1203. Eagan: West Group.
He, Jiahong. 2001. On the Presumption of Judicial Proof. *Journal of National Procurators College* (2).
He, Jiahong (ed.). 2000. *Evidence Forum*, vol. 1, 7. Beijing: China Procuratorate Press.
He, Jianhong (ed.). 2008. *Legal English: American Legal System*, 4th ed, 299. Beijing: Law Press China.
He, Jiahong, and Pinxin Liu. 2004. *Evidence Law*. Beijing: Law Press China.
Long, Zongzhi. 2008. The Concept and Application of Presumptions. *Chinese Journal of Law* (1).
Luo, Zhufeng (ed.). 1990. *The Great Chinese Dictionary*, vol. 6, 673. Shanghai: The Great Chinese Dictionary Publishing House.
Smith, John. 1995. *Criminal Evidence*, 47. London: Sweet & Maxwell Limited.
Waight, P.K., and C.R Williams. 1998. *Evidence, Commentary and Materials*, 5th ed, 109. Australia: The Law Book Company Limited.
Waltz, Jon. 1983. *Criminal Evidence*, 2nd ed, 275. Chicago: Nelson-Hall Press.
Wei, Jiang (ed.). 1999. *Evidence Law*. Beijing: Law Press China.
Wu, Yusu (ed.). 1983. *Study of Evidence*, 98. Beijing: Qunzhong Publishing House.

[40]Published by the Penguin Group (Australia) in 2012.

[41]See Waight and Williams (1998, p. 109).

Chapter 8
The Categories of Presumption

Contents

8.1 Case Illustration

On 7th August 1985, Mr. and Mrs. Bamber, their adopted daughter Sheila and her twin sons all died from fatal gunshot wounds at the Bambers' residence: White House Farm. Police arrived on the scene after receiving a phone call from Jeremy Bamber, the Bambers' adopted son. Based on initial investigation of the scene, police determined that Sheila had killed her parents and her children and then shot herself. But among the family and friends at the funeral were two young people who did not believe the conclusions of the police investigation. They found at the scene of the crime a rifle silencer with traces of blood on it.

The police crime-lab analysis determined that the blood type on the silencer corresponded with the blood type of Sheila. Based on this finding, and on the forensic

J. He, *Methodology of Judicial Proof and Presumption*,
Masterpieces of Contemporary Jurisprudents in China,
https://doi.org/10.1007/978-981-10-8025-8_8

indicating that Sheila's arms were not long enough to have fired the rifle equipped with the silencer, the police believed that it was not a suicide and killing but a homicide with Jeremy as the suspect.

Some time later, Jeremy's girlfriend, Julie Mugford, gave a testimony that she believed Jeremy to be the murderer. On 2nd October 1986, Jeremy was put on trial for murder at the Chelmsford District Court. After the court hearing was concluded, the jury found Jeremy to be guilty of murder by a vote of ten to two. Then, the court sentenced him to life in prison with no parole for a minimum of twenty-five years.[1]

Jeremy steadfastly maintained his innocence and regularly filed appeals. At the beginning of 2011, his lawyers conducted their own investigation and evidence collection, leading them to note 'ten major reasons' why Jeremy's conviction should be overturned, including new evidence indicated that police had damaged the crime scene and new DNA analysis of the blood on the silencer. Though the results of the DNA analysis were uncertain, they indicated that there was a greater chance the blood was from the father, Mr. Bamber, than from his adopted daughter, Sheila.

The UK Criminal Cases Review Commission agreed to hear Bamber's appeal, and after initial examination on 11th February 2011 issued an 'interim decision' against referring the case to the court of appeals.[2] The Commission also gave the claimants three months to plead their case. On 15th April Bamber's lawyers applied to the Director of Public Prosecutions and the Independent Police Complaints Commission to demand the negatives of 198 photographs taken by the police of the crime scene during the year the crime was committed. On 13 May the Criminal Cases Review Commission permitted Bamber's lawyers to examine 406 photographs of the crime scene then in the custody of the Commission. They also announced that they would allow claimants to have two more months to plead their case. On 26th May Bamber's lawyers submitted their final legal opinion to the Commission, which sought to have the Commission pass the case to the Court of Appeals for retrial. Although the appeal was rejected, the Bamber team continues to fight for his innocence.[3]

---

[1]This author wrote an article about the Bamber case, based on a report in *True Detectives*, in late 1980s. See He (2009).

[2]The UK Criminal Cases Review Commission was created by the Criminal Appeal Act 1995 and began formal operations in 1997. Members of the Commission are appointed from among the private citizenry, but the Commission is publicly funded. The Commission has more than 80 staff workers, including lawyers, reporters and accountants. There are nine commissioners. Each case is reviewed by a review group comprised of three commissioners, with one person serving as chairman who listens to all opinions and implements necessary investigations before deciding whether to refer the case to the court of appeal for retrial. In April 2011, this author participated the *2011 Innocent Network Conference—an International Exploration of Wrongful Conviction* in Cincinnati, USA. During the conference, the author met John Weydon, a commissioner serving on the UK Commission. Mr. Weydon was the chairman of the review group for Jeremy Bamber's case.

[3]The narrative related above is based on accounts from British media sources including *The Guardian*, *The Telegraph* and *BBC*. According to an article, "Killer Jeremy Bamber in bombshell bid to be free after 27 years," written by Andy Gardner for Mirror News on Dec. 1, 2013, Jeremy Bamber has launched a fresh appeal against his convictions for murdering his family 27 years ago—citing "bombshell" new evidence.

Was the guilty verdict in this case wrongful? In other words, is Jeremy Bamber innocent? I have no way to answer with certainty, because the evidence includes some material that helps his case, and other things that damage it. Even though there may be evidence to show his guilt, there is also evidence clearing him of guilt. This is what we mean by uncertainty surrounding a conviction. As far as law enforcement is concerned, the facts of a case that occurred in the past are like 'the moon in the water'. The moonlight has an objective existence, but what investigators see is the image reflected and refracted. The water here refers to the evidence. Without evidence, law-enforcement officials have no way of determining the facts, but facts determined through evidence do not necessarily correspond to the objective facts. When the water is murky or choppy, the action of refraction and reflection distorts the image, sometimes so much so that the resulting image of the moonlight is totally different that the reality. Jeremy Bamber's case is a good example of this. The water here is especially turgid, which is to say, the evidence itself suffers from defects and uncertainty. First of all, there is no direct evidence to prove that he carried out the crimes. Second, the evidence is incomplete, and even features a mutually exclusive chain of evidence. Third, the blood-type findings are inconsistent, and so only introduce more uncertainty to the question of determining the perpetrator. Finally, there are many problems with the key pieces of evidence, including the testimony of Julie Mugford, and the questions whether it should be considered hearsay, or an opinion, and whether her she was the best character witness. The evidence does not eliminate the possibility that Jeremy is guilty of murder. Thus, there are two moonlight images in the water: in one, Jeremy is guilty, and in the other, he is not. Which one reflects the truth? We do not yet know, and we may never know.

In the course of Bamber's appeals and the subsequent re-examinations of his conviction, we can detect the signs of opposing parties at work: Bamber and his lawyers, who are trying to prove his conviction to have been wrongful; those others, represented primarily by the police, who take a negative attitude towards review of the case, and who have gone so far as to take steps to obstruct review, for example by refusing to willfully supply all the photographs to Bamber's lawyers. Whether or not he is innocent, it is in the interest of Bamber and his lawyers to try to prove the conviction was wrongful. And if the police have made mistakes, an affirmation of a wrongful conviction would negate their previous work, which would lead to a loss or degradation of their own interests.

8.2 Categories of Presumption in Anglo-American Law of Evidence

In the evidence law of Anglo-American legal systems, presumption poses a constant headache to scholars, for it is a little mess when used not only in itself, but also in its subordinate concept or category. To some extent, the latter may be more serious. For instance, the *Black's Law Dictionary* enumerates many subordinate concepts of presumption, such as presumption of fact or factual presumption and presumption of law or legal presumption; rebuttable presumption and irrebuttable presumption; mandatory presumption and permissive presumption; absolute presumption and conditional presumption; conclusive presumption and procedural presumption; disputable presumption and *presma facie* presumption; conflicting presumption and inconsistent presumption; presumption of general application and statutory presumption; Thayer presumption[4] and Morgan presumption,[5] etc.[6] With so many categories and their semantics intersected and overlapped, no wonder learners or researchers feel dazzled upon entry into this field.

These categories are created by British and American scholars during their years of research for better explaining connotation and extension of presumption concept. In my view, most scholars prefer to create categories: on the one hand, finding that the original categories were not reasonable or accurate during research, they proposed new ones instead following their own studies; on the other hand, a newly created category can become a symbolic achievement for their "creative mind". Scholars[7] who prefer to do something different are never bored with racking their brains, so new categories came into being one after another despite that many of them are only repetitions of old ones. Undoubtedly, many fields in law study exist such kind of "knowledge increment" more in name than in reality, but the complicated concept of presumption provides sufficient space for "creative mind" of scholars. I am convinced that scholars hope to reduce the mess of concepts in use when creating categories, but the result may be totally different. As English presumption categories have a wide influence on Chinese presumption theory, it is necessary for us to analyze those categories carefully. In this paper, my analysis will mainly focus on rationality and irrationality of two couples of Anglo-American presumptions—presumption of law and presumption of fact; rebuttable presumption and irrebuttable presumption—the most influential and controversial categories in Anglo-American law.

8.2.1 Presumption of Law and Presumption of Fact

As editor-in-chief Bray A. Garner has two prestigious dictionaries of Anglo-American law to his credit: *A Dictionary of Modern Legal Usage* and *Black's Law Dictionary*; the former is part and parcel of the English while the latter, of the American. It is worth noting that *A Dictionary of Modern Legal Usage* clarifies different viewpoints on classifying presumption by American and British scholars respectively: "In American law, the most basic distinction is between presumption of law

[4]Proposed by James Thayer in 1898, a presumption that only transfers the burdenof going forward with evidence, but not the burden of proof.

[5]Presumption of transferring the burden of proof, proposed by Edmund Morgan in 1933.

[6]Garner (1999).

[7]Scholars are fond of novelty, so am I; thus "legislative presumption and judicial presumption" are proposed hereby.

and presumption of fact. A presumption of law is a rule of law by which the finding of a basic fact gives rise to a presumed fact capable of being rebutted. A presumption of fact is simply an argument. It is an inference that may be drawn from the establishment of a basic fact, but need not be drawn as a matter of law, e.g. the possessor of recently stolen goods is the thief... British lawyers distinguish between the following types: (1) presumptions *juris et de jure* which are irrebuttable; (2) presumption *juris* which are rebuttable evidence; (3) presumptions of fact which are merely inferences".[8] *Black's Law Dictionary* does not note the difference between American law and British law, only gives respective explanations of the two concepts: presumption of law is "a legal assumption that a court is required to make if certain facts are established and no contradictory evidence is produced", whilst presumption of fact is "a type of rebuttable presumption that may be, as a matter of law need not be, drawn from another established fact or group of facts".[9]

In academic works, explanations of this pair of presumption categories are not as concise as dictionary entries, but implications are the same. For example, professor Waltz points out: "A presumption of fact is one deriving from the mental process by which the existence of one unknown fact is inferred from proof of other known, basic facts because common sense and experience teach that the known, basic facts usually go hand-in-hand with the unknown fact.... A presumption of law is an inference that the law requires the fact-finder to draw once certain basic facts have been established, assuming, of course, that there has been no direct evidence on the particular subject".[10]

Thus it can be seen that cognitive objectives of both presumption of fact and presumption of law are unknown facts by means of deduction, and the cognitive process is from one fact to another. The only difference is absent of explicit provision by law which hereby is in its narrow sense, excluding case law. In my opinion such discrimination in countries of Anglo-American legal system is rational to a certain degree. To begin with, judges in those countries enjoy "power of law-creating" which entitles them, in case of no explicit legal stipulation, to presume and create case law on presumption based on particular case; secondly, such discrimination assists judges to be aware of which presumption basis is associated relationship among clearly recognized facts by law and which are associated relationship among facts subject to judge's discretion; To the former, judges need not any examination or argumentation; to the latter, judges should examine and justify with discretion. From a historical point of view, presumption of law has been evolved or transformed from presumption of fact.

Evidence scholars from mainland China generally agree with the division between presumption of fact and presumption of law. Some scholar pointed out: "the presumption of law is explicitly defined by legal provision"; "as for presumption of fact... refers to that the court is entitled to, based on known facts and empirical rules, logically deduce to draw true or false conclusion from fact to be proved; therefore, it

[8]Garner (2003).

[9]Bryan A. Garner ed., *Black's Law Dictionary*, pp. 1204–1205.

[10]Waltz (1983).

is by explicit provision that distinguishes clearly the presumption of law from the presumption of fact. In evolutionary process, the presumption of fact precedes the presumption of law. Thus, it may be considered that the presumption of law is the legal and finalized form of the presumption of fact which is the preliminary phase of, and to be evolved to, the presumption of law".[11]

Such distinction is too made by scholars of Taiwan. For example, Professor Chen Pusheng pointed out: "Presumption, a legalese by nature, is used for presumption of law and presumption of fact. The presumption of law refers to the presumption process that Fact B, by Fact A's existence or not, can be presumed *to be or not be* under law, unnecessary to produce evidence; while the presumption of fact means that when Fact A has been determined in litigation, Fact B's existence shall be deduced on the basis of ethnic rules".[12]

In studying presumption theory of Anglo-American legal system, I, from the beginning, impressed on the poor rigor of terminologies of presumption of law and presumption of fact, attributing both to the presumption of fact and both on the basis of law, with the exception that presumption of fact is based on case law. For instance, many scholars, when explaining the concept of presumption of fact, cite the presumption example of "that the possessor of recently stolen property is the thief". In U.S., this "presumption of fact" is also based on a number of cases with binding force, such as Barnes cases (1973).[13] In my opinion, their difference is that the presumption of law is determined by legislator whereas the presumption of fact is created by administrator of justice; therefore I advocate the use of categories of "legislative presumption" and "judicial presumption"[14] instead of categories of presumption of law and presumption of fact. Now I realized that my past understanding of this issue was not complete and the expression was inaccurate. In China neither the term nor the concept of "presumption of fact" is appropriate to use, for any presumption shall fall into the category of legal provision.[15]

Some Chinese scholars also questioned the discrimination between presumption of law and presumption of fact. Professor Chen Yiyuan, for example, is not in agreement about using "presumption of fact", holding that every presumption is of law.[16] Again Professor Long Zongzhi objects to use the concept of "presumption of fact", arguing that it may firstly confuse the limit between presuming mechanism and proving mechanism, and then conflict with legal principles of state.[17]

As a matter of fact even in common law countries, there are scholars in opposition to such distinction between presumption of law and presumption of fact. The author

---

[11] Jiang (1999).

[12] Chen (1992).

[13] In this case, the accused was charged to keep and use 4 financial invoices of USA which he was clearly aware of booties. The judge dictated the presumption to jury that was queried by the defender, but the Supreme Court supported judge's viewpoint. See Jones Waltz, pp. 398–403.

[14] See He (2001), He and Liu (2004).

[15] See He (2008).

[16] Chen (2000).

[17] Long (2008).

of *A Dictionary of Modern Legal Usage* admitted that the presumption of law and the presumption of fact: "this distinction is increasingly rejected".[18] Professor John H. Wigmore indicated: "the presumption of law and presumption of fact are nothing but loan words of continental law system which have been wrongly used. In practice only one presumption exists, the phrase 'presumption of fact' shall be discarded as the useless and the confused".[19]

Ronald Allen, professor at U.S. Northwestern University Law School, diverged greatly on this issue in his book *Evidence: Text, Problems, and Cases*. Instead of adopting classification between presumption of law and presumption of fact, he implied discarding the legalese *presumption*—"There is, however, no independent substance that inheres in the concept of presumption and rather, presumption is only a label that cause legislators and commentators attach to a variety of devices that manipulate the process of proof. It would be possible to describe those manipulations specifically and directly and to eliminate the term presumption from legal discourse. Indeed, as the materials throughout this section imply, such a reform would be desirable".[20]

To sum up, the discrimination between presumption of law and presumption of fact is not only of no significance, but also of confusion to presumption concept, especially in such a country like China where case law is not recognized, thus defects being apparently magnified. In a word, it is not necessary for us to introduce into China such a pair of categories, which is not only inappropriate to China's legal context, but also subject to criticism and denunciation in countries of Anglo-American law system.

8.2.2 Rebuttable Presumption and Irrebuttable Presumption

Presumption is no other than made on the basis of normal contact or associated relationship between elemental truth and presumed fact. In different presumptions, the connection or relationship between basic fact and presumed fact are not completely uniform, of which some have high probability and, the others, low; some have stable relationship, whereas others are unstable; thus the certainty or effectiveness of presumption conclusions shall draw differentiated. Moreover, the division between presumption of law and presumption of fact makes felt obligatory to differentiate the effectiveness of the two presumptions. Under this context, some scholar set forth such pair of categories as rebuttable presumption and irrebuttable presumption. In the light of the *Black's Law Dictionary's* entry, the irrebuttable presumption cannot be reversed by other evidence or argument. For instance, children under seven are not capable of committing heinous crime, this is an irrebuttable presumption; whereas the rebuttable presumption, made in accordance with a certain fact and a compo-

[18] Garner (1995).

[19] See Long Zongzhi.

[20] Allen et al. (2006).

nent of *prema facie* proof, can be reversed by providing opposite evidence.[21] For instance, a letter properly mailed from a post office can be presumed to be received by addressee after a certain period. In general, this conclusion is right, for in most instances we may reason as above. But under some circumstances, the letter may be missed or damaged on its way, thus this presumed conclusion is probable and the addressee may rebut, that is to say by means of evidence and argumentation to prove that the letter was not arrived in hand for the sake of some special occurrence.

In retrospecting this pair of categories, the relationship between presumption of law and presumption of fact occurred to me: Can we say, to begin with, that any presumption of law is irrebuttable while any presumption of fact is rebuttable? The answer shall be negative, for many purported presumptions of law are significant to be rebutted. Is the irrebuttable presumption, then, the category excluded from presumption of law and presumption of fact? Based on the above introduction to presumption of law and presumption of fact by *A Dictionary of Modern Legal Usage* and *Black's Law Dictionary*, both shall be rebuttable, so where is the irrebuttable presumption from? In order to expound this perplexed problem, let's take a look at the explanation of *English-Chinese Dictionary of Anglo-American Law* compiled by Chinese scholar: presumption of fact refers to "presume a certain fact stand up from other known and determined fact;... the presumption of fact is unnecessary to stand up and permissive to be reversed by producing contradictory evidence"; presumption of law refers to "when the specified fact has been proved without contradictory evidence produced otherwise, a court is required to make legal assumption, i.e. to rule that the presumed fact stands up. The presumption of law is permissive to refute.[22] It can be seen from the two definitions that the presumption of fact and the presumption of law are both rebuttable. Here a logic issue arises: if the presumption of law and the presumption of fact are the division of presumption concept and both are rebuttable, there will not be an irrebuttable presumption exclusive of the two; if the irrebuttable presumption and the rebuttable presumption are also the distinction of presumption concept, the explanations of above two dictionaries shall not be correct on the presumption of law and the presumption of fact. Till now, we have peeped the chaos caused by the pair of categories.

In epistemology, a presumption is to determine indirect fact by means of deduction, its cognitive conclusion is drawn with chance and sham. To put it another way, the presumed truth shall not be equivalent to occurred objective fact, thus any presumption may be rebuttable. Professor Chen Yiyun opposes to distinguish "rebuttable presumption from irrebuttable presumption", holding that "any presumed truth can be rebutted".[23] The complexity of presumption, however, is a product of not only epistemology but also axiology, as well as the consideration of proving cost and litigation efficiency. So it can be seen that in some laws the definition of "presumption" implies irrebuttable connotation, for example, presumption in *Black's Law Dictionary* about: "Children under seven are not capable of committing heinous crime". In explaining

[21] See Footnote 9.

[22] Xue (2003).

[23] Chen Yiyun ed., pp. 180–181.

irrebuttable presumption, *English-Chinese Dictionary of Anglo-American Law* too sets forth a similar instance–definition of "Child under ten is not able to commit any crime" enclosed in *Children and Teenagers Law* of Great Britain in 1933.[24]. However, scholars may query whether such legal provision falls into presumption category. As stated above, presumption is an indirect determination from elemental truth to presumed fact based on their normal connection or associated relationship; to put it strictly, the above regulation is not deduced on the basis of associated relationship between elemental truth and presumed fact at all, but in consideration of values by law. For the sake of this assumption, perhaps, author of *Black's Law Dictionary* stressed that such kinds of irrebuttable presumptions "are legal provisions in nature".[25] Moreover, author of *English-Chinese Dictionary of Anglo-American Law* holds that such irrebuttable presumptions "shall be more properly termed legal regulations or law drafting".[26] Professor Ronald Allen in his *Evidence: Text, Problems and Cases* provided an irrebuttable presumption which can be probably termed "presumption": *Federal Coal Mine Health and Safety Act of 1969* concerning "Upon proof by X-ray or other clinical evidence that miner has complicated pneumoconiosis the law conclusively presumed that the miner is totally disabled". He admitted, of course, that this presumption "is nothing more than a somewhat awkwardly worded substantive rule of law".[27] By the way, Professor Ronald Allen, instead of simply distinguishing between rebuttable presumption and irrebuttable presumption in his book, adopted such more complicated and incompletely corresponding categories as "irrebuttable or conclusive presumption", "mandatory rebuttable presumption" and "permissive or 'feeble' presumption", etc.

Probably the wide recognition of semantic defect in categories of rebuttable presumption and irrebuttable presumption, scholars in countries of Anglo-American law system intend to describe effectiveness differences of different presumptions by other words and expressions; thus, there appeared a series of categories equivalent or close to rebuttable presumption and irrebuttable presumption, such as mandatory presumption and permissive presumption, absolute presumption and conditional presumption, conclusive presumption and procedural presumption, disputable presumption, *prema facie* presumption, strong presumption and slight presumption, etc. Chinese scholars shall be vigilant to this semantic chaos, advised not to introduce into China presumption categories which are subject to confusion; nevertheless, things will become more complicated because of different legal systems and linguistic contexts.

---

[24]Xue Bo ed., p. 1084.

[25]Bryan A. Garner ed., *Black's Law Dictionary*, p. 1204.

[26]See Footnote 24.

[27]Ronald Allen et al., p. 854.

8.2.3 Practical Categories of Presumption Without Classifications

Some scholars in countries of Anglo-American law system adopted practical evasive attitude toward such chaos of presumption category. They stopped bothering to classify presumption, but to study directly particular presumption "category" instead. Waight and C.R Williams, Australian experts of evidence wrote in their book *Evidence, Commentary and Materials*: "The accuracy of presumption and its classification are so indistinct that in words of Edmund Morgan, 'Every writer with sufficient intelligence to appreciate difficulties of the subject matter has approached the topic of presumption with a sense of hopelessness and has left it with a feeling of despair' (1937). Therefore, we will not intend in the present book to examine those suggestive varieties of presumption, such as rebuttable presumption and irrebuttable presumption, presumption of law and presumption of fact".[28]

After a brief introduction to the definition of presumption, writers of this book set out to discuss "particular presumption", centering on analysis of those presumption principles and their applications on the basis of cases by Australian courts. Such presumptions which are widely applied in judiciary practice include: (1) the presumption of legitimacy, i.e. under the condition of no contradictory evidence provided, it shall presume that her husband is father of the children whom the wife gave birth to during legitimate marriage; (2) the presumption of the validity of marriage, i.e. if an evidence is provided that a couple held wedding ceremony and lived together in their capacity as husband and wife, it shall presume that their marriage is legitimate; (3) the presumption of life of continuance, i.e. if an evidence is produced that someone is alive at a specified time, it shall presume that he/she remains alive afterwards; (4) the presumption of death, i.e. one who was missing at his/her residence of everyday life and no tiding heard for a certain period (seven years in general), it can be presumed that he/she was dead; but the exact dying time must be proved instead of presumed; (5) the presumption of survivorship, i.e. to presume that a person was alive when another person was dead. For issues of succession, should two persons were dead in the same accident and cannot prove the dying order of priority, it can be presumed that one was dead later than the other based on their different ages, genders, strengths or body conditions; (6) the presumption of regularity, i.e. if no contradictory evidence produced, it shall presume that an administrative official performed his function in legitimate forms; or, administrative regulations, decisions and orders, etc. meet its statutory rights, thus being legitimate and effective; (7) the presumption of accuracy of scientific instruments, i.e. under circumstances of no opposite evidence produced, it can be presumed that a scientific instrument is accurate and its recordings are reliable.[29] I argue that we should draw lessons from the authors of this book who free from the entangled presumption categories.

[28]...in the words of Edmund Morgan, "Every writer of sufficient intelligence to appreciate the difficulties of the subject matter has approached the topic of presumption with a sense of hopelessness and has left it with a feeling of despair".... Waight and Williams (1998).

[29]P. K. Waight and C. R. Williams, pp. 110–128.

8.3 Natural Presumption and Artificial Presumption

Another pair of presumption categories, natural presumption versus artificial presumption in Anglo-American law of evidence, seems not to be drawn attraction by Chinese evidence scholars in particular. Perhaps English works on law of evidence usually give simple introduction to the pair of concepts, and some equate them to presumption of fact and presumption of law,[30] making us neglect them in presumption studies; nevertheless, a thorough probe into original significance and correlation of this pair of categories[31] is of great benefit to presumption studies.

8.3.1 Definition of Natural Presumption

Natural presumption, as the term suggests, is a presumption made in accordance with natural law. *Nature* here refers to nature proper or by its nature instead of natural world or natural science. In the context unconcerned of law of evidence, concept "natural presumption" sometimes is employed. For example, Alexander Hamilton, famous U.S. jurist, once in expounding relationship between the legislature and the judicature wrote in *the Federalist Papers*: "if the legislature itself is a constitutional judge of its power and other departments are not entitled to inquire the law made by itself, response to this shall be that this cannot be the natural presumption".[32] In his wording, natural presumption can also be rendered "natural assumption", or translated into assumptions of either "principles of heaven and earth" or "undoubted logic". However, we can still figure out the original sense as a legalese of law of evidence, i.e. a presumption made beforehand in the light of natural law.

To expound natural presumption within realm of law of evidence, it is necessary for us to analyze its connotation and extension instead of limit to literal rendering. Let's take a look at explanations of *natural presumption* by specialized dictionaries. *Black's Law Dictionary* goes: "a deduction of one fact to another based on common experience";[33] while *English-Chinese Dictionary of Anglo-American Law* notes: "a presumption made from a certain proved fact; according to this fact, existence of another fact can be directly deduced".[34] From above quotations we may see the similarity between natural presumption and "presumption of fact" used by some scholars. Both are inferences or deductions made under empirical rules, but natural presumption is much clearer in semantics than presumption of fact. More important

[30]For example, *Black's Law Dictionary* terms simply artificial presumption as presumption of law; while in its explanation of natural presumption, presumption of fact is implied.

[31]In addition, there is mixed presumption in English, i.e. one between natural presumption and artificial presumption or one denotes legal factor and fact factor. See Bryan A. Garner: *Black's Law Dictionary*, p. 1204.

[32]...that this cannot be the natural presumption. *The Federalist* (New York: Tudor, 1937), p. 78.

[33]See Footnote 25.

[34]Xue Bo ed., p. 950.

is that natural presumption lays stress on presuming process based on law of matter itself instead of on artificially prescribed norms. All in all, natural presumption is of *pure nature*.

To sum up, presumption is the cognition for case fact or disputable fact. Based on natural relationship and law among objective matters, the cognition of natural presumption depends completely on mode and effectiveness of its own. As a kind of presumption, natural presumption is to functionally determine facts under obscure state, and the determining criteria are natural attribute and state of connections among matters, aimed at determining relevant fact as accurate as possible. In other words, the basic principle of natural presumption is to guarantee that the cognitive conclusion approaches to objective truth as close as possible. According to case law of countries of Anglo-American law system, for instance, a judge can presume that a person who holds recently stolen property and fails to justify his possession to the court is thief or a participant to the theft. In the first place this is an identification of fact under indistinct state, for there is no sufficient evidence to prove directly that the person with stolen goods is actually the thief or not; in the second place this is a kind of natural presumption, as the basis is natural connection among facts. As a matter of fact, no matter whether there is such regulation of case law and no matter whether the umpire is a professional judge, any person in charge of judgment will deduce that he/she who holds recently stolen goods and fails to justify him/herself is thief or a participant to theft.

It is a common sense that in our world exists objectively natural law and natural connections which cannot be realized without efforts made by human being; while the human cognition shall not be all correct or accurate. Generally speaking, the human cognition of natural laws and natural contacts is demonstrated by experience of common sense or empirical rules endowed with social members, the task of justice is to make the empirical rules applied to determining particular case facts or disputable facts. It is noted that the empirical rules owned by social members may change with social development. Such change results in two aspects: one is that past empirical rules had errors which are rectified with cognitive capacity upgraded; the other is that law of goods itself changed, thus empirical rules shall alter accordingly. In all, standards of natural presumption are by no means unchangeable.

8.3.2 Definition of Artificial Presumption

Literally speaking, artificial presumption is a presumption made by human. As we conduct our discussion in the sphere of law, the artificial form is law. Just because artificial presumption is under the garb of law, some scholars from countries of Anglo-American law system equate it with alleged "presumption of law". In accordance with *English-Chinese Dictionary of Anglo-American Law,* artificial presumption is a "lawful presumption" or "assumed deduction", i.e. "presumption is made in the light of legal provision instead of language logic".[35] In place of commenting on defects and slips in expressions of "assumed deduction" and "made instead of language logic" I would like to explore from "artificial" point of perspective the system and law which constitute such kind of presumption.

The artificial presumption is too a cognition of unknown facts. This cognition does not rely completely on mode and efficiency of its own, but intermingled with technological processing by human. To put it another way, the conclusion is drawn from not only natural relation and law of matters, but also subjective faith and values under which the legislator set up presumption rules. For instance, under law a person whose whereabouts have been unknown for seven years can be presumed dead. To begin with, natural presumption is built on the presumption base, as a person whose whereabouts have been unknown for many years, in accordance with empirical rule, has been dead in general; in the second place artificial traces exist herein, for a person not heard from for five, six, six and half or seven years, viewed from natural law, may have been dead already; but this presumption rule is artificially set for seven years, prescribed to reach seven years. This means that as long as one day left is on the expiry of seven years, the judge is not able to presume that the missing is dead. Apparently the time demarcation line falls into artificial category. However, because presumption belongs to means of identifying fact under indistinct state, the artificial demarcation line becomes necessary to presiding judge. The judge in charge does not know exactly whether the missing is dead, so he is not able to determine exact time of death, but in consideration of social stability, the legislature requires judges to announce dead on expiry of the time period. If such a period is not prescribed explicitly, judges will not know, in the face of such circumstance, how on earth to behave even give different judgments.

To sum up, the artificial presumption is to artificially set up rules of judgment under indistinct state to avoid a decision impasse. Example is taken for that mother and baby were both dead in the same accident and no evidence proved the order of priority of their death, so a judge could presume that the baby preceded the mother in death. Indeed, in consideration of that mother is superior to baby in life, it meets natural law to presume that mother followed baby in dying. Life experience tells us, however, that at that very instant of accident mother will protect her baby by instinct, thus preceding baby in death. In this instance, presumptions that mother preceded baby, or vice versa, are both rational in some ways. If no artificial defining criterion presents, the disputable parties will set forth their own opinions and plunge the judgment into a "deadlock". It is artificial presumption that provides a deciding criterion to break "deadlock", in addition to take values of natural law and legal norms into consideration in setting up such criterion. Because disputes on dying order often involve in heritage, and the practice of mother as decedent meets values of social stability under such circumstances, the legislature stipulates artificially that under such cases mother should be presumed to die afterwards, thus guaranteeing that heritage belongs to successor of mother.

---

[35] Xue Bo ed., p. 102.

The means by artificial regulation to break deadlock is also seen in other domains of social life. In football match, for example, if two teams play even first in normal time then in overtime and the match is of a tiebreaker, penalty kicks shot by either team will be adopted to decide which team will win under rules. By this practice it seems not to win "natural" in football match, but it can avoid a deadlock in which it is impossible to umpire or may plunge the match into restless play. The artificially stipulated rule shall be agreed or recognized by parties concerned by two approaches: one is to conclude a "treaty" under consultation and consensus; the other is that a power organ constituted in accordance with law makes and promulgates, on the basis of procedures concerned, "law" to follow. In all, artificial presumption is a artificially set method to determine fact, and is capable of playing "decision rule" role in the face of "even game", thus also termed *decision rule presumption.*

8.3.3 Relationship Between Natural Presumption and Artificial Presumption

The natural presumption and artificial presumption are both distinct and correlative. The basic distinction lies in that: natural presumption is of natural produce whereas artificial presumption is of artificial product. This abstract generalization may demonstrate semantic differences, and evolve into differences of content. As an ought-to-be presumption, natural presumption exists against human act; as an actual presumption, however, natural presumption cannot work without human act. On the one hand, natural presumption cannot part human act when applied in judicial activity; on the other hand, nor does it when transformed into legal regulations of general application. In this regard, all presumptions applied in legal practice are of artificial component, thus attributed into artificial presumption. Presumptions discussed in law of evidence, to put it another way, are all of legal provisions and of artificial presumptions, any pure natural presumption exists only as a prototype or base of artificial presumption.

The artificial presumption and natural presumption have close relationship. In the first instance, artificial presumption is generally evolved from natural presumption; secondly, artificial presumption contains natural presumption, or, in other words, artificial presumption meets natural presumption, though the conformity varies in degree. For example, an old legal proverb in English goes: *Possession is nine tenth of the law*, meaning that a person in possession of property in most cases is the legitimate proprietor of this property, thus in the face of ownership dispute the judge can presume that the possessor is the lawful owner. This is a natural presumption in content, and many countries have set up relevant presumption rules on its base; therefore, a natural presumption is transformed into an artificial one. When a real estate registration system is not established, this presumption rule is applied to all property disputes including real estate. If no evident and convincing verbal testimony or documentary evidence is produced against contradictory case, the property possessor is presumed to the legitimate possessor of the property. For example, the clothing you wear is your garment, the chariot you drive is yours and the house in which you live is your residence, unless someone produces contradictory evidence. But when the real estate registration system has been established, this presumption rule is applied to personal property only; for in accordance with real right disclosure principle, the real right disclosure for real estate is of registration whereas the real right disclosure for personal property is of possession, and real right with disclosure can be presumed to be correct legitimate right. As far as real estate is concerned, people with such registration as "appearance of right" can be presumed to correct proprietor. For example, people with "Certificate for Housing Property" issued by state organ is owner of the house, unless someone otherwise proves that the registration is wrong. This legal regulation is too based on empirical rules, thus connoting natural presumption; because of its "garb of law", it became artificial presumption. The change to presume property right of real estate above indicates that this presumption is artificial and criteria of natural presumption are changeable.

The artificial presumption is a variety of legal provision. So are these legal provisions created by human being? This is a rather old issue with regard to fundamental character of law. Outwardly, law is made and promulgated by man, so it seems that law is "artificially made". Alternatively, law also denotes or shall denote "law of nature" which transcends human will or intentions. Early in the ancient Rome, some jurists pointed out that law of nature, discovered by man with its reasons, is a set of values on human right and social justice, which are superior to real law and generally applicable. Cicero, representative jurist in ancient Rome, had: "law of nature is the only criterion to weigh artificially made law; for law is aimed at maintaining state unification as well as security and happiness of people, therefore any state-made law up to this aim deserves "genuine law".[36] Ancient Chinese thinkers also put forward similar views on law of nature. For instance, Lao Zi (also known as Li Er, about 571–471 B.C.), founder of Taoism, made great efforts to advocate his thought of "The law of Tao is its being what it is", holding that heaven takes its law from nature without artificial component.

Nature precedes human being in existence, so does natural law. In natural world, both cosmos the largest and gene the tiniest follow objective law of their own. Since thousands of years, our mankind has been persistent to explore those laws from different point of view, and achieved many results in different fields of scientific research. These results, of course, are announced by man though, not "created" by man, but innate in "nature". Human being only discovers in its scientific research the natural law which objectively exists; in addition such discovery, either right or wrong, is a stage by stage process. An example is given that in the long course of history, man has been convinced that "heaven is round and earth is square" with the earth as center of the cosmos. But early in the sixteenth century, Nicolaus Copernicus reversed the theory of "the earth as center of the cosmos", and set forth the theory that "the sun is center of the cosmos". Moreover, in the beginning of the seventeenth century, Galileo observed celestial bodies through astronomical telescope made by

[36]Zhang (1983).

himself and scientifically proved Copernicus' theory. Afterwards their theory was again canceled, for man discovered finally that the solar system is but a small part of the cosmos. Up to now, man still fails to realize the whole story of the cosmos. Indeed, "The sun as center of the cosmos" is a theory set forth by Copernicus and Galileo, but the law "the earth revolves round the sun" is not created by them, they only discovered it first. Should no Copernicus and Galileo exist, the law exists objectively and would be found by other(s), just as the saying goes that the earth will rotate always no matter who leaves.

"Law" can be taken "regular pattern of statute", i.e. the law to respect in coordinating rights and obligations and regulating behaviors of social members. Seemingly, law is "artificially" enacted by a part of people in accordance with their subjective will. But when enacting law, man must follow given law and show some spirit, or, put it another way, man shall continue to find law and spirit of statute upon legislation. The fundamental spirit and inherent law of statute is to seek values of fairness, justice, equity and rationality. In form, law is artificial and social; in content, law is objective and natural. With advances of society and human being as a whole, the man-made law will definitely better meet the elemental spirit and inherent pattern. Law is like this, so is presumption as one of legal forms.

In a nutshell, presumption is, but not completely, artificial. In law it is not a pure creation or illusion to enact presumption rules, nor designed in accordance with man's will. On the contrary, it shall be a discovery in which man "makes" based on objective law and basic principles of presumption. The artificial presumption and natural presumption are distinct, for the former is evolved from the latter, thus denoting natural presumption in artificial presumption. Whether in conformity with principles and law of natural presumption constitutes our criterion to draft and examine artificial presumption—though it may not be the only one.

8.4 Categories of Presumption in Chinese Law of Evidence[37]

8.4.1 Description of Current Presumption Categories

The presumption theory of Chinese law of evidence is basically learned from countries of Anglo-American law system, so the presumption category of Anglo-American law of evidence is received by Chinese scholars. Indeed, we have in Chinese law of evidence circle such scholars as Professor Chen Yiyun who objects to distinguish presumption of law from presumption of fact as well as classify as rebuttable presumption and irrebuttable presumption.[38] But they are few and most

[37]The data on Chinese law and legal interpretations were collated by Mao Shuling and Zhang Junzhou, Ph.D. students at the Law School of Renmin University of China from 2005 to 2009.

[38]Chen Yiyun ed., pp. 178–181.

scholars are to some degree in agreement with such categories as presumption of law and presumption of fact, rebuttable presumption and irrebuttable presumption.[39] I have set forth in present article my current views: first we shall not introduce into China such a category that is not only inappropriate to China's legal context at all but also subject to criticism and denunciation in countries of Anglo-American law system and second, some Anglo-American law scholars have practical evasive attitude towards the chaos of presumption category, which affords us lessons that merit attention.

Many Chinese scholars, upon expounding varieties of presumption, use respectively such categories as mandatory presumption and permissive presumption, absolute presumption and relative presumption, conclusive presumption and persuasive presumption, etc. Because these categories basically are of imports, and affiliated to the two categories above. As mentioned in Chap. 7, some scholars in their works use "direct presumption" and "deductive presumption", which are allegedly said from law of evidence of continental law system, of which I think it necessary to give my analysis.

Scholars in support of such point of view point out upon classifying "presumption of law": "Based on the criterion that whether prerequisite fact is necessary, it can be divided into direct presumption and deductive presumption. The direct presumption refers to a presumption made without prerequisite fact to be proved. The presumption of innocence and presumption of sound mind are the most well-known ones. This is termed "provisional authenticity" in continental law system.... by comparison, the deductive presumption is based on already proved prerequisite fact. This presumption may transform the responsibility of evidence producing from one party to another, meeting completely essence of presumption, thus termed as "real legal presumption"[40] by continental law scholars. In his book *British Law of Evidence*, Professor Qi Shujie termed "direct presumption" and "deductive presumption" as two forms of presumption, and the latter is also called "inferential presumption" by British scholars. Although the author gives some words for the concepts of direct presumption and inferential presumption, it is a pity that no source is spotted.[41]

If the two concepts indeed exist in Anglo-American law of evidence, "inferential presumption" is logical in English. As discussed in Chap. 7, presumption in English means "pre-assumption", therefore, "inferential pre-assumption" or "pre-assumption based on inference" is appropriate. On the contrary, "presumption" (*tuiding*) in Chinese language means "inference and determination", so the "inferential presumption" becomes "inference and determination based on inference", and the semantic repetition is obvious. As for the term of "direct presumption", I insist that this concept is self-contradictory with presumption. As mentioned in Chap. 7, presumption is the cognition to deduce unknown presumed fact from basic known fact, and the determination of presumed fact depends on proof of elemental truth; in other words, without elemental truth neither the presumed fact produces nor presumption follows, but there

[39]See Jiang Wei ed., pp. 130–142; Bian (2000), Fan (2001).

[40]Jiang Wei ed., p. 135.

[41]Qi (2002).

is not any basic fact in "direct presumption" at all. How can be termed "presumption" without basic fact? So "direct presumption" is not a real presumption. This classification is equal to divide presumption into "false presumption" and "genuine presumption".

As legal provisions, presumption rules are scattered in departments of law, including substantial law and procedural law, criminal law and civil law, rules of general application such as general principles of civil law and particular regulations applied to some fields such as rules concerning contract law, law of succession, environmental protection law, copyright law, patent right law, etc. Thus we find it very difficult to study presumption rules, for it needs a comprehensive means of research with a good command of departments of law. To solve this problem, some Chinese scholars, in lecturing presumptions, adopt a method of "thematic class", i.e. classifying presumption in accordance with the theme of presumption items, such as presumption of behavior, presumption of state, presumption of causality and presumption of fault, etc.[42] In my view such explanation of particular category is significant for judiciary practitioners to apply presumption rules.

8.4.2 Two Modes of Presumption Rules

As aforementioned discussion, presumption rules as legal provisions, though not completely, are artificial. The principles and law on which presumption is based are objective. The reason why men set up presumption rules by means of law is that they "make" them on the basis of discovering these principles and law. In this regard anyone who participates in this activity may find those principles and rules, then "makes" such rules. However, legal rule is the universal applicable code of conduct that is enforced by the state, so it must be unified and authoritative. Objective as principle and law of presumption are, different people could not find the same principle and law under specific circumstance. In order to prevent from confusing legal rules, presumption rules must be "made" by some people under unified requirements and procedures. Specifically speaking, two entities are in charge of setting up presumption rules: the legislature and the judicature. The former produces the "legislative presumption", and the latter, "judicial presumption".

The legislative presumption refers to presumption rules clearly prescribed in relevant laws by the legislature; while judicial presumption means presumption rules are determined by means of explaining law and establishing case law by the judicature. The legislative presumption may safeguard better the rules generally applicable and relatively stable whereas the judicial presumption is well accomplished in giving consideration to the rules both applicable to an individual case and flexible to general application. It is beyond all doubt that legal rules shall be generally applicable and relatively stable, but this is limited. On the one hand, under horizontally complicated and diversified conditions of society, it shall be necessarily abstract and vague to

[42] See Jiang Wei ed., pp. 141–142.

keep legislative presumption generally applicable, thus impossible to make different rules for each particular condition or each particular case. On the other hand, under vertically constant change of society, to keep legislative presumptions relatively stable it is impossible to design them in detail, but leave a tolerant space for evolution instead. In addition, it is a constant progress for mankind to find presumption principle and law which shall get perfected nonstop with social development. In other words, legislative presumption may lag behind and have limitations even with flaw or blank, thus judicial presumption constituting complementary in particularity and flexibility.

The cognitive process or thinking form of legislative presumption and judicial presumption both demonstrate: as long as Fact A exists, Fact B can be presumed to exist. But they two have different effectiveness. The legislative presumption is more effective than judicial presumption. Because the presumption is based on normal relation or probable association between basic fact and presumed fact, the mode of legislative presumption may be adopted under the condition that the associated relation is stable or the probability is higher between elemental truth and presumed fact. On the contrary, when associated relation is unstable and probability is lower between basic fact and presumed fact, the mode of judicial presumption is taken. In addition, some presumption is set up not only in consideration of epistemology, but also of values or policy, such as judiciary equity, litigation efficiency, social stability, etc. In such kind of presumptions, the difference between legislative presumption and judicial presumption cannot rely on the probability of associated relation. Anyway, a good understanding of discrimination of the two modes does benefit constitution and application of presumption rules.

8.4.3 Eight Paradigms of Presumption Rules

There are numerous and complicated presumption rules in law and legal interpretations. In benefit of analysis and command, we classify presumption items in the light of themes based on which presumption paradigms are described. In general, presumption items can be divided into first objective fact such as the state of existence of some matter, characters of some behavior, etc.; and second subjective fact such as subjective fault, whether knowing or not, etc. We divide presumption rules into eight paradigms in accordance with subject matters: presumption paradigm of state, presumption paradigm of right, presumption paradigm of behavior, presumption paradigm of cause, presumption paradigm of fault, presumption paradigm of meaning, presumption paradigm of knowing and presumption paradigm of purpose. The following will address each paradigm by means of related regulations of China's current law and judicial interpretations.

8.4.3.1 Presumption Paradigm of State

The presumption of state is made, when content, quality, character or status of cognitive objectives such as people, matter and thing are not clear, to the given situation in accordance with certain basic fact. For example, Article 23 of GPCL prescribes: "Under either of the following circumstances, an interested person may apply to the people's court for a declaration of a citizen's death: (1) if the citizen's whereabouts have been unknown for four years or (2) if the citizen's whereabouts have been unknown for two years after the date of an accident in which he was involved. If a person's whereabouts become unknown during a war, the calculation of the time period in which his whereabouts are unknown shall begin on the final day of the war." This is the legislative presumption about life state. Article 395 of CLreads as follows: "Any State functionary whose property or expenditure obviously exceeds his lawful income, if the difference is enormous, may be ordered to explain the source of his property. If he cannot prove that the sources are legitimate, the part that exceeds his lawful income shall be regarded as illegal gains…". This is the legislative presumption about property character. Some scholars attribute "enormous property of unknown source" to "possessing crime", holding that the provision of Article 395 of the *Criminal Law* is of "knowing" presumption.[43] In my opinion, the presumption item hereby is of property, i.e. illegal gains, really not whether knowing or not by the accused. Article 2 of the *Opinions of SPC on Several Issues concerning the Implementation of the Law of Succession* prescibes: "Persons who are in succession relationship each other were dead in the same accident, if the dying time cannot be determined in order of priority, it shall be presumed that the person without successor was dead first. Where the dead had their own successor, if they belong to different generations the person of senior generation is presumed to be dead first; if they are at the same generation, they are presumed to be dead at the same time and no succession will be open among them, their successors will take legacy respectively".This is the judicial presumption of time sequence on life state or life in dying state. Article 75 of PECP reads as follows: "Where there is evidence proving that a concerned party refuses, without any justifiable reason, to provide evidence that he controls, and the opposite party alleges that contents of such evidence are disadvantageous to the evidence holder, such allegation can be construed as justifiable". This is the judicial presumption on evidence content.

8.4.3.2 Presumption Paradigm of Right

The presumption of right is made, when some ownership is not clear, to the given right in accordance with certain basic fact. For example, Article 250 of the *Contract Law* prescribes: "The lessor and the lessee may agree on the ownership of the lease item at the end of the lease term. Where ownership of the lease item was not prescribed or clearly prescribed, and cannot be determined in accordance with Article 61 hereof,

---

[43] See Long Zongzhi.

title to the lease item shall vest in the lessor". This is the legislative presumption on ownership of lease item. Article 11 of the *Copyright Law* reads: "The citizen, legal person or entity without legal personality whose name is indicated on a work shall, in the absence of proof to the contrary, be deemed to be the author of the work". This is the legislative presumption on copyright ownership. Article 88 of the *Opinions of SPC on Several Issues concerning the Implementation of the GPCL* prescribes: "For a joint property, where some co-owners advocate ownership by shares and other co-owners advocate common ownership, if the property cannot be proved to owned by shares, it shall be deemed to be common ownership". This is the judicial presumption on ownership of common property.

8.4.3.3 Presumption Paradigm of Behavior

The presumption of behavior is made, under condition whether some behavior exists and when objective, quality or character of some behavior are not clear, to the given behavior in accordance with a certain basic fact. For example, Article 25 of *Law of Succession* prescribes: "A successor who, after the opening of succession, disclaims inheritance should make known his decision before the disposition of the estate. In the absence of such an indication, he is deemed to have accepted the inheritance. A legatee should, within two months from the time he learns of the legacy, make known whether he accepts it or disclaims it. In the absence of such an indication within the specified period, he is deemed to have disclaimed the legacy." This is the legislative presumption on acceptance of inheritance and disclaim of legacy. Article 22 of the *Interpretation of SPC on Several Issues in the Application of the Marriage Law* prescribes: "before marriage of the parties in question, where parents of either party invested in housing for the couple, the investment shall be deemed to personal gift to offspring of their own, except that the said parents explicitly express their gift to the couple. After marriage, any investment by parents of either party in housing for the couple shall be deemed to the couple, except that the said parents explicitly express their gift to one party of the couple." This is the judicial presumption on gift. Article 119 of the *Interpretations of SPC on Several Issues in the Application of the Security Law* prescribes: "actually paid deposit is more or less than the prescribed amount, it is deemed to deposit alteration contract". This is the judicial presumption on contract alteration.

8.4.3.4 Presumption Paradigm of Cause

The presumption of cause is made, when cause of some effect is not clear, to determine that some fact is the cause in accordance with causality. Because this presumption is based on causal relationship between two facts, it is also termed presumption of causality.[44] For example, Item 3 of Article 4 of PECP reads: "In a compensation lawsuit for damages caused by environmental pollution, the infringing party shall be responsible for producing evidence to prove the existence of exemptions of liabilities as provided in laws or that there is no causal relationship between his act and the harmful consequences". Although this article does not apply "presumption" or "be deemed to" thereof, the provision of responsibility for producing evidence implies judicial presumption on damages caused by environmental pollution, i.e. as long as some evidence proves the fact of environmental pollution and related damage, presumption can be made that the latter is caused by the former, or, the two exist causal relationship, thus the infringing party shall be responsible for producing evidence of "no causal relationship". In addition, Item 7 of Article 4 of PECP prescribes: "In an infringement action of damages caused by common danger, the persons who commit the common danger shall be responsible for producing evidences to prove that there is no causal relationship between the act thereof and the harmful consequences." Item 8 of Article 4 of PECP reads: "In an infringement action of damages caused by medical acts, the medical institution shall be responsible for producing evidences to prove that there is no causal relationship between the medical act and the harmful consequences or it is not at fault." These are all judicial presumptions on causes of civil infringement damages. Article 18 of *Several Provisions of SPC on the Trial of Cases on Civil Compensation for False Statement in Securities Market* prescribes: "In any of the following circumstances, the people's court shall deem that causal relationship exist between false statement and damage result: (1) securities that investor purchased are directly related to false statement; (2) investor bought these securities on or after the date of the false statement until disclosed date or before corrected date; (3) on the date or after the corrected date of false statement disclosed, investor suffered loss because of selling these securities or holding continuously these securities." This is the judicial presumption on causal relationship between false statement by listing company and investor's damages. In other words, as long as the prescribed elemental truth mentioned above exists, it shall presume that the false statement by listing company is the fact that caused investor's damages.

8.4.3.5 Presumption Paradigm of Fault

The presumption of fault is made, under the condition that it is not clear whether the tortfeasor has subjective fault or not, to identify that he/she has subjective fault based on some basic truth. For instance, Article 126 of GPCL prescribes: "If a building or any other installation or an object placed or hung on a structure collapses, detaches or drops down and causes damages to others, its owner or manager shall bear civil Liability, unless he can prove himself not at fault". This is the legislative

[44]Because the basic paradigm of presumption is based on contact or relationship between Fact A and B, should Fact A exist, it can presume that Fact B exists too. On the contrary, causality, not a fact at all, is a kind of relationship between facts, which can be a basis to presume caused fact, but cannot be a presumed fact. Thus, "presumption of causality" is not rigorous in expression.

presumption on subjective fault leading to above-mentioned damages by building owner or manager. Article 16 of the *Interpretations of SPC on Some Issues concerning the Application of Law for the Trial of Cases on Compensation for Personal Injury* stipulates: "Under any of the following circumstances, Article 126 of GPCL shall apply, and the owner or caretaker shall bear the compensation liabilities, unless he can prove that he has no fault: (1) a road, bridge, tunnel or any other artificial building injures someone due to a blemish in maintenance or management; (2) a piled-up article rolls or slides down or collapses, and injures someone; (3) a tree falls down or is broken or a fruit drops, and injures someone. Where, in the event of a circumstance in sub-paragraph (1) of the preceding paragraph, an injury occurs due to a defect in design or construction, the owner and the caretaker shall bear joint liabilities together with the designer or constructor. This is the judicial presumption supplementing and detailing the legislative presumption.

8.4.3.6 Presumption Paradigm of Meaning

Under the condition that the actor's expression of meaning is not clear this presumption is made to identify his expression of meaning based on certain basic facts. For instance, Article 66 of GPCL prescribes: "...If a principal is aware that a civil act is being executed in his name but fails to repudiate it, his consent shall be deemed to have been given. This is the legislative presumption about expression of agency intent. Article 211 of the *Contract Law* prescribes: "Under a contract for loan of money between natural persons, if payment of interest was not prescribed or clearly prescribed, the loan is deemed interest free". This is the legislative presumption on expression of meaning for loan interest. Article 177 of the *Opinions of SPC on Several Issues concerning the Implementation of the GPCL* prescribes: "...if any heir does not explicitly express to give up the succession after the succession begins, he shall be deemed as accepting the succession..." This is the judicial presumption about meaning expression of succession. Article 54 of the *Judicial Interpretations of SPC on Some Issues regarding the Application of the Security Law* stipulates: "Where the common owner mortgages the jointly owned property without consent of other owners, such mortgage is invalid. If the other common owners know or should know about such mortgage and do not object it, such act will be deemed as consent, and the mortgage shall be valid". This is the judicial presumption about meaning expression of mortgage.

8.4.3.7 Presumption Paradigm of Knowing

The presumption of knowing mainly refers to identify his knowing based on certain basic facts under the condition that the defendant of criminal litigation is not clear about constitutive elements of crime in his subjective cognition. For instance, Article 10 of the *Interpretations of SPC on Some Issues concerning the Specific Law Application for Trial of Criminal Cases of Destroying Forest Resources* stipulates:

"in Article 345 'illegally purchases in a forest area trees, bamboo, etc., which he knows are felled stealthily or arbitrarily', of which *knows* means the act of *know or shall know*. In any of the following circumstances, the violator shall be determined to "shall know the fact" as prescribed, unless otherwise proved be deceived: (1) purchases woods in an illegal wood trading place or selling unit; (2) purchases woods sold at a price which is obviously lower than market; (3) purchases woods sold against regulations." This is the judicial presumption about "clearly know stealthily or arbitrarily felled trees".

Article 9 of the *Interpretations of SPC and SPP Concerning Some Issues on the Specific Application of Law for Handling Criminal Cases of Infringement upon Intellectual Property Rights* prescribes: "In any of the following circumstances, the violator shall be determined to "clearly know the fact" as prescribed Article 214 of the *Criminal Law*: (1) He/it knows that the registered trademark on the merchandise he/it sells is altered, changed or covered; (2) He/it has ever been imposed upon administrative penalties or has borne civil liabilities due to sale of merchandise under a counterfeited registered trademark, but again sells the merchandise under the same counterfeited registered trademark; (3) He/it forges or alters the authorization document of the trademark registrant or knows that the said document is forged or altered; (4) Other circumstances in which he/it knows or ought to know the merchandise under the counterfeited registered trademark." This is the judicial presumption about the sale of merchandise under a counterfeited registered trademark. However, sub-paragraph (4) of this article does not belong to presumption, for the diction describing basic facts in presumption rule shall be specific and clear. The "miscellaneous provisions" make regulations allowing the judiciary to use their discretion to presume mixed with presumption rules.

Article 6 of *the Interpretations of SPC and SPP on Issues concerning the Specific Application of Law in Handling Criminal Cases Involving Stealing, Robbing, Swindling or Forcibly Seizing Motor-vehicles* prescribes: "Where the motor vehicle involved in any act prescribed in Article 1 or Paragraph 3 of Article 3 of this Interpretation falls into any of the following circumstances, the doer shall be determined as 'knowingly' as mentioned in the preceding articles: (1) There is no legal and valid voucher on its origin; or (2) The engine number or the vehicle identification code number has been obviously changed and there is no legal certificate for the change. This is the judicial presumption of "knowing" to buy stolen cars.

8.4.3.8 Presumption Paradigm of Purpose

The presumption paradigm of purpose mainly refers to identify, based on given basic facts, whether the defendant of criminal litigation has "illegal possession purpose" where it is not clear. For instance, Article 2 of the *Interpretations of SPC on Several Issues Concerning the Specific Application of Law in the Trial of Cases on Swindling* prescribes: "In any of the following circumstances, the doer shall be determined to illegally possess by means of swindling through economic contract: (I) Clearly know that he/it is not capable of performing the contract or offering effective security, but adopted the following deceitful methods to sign contract with other(s) to swindle property or money which is large in sum or caused bigger damages: (1) Fabricate entity; (2) Pretend another name; (3) Use forged, altered or invalid invoice, letter of introduction, stamp or other certified document; (4) Conceal truth, using knowingly invalid bill or other settlement voucher as contract performance bond; (5) Conceal truth, using knowingly unqualified security mortgage, securities document as contract performance bond; (6) Use other deceitful method to make the other party pay money or offer goods; (II) Flee with, after the contract was signed, goods, money, down payment or deposit handed by the other party for the sake of guaranteeing the contract performance; (III) Squander goods, money, down payment or deposit handed by the other party for the sake of guaranteeing the contract performance and make the above items impossible to return; (IV) Use goods, money, down payment or deposit handed by the other party for the sake of guaranteeing the contract performance to commit crime and make the above money or property impossible to return; (V) Conceal goods, money, down payment or deposit handed by the other party for the sake of guaranteeing the contract performance and refuse to return; (VI) After contract was signed, by paying partial payment for goods to begin contract performance as a bait so as to swindle all money for goods, and refuse to pay the rest of money for goods without reasonable grounds during the prescribed time limit or payment period otherwise agreed by two parties."

Article 3 of the same *Interpretations* stipulates: "In any of the following circumstances, the doer shall be determined to 'aim to illegally possess and illegally raise funds by deceptive method: (1) flee with raised funds; (2) squander raised funds to make it impossible to return; (3) use raised funds to commit crime and make it impossible to return; (4) commit other frauds and refuse to return raised funds or make it impossible to return." For the two regulations, the former is the judicial presumption that the defendant in contract fraud crime has the "illegal possession purpose"; the latter is the judicial presumption that the defendant in funds-raising fraud is for the "illegal possession purpose". However, there are unclear "miscellaneous provisions" describing basic facts in both presumption rules, which is a clear indication of confusing presumption regulations in legal and judicial explanations, thus uniformity and formalization are badly needed.

References

Allen, Ronald J., et al. 2006. *Evidence: Text, Problems, and Cases*, 3rd ed, 852, trans. Baosheng Zhang et al. Beijing: Higher Education Press.

Bian, Jianlin (ed.). 2000. *Evidence law*, 373–374. Beijing: China University of Political Science and Law Press.

Chen, Pusheng. 1992. *Criminal Evidence Law (Revised)*, 171. Taiwan: Sanmin Press.

Chen, Yiyun (ed.). 2000. *Study of Evidence*, 2nd ed., 180–181. Beijing: China Renmin University Press.

Fan, Chongyi (ed.). 2001. *Evidence law*, 256–257. Beijing: Law Press China.

Garner, Bryan A. (ed.). 1999. *Black's Law Dictionary*, 7th ed., 1204–1205. St. Paul: West Group.

Garner, Bryan A. (ed.). 1995. *A Dictionary of Modern Legal Usage* 2nd ed., 689. Beijing: Law Press China.

Garner, Bryan A. (ed.). 2003. *A Dictionary of Modern Legal Usage*, 2nd ed., 689. Beijing: Law Press China.

He, Jiahong. 2009. *Distorted Souls: Empirical Studies of Criminal Cases in Foreign Countries*, 180–192. Beijing: China Renmin Public Security University Press.

He, Jiahong. 2001. On the Presumption of Judicial Proof. *Journal of National Procurators College* (2).

He, Jiahong. 2008. On Defining Norms of Presumption, *Science of Law* (10).

He, Jiahong, and Pinxin Liu. 2004. *Evidence Law*, 271–277. Beijing: Law Press China.

Jiang, Wei (ed.). 1999. *Law of Evidence*, 130–138. Beijing: Law Press China.

Long, Zongzhi. 2008. Presumption: Limits and their Application. *Chinese Journal of Law* (1).

Qi, Shujie (ed.). 2002. *British law of evidence*, 722. Xiamen: Xiamen University Press.

Waight, P.K., and C.R Williams. 1998. *Evidence, Commentary and Materials*, 5th ed., 109. Australia: The Law Book Company Limited.

Waltz, Jon. 1983. *Criminal Evidence*, 2nd ed., 275–276. Chicago: Nelson-Hall Press.

Xue, Bo (ed.). 2003. *English-Chinese Dictionary of Anglo-American Law*, 1085. Beijing: Law Press China.

Zhang, Hongsheng (ed.). 1983. *Western History of Law Thought*, 59. Beijing: Peking University Press.

Chapter 9
The Rules of Presumption

Contents

9.1 Case Illustration

On 12th February 2014 in Hebei Province, a joint action was taken by the local Commission for Discipline Inspection, the local Procuratorate and the PSB to arrest Ma Chaoqun, a deputy researcher in the Urban Management Department of Qinghuangdao city and also General Manager of Beidaihe Water Company. A search of Ma's family homes was carried out and over 100 million RMB in cash and a large quantity of gold was discovered at his mother's residence. The case caused a sensation and became known as "Little Official, Giant Corruption".

Ma Chaoqun was born in 1967 in Funing county near Qinhuangdao. In 1985, after graduating from technical school, he joined the city's water company as a furnace technician, later switching to an administrative role, and gradually rising from the ranks of ordinary employee to become section chief. In 1997, Ma Chaoqun took over the running of the Beidaihe branch of the water company and a few years later took up the concurrent position of assistant general manager of the whole water company. In October 2005, the water company restructured; the publicly listed Beijing Capital Group bought 50% of its shares, and set up Qinhuangdao Shouchuang Water Company, with a 25 year franchise on Qinhuangdao's running water. Ma

J. He, *Methodology of Judicial Proof and Presumption*,
Masterpieces of Contemporary Jurisprudents in China,
https://doi.org/10.1007/978-981-10-8025-8_9

Chaoqun was promoted to vice president of the new company and, also, president of the Beidaihe branch. In November 2010, the Qinhuangdao municipal government approved the establishment of Beidaihe Water Company, which split from Qinghuangdao Shouchuang and ran itself independently. In January 2011, the Beidaihe branch office became the Beidaihe Water Supply Company (similar to the Qinhuangdao Shouchuang Water Company), and Ma Chaoqun was appointed president. This company was a state-owned subsidiary of the Qinhuangdao municipal government, responsible for ensuring the safety and quality of Beidaihe's water supply and infrastructure construction, and for the maintenance and management of state-owned assets. In 2012, Ma Chaoqun was promoted to deputy director of the Qinhuangdao Urban Management Bureau, but still retained his position as general manager of Beidaihe Water Company. Although his position was not too senior, he had a lot of power. If a work unit in Beidaihe needed water, it had to submit an application to Ma Chaoqun's company, and it was completely up to him whether or not they received any. He was once heard to say, "If you don't pay, you don't get any water. And if you don't pay enough, we'll cut you off."

On 12th November 2014, Hebei Province's Commission for Discipline Inspection (CDI) announced that it was investigating Ma Chaoqun for the alleged corruption of assets including 120 million RMB in cash, 37 kg of gold and 68 properties (with 7 in Beijing alone, including an apart-hotel near Sanlitun and six houses near Chongwenmen).

In March 2015, the Supreme People's Procuratorate also made a statement regarding Ma Chaoqun: Ma Chaoqun had taken advantage of his office to ask for huge sums of money from successive work units and individuals; he had ordered company employees to defraud huge amounts of public funds through false invoicing, payments to fictitious temporary workers, false inflation of engineering projects and other means; and without authorization had lent huge amounts of public funds to others which were not returned over the long term.

In June 2015, some media reported that the investigation into Ma Chaoqun, deputy director of Urban Management for Qinhuangdao and general manager of Beidaihe Water Supply Company, for corruption, bribery, misappropriation of public funds, property and huge sums of money of unclear origin was closed and being transferred for prosecution. But a year and a half has now passed and no judgment has been announced. It is said that, apart from obstruction to the investigation, the other difficulty is the origin of the huge sums of money.[1]

Presumption is an epistemological activity that draws fact B from fact A through inference. In the field of Law, as discussed in Chap. 7, presumptions are inferential findings of fact made by judicial personnel in accordance with legal rules. The form of such rules could be statutes enacted by the legislature, or interpretations and binding precedents made by the judiciary, if the legal system admits the validity of precedents. Admittedly, to study presumption activities in the light of epistemology is the basis for our study of presumption rules from the standpoint of application of law, but the latter assumes a more important practical significance. In the current judicial practice in

[1]Zhao (2015).

China, the application of presumption rules is sometimes in a muddle. This is partly because of different understanding of the concept and the unclearness of relative laws and regulations, and partly because of the lack of common understanding of the principles, patterns, circumstances, procedures, etc. of the application of presumption rules.

9.2 The Structure of Presumption Rules

As a rule of law, a rule of presumption is also a code of conduct that specifies the rights and obligations of the persons concerned and defines the corresponding legal consequences. Here the word “rights” mainly refers to the rights to assert and invoke a specific presumption; the word “obligations” encompasses the obligation of the party invoking a presumption to prove the basic fact, the obligation of the opponent to present evidence to rebut, and the obligation of the judge to make a finding; the term “legal consequences” refers to whether a presumption stands as fact or not. Thus, a rule of presumption constitutes a code of conduct to standardize the use of this device by the concerned parties in the finding of a fact or a disputed fact during litigious proceedings.

The general logical structure of a legal rule consists of three elements, i.e., the condition (or “hypothesis”), the mode (or “disposition”), and the consequence (or “sanction”). So does a rule of presumption. The “condition” refers to the conditions or circumstances to which the rule applies; the “model” states certain patterns of conduct, primarily involving “may”, “shall”, and “shall not”; and the “consequence” means the legal consequences that come into effect when people’s conduct comply with or break such norm. For instance, Article 75 of PECP states: “Where evidence exists demonstrating that one party is in possession of evidence but refuses to provide it without good cause and the other party claims that such evidence is unfavorable to the party in possession of the evidence, a presumption that the other party’s claim is valid may be drawn”.

This is the rule of presumption regarding the content of evidence. The condition is “where evidence exists demonstrating that one party is in possession of evidence but refuses to provide it without good cause” and “the other party claims that such evidence is unfavorable to the party in possession of the evidence”; the mode is “may”, i.e., “may be presumed”; and the consequences is “the claim is valid.” The author believes that a rule of presumption should generally take the pattern of “shall” rather than the pattern of “may”. That is, as long as the conditions for a presumption are met, the judicial officer should accordingly make the appropriate presumption, rather than the optional “may make”. This issue cannot be confused with the rebuttal by the opposite party, as the consequence of a valid rebuttal is that a presumption cannot stands instead of the judicial officer choosing not to establish such presumption.

9.3 The Clarity and Fuzziness of Presumption Rules

As a legal rule to regulate presumption activities, a rule of presumption should be clear, operable, and predictable, among which the clarity is the core, as it is the foundation for operability and predictability. If it is clearer, the operability and predictability would be accordingly higher. In a sense, the clarity degree of legal rules marks the level of legislative technique and sophistication of a legal system. Therefore, when we define a rule of presumption, it should be expressed as exact as possible. However, subject to the fuzziness of concepts, polysemy of words and phrases, and the development of and change in social language, etc., legal rules tend to have certain openness. That is, the main meaning is relatively clear while the periphery meaning is relatively obscure, or, at a more abstract level it is relatively clear and at a more specific level it is relatively fuzzy. For example, Article 395 of *Criminal Law* provides: "Where the property or expenditure of any State functionary obviously exceeds his legitimate income and the difference is huge, he may be ordered to explain the sources thereof. If he fails to prove that the sources are legitimate, the difference shall be deemed as illegal gains..."

This is the presumption rule for the so-called "the crime of holding a huge amount of property from unidentified sources". At first glance, this rule is clear, as long as a State functionary holds a huge amount of property from unknown sources, such property would be presumed to be illegal gains and the person would be convicted and sentenced accordingly. However, fuzziness still exists when it comes to specific cases. For example, how much value does it require to amount to a huge amount of property? It will be agreed that 100RNB is certainly not huge and 1000RMB is not too huge. It is also agreed that 1,000,000RMB can be considered as huge, and 10,000,000RMB is certainly huge. What about 10,000RME and 100,000RME? Perhaps there would be different answers to these questions. If it is specified that an amount higher than 100,000RMB is huge, then does 99,999RMB make a big difference? Take the aforementioned presumption rule regarding evidence as another example, what is "refuses to provide it without good cause"? If the party concerned claims that he lost the evidence but could not prove it, can this be considered as a "good cause"? Thus, the clarity and fuzziness of a presumption rule are correlative, and the two are mutually reinforcing. Just because of the fuzziness, serious interpretation is required during the application of presumption rules.

It has been pointed out by some expert that "sometimes people see fuzziness as a physical phenomenon. Things near may be clearly seen, while things far away may not, in general, the farther, the fuzzier; however, there are exceptions. Standing on the beach, the coastline is fuzzy; gazing down from high above, the coastline would become very clear. But if it is too high, the coastline would be fuzzy again. Accuracy and fuzziness are essentially different yet interrelated; the two are contradictory, interdependent, and convertible to each other. Thus, the other half of accuracy is fuzziness."[2] This is also enlightening for our understanding of the clarity of a rule of presumption. If a rule is to have operability and predictability, it must be clear; how-

[2]Liu Yingming, *Fuzziness: the Other Half of Accuracy*, Beijing: Tsinghua University Press, p. XIII.

ever, in order to be generally applicable, it must have a certain degree of fuzziness. On this issue, I am glad that it is humans, rather than computers, who apply presumption rules, because "so far, even the most advanced computer has a fundamental flaw that it cannot be programmed to have the abilities of fuzzy reasoning and fuzzy decision which are specific to the human brain; it cannot, like human, process knowledge expressed in natural language under a fuzzy environment; it cannot, like human, flexibly do approximate reasoning or talk to human in natural language. Although computers can accurately control the lunar landing of a spacecraft, to identify human voice and countenance remains somewhat difficult. In a sense, its 'intelligence' level is lower than a baby. In fact, even all the super computers in the world are 'mobilized' up; certain issues which look easy such as a baby recognizing its mother cannot be solved."[3]

However, I also feel anxious and confused while I am glad. On one hand, certainly I do not hope that the person applying the rule presumes a person holds 100,000RMB from unidentified sources as guilty while presumes a person holds 99,999RMB from unidentified sources as not guilty because of the difference of 1 yuan only; on the other hand, I also worry about what exactly the standard is if it continues to be fuzzy, as following 99,999RMB, there are 99,998RMB, 99,997RMB... and during this "fuzzy presumption" process, various unreasonable or even illegal "data" may be mixed into it. Sometimes, I wish half of the human brain is a computer, so that it could be unbiased like a computer to handle certain issues; sometimes, I wish half of the computer is the human brain so that it could be as flexible and compassionate as the human brain in handling certain information. Hence it can be seen that while we strive to use accurate language to define a presumption rule, in the application of a presumption rule, there are always a number of specific issues left to the judges to make "fuzzy recognition" and "fuzzy reasoning". We can give it a quite professional appellation—"free proof with intimate conviction".

9.4 The Conditions for Applying Presumption Rules

In earlier discussion about the logic structure of a presumption rule, "condition" was mentioned as one of the constituting elements of legal rules. While the applicable "conditions" for a presumption rule dealt with in this section is related to yet different from the "conditions" as an element of legal rules. The former includes the connotation of the latter, while the latter serves the purpose of the former; the denotation of the former is larger than the latter, while the latter is only a part of the former. When judges review whether in a case the applicable conditions of a presumption rule are met, the following three aspects should be referred to.

[3]ibid, p. XV.

9.4.1 Sufficient Proving of Basic Facts for Presumption

The basic function of presumptions is to provide convenience for the proving of certain specific facts. It is to substitute the proving of facts to be proved by the proving of basic facts. For the party relying on the application of a presumption rule, though it has been relieved of the burden of proof for the facts to be proved, it still has to bear the burden of proof for the basic facts. For example, Article 126 of GPCL provides: "If a building or any other installation or an object placed or hung on a structure collapses, detaches or drops down and causes damage to others, its owner or manager shall bear civil liability, unless he can prove himself not at fault."

In a tort case, the burden of proof for the essential facts of specific damage generally lies on the plaintiff, including acts of tort, damage caused, causation between the act and damage, and the actor's subjective fault, etc. Under the above provision, the plaintiff does not have to prove the subjective fault of the indirect actor, but he still has to prove a series of basic facts that can lead to the presumption of the subjective fault of the indirect actor, such as the detachment of the object placed on the building, the head injury of the plaintiff, the causation between the detachment and the injury, and the defendant being the owner of the building, etc. Only when those basic facts have been sufficiently proved, the judge may consider the presumption of fault.

9.4.2 Compliance of the Basic Facts with "Conditions" of Presumption Rules

As mentioned earlier, the "conditions" of a rule of law describe the circumstances under which the rule may apply, while the language describing the rule tends to be somehow abstract or fuzzy; therefore, whether the basic facts proved by the party relying on a presumption comply with the "conditions" also require the judge' s careful review. I introduce Article 126 of GPCL as presumption paradigm of fault in Chap. 8, I still take that Article as an example here. If a plaintiff alleges that he was injured by a log rolling down from roadside, after confirming the sufficient proving of basic facts, the judge needs to work on whether such facts comply with the "conditions" set forth under Article 126. For example, is the road a "building or other installation"? Is the log "an object placed"? In answering these questions, the judge may refer to the *Interpretations of SPC on Some Issues concerning the Application of Law for the Trial of Cases on Compensation for Personal Injury*. As mentioned in Chap. 8, Article 16 of the Interpretations provides: "under any of the following circumstances, Article 126 of GPCL shall apply, and the owner or caretaker shall bear the compensation liabilities, unless he can prove that he has no fault: (1) a road, bridge, tunnel or any other artificial building injures someone due to a blemish in maintenance or management[4]; (2) a piled-up article rolls or slides

[4]The author believes that the expression "blemish in maintenance or management" used herein is not quite appropriate, as this expression already contains the meaning of subjective fault, and this

down or collapses, and injures someone; (3) a tree falls down or is broken or a fruit drops, and injures someone. Where, in the event of a circumstance in Item (1) of the preceding paragraph, an injury occurs due to a defect in design or construction, the owner and the caretaker shall bear joint liabilities together with the designer or constructor."

Although this interpretation supplements and elaborates the provisions of Article 126, it is still not clear enough to answer the above questions, because, although the interpretation uses the expression of "road" and "roll", it does not directly answer the question that whether a "log from roadside" falls under the provision, so the judge still needs to determine whether the basic facts comply with the "conditions" of this presumption rule under specific circumstances.

9.4.3 No or Insufficient Contrary Evidence for Rebuttal

Presumptions are indirect findings of fact based on reasoning, and it is "false-able"; in other words, the presumed facts are not necessarily the truth, therefore, a judge cannot apply a presumption rule before confirming the contrary evidence is insufficient to rebut such presumption. Generally, such contrary evidence is all provided by the opponent of a presumption. Specifically, introduction of contrary evidence aims to achieve either of the following two goals: one is to demonstrate the basic facts cannot be established; the other is to prove the presumed facts cannot be established. In the previous example, the defendant may present evidence that the injury suffered by the plaintiff was not caused by the rolling log, i.e., the basic fact cannot be established; or produce evidence that the log did roll down from a passing vehicle and they were not at fault as road managers, i.e., the presumed facts cannot be established. In order to decide whether the presumption applies, the judge must carefully review the evidence to the contrary.

9.5 The Standardization of Presumption Rules

Currently, the chaos of presumption rules in legal and judicial explanations is that which items shall need presumption rules are not clear, wordings to express presumption rule are not uniform, and abuse of "miscellaneous provisions". Therefore, three questions shall be answered carefully in study of normalizing presumption rule: first, which items are necessary and possible to establish presumption rules? Secondly, what kind of logic and language norm shall be observed when establishing presump-

---

is a matter of which the burden of proof lies on the plaintiff. Thus such content deviates from the purpose of the presumption of fault. This is also an example of the lack of standardization in the current expression and formulation of the presumption rules in China.

tion rules? Lastly, whether have social life and judicial practice accumulated enough experience for establishing presumption rules?

To begin with, the legal presumption is a convenient approach for the judiciary to identify case facts or dispute facts. In judicial practice, the judiciary needs to identify many matters, but not all matters are necessary and possible to establish presumption rules. In my opinion, the matter necessary and able to establish presumption rules shall meet the following conditions: firstly, the subject matter cannot be proved directly by evidences or no direct evidence existed. Presumption is made to identify fact B indirectly based on relationship between Fact A and B; therefore, presumption is needed only under the case that Fact B cannot be proved directly. If Fact B can be proved directly through evidence, it is not necessary to set up presumption rule. For instance, in intentional homicide cases, under the condition that voluntary guilty statement with evidence of the defendant has directly proved his homicide intention, there is no need to establish rule to presume intention to kill. Secondly, the judiciary is inclined to reach different conclusions about the subject matter. Presumption is a cognition based on reasoning, aiming to normalize fact identification of the judiciary; therefore, the presumption rule needs to be established only under the condition that reasoning is some kind fuzzy or uncertain. If it is very clear to reason some matter, no matter which judge will come to the same conclusion, there is no need to establish presumption rule. For instance, although no direct evidence is produced to prove intention to homicide of the defendant, evidence can prove that the defendant fired at the head of the victim close at hand and this incident did not discharge accidentally in joking, the judge, under this situation, generally identifies that the defendant has intention to homicide, therefore there is no need to establish presumption rule to deduce intention to homicide. Thirdly, the matter has stable or associated relationships required by presumption rule, and objective law or empirical rule is in support of such connections or relationships. If the associated relationship between the fact as deductive basis and the fact to be proved is unstable or in low probability, there is no possibility of establishing presumption rule. For instance, some one drove to knock down a person and caused the latter dead, but he denied his intent to kill. Although the matter accords with the first two conditions of establishing presumption rules, the associated relationship between driving to knock and intent to kill is not stable at all; put it another way, the driver may or may not have intent to kill. Therefore law cannot establish presumption rule for the matter, and the case can be only deduced by judge according to specific condition. Indeed, legislator and judge can take values or policies into consideration of establishing presumption rules, and these considerations will decline stability or probability, required by presumption rule, of the relationship between basic fact and fact to be proved; but the necessity to consider is not seen in this instance, unless law inflicts severe punishments on the driver so as to contain the act of knocking into people.

As for second question, careful readers can find that in the expression of presumption rules of legal and judicial interpretations above the keywords employed are not unified at all, such as “presumption”, “deemed” or “can be viewed”, “shall be determined”, “be regarded as”, and some without any presumption connotation at all. Besides some presumption rules are not rigorous in expression with miscellaneous provisions mixed with presumption rules, the logical relations in connotation are in chaos. This will cause not only chaos in understanding presumption concept, but also in applying presumption rule. Currently, Chinese legal scholars and judicial personnel do not have a unified understanding of the presumption rules of legal and judicial explanations. Therefore, to standardize presumption rules we need to unify the textual paradigm of presumption rule based on affirming presumption matters, which shall include the following aspects: in the first instance, to describe the fundamental facts accurately; second to express presumption facts explicitly; third to explain the relationship of both properly; fourth to observe logical rules of presumption such as law of identity, non-contradiction law and law of excluded middle, for instance; and finally, it had better use "presumption" as the unified keyword. Where "presumption" is improper in use due to context, substitute for "be viewed as".

The last question: it is beyond all doubt to be careful to establish presumption rules. Under the situation that experience is not sufficient, it had better not to be stipulated by law, and leave the question for judicial personnel at their discretion. However, job cannot lag behind too much. When experience is sufficiently accumulated, law should be in place to work as soon as possible. Experts and scholars can and should play a more positive role in summarizing the judicial practical experience. For instance, in identifying whether the defendant "clearly knows" in possession crime, experts and scholars familiar with such issues shall accelerate to conclude experience so as to establish rational presumption rules to meet judicial practice. Besides, when studying and reviewing experience accumulated already, we need to conclude domestic judicial practical experience as well as learn legislative experience from overseas. For instance, in tort ligation of environmental pollution, many countries have established relatively perfect presumption rule of damage reasons, which is worth a study in enacting and revising our relative law.

As mentioned in Chap. 8, although the presumption rule is "artificial" in appearance, its connotation is natural. How to find those rationally and effectively "natural presumptions" and transfer them into "artificial ones" in time is a common undertaking of experts and scholars who engage in presumption issue, and at the same time the theme for the next chapter.

Reference

Zhao, Qingbin. 2015. The Little Official with Giant Corruption. *Teahouse Jurists* 2: 51–53.

Chapter 10
The Creation of Presumption Rules

Contents

10.1 Case Illustration

Wang Yahui, a 28 year-old male from Lushan County in Henan Province, was arrested and detained by police on suspicion of theft on 18th February 2010. Three days later his family was told that he had died in detention. The cause of death was cited as sickness brought on from drinking boiled water when in custody.

On 22nd February, the family visited the hospital mortuary. When Wang's clothes were removed, they found scars covering his body. Photographs of the corpse also show large bruises and scarring on Wang's back and arms, a wound to the head, severed nipples, and scarring on his reproductive organs. Because of this, the family challenged the cited cause of death. The Public Security Bureau (PSB) of Lushan County, however, continued to claim that Wang Yahui was taken ill suddenly when he was about to appear in court, and later died.

Director Yao, head of the Political Department of Lushan PSB, told Wang's family that on 18th February Wang Yahui was arrested by police on suspicion of theft. On 21st February, he was brought for interrogation at the detention center. "When he said he was thirsty, a police officer poured him some boiled water, which was still warm. One of the officers present had a cold, for which he was taking soluble medicine. As this solution was cool, he added some (to Wang Yahui's drink). As soon as Wang

J. He, *Methodology of Judicial Proof and Presumption*,
Masterpieces of Contemporary Jurisprudents in China,
https://doi.org/10.1007/978-981-10-8025-8_10

drank the mixture he changed—both emotionally and physically—so no time was lost in transferring him to hospital (where he later died)." Director Yao also said it was not clear how so many scars had come to be present on Wang's body. Deputy Chief Li of Lushan PSB, told the family that four of the police officers involved had already been detained. "If they are suspected of crimes committed on duty, the Procuratorate will certainly investigate."

The case elicited a strong response from the community, and was satirically renamed "Death by Drinking Boiled Water" online. The leadership of the Henan Province General Policing Department took the case seriously, stating that they would start an investigation to discover the facts of the case promptly, would impose strict penalties on any guilty parties in accordance with the law, and would certainly not cover up any wrong-doing. The Disciplinary and Supervisory Devision of PSB of Henan Province set up a Joint Investigation Team and began investigations in Lushan County. On 28th February, the team decided that there was a possibility that the officers who had handled the case had tortured the suspect Wang Yahui during interrogation, at which point the four officers concerned were handed over to the Procuratorate for investigation in accordance with the law. The Joint Investigation Team also ordered Director Yao to resign, and sacked and disciplined the Deputy Chief who had been in charge.[1]

There have been occasional incidents of detained criminal suspects dying in strange circumstances in China in recent years, and these have provoked heated words online. Take for example the cases known as: Death by Jumping off a Building, Death from Sudden Illness, Death by Tying Shoelaces, Death by Hide-and-Seek and Death by Drinking Boiled Water. This succession of events has made the issue of forced confession a focal point of interest in Chinese society. Indeed, the very phrase "stopping forced confession" has become a platitude. Each shocking miscarriage of justice has stirred up a tidal wave of denouncements against the use of torture. But the practice seems to have exceptional endurance, both odious and unstoppable, nefarious and hidden.

10.2 Conditions for Creating Presumption Rules

I have overseen an empirical study into the question of forced confession with torture in cases of wrongful conviction. We found that, for certain investigators, torture had become an ingrained habit. The cultivation of this sort of habitual behavior was the result of influence from environmental factors both large (e.g. society) and small (e.g. work units). And "difficulties in investigation and prosecution" at a certain level can lead to the aiding and abetting of torture. For instance, in our analysis of 50 cases of wrongful conviction where the murder suspect had been the subject of media

[1] See BAIKE SOGOU ENCYCLOPEDIA, entry for 'Death by Drinking Boiled Water', last updated 28th October 2016, at baike.sogou.com/v8435242.htm?fromTitle=%E5%96%9D%E5%BC%80%E6%B0%B4%E6%AD%BB%E4%BA%A1, retrieved on 28th October 2016.

exposure, we found evidence of the existence or possibility of torture in 47. But only four cases were officially investigated by the procuratorates, and in one of them, the procuratorate decided not to prosecute.[2]

Difficulties in the investigation and prosecution of forced confessions are primarily those of verification. There are two ways of verifying if a confession has been obtained by torture. First, checks during trials to determine whether illegal evidence should be excluded in cases where there is a possibility that confessions may have been forced (hereinafter referred to as ‘primary cases’). And second, checks during trials to establish whether a defendant was indeed guilty in cases found to have involved torture (hereinafter referred to as ‘secondary cases’). In primary cases, judges will usually demand that the defendant supplies evidence to prove that torture took place. In secondary cases, the prosecution will bear the burden of proof of torture. Practical experience shows that it is often difficult to provide sufficient evidence to prove that a confession was forced, either by defendants in primary cases or prosecutors in secondary cases.

The difficulties of verification of forced confessions are mainly because: (1) Torture happens in places that are typically far removed from detention centers, the only eye-witnesses are investigators, and the “team spirit” cultivated during investigators’ day-to-day work can very easily become a “pact of protection” when faced with an investigation into the use of torture. (2) There is often a long time interval between the occurrence and investigation of torture, which makes it difficult to collect relevant evidence promptly. (3) Often the only people who are willing and able to prove that a confession has been forced are the criminal suspects who have suffered the torture, and it is difficult for this sort of “isolated evidence” to be accepted as true by a judge. (4) The professionalism and self-control of those who force confessions makes them proficient in deterring investigations. (5) There is often interference from many quarters in the investigation and evidence-gathering around forced confession.

Verification is, however, essential if the practice of forced confessions is to be corrected. The principles of behavioral science suggests that, to do this, the real cost of obtaining forced confession must be increased by strengthening the institutional constraints of the law on interrogations, and also the risk costs of forced confession must be increased by effective investigation. The direct profit of torture is the suspect’s confession—therefore, to lower the gains of forced confession, evidence obtained by torture must be excluded from lawsuits. And, the basis of the exclusion of such illegal evidence must be verification of torture. From this we can see that both the increase in the cost of behavior and the reduction of its profit are inseparable from effective verification that torture did in fact take place. In other words, difficulties of verification become a bottleneck in the correction of the practice of forced confession. How can this predicament be resolved? One viable path is to create rules of presumption around forced confession, which immediately demands the resolution of basic questions around the creation of such rules.

---

[2]See He Jiahong, Lv Zehua, and Liang Kun, ‘The Cultivation and Curbing of Confessions Obtained through Torture—A Discussion Of Two Torture Cases’, *Evidence Forum*, Volume 14. See also He and He (2008).

I believe that there are three basic conditions must be answered when creating rules of presumption in the determination of certain facts in judicial decisions. That is to say, whoever creates the rules should seriously consider how to answer the following three questions: (1) Does the matter *necessitate* the creation of rules of presumption? (2) Is the creation of rules of presumption *possible* in this matter? (3) Does the matter have the *maturity* required to create rules of presumption?

10.2.1 "Necessity" for Creating a Presumption Rule

In a legal sense, presumption is defined as a convenient way for the judiciary to determine the facts of a case or of a dispute. There are many matters which require decisions by judges, but not all necessitate the creation of a presumption rule, nor is it possible in all cases. I believe that the matters where it is both necessary and possible to create rules of presumption should meet the following conditions:

First, the matter should not be able to be proved by direct evidence, or there is no evidence available. Presumption is based on the relationship between fact A and fact B and the direct determination of fact B—therefore, presumption is only required when there is no means of directly proving fact B. If evidence exists which proves fact B, there is no need to establish rules of presumption. For example, take a case of intentional homicide. If evidence such as a voluntary confession of guilt by the defendant exists, there is no need to create a rule presuming intentional homicide.

Secondly, it would be easy for different judges to make different rulings on the same matter. Presumption is a cognitive activity based on reason, and its basic function is to standardize judicial rulings on facts. It is, therefore, only necessary to create rules of presumption in situations where there exists a certain degree of ambiguity or uncertainty in reasoning. If the reasoning set out for determining the facts of a matter is clear, and all judges will reach the same conclusion, then it is not necessary to create rules of presumption. For example, although there might be no direct evidence to prove that a defendant had the intention to kill, if there is evidence to prove that the defendant fired a gun in close proximity to the victim's head and the firearm was discharged in a moment of gravity, a judge will usually conclude that the defendant intended to commit murder. In this situation there would be no need to establish a rule presuming intent.

10.2.2 "Possibility" for Creating a Presumption Rule

Matters where rules of presumption are created ought to possess either the accompanying relationship or normal linkage required by such rules. Moreover these links or relationships should be supported by objective laws or experiences. If the "accompanying relationship" between the facts used as the basis for reasoning and the facts that require proof is not steady, or has only a low probability, it is not possible to create rules of presumption. For example, a driver could run a person over causing the latter's death, but not admit intention to kill. Although cases like this match the two conditions set out above in terms of the creation of rules of presumption, the accompanying relationship between a driver hitting another person and intentional homicide is not steady—so the law cannot, therefore, create rules of presumption around such matters and only the judge involved who can make presumptions based on the specific circumstances of a case. It is true that, in the creation of rules of presumption, those who set laws and those who administer them can increase the value considerations or political considerations, and that these can reduce the stability or probability requirements that rules of presumption have with regards to the relationship between the basic facts of a case and those requiring proof. However there is no need in these matters for such considerations unless the law is to dispense severe punishment to firmly control the action of running people over by car.

10.2.3 "Maturity" for Creating a Presumption Rule

Here, maturity means that both society and judicial practice have acquired the full experience needed to create rules of presumption. In other words, rules of presumption must not be rashly created. In situations where experience is not sufficient, it is best that the law make no stipulation and leave judges to use their discretion in resolving questions. However, the creation of rules of presumption must not be overly delayed either. Where experience is plentiful, it is best that the law makes stipulations as soon as possible, in order to allow presumption to be deployed freely. On the question of the practical needs and experience of the judiciary in making rulings, experts and scholars can and ought to play a more active role. For example, take a case of corruption and the question of whether one of the defendants charged with illegal possession had intent. Those experts and scholars familiar with the relevant issues should accelerate how they sum up their experience in order to quickly design rules of presumption that meet the judiciary's practical needs. Moreover, when assessing experience, scholars should take stock of the practical experience of China's judiciary, and study and draw lessons from other countries' legislative experience. For example, in litigation dealing with the infringement of environmental pollution law, the laws of many countries have established relatively sound rules of presumption around the cause of damage, so it is worth China drawing lessons from these when drafting and revising its own laws.

10.3 Creating a Presumption Rule About Forced Confessions

The above cases and the results of empirical research show that it is both necessary and possible to create rules of presumption to deal with the problem of forced confessions. Therefore, we must both sum up the relevant practical experience and create the rules in accordance with the logical and linguistic norms of rules of presumption. As explained in Chap. 8, the rules of presumption can be prescribed either in legislation or in judicial interpretations. Given China's legislative and judicial *status quo*, I suggest that the SPC and SPP use judicial interpretations to formulate rules of presumption as follows.

If any one of the following circumstances exists and the investigators cannot supply sufficient rebuttal evidence, it should be presumed that a confession was forced: (1) The suspect died suddenly during interrogation. (2) The suspect sustained a non-self-inflicted injury during interrogation. (3) The investigators did not send the suspect to the detention center in accordance with the law or, after taking the suspect to the detention center, did not conduct the interrogation there in accordance with the law. (4) The investigating authorities extended the detention period of the suspect and did not inform the suspect's family and work unit nor did they arrange for a meeting with a lawyer.

In the four basic circumstances of presumption above, points (1) and (2) have a high probability of "association relationship" with forced confessions. Although this probability is slightly lower with points (3) and (4), in the interests of strengthening the legal handling of cases by investigators and protecting the value considerations of the legal rights of criminal suspects, they also have a regulatory necessity. Moreover, although it is not always necessarily the case that these situations are accompanied by the "hard torture" of corporal torment, they are often accompanied by grueling trials and the "soft torture" of "baking in the sun, starving, freezing, roasting" and other mental torments.

When applying these rules of presumption, defendants in primary cases or public prosecutors in secondary cases must bear the burden of proof of the basic facts, but should not bear the burden of proof of the presumed facts. That is to say, as long as a defendant in a primary case or a prosecutor in a secondary case provides sufficient evidence to prove the existence of one of the above mentioned basic facts, they can then request that the judge presume the existence of torture. Presumption can, therefore, be rebutted. Before making a decision on presumption, a judge must give an opportunity for rebuttal to the presumed adverse party. In primary cases, the presumed adverse party is the public prosecutor, but the actual subject of the rebuttal is the investigators accused of torture. In secondary cases, the presumed adverse party is the defendants, i.e. the investigators.

Rebuttal by investigators can take two directions: either rebuttal of the basic facts, or of the presumed facts. The former can be rebutted by, for example, proving that the suspect's death or physical harm did not occur during an interrogation, or by proving that the investigators did not extend the period of detention, or did in fact notify family and work unit of such an extension in accordance with the law. The latter can be rebutted by, for example, proving that the cause of death of the suspect was not torture but sudden illness, or by proving that the injuries on the suspect's body were not the result of torture but were "self-inflicted". If investigators cannot provide sufficient evidence for a rebuttal, the judge must then infer that the confession was forced. The real question that the judiciary face here is: what is "sufficient"?

The rebuttal evidence provided by the investigators must be deemed to be "sufficient," but there is a difference in the standards of what is considered sufficient in primary and secondary cases. In primary cases, the rebuttal evidence is for the prosecution to provide, therefore the standard of proof must be that of the prosecution. In secondary cases, the rebuttal evidence is for the defendant to provide, therefore the standard of proof must be that of the defendant. Although China's current laws do not make a clear distinction between these two standards of proof, a distinction of this kind is more than necessary from both a theoretical and a practical perspective. Here, we can borrow from the Anglo-American legal systems to express these different standards of proof: for the prosecution this would be "beyond reasonable doubt" and for the defendant, "the preponderance of the evidence". The former is a very high standard of proof, with a probability of more than 90%; the latter is a relatively low standard of proof, with a probability of 51% and above. So, in secondary cases, if an investigators' rebuttal probability reaches 51% or above, a judge cannot on the basis of presumption find that a confession was forced. But in primary cases, if an investigators' rebuttal probability does not reach 90%, a judge must presume torture and exclude the illegal evidence of the confession.

Rules of presumption around forced confession are then supplementary to the rules around the exclusion of illegal evidence. They have a positive effect on both the problems faces in excluding illegal evidence and on curbing forced confessions and preventing wrongful convictions. Naturally, other rules of presumption designed to curb the practice of forced creation should be created, such as rules of presumption around the recording of interrogations.

10.4 Creating a Presumption Rule About Compulsory Recording of Interrogations[3]

Article 121 of CPL states: "Investigators, when interrogating a criminal suspect, may record or videotape the interrogation process, and shall do so where the criminal suspect is involved in a crime punishable by life imprisonment or capital punishment or in an otherwise major criminal case." Although legislators have made it a mandatory requirement for audio-video recordings to be taken during the interrogations of major criminal cases, they have not clearly specified the consequences of transgression. In October 2013, *the Opinions on Establishing and Improving Working Mechanisms for*

[3]The basic research for this part was done by Wang Aiping, Ph.D. student at the Law School of Renmin University of China from 2012 to 2015.

the Prevention of Miscarriages of Justice in Criminal Cases issued by SPC contained an additional stipulation: "With the exception of emergency situations necessitating at the scene interrogations, confessions obtained during interrogations which occur in places other than the designated case-handling location, and confessions obtained during interrogations in which a full audio-visual recording was not made in accordance with the law, shall be excluded." However, by its nature this document is merely an internal "Guidance Opinion" published by the higher authorities and is not a formal "Judicial Interpretation", moreover the creator of the document is one body only—SPC—and so its provisions have failed to be strictly enforced.

In fact, China's procuratorates began the use of synchronous audio-video recording system for duty-related crime interrogations as early as 2007. But in practice, the practice of selective recording is nothing new and investigators adopt the "normative" interrogation process when conducting audio-video recordings, which includes methods such as "ask much, record little" and "ask first, record later". For example, a defendant Chen, the head of a local police station in Dongfang City, Hainan Province, together with another defendant Lei, the deputy director of the anti-riot brigade, were suspected of abuse of power. Chen claimed in court that he had himself had been tortured by investigators. According to the interrogation transcript, the investigators conducted a total of ten interviews with Chen, but there were only recordings of five. In another example, in the case of corruption and bribery involving a defendant Liao, director of the Civil Affairs Bureau in Ezhou City, Hubei Province, both the defendant and counsel for the defense raised the question of torture in court, and pointed out that recordings of the three interrogations were amended after questioning had concluded, and moreover "superfluous parts had been cut out". The public prosecutor also admitted in court that there were imperfections on the video recording, but believed that the court could not presume torture on the basis of a lack of a whole synchronous recording.

As audio-video recordings of interrogations are not yet legally mandated, when the defense raises in court the that the defendant has been a victim of torture and points out that audio-video recordings supplied by the prosecution are incomplete, the prosecution usually cites equipment issues or technical failures as mitigation, and judges often accept the prosecution's explanation, and do not find the evidence to be illegal on the basis of deficiencies in audio-video recordings. As a result, the effects of the system of making audio-video recordings of interrogations are greatly reduced in practice. In order to counter vulnerabilities in the system of selective audio-video recordings, SPP set out clear requirements in its *Relevant Rules On Synchronous Audio-Video Recordings During Interrogations of Duty-Related Criminal Suspects by Procuratorates* in May 2014. This states that audio-video recordings of interrogations must be complete, synchronous and uninterrupted and, furthermore, makes clear stipulations around such things as the truncating of the main part of recordings, the standardization of recording sequencing and the management of technical failures. Although this type of regulation has a certain impact on the standardization of investigative interrogation conduct, because it lacks clear rules around eliminating "gain", its effectiveness is still unsatisfactory.

Because of insufficiently clear laws and regulations, there are variations in the attitude of judges when dealing with these sorts of questions, and rulings can differ widely. For example, in a 2011 bribery case in the Junshang District of Yueyang, Hunan Province, the defense suggested in court that the defendant, when in the prosecution room of the detention center, was subjected to corporal punishment including being forced to kneel for protracted periods. The prosecution then supplied physical examination reports, an account of the event, and testimony of the disciplined used as counter-evidence. The judge, giving as reasons "the prosecution has not as yet supplied the audio-video recording equipment from the day in question, thus failing to meet the requirements of the Procuratorate's internal regulations", and "the evidence supplied by the prosecution is neither credible nor sufficient enough to rule out forced confession", ruled in favor of excluding the confession. However, in the 2013 case involving defendant He, a technical manager at the Yantai Port Power Company in Shandong Province, the suggestion of the defense and the counter-evidence provided by the prosecution was essentially identical to the previous case, but here the judge did not accept the defense's position and did not exclude the defendant's confession. In another example from 2013, a defendant Wang was accused of selling drugs in Heze, Shandong Province. The defense in a court hearing raised the fact the defendant's confession had been obtained through torture, that the Procuratorate had not carried out audio-video recordings in line with Article 121 of China's Criminal Procedure Law, and requested that the court exclude the defendant's confession of guilt. The court did not accept the defense's suggestion. However, in a joint robbery case in Zhoukou, Henan Province in 2014, the Procuratorate failed to supply audio-video recordings of interrogations and judge ruled to exclude the defendants' testimony. These examples demonstrate the phenomenon of "same case, different judgments" in judicial practice. The creation of rules of presumption which make audio-video recordings of interrogations mandatory would be an effective way to eliminate this chaos.

A logical structure for rules of presumption around mandatory audio-video recordings of interrogations can be expressed as follows: As the law clearly stipulates that synchronous audio-video recordings of suspect's interrogations must be made, the prosecution should supply the court with complete recordings of all interrogations. If the prosecution is unable to supply these, or if the audio-video recordings are incomplete, the court should presume that the interrogations "used torture or other illegal methods of obtaining a confession" and should not allow any confessions obtained during these interrogations to be heard.

The creation of this rule of presumption would be beneficial not only in tackling the difficult issue of how to determine the facts of a case when there is a shortage of evidence, but also in setting just procedures in the curtailment of forced confessions and in the safeguarding of the judiciary. In other words, the creation of this legal rule would be both valuable and epistemological. Moreover, if the rule were to be established firmly, it would be conducive to the regulation of behavior during interrogations, thus raising the competence and standard of criminal investigations.

The creation of presumption rules ought to observe the logic rules and the linguistic norms, and should meet the following requirements: (1) There must be an accurate description of basic facts. (2) There must be a clear expression of the presumed facts. (3) The relationship between the two must be legitimately explained. (4) The facts must observe the laws of logical thought, i.e., the law of identity, the law of non-contradiction, and the law of the excluded middle. (5) It is best to uniformly use "presume" as the key word; if the use of "presume" is inappropriate in a particular context, then the word "deem" can be substituted. These are the prerequisites for the correct application of the rules of presumption in judicial practice.

Reference

He, Jiahong, and He, Ran. 2008. Problems of Evidence in Wrongful Convictions—Empirical Studies and Economic Analysis. *Tribune of Political Science and Law* (2), vol. 2008.

Chapter 11
The Application of Presumption Rules

Contents

11.1 Case Illustration

Before dawn on 2nd June 2009, there was a road traffic accident at an intersection in the Chaoyang District of Beijing—a Mercedes Benz car traveling straight ahead hit a taxi turning left which caused the taxi to hit an electricity pylon by the roadside, writing the vehicle off and causing injuries to the two passengers. Zhou, the driver of the Mercedes, left the scene after reporting the crash to the police by telephone. When police from the Chaoyang road traffic division arrived on the scene, an investigation of the scene was conducted, and a (negative) alcohol-level test on the driver of the

J. He, *Methodology of Judicial Proof and Presumption*,
Masterpieces of Contemporary Jurisprudents in China,
https://doi.org/10.1007/978-981-10-8025-8_11

taxi was performed. Officers repeatedly called the number that Zhou had called from, but the phone was switched off. Later that morning, police searched the address that Zhou's car was registered to, but did not find Zhou. At around 4 p.m. that afternoon, Zhou turned himself in for questioning at the Chaoyang Traffic Department. The police immediately conducted an alcohol test, but found nothing. The case attracted a lot of public interest, because Zhou was a famous actor. For a time, the "Zhou Hit and Run" case was an internet sensation.

On 25th June, the Road Traffic Accident Expert Center issued its report on the speed the two vehicles had been traveling at when the crash occurred: the Mercedes Benz had reached 78.8 km/h, the taxi no more than 32.2. The speed limit on the road where the incident took place was 70 km/h. On 1st July, Chaoyang Traffic Department published its Accident Liability Conclusion: Zhou was found to be responsible in the most part, with the taxi driver bearing secondary responsibility. The two passengers in the taxi were innocent. With regards to the question that had been attracting special interest from the public—whether or not Zhou had been drinking—the department's conclusion was as follows: "There is currently insufficient evidence to prove whether Mr. Zhou was driving under the influence of alcohol at the time of the incident." There was much widespread comment about this conclusion online. Because of his actions—fleeing the scene after the crash and only turning up and accepting tests at the traffic department 12 h later—many people believed that he must have been drink driving.

On 6th July, Zhou applied for a review of the Accident Liability Conclusion, but the review upheld the original conclusion. On 26th July, Beijing's Chaoyang Road Traffic Department published a "Decision on Administrative Punishment", imposing a five-day detention and a 1800RMB fine on Zhou. Zhou applied for an Administrative Reconsideration. On 10th November, the review body upheld the sentence. Shortly after this, at Chaoyang District Court, Zhou brought a lawsuit asking for a deferment of the five-day imprisonment sentence. On 25th November, Zhou withdrew the case. On 2nd December, the traffic department started procedures for the five-day detention in accordance with the relevant regulations.

Around this time, the civil lawsuit was progressing in a series of twists and turns. On 21st July, in Chaoyang District Court, Zhou sued the Beijing-based Xinyue United Car Limited Company, asking for compensation for the loss of a vehicle of 200,000RMB. On 13th August, Zhou withdrew the case. On 19th August, Xinyue submitted a counterclaim at the district court, asking that Zhou pay for the company's vehicle loss at a cost of more than 97,000RMB. Soon after this, Zhou expressed willingness towards reconciliation and compensation, and the two parties started negotiations. At the beginning of November, two taxi drivers (who shared the same taxi) also sued Zhou after five months of inactivity, asking for vehicle rental fees and compensation for loss of earnings of more than 60,000RMB (the taxi driver who had been hit had still not recovered). On 26th November, the case was heard at Shuangqiao Court in Chaoyang District, but despite many delays did not reach a conclusion. On 19th May 2010, Chaoyang District Court decided to once again schedule hearings between Zhou and Xinyue, and Zhou and the two taxi drivers. At nine a.m. a throng of reporters was waiting outside the courtroom when Zhou's lawyer came into court. She told the judge that she was there to handle formalities around the withdrawal of charges, as Zhou had reached a settlement in both cases. Zhou's lawyer did not reveal the content of the agreement reached.

Although the cases were settled, the question of whether or not Zhou had been driving under the influence of alcohol still attracted media interest, it being felt that Zhou's behavior was not a positive model. The conclusion reached by Chaoyang traffic department was that "There is currently insufficient evidence to prove whether Mr. Zhou was driving under the influence of alcohol at the time of the incident." In other words, a shortage of evidence had led to ambiguity over whether or not Mr. Zhou had in fact been drinking. That is, it could be neither confirmed nor denied. When it comes to difficult questions of proof such as this, some people suggest applying rules of presumption around unfavorable evidence. In Chap. 8, when I deal with the "resumption paradigm of state", I refer to Article 75 of PECP. "Where there is evidence proving that a concerned party refuses, without any justifiable reason, to provide evidence that he controls, and the opposite party alleges that contents of such evidence are disadvantageous to the evidence holder, such allegation can be construed as justifiable." In this case, the evidence as to whether not Mr. Zhou was drinking alcohol (i.e. his breath and/or his blood) was in his control, moreover he avoided the alcohol test for no proper reason which resulted in there being no way to acquire the evidence. This ought to be viewed as "a concerned party refusing, without any justifiable reason, to provide the evidence that he controls" and it should, therefore, be presumed that the content of that evidence was disadvantageous to him. That is, it should be presumed that Mr. Zhou was indeed driving under the influence of alcohol. However, some people believe that applying rules of presumption in this way is rash.[1]

As concluded in Chap. 7, presumptions are inferential findings of fact made by judicial personnel in accordance with legal rules. Generally speaking, since presumptions are based on legal rules, finding the case facts or disputed facts by presumption in judicial activities is presented as applying the presumption rules. The presumption rules can be in the form of laws formulated and promulgated by legislature, as well as in the form of legal interpretations made by judicial organs.

11.2 Principles for Applying Presumption Rules

As mentioned in Chap. 9, besides other essential features, a rule of presumption should be clear, operable, and predictable, but influenced by various factors including language, the expression of a presumption rule tends to have a certain degree of fuzziness. Moreover, in judicial practice, the circumstances where facts require the application of a rule of presumption are complex and diverse. Thus, fuzziness of the expression of a rule and complexity of the cognitive object determine that the application of a rule of presumption can never be a simple repetition or mechanical

[1] Huang (2010) and Zhang (2012).

activity; instead, to accomplish the mission, it requires a judge to fully deploy subjective cognitive ability and professional knowledge and skills. Within this context, laying down certain basic principles is essential for the purpose of guidance. The author believes that in judicial practice the application of a presumption rule should comply with the following basic principles.

11.2.1 The Principle of Strict Application

Established on certain objective laws or rules of thumb, a rule of presumption should be scientific and rational. However, it is also limited in the aspect that the conclusion it draws is not necessarily consistent with the objective truth; in other words, the conclusion is "false-able". This means the application of a presumption rule has its "double sword" effect: on one hand, it can provide a shortcut for identification of a fact which is difficult to prove; on the other hand, it may also make the finding of a fact fall into trap or go astray. To prevent the happening of the latter, or to reduce such possibility to a minimum, a judge must strictly comply with the applicable conditions in the application of a presumption rule, and when the specific circumstances of a case are not fully in line with the applicable conditions, compelled application or extension of application is inadvisable, which is especially the case in criminal proceedings. The application of a presumption rule often leads directly to the "presumption of guilt" of the defendant,[2] which to some extent is contrary to the rule of presumption of innocence, though it is legal, wherefore the application of a presumption rule must be strictly regulated in prevention of misuse.

Meanwhile, we should make a distinction between presumptions and inferences. An inference refers to the referential assessment concluded by a judge in specific cases as to the fact to be proved based on certain basic facts; presumptions may be viewed as inferences fixed down in legal form. A judge may enjoy a greater discretion in making inferences to find a fact, as the judge must give the reasons behind an inference as per the particulars of a case, and then the parties and other interested persons can review the correctness and reasonableness of the inference. In contrast, the judge does not have to do so in the application of a presumption rule; only accurate citing of the relevant provisions of legislation or judicial interpretation will do, as whether the chain of reasoning is scientific and rational is the problem should be considered in the establishment phase of the rule, rather than in the application of the rule. Briefly, a judge is free to use the device of inferences, but he/she must be strict in applying the presumption rules.

---

[2]E.g., as per the presumption rule of the "crime of holding a huge amount of property from unidentified sources", as long as the defendant could not prove the "huge amount of property" is lawfully obtained, such property is presumed to be unlawfully obtained, hence the defendant is presumed guilty. In a certain sense, this is a "presumption of guilty", i.e., the defendant is presumed guilty as long as he cannot prove his innocence.

11.2.2 The Principle of Fair Application

Fairness is the essence of justice. In judicial activities, judicial officers should abide by the principle of fairness, and applying presumption rules is no exception, as it should be. Yet there is still a point in additionally emphasizing on the principle of fairness in the application of a presumption rule, as the establishment of a presumption rule is grounded not only on certain objective laws or rules of thumb, but also on certain values and social policies, and the value orientations and policy considerations tend to incorporate certain "inclined fairness" and "epoch character". The "inclined fairness" means that though the underlying connotation of the values of law is fairness, the value orientation for the establishment of a rule of presumption is not absolutely fair; there is a certain tendency that some values are attached with priority or emphasis. For example, the value orientation for the legislative presumption rule as to the "crime of holding a huge amount of property from unidentified sources" is to strengthen the crackdown on corruption, and the protection of the rights of the accused are therefore weakened. This is not absolute justice, not absolute injustice, so I call it "inclined fairness". As for the "epoch character", it means that values and social policies change with the development of society, and different historical periods carries different values and social policies. For example, in the 1980s, the mainstream values of Chinese society was "maintenance of state power" and "to fight against crime", the corresponding criminal policy was "severe blow"; but today, 20 years later, the mainstream values of Chinese society are "harmonious society" and "to protect human rights", the corresponding criminal policy turns to "justice tempered with mercy". Value orientations and policy considerations for the establishment of a rule of presumption would also be attached with such "epoch character", bearing features meeting the demands or circumstances of a particular historical era.

Article 23 of GPCL stipulates: "Under either of the following circumstances, an interested person may apply to the people's court for a declaration of a citizen's death: (1) if the citizen's whereabouts have been unknown for four years or (2) if the citizen's whereabouts have been unknown for two years after the date of an accident in which he was involved. If a person's whereabouts become unknown during a war, the calculation of the time period in which his whereabouts are unknown shall begin on the final day of the war".

This rule of presumption of death is established out of policy considerations to maintain a stable of social life. In fact, many countries have similar laws, but the time span is generally prescribed as 7 years. GPCL was enacted in 1986. At that time, the social mobility of population in China was quite low, and household registration system was very tight, if a person's whereabouts has been unknown for over 4 years, in general the death of such person could be concluded. However, nowadays in China, mobility of the population has greatly increased, and household registration system has become looser, so it is not rare that a man missing for over 4 year is not dead. The sensational wrongful conviction of She Xianglin discovered in 2005 was a good example. The man served 11 years in prison after being wrongly convicted of murdering his wife in 1994, while the "victim" Zhang Zaiyu, the wife, returned to home in 2005, who was proven to be alive after 11 years missing.[3] Although there are not many cases in China that people petition the court to presume the death of their relatives, the statutes should try to be in accord with changes in social circumstances, and provisions like a person whose whereabouts has been unknown for over 4 years can be presumed as dead is clearly characterized by the past era.

The "inclined justice" and "epoch character" of the value orientations and policy considerations embodied by a rule of presumption may, to a certain degree, tip the "scale" of law, and the judges, in the application of a presumption rule, must strive to maintain the fairness of law. This is mainly manifested as the balance of the rights and interests between litigant parties. Since the establishment of a presumption rule is often in favor of the party that espouses the presumption, thus, in applying a presumption rule, a judge should give priority to the interests of the opponent to make the "scale" of law return even, and it is especially the case in criminal litigation. This guarantee of fairness is mainly reflected in two aspects. One is that the procedures should be configured to protect the right and opportunity of an effective rebuttal by the opponent; the other is that in the finding of a fact, when the evidence and arguments of both parties are well-matched, a ruling in favor of the opponent should be made. Take criminal proceedings for example, as long as the rebuttal by the defendant achieves the effect that the authenticity of the basic fact is uncertain, or it is able to prove that the possibility of the existence of the presumed fact under a given case is not significantly greater than the likelihood of other potentialities, the judge should rule that the presumption cannot stand.

11.2.3 The Principle of Open Application

Open trial is a fundamental principle for litigation proceedings; it should also be a fundamental principle for a judge in the application of a presumption rule during the proceedings. As mentioned earlier, the application of a presumption rule, as an important part for identifying a fact to be proved, will directly affect the outcome of a trial and the rights of the litigants, so a judge must abide by the principle of open application, which includes three aspects. First, the applicable procedures should be open, which requires a judge to inform the litigant parties of the decision to apply a presumption rule, especially to the adversely affected party; in other words, the adversely affected party should enjoy the right to be informed when the judge applies a presumption rule; secondly, the basis for the application should be disclosed, which requires a judge to openly inform in court the parties of the law or judicial interpretation that such application of a presumption rule is based on; and finally, the conclusions drawn from the application should be made public, which requires a judge to openly state the conclusion from and reasons for the application of a presumption rule in court or in judgment.

---

[3] See He (2016).

As mentioned earlier, on some occasions a judge need to make certain "fuzzy recognition" and "fuzzy reasoning" in deciding whether to apply a presumption rule, or, to put it in another way, a judge is allowed to some extent to make a "free proof with intimate conviction (*l'intime conviction*)". In judicial proof, "*l'intime conviction*" refers to a judge's subjective or inner cognitive status with respect to the facts to be proved. Indeed, a judge's "*l'intime conviction*" is not directly perceived by outsiders, but it can and should be disclosed in a certain way. Specifically, the conclusions from and reasons for the application of a presumption rule should be disclosed to the litigants and the public at large. There could be two ways of such disclosure. One is to disclose it in court trial, that is, to make it open through the admission of evidence; the other is to disclose it in written judgment, that is, to make it open by illustrating the conclusions from and reasons for the application of a presumption rule. In brief, the application of a presumption rule should not just occur within the mind of a judge, but also occur in an openly manner. This is also an important guarantee for the standardization of the application of presumption rules.

11.3 Procedures for Applying Presumption Rules

In China, procedures for application of presumption rules are not specifically provided in the legislation currently in force. Evidence scholars have not clearly elaborated on the subject either. Some scholars, in discussion of "application of presumptions", emphasize that the basic facts must be confirmed at first, meanwhile, there has to be no contrary evidence to rule out the presumption.[4] This carries a sense of application procedures. Due to the absence of legislation and theoretical interpretation, there is no universal judicial practice when it comes to procedures for application of presumption rules. Some judges explicitly state the application of a presumption rule in the course of a trial; some judges merely mention it in rulings; some even only use with no mention of it. The author believes that it is still adequately necessary to clarify the procedures for application of a presumption rule. According to the general rules of litigation activities and judicial proving, the procedures to apply a presumption rule should include the following three phases.

11.3.1 Initiation

To apply relevant presumption rules in litigation activities is both the right of the concerned litigants and the power of the judge. The litigants have the right to request the judge to apply a certain presumption rule in the finding of a fact or a disputed fact, and the judge may also at his/her discretion apply a certain presumption rule in fact-finding. Yet when a litigant party requests application, the final decision rests

---

[4]See Chen (2000), Bian (2000, p. 376).

on the judge. Upon receiving such request, or at his/her own discretion to apply a presumption rule, the judge should first review the proving of basic facts so as to determine whether the basic conditions for application of a presumption rule are met.

11.3.2 Rebuttal

The phase of initiation should be followed by rebuttal, no matter the request is made by a litigant party or the decision is made by the judge. This means the adversely affected party should be given the opportunity to rebut. The target of such rebuttal could either be that the basic facts to which the presumption applies cannot be established, or that such basic facts do not fit the conditions of the presumption rule, or that the outcome of the presumption does not match the specific circumstances of the given case. The manifestation of rebuttal can be offering of evidence, explanation, or debate. Judges should hear the rebuttal of the adversely affected party observantly.

11.3.3 Ruling

If the adversely affected party does not make any rebuttal after given the opportunity, the judge may directly render the application of a presumption rule. If the adversely affected party makes a rebuttal, the judge will review and determine whether such rebuttal is valid and whether it is sufficient to prevent the application of a presumption rule. Based on an integrated weighing of the opinions from both parties, the judge will rule whether a presumption rule shall apply.

In judicial practice, the procedures for application of a presumption rule may be a continuous dynamic process. The proponent may request the application, the opponent party rebuts, both parties presenting evidence and offering arguments, until the judge reach a decision. In this scenario, the borderline between the phases of the above procedures might not be very distinct; yet for the standardization of the application of presumption rules, it is still meaningful to clarify these three phases in terms of jurisprudence. Since the main effect of applying the presumption rules would be on the allocation of burden of proof, I shall now discuss the application with regard to the burden of proof.

11.4 Application of Presumption Rules and the Burden of Proof

11.4.1 The Burden of Proof in Application of Presumption Rules

Although presumption is an approach for a judge to conduct fact-finding activities, the immediate effect of applying the presumption rules, in the proceedings, is to exempt the burden of proof from one party and add it to the other. For example, as mentioned in Chap. 8, Item 3 of Article 4 of PECP stipulates that, in a compensation lawsuit for damages caused by environmental pollution, the infringing party shall be responsible for producing evidence to prove the existence of exemptions of liabilities as provided in laws or that there is no causal relationship between his act and the harmful consequences. This is the judicial presumption rule related to the causality of environmental pollution.

It is well known that the general principle of the distribution of the burden of proof in civil procedures is "who claims, who has the burden of proof". In the civil litigation caused by environmental pollution, the plaintiff (the victim) should have borne the burden of proof of all facts, including the causality between the polluting action and the damage results. But in the case related to environmental pollution, the damage is caused by several factors in a relatively long term, and the causality is fairly complicated with some expertise, so that ordinary victims usually fail to prove. To better protect the rights and interests of the victims of the environmental pollution and further strengthen environmental protection, some countries rectified the principle of "who claims, who has the burden of proof" and required the defendant (the injurer) bearing the burden of proof that there is a causality between the polluting action and the damage results. The above-mentioned presumption rule is just the case. According to the rules, the plaintiff no longer bears the burden of proof that there is causality between pollution action and damage results, and meanwhile, the defendant shall bear the burden of proof that there was not. If the defendant doesn't present evidence or it isn't sufficient to persuade the judge to accept his claims, the judge should presume that the pollution action is the cause for the damage results and make the decision that the defendant shall take compensation liability.

In the lawsuit of compensation for environmental pollution and some other similar lawsuits, applying presumption rules can allocate the burden of proof in a more fair and reasonable manner. On one hand, it's difficult for the plaintiff to prove the facts, such as causality; applying presumption rules can avoid losing the lawsuit due to the failure to present evidences caused by objective reasons. On the other hand, in such kind of cases, the defendant usually has the information and ability to proof relevant facts, and applying presumption rules can prompt the defendant to actively participate in proof-taking activities, or force the defendant to provide information that can prove the truly facts, so that the judge can properly conduct fact-finding activities and make fair and reasonable judgments. It follows that the presumption rules have the function of reallocating the burden of proof among parties according to particular circumstances. And after that, we need to answer two questions underlying in the above context and interweaving in the related concepts—careful readers may have realized their very existence, and deduced their diversity from the caution of the author in choosing vocabularies. Questions one: is the target of reallocation the burden of proof or the burden of producing evidence? Question two: is such reallocation a shift or an inversion of the burden of proof. Now, I will discuss the two questions respectively. Due to their interrelations, this author will use temporarily the word of "shift" when discussing the first question.

11.4.2 The Burden of Proof or the Burden of Producing Evidence

There are some discussions about the two concepts, the burden of proof and the burden of producing evidence, in Chap. 5, and the opinion of this author is that the two concepts are generally used as the same in Chinese. Here, some readers may raise a question: since the burden of proof and the burden of producing evidence are the same, why it is necessary to discuss which, the former or the latter, should be shifted when applying the presumption rules? This doubt has its own ground, so does the questions mentioned above. Because in China, many scholars view that, just part of the burden of proof will be shifted, which is considered as "the burden of producing evidence". Professor Bian Jianlin said: "the author holds that, with the shift of the burden of proof, just the shift of the burden of proof will be mentioned except the shift of the burden of persuasion; in other words, the shift just happens to be subjective or the burden of proof in an action sense, and objective the burden of proof or the burden of proof in a result sense always fix to the prosecution."[5] Professor Long Zongzhi points out that, "generally, people think the burden of producing evidence can be shifted in the criminal burden of proof, but the burden of persuasion belongs to the prosecution. The author disagrees with this point. The accused takes the burden of proof effectively, which also convinces the judicial organs to confirm his innocence. The 'explanation' stipulated by law can be viewed as including both the burden of producing evidence and the burden of persuasion."[6] The author agrees with this point, but also appreciates the caution of Professor Bian in choosing words. In the above citation, we can see that, Professor Bian uses "the duty of presenting evidence" carefully to avoid involving into the conflict with "the burden of producing evidence", but his statement about "the shift of the burden of proof" seems stay contradictory with the viewpoint that "the burden of proof is the integration of the burden of presenting evidence and the burden of persuasion". Professor Long uses "the burden of producing evidence" directly, which stays parallel with "the burden of persuasion". To be frank, it isn't an initiative from Professor Long and many scholars use "the

[5]ibid, p. 229.

[6]Long (2008).

burden of producing evidence" in this sense. But this stands obvious differences with the legal practitioners mentioned-above (including legislators) who have been used to "the burden of producing evidence". "the burden of producing evidence" mentioned-above includes the burden of persuasion while "the burden of producing evidence" mentioned in Long's context stay parallel with the burden of persuasion. To distinguish, the former is called as "the broad burden of proof" and the latter "the narrow burden of proof". Till now, we have realized the divergence in the mentioned questions, namely, the presumption rules shift all the burden of proof or part of it ("the narrow burden of proof"). But this one implies another deep question: can the three meanings of the burden of proof be separated and maintain independent?

As the author mentioned above, whatever we choose, the burden of proof or the burden of producing evidence, it should involve the burden of action, the burden of persuasion and the burden of results. Here, the author clearly points out that, the duty implied in the three meanings can't be divided. This is to say, in the proceedings, the burden of proof borne by any party (in the principle of general allocation or by shift or inversion) involve all the three meanings together. To be frank, in some circumstances, we can feel that one party bears relatively slight duties but no matter how slight it can be, the burden of proof should include the three complete meanings. We assume that one party only bears the burden of action, excluding the burden of persuasion and the burden of results; this means one party is allowed to provide any evidence (no matter it is true or false or have the slightest credibility), and the judge declares that he has fulfilled the proof task and shifted the task to the other party. As a result, the proof of both parties will become an alternate behavior casting the evidence at random, and the allocation of the burden of proof would lose its meaning. I think the burden of action, the burden of persuasion and the burden of results can't be divided. Even though there is the only one evidence, parties shall bear the burden of persuasion, namely persuading the judge to believe the facts are true, and can prove pending facts to some extent; and parties shall bear the unfavorable results in case of the failure to persuade the judge.[7] Some parties bear relatively slight the burden of proof, but it doesn't mean that he only bears the burden of action; it just indicates that he bears relatively slight burden of persuasion. In fact, when we answer this question, the focus of statement has shifted from the burden of proof to the standard of proof, which I will discuss later in this chapter.

The scholars, who support the burden of proof can be partly shifted, may take relevant theories concerning presumption and the burden of proof in Anglo-American evidence law as arguments. In fact, the view "only shifting the burden of producing evidence" of Chinese scholars is probably influenced by their counterparts in the Anglo-American countries. Here we need to mention two scholars from America, because their names gained the "naming rights" of some kind of presumption. The first one is James Thayer; in 1898, he proposed only shifting the burden of producing

[7]Here we need to differentiate the burden of proof and the right of proof. For example, in criminal lawsuits, the accused generally doesn't bear the burden of proof but has the right of proof. When exercising this right, the accused also attempts to persuade the adjudicator, but this is not duty so he don't need to accept unfavorable lawsuit result in case of the failure to persuade the adjudicator.

evidence but not the burden of proof and relevant series. Such kind of presumption was called "Thayer presumption" later. The second one is Edmund Morgan; in 1933, he proposed not only shifting the burden of producing evidence but also the burden of proof and relevant theories. It is called "Morgan presumption".[8] When first saw these two concepts, the author was also confused: don't they understand that the burden of producing evidence and the burden of producing evidence can't be divided? Or they were so ignorant that they can't realize the deep meanings? With in-depth research, the author understood that it was just a misunderstanding due to different languages. In English, "the burden of producing evidence" and "the burden of persuasion" is not entirely equal to the corresponding concepts in Chinese. Although the concepts we use in Chinese may be introduced from English, we interpret them according to Chinese meanings, which depart from their original meanings in English to some extent.

There are three relevant concepts in the field of Anglo-American evidence law: burden of proof (onus of proof), burden of producing evidence (burden of production or burden of evidence), and burden of persuasion. The burden of producing evidence can also be referred to the burden of initially producing evidence or burden of going forward with the evidence or burden of coming forward with the evidence. In the field of the Anglo-American evidence law, some scholars hold that the burden of producing evidence is a general concept, and the burden of producing evidence and the burden of persuasion are two branches. Others view that the three concepts are independent and different.[9]

To correctly understand the meanings of these concepts, it is necessary to look up related explanations in dictionaries and academic monograghs. According to the explanation in the *Yuanzhao English-Chinese Dictionary of Anglo-American Law,* the burden of proof refers to a burden that "to avoid unfavorable judgment, parties provide evidence to prove their claims and persuade the fact-finders to believe"; the burden of producing evidence refers to the burden that "parties, who support some facts or propose arguments, produce sufficient evidence to confirm the facts or obtain favorable judgments in terms of arguments. If parties fail to bear the burden of producing evidence, the lawsuit will be dismissed or the court will make instructing judgments"[10]; the burden of persuasion refers to the burden that "to persuade fact-finders (the judge or the jury) to believe that the facts proved by the evidence or elements (such as the criminal elements) are true. If parties fail to bear the burden of persuasion, fact-finders must make unfavorable judgments to a party in terms of facts or elements".[11]

---

[8]Garner (1999, pp. 1026, 1486).

[9]See Waltz (1983, p. 273).

[10]It means that the jury doesn't need to examine the evidence and makes judgments directly under the judge's instruction. In such case, the judge replaces the judge who plays a role as fact-finder, because the evidence is obviously insufficient so that it doesn't need to go through the formal jury trial.

[11]Xue (2003, p. 179).

With regard to the burden of producing evidence and the burden of persuasion, Professor Whalz indicates that "the burden of producing evidence refers to proposing or performing the duty to present the evidence of some specific questions; this is to say, the present has enough weight to require submitting this disputed question to the jury … The burden of persuasion refers to a duty that persuading the fact-finders believe the evidence presented in the court are true. In other words, the burden of persuasion require the lawyers to show their argue techniques, which is mainly in the closing statement to the jury".[12]

When explaining these two concepts, professor Allen points out: "any dispute in lawsuits, no matter one factor or a positive defense, is related to the burden of producing evidence to require one party or the other to provide evidence for some specific disputes (so referred to 'the burden of producing evidence'). If the party, who bears the burden of producing evidence, fails to provide sufficient evidence for specific disputes, the judge would not allow submitting this question to the jury … To decide whether there are justified divergences on which party should win the case, the judge must take the burden of persuasion into consideration … To make the jury confirm more than half of the facts are true, the plaintiff (or the prosecutor) must provide sufficient evidence. If, as reasonable person, people fail to confirm that the plaintiff (or the prosecutor) has performed the burden of persuasion, there was no reason to further consider any legal procedure of the fact and the judge should suspend any procedure favorable to the defendant (or the accused). Similarly, if the evidence of the plaintiff (or the prosecutor) is overwhelming, reasonable person may not confirm the truth in the facts are less than 50%, and the defendant (or the accused) can't doubt or refute the evidence of the opposite, the judge should suspend any procedure favorable to the plaintiff (or the prosecutor). In short, as Professor McNaughton states in an important paper, the burden of producing evidence plays a role as saying performing duties".[13]

Whereas the explanation and indication above-mentioned, we can see that, the burden of producing evidence and the burden of persuasion actually contains the meaning of "producing evidence" and "persuasion" in Anglo-American evidence law. On one hand, the burden of producing evidence also require the parties to present sufficient evidence to persuade the judge, or their claims and evidence would never get through the judge's examination so as to be examined by the jury. On the other hand, although the burden of persuasion mainly the persuasion to the jury conducted by lawyers before the trial investigation but it is on the basis of producing evidence in the course of investigation. This author holds that, the differences between the two concepts mainly include the following three aspects: (1) judge is the object of the former, while jury is the object of the latter; (2) the former usually happens before the court hearing, while the latter happens after the court hearing; (3) the latter has a higher standard of proof than the former. Therefore, the so-called "the burden

[12]See Waltz (1983, pp. 393–394).

[13]Allen et al. (2006, pp. 801–802).

of producing evidence" is equal to the initial burden of proof,[14] and the so-called "the burden of persuasion" is equal to the final burden of proof. They aren't two layers of meanings but two stages of the burden of proof. Making it clear, we can understand why the burden of producing evidence and the burden of persuasion can be divided and be independent in Anglo-American legal system. Furthermore, the jury trial in common law countries also needs such kind of division. Before the jury trial, the judge preliminarily examines the evidence submitted by the plaintiff (or the prosecutor) to avoid the jury trial wasting resource and time. If there is no jury, it would not need to divide the burden of proof into the burden of producing evidence and the burden of persuasion.

Therefore, "the burden of producing evidence" and "the burden of persuasion" in Chinese are different from those in the Anglo-American evidence law. We can't use the Chinese meaning to understand its English meaning, and can't apply the Chinese concept to English concept. China doesn't adopt the model of jury trial and the proceedings in China don't accurate to dividing the burden of proof into two stages, thus we don't need to introduce such division in the Anglo-American evidence law. More importantly, using such words to divide the proof stage easily lead to misunderstand; it seems that the former stage just needs "producing evidence" and the latter just needs "persuasion". Let's come back to the question of presumption again. The presumption of shifting the burden of producing evidence can be found only in the context of Anglo-American evidence law but not the Chinese evidence law. In other words, in the context of Chinese evidence law, applying the presumption rules is to shift the complete burden of proof, including the burden of action of producing evidence, the burden of persuasion that making the adjudicator believe parties' claims and the corresponding burden of results. Of course, if we use "the burden of producing evidence" which is equal to the part of "the burden of proof", it is no doubt that the application of the presumption rules will shift the burden of producing evidence, because it still be the burden of proof in a complete sense.

11.4.3 Shift or Inversion of the Burden of Proof

Now I move on to the second question, whether the reallocation is a shift or an inversion of the burden of proof. Undoubtedly, there is close relation between the presumption and the burden of proof. As some scholars point out: "we should first study the presumption when it comes to the burden of proof. On the premise of presumption, the burden of proof can be possible and necessary. Without the real existence and the scope of presumption, the institutions and procedure establishment of the burden of proof will lose support and grounds. The burden of proof is on the basis of presumption and also serves for it. They are always integrated with each

[14]Therefore, in Anglo evidence law, the burden of persuasion is also called the ultimate burden or the general burden. See Qi (2002).

other".[15] To be sure, presumption is referred to the prerequisite of the institutions and procedure establishment of all the burden of proof, which seems "exaggerate" the role of presumption. But the presumption rules indeed determine the allocation of the burden of proof, or in other words, the basic function of the presumption rules is reallocating the burden of proof. Scholars hold different views on whether such kind of reallocation belongs to the shift or the inversion of the burden of proof.

In the *Law of Evidence* edited by Professor Jiangwei, the author indicates that: "specifically, the relation between presumption and the burden of proof can be presented form the following three aspects: (1) in special cases, presumption determines the allocation of the burden of proof … (3) presumption determines the shift and changes of the burden of proof. In the proceedings, the burden of proof always moves around between the two sides, because presumption plays some roles".[16] If the views from this statement are somehow ambiguous, what Professor Long Zongzhi thinks is much more clear. He holds that, one feature of presumption to be different from proof methods such as inference is that "presumption shifts the burden of proof".[17] Yet Professor Long doesn't specially discuss "shift or inversion" in that article, so I don't know whether such statement reflects his original intention. In fact, without noticing, the author sometimes says some word like this "the basic function of presumption is to shift the burden of proof", although my original intention is to use "inversion". Some scholars clearly tend to "inversion". For example, Professor Bian Jianlin points out that: "in view of allocating the burden of producing evidence in a fair and reasonable manner, legislators may inverse the burden of producing evidence by presumption, so the burden of proof shall be borne by the party who have the evidence and the ability to prove".[18]

So long as I know, there is no "inversion of the burden of proof" in the Anglo-American evidence law, and the scholars would use the term of "shifting the burden". The basic meaning is "in the proceedings, the court must prove that the liability can be shifted from one party to the other. Through presenting the evidence, one party completes the preliminary proof, after which the other party presents the opposite evidence to argue. This is the shift of the burden of proof".[19] In fact, it's more sensible not to differentiate "shift" and "inversion", because it can eliminate the trouble that determining "shift" or "inversion" in face of complicated cases. As long as the allocation of the burden of proof changes between the two parties, that is "shift"—the answer is very simple, so does the question.

However, influenced by the allocation of the burden of proof of the continent legal system, scholars in China use "shift" and "inversion". Some scholars summarize the differences between the shift and the inversion of the burden of proof as the following seven aspects: different jurisdiction, different value, different enforcement power, different legal results, different origins, the differences between unidirectional and

[15] Jiang (1999).

[16] ibid, pp. 122–123.

[17] Long Zongzhi.

[18] Bian (2000, p. 375).

[19] Xue (2003, p. 1254).

bidirectional nature and between static and dynamic state.[20] Since using these two concepts, we have to answer which question is about "shift" and which one is related to "inversion", and also have to answer that whether the changes of the burden of proof from the application of presumption rules belong to "shift" or "inversion". As a result, we unconsciously make the easy questions complicated.

As mentioned above, the general allocation principle and the initial allocation principle of the burden of proof is "who claims, who bears the burden of proof". In a civil litigation, the burden of proof shall at first or generally be borne by the plaintiffs who file the claims. In the criminal lawsuits, according to the presumption of innocence, the burden of proof shall generally be borne by the prosecutors[21] who file the criminal charges. However, this doesn't mean that in all proceedings, the plaintiffs and the prosecutors always bear the burden of proof. In some cases, the burden of proof shall be borne by the defendants (or the accused). This is the shift or the inversion of the burden of proof. The author will indicate this issue from the perspective of criminal lawsuit.

The shift of the burden of proof refers to that according to the needs in the proceedings and the convenience of producing evidence—which party produces the evidence facilitates the advancing of the proof, the burden of proof is shifted from the prosecutor to the accused. For example, the accused in a murder case states that he was not at the scene of crime. For this fact claim, the accused should bear the burden of proof, namely, producing evidence to prove that he was not at the scene of crime. In such case, the burden of proof shall be shifted form the prosecutors to the accused. Such kind of shift complies with the law of judicial proof. Since the accused file a positive claim to defense, he should submit the corresponding evidence to support his claim and obviously, he is in the favorable position. But after the accused fulfilled the burden of proof, the burden of proof in the case would be shifted to the prosecutors. In addition, the prosecutors should take use of sufficient evidence to prove all the charged criminal facts, including the accused was on the scene when the crime happened.

The accused doesn't bear the burden of proof for all claims. If the accused just negatively object the claims filed by the prosecutors, for example, if he claims he didn't kill anyone, he doesn't bear any burden of proof fro this kind of fact; in other words, there exists no shift of the burden of proof. Only when the accused file the specific facts with positive defense meaning, the burden of proof can be shifted to the accused. In the legal practice, the common defense claims, which can lead to the shift of the burden of proof, include the following four categories: (1) facts related to the capacity for liabilities of the accused; for example, the accused have mental disorder or he is in an abnormal mental state when committing the crime; the accused don't reach the age which he should take the criminal liabilities when committing the crimes. (2) Facts related to the legality and the legitimacy of the behavior; for

[20]Bian, Jianlin (ed.). 2004. *The Theory of Criminal Proof*, pp. 226–227. China Renmin Public Security University.

[21]If it is a private prosecution case, the prosecutor should bear the burden. To make the expression clear, the author only uses the "prosecutor".

example, the killings or the injuries of the accused belong to self defense; and the property damage committed by the accused belong to necessity. (3) Facts related to the illegality of the investigators' and the law enforcement officials' behavior; for example, the reason for the accused to commit the charged crime is the "investigation trap" of public security officers; the reason for the accused to admit guilty is the torture from interrogators. (4) Facts related to the impossibility for the accused to commit the charged crime; for example, the accused is impossible commit robbery, because he was not at the scene when the crime occurred; and the accused is impossible to commit murder, because the victim was murdered by someone else. In criminal lawsuits, whether the shift of the burden of proof is shifted or not depends on the specific analysis of the facts proposed by the accused.

The inversion of the burden of proof refers to that in some cases, the accused shall bear the burden of proof pursuant to law. Some scholars suggest that: "the inversion of the burden of concept is belong to the Germany federation law, which is proposed for the amendment of classifying the elements and the need to maintain legal policies and order; it isn't complied with the basic principle of the allocation of the burden of proof and make some additional stipulations for the opposing party to bear the burden of proof".[22] To sum up, the inversion of the burden of proof is the informal allocation of the burden of proof. Legislators determine to apply the inversion of the burden of proof for the following reasons: the need of judicial proof, the convenience for producing evidence and the consideration about social policies which reflect some social values. For example, the stipulation concerning "the crime of holding a huge amount of property with unidentified sources" in the Article 395 of CL belongs to the inversion of the burden of proof. In such cases, to crack down on the embezzlement and bribery, legislators stipulate the accused shall bear the burden of proof and meanwhile, this stipulation also take the convenience for producing evidence into consideration. In such cases, even the huge amount of property of the accused is the illegal income, it's difficult for the prosecutor to prove. However, if these property has its legal source, it is much more reasonable and convenient for the accused to producing evidence.

The author holds that, main differences between the shift and the inversion of the burden of proof is that, the former still conforms to the general principle of "who claims, who bears the burden of proof", and the latter is just the contrary to this principle, namely, I claim, but you have the burden of proof. In the case concerning "the crime of holding a huge amount of property with unidentified sources", the prosecutor claims these properties are illegal income, but the accused shall bear the burden of proof to prove that it is not illegal income according to law. The accused fails to submit a positive fact to defense but law forces the accused to bear the burden that facts claimed by the prosecutor cannot be confirmed. As long as the accused fails to use sufficient evidence to prove the huge mount of property has its legal source, the judge would presume that these properties are illegal income and convict the accused. So far, our discuss comes back to the relations of presumption and the burden of proof and after making it clear the differences between the shift

[22] Bian, Jianlin (ed.). *The Theory of Criminal Proof*, p. 227.

and the inversion of the burden of proof, we can answer the above questions much more easily. The prerequisite to the shift of the burden of proof is the accused files positive facts claims and the prerequisite to the inversion of the burden of proof is the presumption rules, so it is the shift not the inversion of the burden of proof is leaded by the application of presumption rules. According to presumption rules, the party who confirms the fact claims doesn't bear the burden of proof; the party who doesn't confirm the fact claims should bear the burden of proof. To sum up, the saying of "I claim but you prove" obviously belongs to inversion of the burden of proof.

11.5 Application of Presumption Rules and the Standard of Proof

11.5.1 The Standard of Proof with Presumption Rules

The application of the presumption rules has close relationships with the standard of proof. However, in the theoretical studies of the issue, scholars pay more attention to the relationships between presumption and the burden of proof, and rarely discuss the relationships between presumption and the standard of proof. For example, when scholars in China feel confused about the division of "the burden of producing evidence" and "the burden of persuasion" in the Anglo-American evidence law, the solution always focuses on sharing the two burdens, namely, who should bear "the burden of producing evidence" when applying the presumption rules and who should bear "the burden of persuasion" when applying the presumption rules. In fact, people ignore a more important question: the difference in proof standards. As this author mentioned above, in the Anglo-American evidence law, one of the differences between "the burden of producing evidence" and "the burden of proof" is proof standard. The so-called "the burden of producing evidence" is just the burden of proof with lower proof standard.

In the textbooks of Chinese evidence law, the burden of proof and the standard of proof usually represented as two independent topics. For example, in the invoked works on evidence law, Professor Jiangwei and Professor Bian Jianlin opened independent chapters respectively in the textbooks edited by them to discuss the burden of proof and the proof standards; in the textbooks edited by Professor Chen Yiyun, even though no special chapter was opened for the proof standards, but it has been included in the chapter called "the proof task", which is actually separated with the burden of proof. In addition, in the textbooks of the evidence law edited by the author, the burden of proof and the proof standards are also discussed in different chapters.[23] However, in the works on the Anglo-American evidence law, the proof standards generally aren't discussed in independent chapters but under the theme of the burden of proof. For example, in the book of Professor Whalz and of Professor Allen, we can't

[23] See He and Zhang (2007), He and Liu (2007).

see the words "the proof standards" in the chapter title, but we can find some discussions about the proof standards in the chapter on the burden of proof. Under the title "the allocation of the burden of proof in criminal cases", the former mainly discusses the burden of proof[24]; in the two sections "the burden of proof in civil cases" and "the burden of proof in criminal cases", the latter devotes pages to the proof standards, and even regards "preponderant evidence" and "excluding reasonable doubts" of the proof standards as the rules of "the burden of persuasion".[25]

To be sure, in term of the logic of content system, the chapters are more specific and reasonable—first, the burden of proof and then, the proof standards, so that it can facilitate imparting knowledge and learning. But the teaching model, which is dedicated to separated discussion, makes us develop a thinking habit and naturally think that the burden of proof and the proof standards are two independent questions, and ignore the close relationships between the burden of proof and the proof standards. To be frank, the burden of proof and the proof standards are indivisible and the relationship between them can really be deemed as "always be together and indivisible". The proof standards always rely on the burden of proof; without the proof standards, the burden of proof would lose its realistic meanings. As above-mentioned, "the burden of producing evidence" and "the burden of proof" in the Anglo-American evidence law contains the meanings that using "sufficient" evidence to "persuade" fact-adjudicators. So what is "sufficient" or "insufficient"? What is "persuading" or "failing to persuade"? Some proof standards are needed to answer these questions. From pragmatic viewpoint, it has some sense to involve the proof standards into the burden of proof and discuss it and even regard it as a part of the burden of proof. Such difference between the textbooks of Chinese evidence law and those of the Anglo-American evidence law reflects, to some extent, that Chinese scholars focus on theory while scholars from Anglo-American countries focus on practice.

When the presumption rules are applied, the proof standards are also by the side. For example, in the above "the civil compensation litigation caused by the environmental pollution", the defendant (or the accused) attributed to the environmental pollution should bear the burden of proof without causal relationship, or else presume the existence of causal relationship. However, in the course of applying the presumption rules, the plaintiff (or the prosecutor) also bears the initial burden of proof, namely, using "sufficient" evidence to prove that he has suffered from damage, which has some relations in time and space with the environmental pollution ever happened. If the defendant (or the accused) doesn't want to take the civil compensation liability, he must submit the opposite evidence. In other words, the party who files claims of the presumption rules has the duty to use the "sufficient" evidence to prove basic facts: the opposite party of the presumption rules has the duty to use the "sufficient" evidence to refute. Therefore, the burden of proof of both parties cannot be separated with the proof standards—"sufficient" evidence. But is the standard for the two "sufficient" the same? As discussed in Chap. 6, the standards of proof may be

[24]See Waltz (1983, pp. 274–275).

[25]See Allen et al. (2006, pp. 801–821).

different in different cases and at different litigation stages. So the two "sufficient" may have different meanings here.

11.5.2 The Standard of Proof in the Application of Presumption Rules

In all proceeding activities, the plaintiff or the accused should bear the burden to prove the facts so that the court can support his claims, so the proof standards in the proceedings are generally set for the proof activities of the plaintiff or the accused. For example, the proof standard for conviction in a criminal case is "proof beyond a reasonable doubt". This is to say, the prosecutor should use the evidence which should meet the standard of "proof beyond a reasonable doubt" to prove the accused committed the charged crime. In applying the presumption rules, the burden of proof is inverted to the opposite party. Does it mean that the same proof standard in the proceedings can only be applied to the defendant's proof? The question is not that simple. First, when applying the presumption rules, the plaintiff (or the prosecutor) should bear the initial burden of proof or the burden of proof of basic facts, thus there are still questions about the proof standard. Secondly, the proof standard which is applied to the general burden of proof of the plaintiff (or the prosecutor) may not be applied to the burden of proof inverted to the opposite party. Finally, different proof standards of various proceeding activities also influence the proof standard in applying the presumption rules. Specifically, there are two questions about the proof standards when applying the presumption rules: one is the proof standard for basic facts; the other is the proof standard for rebuttal. The author will discuss the two questions in the following context.

11.5.2.1 The Proof Standard for the Basic Facts

Professor Allen once pointed out that: "when we begin to think about presumption, we should bear in mind two questions that can influence the operation of presumption but rarely be talked about by the court and commenter. Firstly, who has what kind of the burden of persuasion for the facts leading to presumption? … "Who" in this question is beyond doubt; people who want to use this presumption have the duty to prove the confirmation of presumptive facts. The preponderant evidence could answer "what" in this question; for most of preparatory facts, although rarely declaring the proof standards, it's a common sense. However, there are also cases in which the court set higher standards. (… using clear and convincing evidences to prove that…) Secondly, who will decide whether the party who wants to use the presumption meets the proper burden of persuasion? For example, presuming that a woman want to take use of the presumed death of her husband (fact B). If there are contradictory evidences regarding whether it has been 7 years since his missing (fact A), can the question be decided by the judge or the jury"?[26] What we are talking about here is that the standards of proving basic facts when the plaintiff (or the prosecutor) require to apply the presumption rules.

The proof standards of basic facts when people apply the presumption rules should meet the proof standards of different proceedings. As we mentioned above, the existing statutory proof standards in three procedure laws can be summarized as "the facts are clear and the evidences are true and sufficient". However, the "unified" proof standards can't reflect the differences between the features of three kinds of lawsuits and value orientation and we need to establish a "diversified" system. The author holds that, without changing articles in the existing procedure laws, we can, by legal interpretation, make different definitions for the proof standards in three kinds of lawsuits. Specifically, the proof standards in criminal lawsuits can be expressed as the proving "sure"[27]; the proof standards in civil litigation can be expressed as the proving "preponderant evidence"[28]; administrative lawsuits combine the features of proving private rights and public powers, so we can use "dichotomy", namely, in civil lawsuits, the proof of the plaintiff can use the proof standards of "preponderant evidences", and the proof of the defendant can use the proof standards higher than those of civil lawsuits but lower than "clear and convincing" in criminal lawsuits.[29] By the way, in accordance with the Article 32 in *the Administrative Litigation Law*, the burden of proof borne by the defendant aims at specific administrative actions, so "be sure and convincing" can also be deemed as the proof standards to confirm relevant facts when the administrative organs make specific behaviors (such as administrative punishments). If we use the language in probability to explain the three standards, the possibility that the claims proved by the standard of "preponderant evidences" are true is 60%; "be clear and convincing", 80%; "be sure", 90%.

The author holds that, no matter "be sure", "preponderant evidences" or "be clear and convincing", they don't conflict with the standard of "evidence is true and sufficient" in nature, for which it can be considered as the expression of the abstract proof standards; and "be sure" explains and states it from different perspective.

---

[26] Allen et al. (2006, p. 853).

[27] Some scholars in China have prejudice against the standard of "proof beyond a reasonable doubts" in Anglo-American Legal system countries, so we can use the expression of "be sure" with Chinese characteristics. With regard to the information conveyed by the word, "be sure" can be understood as the summary and integration of criminal proof standards in two legal systems, because it contains the concept of "inner conviction" as well as "excluding reasonable doubts".

[28] In fact, Some Provisions of the Supreme People's Court on Evidence in Civil Procedures has contained such "explanation". The Article 73 stipulates that: "Where both parties concerned produces contradicting evidences to prove a same fact but neither has enough evidence to rebut the evidences of the other party, the People's court shall determine which evidences are obviously more forceful than the other evidences by taking the case into consideration, and shall affirm the evidences that are more forceful."

[29] This is the proof standard, which can be applied to some special civil lawsuits it is higher than the standards of "preponderant evidence" in ordinary civil lawsuits, but lower than those of "excluding reasonable doubts" in criminal lawsuits. The original context is Clear and convincing proof or clear and convincing proof". It means that the evidence shows that there is high possibility for the pending proved facts or reasonable certainty. See Garner (1999, p. 577).

Although the proof standards of "be sure" are higher than those of "be clear and convincing", and the proof standards of "be clear and convincing" are higher than those of "preponderant evidences", the evidences the three proof standards rely on should have some credibility to some extent. But in the civil and administrative proceedings, as long as the probative forces of these evidences have reached a level of "preponderant evidences" or "be sure and convincing", law would think it is "sufficient"; while in the criminal proceedings, that thing would happen only when the probative force has reached a level of "be sure". Such explanation is just the expedient and it would better for the legislature to reset the proof standards when modifying the litigation laws.

Come back to the proof standards of basic facts when applying the presumption rules. In the civil proceedings, it should be "be sure". For example, in the criminal presumption of "the crime of holding a huge amount of property with unidentified sources", the prosecutor should prove that the property or the income of the accused "surely" exceeds legitimate income and the difference is huge. When coming to civil lawsuits, it would become "preponderant evidences". For example, in accordance with the Article 22 of the *Interpretation of the Supreme People's Court about Several Problems Concerning the Application of the Marriage Law*: "if, before the parties concerned get married, his or her parents contributed money for purchase of housing by both parties, such contribution shall be determined as a personal bestowal on their own child, unless the parents expressly indicate such contribution as a bestowal on both parties." If the plaintiff of divorce litigation requires the court to apply the legal presumption rules related to bestowal, he (or she) would use the preponderant evidence to prove that his or her parents contributed money for purchase of housing before the parties concerned get married. In the administrative litigation, the aim of presumption rules is to relieve the burden of proof borne by the plaintiff, so the proof of basic facts target at the plaintiff which can also use the proof standards of "preponderant evidence". For example, Article 69 of PEAP stipulates: "the plaintiff surely has evidence to prove that the evidence held by the accused is favorable to the plaintiff; and if the accused refuses to provide evidence without justification, the court could presume the facts are true." According to the standards of "preponderant evidence", the plaintiff complete the task of proving the basic facts as long as he provides evidences to prove that the possibility for the accused to hold this evidence is higher than that of not holding the evidence.

11.5.2.2 The Proof Standard for an Effective Rebuttal

As mentioned above, to prevent the application of the presumption rules, the party with unfavorable presumption can refute the basic facts. But the unfavorable side doesn't bear the burden of proof of the basic facts, so the rebuttal to the basic facts isn't concerned with proof standards. The unfavorable side can provide opposite evidence to prove that the basic facts don't hold but such kind of providing the evidence is right rather than duty and the main purpose is to prevent the proof submitted by the opposite party meeting the standards stipulated by law. For example, in the proof of "the crime of holding a huge amount of property with unidentified sources", the accused can refute the basic facts, namely, his property or income doesn't greatly exceed his legitimate income. He can prove that some properties confirmed by the prosecutor aren't in his possession, and his expenses confirmed by the prosecutor don't belong to him. In addition, the prosecutor require the proof of the basic facts to reach the standard of proof beyond a reasonable doubt, so an effective rebuttal can be formed as long as the accused can make the judge have a reasonable doubt by evidence.

The rebuttal against the presumed facts of the unfavorable side of presumption belongs to his burden of proof, for which it has to meet some certain standards. Generally speaking, such refutation of the unfavorable side will propose a fact claim against the presumed facts, namely, by proving the existence of the opposite fact to prove that the presumed fact cannot be established. For example, in the criminal presumption of "the crime of holding a huge amount of property with unidentified sources", the presumed fact is that the huge amount of properties of the accused is illegal income. If refuting this fact, the accused has to prove these properties have legal sources, such as given by the overseas relatives and friends. For this fact claim, the accused should bear the burden of proof. But considering the value of protecting the rights of the accused, the proof standards applied to the accused should be lower than those applied to the prosecutor, and therefore, the proof of this fact claim doesn't have to meet the standard of proof beyond a reasonable doubt, and it only needs to meet the standard of "preponderant evidence", namely, the possibility that the huge properties were given by overseas relatives and friends is bigger than that of illegal income.

To take another example, in the civil presumption of "his or her parents contributed money for purchase of housing before the parties concerned get married", the presumed fact is that the contributed money is the bestowal to their son (or daughter). If the unfavorable side of presumption wants to refute against the fact, he has to prove that the money contributed by his or her parents is clearly bestowed on both parties. For this fact claim, the proof of the unfavorable side should also meet the standard of "preponderant evidence". In addition, in the administrative litigation presumption of the "evidence content", the presumed fact is that the content of this proof is unfavorable to the defendant. If the defendant wants to refute this presumed fact, he has to prove that the proof content isn't unfavorable to him. He can prove the content through providing testimonies or proving the justifications for the failure to provide such evidence, but his proof must meet the standard of "preponderant evidence". To sum up, in criminal, civil, and administrative lawsuits, the proof standard of "preponderant evidence" can be applied to the effective rebuttal against presumed facts.

In the course of applying presumption rules, the rebuttal against the basic facts of the unfavorable side doesn't take any burden of proof and has no proof standard, while the rebuttal against the presumed facts just handles the reverse situation. Therefore, it's of great significance to define the basic facts and the presumed facts of the presumption rules, especially in the criminal lawsuits. As said in Chap. 9, the presumption rule is composed of three elements: the condition (or "hypothesis"), the mode (or "disposition"), and the consequence (or "sanction"). This author takes it again for example that "the crime of holding a huge amount of property with unidentified sources". The "condition" of the presumption rule is that the accused has huge amount of properties which exceed his legal income and have unidentified sources; however, if all these facts are considered as the basic facts of the presumption rule, the prosecutor shall bear the burden of proof of "the unidentified sources", while the refutation of the accused can prevent the application of the presumption rules as long as it has reached the level of "raising a reasonable doubt". In other words, the possibility of the defendant's proof has decreased from 60 to 20%, which doesn't conform to the original meaning of legislation.

For a long term, we focus on the burden of proof when studying the presumption rules and it seems that as long as the judge identifies the allocation of the burden of proof, he can make the judgment in the case of unclear facts. But as we just mentioned, the burden of proof cannot be separated form the standard of proof, and without the clear proof standards, it's difficult for the judge to decide whether the parties effectively bear the burden of proof. In this sense, this author may say that the standard of proof has more important realistic meanings than the burden of proof. Therefore, we should shift our focus from the burden of proof to the standard of proof when studying the application of presumption rules.

References

Allen, Ronald J., et al. 2006. *Evidence: Text, Problems, and Cases*, 3rd ed, 801–802. Translated by Zhang Baosheng et al. Beijing: Higher Education Press.

Bian, Jianlin (ed.). 2000. *Evidence Law*, 376. Beijing: China University of Political Science and Law Press.

Chen, Yiyun (ed.). 2000. *Study of Evidence*, 2nd ed, 183. Beijing: China Renmin University Press.

Garner, Bryan A. (ed.). 1999. *Black's Law Dictionary*, 7th ed. St. Paul: West Group.

He, Jiahong. 2016. *Back from the Dead: Wrongful Convictions and Criminal Justice in China*, 81–146. Honolulu: University of Hawai'I Press.

He, Jiahong, and Pinxin Liu. 2007. *The Evidence Law*, 2nd ed. Beijing: Law Press China.

He, Jiahong, and Weiping Zhang (ed.). 2007. *The Concise Evidence Law*. Beijing: China Renmin University Press.

Huang, Shuo. 2010. Zhou Jie Crash Compensation Case Withdrawal of Charges and Three Party Agreement. *Beijing Daily News*, published on the 'Culture China' website on May 20, 2010 culture.china.com.cn, accessed on January 4, 2017.

Jiang, Wei (ed.). 1999. *Law of Evidence*, 122. Beijing: Law Press China.

Long, Zongzhi. 2008. Presumption: Limits and their application. *Chinese Journal of Law* 1.

Qi, Shujie (ed.). 2002. *British Law of Evidence*, 179. Xiamen: Xiamen University Press.

Waltz, Jones. 1983. *Criminal Evidence*, 2nd ed. Chicago: Nelson-Hall Press.

Xue, Bo (ed.). 2003. *English-Chinese Dictionary of Anglo-American Law*, 179. Beijing: Law Press China.

Zhang, Weiping. 2012. Legal Techniques in the Identification and Handling of Facts in the Zhou Jie Crash. Caijing Blog, published on July 9, 2012, accessed on January 4, 2017. http://blog.caijing.com.cn/topic_article-151627-38309.shtml.

Chapter 12
The Proof of Wrongful Convictions

Contents

12.1 Case Illustration

At around 5 pm on 5th August 1994, a woman by the surname of Kang, who worked at a hydraulic parts factory in Shijiazhuang, Hebei province, was raped and murdered in a cornfield by the side of a road in the outskirts of the city. Based on tips from the public, police identified Nie Shubin as a suspect, and obtained a confession to the crime. On 15th March 1995, the Shijiazhuang Intermediate Court found the defendant Nie Shubin guilty of premeditated murder and sentenced him to death. They also found him guilty of rape and sentenced him to fifteen years in prison for that crime, with the primary evidence being his confession. On 25th April the High Provincial People's Court of Hebei released its final verdict approving the death sentence and two days later Nie Shubin was executed.[1]

In March 2005, the alleged serial rapist, Wang Shujin, was arrested for other crimes, and while being interrogated confessed that he had raped and murdered a

[1] See Zhao (2007).

J. He, *Methodology of Judicial Proof and Presumption*,
Masterpieces of Contemporary Jurisprudents in China,
https://doi.org/10.1007/978-981-10-8025-8_12

young woman in a cornfield by the side of the road in the outskirts of Shijiazhuang. His narration of the crime and knowledge of its location, which he identified, agreed with details of the rape-murder of the female Kang. Nie Shubin's mother had never believed that her son, who had always been an honest and timid boy, could have committed rape and murder, and so upon hearing this news made even more insistent appeals on her son's behalf, nevertheless to no avail.[2] A police officer involved in the case said: "If this had happened ten years ago we might well have determined Wang to be the murderer with only his confession to go on, and no other corroborating evidence. But cases can no longer be made with confession alone, not to mention this case has already been closed, and one person has been executed".[3]

On 25th June 2013, the second-instance trial of Wang Shujin for rapes and murders finally began. Six years after Wang's shocking confession, the Hebei High People's Court tried the case again at the Handan Intermediate People's Court. The event garnered much public attention. Arguments in the retrial instigated a fresh outlook: the defendant maintained that he was indeed the true culprit Kang's case, while the prosecution making the charges maintained that he was not. Public attention focused not on whether Wang Shujin was guilty, but whether Nie Shubin was guilty.

In the courtroom on 25th June the prosecution supplied four reasons why Wang Shujin could not have raped and murdered the victim Kang. First, Wang Shujin's testimony regarding the body did not correspond with the facts of the case. The corpse was clothed with a white undershirt; the neck had been obscured by corn stalks, which when removed, revealed that a flower-printed shirt. Wang Shujin's testimony lacked these details. Second, Wang's testimony as to the method of the murder did not correspond with the facts. The cause of death was strangulation but Wang said he had first choked the victim, then stomped her on the chest until she died. But apart from the shirt wrapped around the victim's neck, there were no bone fractures found at the autopsy. Third, Wang's testimony as to the time of the victim's death did not accord with the facts. Fourth, Wang's description of the victim's height was incorrect. The prosecution also pointed out that, when the events occurred, Wang was at work at a factory nearby and familiar with the area around the crime scene, and when law enforcement authorities were examining the crime scene considerable numbers of public onlookers gathered around. In this way, Wang could have learned some of the details of the case in this way.[4]

So is Wang Shujin the true culprit, or not? We have no way of knowing. Based on the case presented by the prosecution, there is insufficient evidence to prove him guilty, or not guilty, or innocent. It is possible that he is lying—if, indeed, Wang could be so conniving; however, it is common for the actual criminal to make some errors when recounting the events of the crime—and it should be remembered that Wang's confession came more than ten years after the crime had been committed. Moreover, in the meantime he had committed rape and murder on three other occasions and rape on two other occasions. It would have been surprising if some of his testimony

---

[2]See Zhao (2009).

[3]See Zhou (2005).

[4]See a news report by Lei Hongtao, Legal Weekly, 26 June 2013.

had not been confused, if some of the details had not been mistaken, in his memory. In sum, given the evidence at hand, it cannot be certain that Wang Shujin committed the murder and rape against the victim Kang, nor can it be certain that he did not. Roughly, let us assume that chance Wang did commit the crime was about 60%. In other words, the chance that he is the true culprit is slightly higher than the chance he is not.[5]

In Chinese criminal procedure, the standard for proving a defendant guilty of a crime is that 'the facts of the case be clear, the evidence reliable and sufficient'. In terms of probabilities, the chances that the defendant committed the crime must reach at least 90%. According the principle of presumption of innocence, or 'no conviction in a case of doubt', whenever the chances that the defendant is guilty drop below 90% the court should find the accused not guilty. In the case at hand, and if it can be assumed that Wang Shujin's chance of being the true culprit is only 60%, the court should find Wang 'not guilty' in the case of the rape and murder of the victim Kang. However, the next question is, what to do in the case of Nie Shubin? Some believe that Nie's case cannot be overturned as long as Wang Shujin cannot be identified as the true culprit. But not being able to confirm Wang Shujin as the true culprit is not equivalent to confirming Nie Shubin as the true culprit. When using counter-evidence to give indirect proof of wrongful conviction, an increased chance of one suspects committing the crime corresponds to a decreased chance that the other suspect had committed the crime. In this case, if there were a 60% chance that Wang Shujin committed the crime, and if this were not enough to determine his guilt, then Nie Shujin's 40% chance is also not enough to determine Nie's guilt.

On 27th January 2013, the Hebei High People's Court opened trial proceedings against Wang Shujin in the Handan Intermediate People's Court for the crimes of rape and murder. The court ruled that the evidence was insufficient to prove that Wang Shujin committed rape and murder against the victim Kang, and so rejected the appeal and re-affirmed the original verdict convicting him for other five charges of rape and murder. Wang Shujin was sentenced to death.[6]

On 12th December 2014, the Supreme People's Court of China made a decision to appoint the High People's Court of Shandong Province to review the case of Nie Shubin. On 28th April 2015, the High Court held a special hearing on the case, for which the Court invited 15 representatives of the people including law professors, journalists, members of the people's congress, and local residents. It is the first time for Chinese courts to hold such a hearing in a criminal case, and it may illustrate the direction of the related judicial reform.[7]

On 11th June, the High Court decided to extend the review time for three months, till 15th September 2015. The extension was approved by SPC. Then the High Court asked for more extensions, and was approved by SPC.

On 6th June 2016, the High Court concluded the review. Based on the review conclusion, SPC decided to retry the case. After careful assessment of the evidence

[5]See Zhang (2013).

[6]See Li (2013).

[7]See news report, 'Court's transparency in trial welcomed', China Daily, 30 April 2015.

in the case, the Second Circuit Court of SPC declared innocence for Nie Shubin on 2nd December 2016.[8]

At all times and in all lands, wrongful convictions are like a spirit that haunts the castle of criminal justice. They are certainly unexpected disasters to the wrongfully convicted and their families but, at some point, they push the criminal justice system towards a progress and development. In recent years, with the disclosure of the wrongful convictions in the media, the topic has become a grim and sad focus of attention in China. There seemed to be a proliferation of wrongful convictions overturned, which led people to ask: what is going wrong in Chinese criminal justice system? Since late 1995, this author led a group of researchers and embarked upon an 'Empirical Study of Wrongful Convictions in China'. In one instance, we distributed questionnaires to some 2000 law enforcement professionals, including judges, prosecutors, police, and lawyers, with which data we discovered that over half believed, directly or indirectly, that torture and forced confession were a major factor leading to wrongful convictions. In addition, we analyzed fifty murder cases of wrongful conviction already exposed by the media, establishing that the proportion of cases in which there existed false confessions made by the defendant, as well as the possibility of, if not certainty of, torture and forced confession, was 94%.[9]

12.2 The Ambiguousness of Facts and the Antagonism Between Parties in Redressing Wrongful Convictions

Wrongful convictions are frequently covered up, easily concealed amidst the magnitude of correct verdicts. Some of dormant, or cold, cases do occasionally rise to the surface, gain the attention of law enforcement or the public, and so encounter an opportunity for rectification. In China, the cases of Teng Xingshan,[10] She Xianglin[11] and Zhao Zuohai,[12] for example, were all exposed to the world when the alleged 'victim' came 'back from the dead'. Indeed, cases of wrongful conviction often lay dormant for long periods before they are discovered. As part of our Empirical Study on Wrongful Convictions in China, the research team gathered 55 sets of case materials from wrongful conviction cases in China that had the rulings overturned and which resulted in compensation issued by the national government between 1995 and 2007. Among these cases, one salient trait was clear: violation of the prescribed custody in 48 cases involving 60 people. The average custodial period was five years. The case with the most egregious example of this was that of Li Huawei of Liaoning Province, accused of premeditated murder and held in custody for sixteen years. The

[8]See He (2017).

[9]See He and He (2012).

[10]I mentioned this case in Chap. 1.

[11]I mentioned this case in Chap. 9.

[12]Zhao Zuohai was sentenced to death with two-year suspension in a murder case in Henan in 1999, and exonerated in 2010. See He (2016, pp. 149–151).

shortest time involved the case of Zhu Mingli of Sichuan Province, accused of rape and held in custody for 372 days. Five people had been in custody for over ten years, fifty persons between five and ten years, and twenty-five had been in custody fewer than five years.[13]

Determination of the true facts behind a case of wrongful conviction is not always a black-and-white process; sometimes there is a gray zone, meaning that there is no way to determine with accuracy whether the defendant is guilty or not. In other words, the line between good guys and bad guys is not clear-cut, but rather fuzzy, and vague. As a result, coming up with standards regarding the rectification of wrongful conviction becomes problematic. In what follows, I will discuss the standard for determining the facts leading to wrongful conviction cases. This discussion represents the level and degree of knowledge that law enforcement officials must bring to their roles within the judiciary.

As previously mentioned, judicial proof is a reverse mental activity, in that it uses evidence to prove the facts of past events. Likewise, wrongful conviction is frequently only apparent many years after the event, which means that discovery of the miscarriage of justice is a second reverse mental activity performed on a past mental activity. Given the passage of time and change of location, the difficulty of the mental work involved is understandable, even if there is new evidence or newly discovered evidence. Certainly, in some wrongful conviction cases newly discovered evidence is substantial, even ironclad, but in the majority of wrongful convictions, new evidence does not constitute 100% proof of guilt or innocence, and so add varying degrees of ambiguity or uncertainty.

In the case of Nie Shubin, it is difficult for people to answer this question with certainty, because the evidence includes some material that helps his case, and other things that damage it. Even though there may be evidence to show his guilt, there is also evidence clearing him of guilt. This is what we mean by uncertainty surrounding a conviction. As far as law enforcement is concerned, the facts of a case that occurred in the past are like ‘the moon in the water’. The moonlight has an objective existence, but what investigators see is the image reflected and refracted. The water here refers to the evidence. Without evidence, law-enforcement officials have no way of determining the facts, but facts determined through evidence do not necessarily correspond to the objective facts. When the water is murky or choppy, the action of refraction and reflection distorts the image, sometimes so much so that the resulting image of the moonlight is totally different that the reality. In the case of Nie Shubin, the water is turgid, which is to say, the evidence itself suffers from defects and uncertainty. First of all, there is no direct evidence to prove that he carried out the crimes. Second, the evidence is incomplete, and even features a mutually exclusive chain of evidence. Finally, there are many problems with the key pieces of evidence. However, the evidence does not eliminate the possibility that Nie is guilty of murder. Thus, there are two moonlight images in the water: in one, he is guilty, and in the other, he is not. Which one reflects the truth? We do not yet know.

[13]See Liu (2009, pp. 364–367).

It is human nature to pursue one's own interests and to try to avoid harm. It is instinctive to deny or cover up our mistakes. For this reason, those whose work leads to wrongful convictions frequently do not wish to admit to this; some will even go to great lengths to prevent the cases from being overturned. Thus, work on such cases becomes a struggle, both overt and covert, between two collective and competing interests, especially in China. In the case of Nie Shubin, it is clear that "insufficient evidence" was just an excuse for not overturning the conviction, and that a much deeper factor was the relevant officials' fear of and even resistance towards the responsibility to investigate and uncover the wrongful conviction.

12.3 The Standard of Proof for Redressing Wrongful Convictions in USA

With my limited research ability in English, I have not found a clear provision about the standard of proof for redressing a wrongful conviction in American laws. According to Mark Godsey, Professor of Law at the University of Cincinnati College of Law, the standards for determining wrongful conviction in the United States are not uniform, and generally depend on whether new evidence (such as DNA analysis) could lead to reasonable doubt. This is much less than a demand that evidence be sufficient to prove innocence; rather, it only requires the claimant to supply evidence that forms a reasonable doubt with regard to the perpetration of the original crime. This is the standard according to the law. In practice, courts are allowed the flexibility to raise the standard, which they do frequently. If the evidence proves reasonable doubt but does not meet the standard for 'preponderant evidence' (meaning able to prove that the prisoner has a more than 50% chance of being innocent), the courts will rule that 'it has not formed a reasonable doubt'. In this we can see that the standard according to the law and the standard applied in reality manifest some difference. Moreover, even if a prisoner appealed successfully, he would have won only the right to a retrial. If the evidence of innocence is strong (as in high-certainty DNA analysis), then the prosecution would generally forego a retrial and the prisoner may be declared innocent. But if the evidence is weak or uncertain the prosecution may decide to hold a second trial by jury. If the jury at this second trial issued a verdict of not guilty, the prisoner would be declared innocent. If the jury issued a guilty verdict, then he must be declared guilty.[14]

The standard for determining a wrongful conviction in the USA is generally "the formation of reasonable doubt", but the standard held by the courts in practice is generally one demanding 'preponderant evidence'. Whether it is the standard of the law or the standard held in fact, both are perceptibly lower than the standard of criminal proceedings, which must prove the defendant guilty 'beyond reasonable

[14]Professor Godsey is Director of the Ohio Innocence Project. The statement quoted above comes from his answers to the question of this author regarding to the standard for proving a wrongful conviction in the USA in July 2010.

doubt'. If based on new evidence the court determines the original verdict to have been a wrongful conviction, they may cancel the original verdict and immediately release the person in custody. This does not certify 'with finality' that the claimant is innocent. If the prosecution believes that a jury might find the claimant guilty despite the existence of new evidence, they can begin new prosecution proceedings. Because this would be a new trial after the cancellation of the original verdict, it does not violate the concept of "double jeopardy". In this second trial, if the jury found the defendant guilty in light of all the evidence—both new and old—the court would once again issue a sentence of guilt. If the jury found the defendant not guilty, the defendant would be declared innocent "with finality". In practice, cases in which the prosecution begins new proceedings are rare, especially when analysis of DNA evidence certifies the claimant to be not guilty.

12.3.1 The Case of Robert McClendon

On 25th April 1990 a ten-year-old girl was kidnapped from the back yard of her own home in Columbus, Ohio, taken to an empty residence nearby, and raped. The victim's parents learned of the incident the next day, took her to the hospital for an examination and reported the crime. Based on the victim's statement and her positive identification of her assailant, police arrested thirty-two-year-old Robert McClendon. Crime-lab analysts failed to identify the presence of semen from the victim's underwear on the swabs collected from the hospital. Nevertheless, on 21st May prosecutors issued formal charges against Robert McClendon for the crimes of kidnapping and rape. On 26th August 1991, trial proceedings began in the county court. Since McClendon waved his right to a trial by jury, the case was heard by a sole presiding judge, David L. Johnson.

The evidence for the prosecution included photographs were taken at the crime scene, testimony by the victim's mother and the report of the hospital examination; however, the evidence that formally tied the accused to the crimes of kidnapping and murder were the statement and positive identification by the victim, as well as the defendant's poor performance in a lie-detection test.[15] McClendon maintained his innocence. After just two days of trial, Judge Johnson found the defendant guilty of kidnapping and rape and sentenced him to life in prison, stipulating that he serve a minimum of fifteen years before becoming eligible for parole. McClendon filed an appeal, but the appeals court upheld the original verdict.

On 13th October 2004, McClendon requested that the DNA evidence be analysed again, but he was not granted his request. In April 2008 the Ohio Innocence Project represented McClendon's second request, which was granted. On 16th July DNA

[15]On 4 February 1991, McClendon agreed to the suggestion of the prosecution that he should undergo a lie-detection test, and further that the results of the test could be admitted as evidence in court. The test was administered by a specialist for the Ohio Highway Patrol, who noted in the results that McClendon "might possibly have deliberately lied" in his answers to relevant questions.

analysis experts determined that there were indeed traces of semen in the victim's underwear but that it could not have been McClendon's. On 11th August Judge Schneider announced the cancellation of the original verdict. Because the prosecution had already announced that it would not pursue new prosecution proceedings, but would rather use the DNA evidence to seek the true perpetrator, Robert McClendon, aged fifty-two and wrongfully held in custody for seventeen years, was released from prison and exonerated.[16]

12.3.2 The Case of Joseph Abbitt

Early in the morning of 2nd May 1991, two girls aged thirteen and sixteen were tied up and raped in their own home in Winston-Salem County, North Carolina. One of the girls subsequently reported the crime and claimed their assailant had been a Joseph Abbitt, who had lived in the area and done odd jobs at the girls' home. When the police showed the girls a mixed photograph line-up, they identified Abbitt. Since Abbitt had left North Carolina, a wanted bulletin was issued for his arrest. In October 1994, Abbitt was arrested at a dog-walking park in Texas and transported to North Carolina for trial on the charges of burglary, kidnapping and rape. In June 1995, the Winston-Salem County Court formed a jury and opened trial proceedings. The main evidence for the prosecution was the statements of the two victims and their identification of Abbitt during court proceedings. Despite collection of material evidence, including the underwear and bed sheets of the victims from the scene of the crime as well as the positive identification of semen traces, the results of DNA analysis had been inconclusive, and could only show that the semen might have been Abbitt's. The jury found Abbitt guilty, and he was sentenced to two life sentences plus an additional 110 years. Abbitt appealed unsuccessfully.

In 2005, the North Carolina Center on Actual Innocence appealed on Abbitt's behalf and was granted permission to have the DNA evidence re-analyzed. They obtained material evidence, including the underwear of the victims; however, the conclusion from the first 're-analysis' was not strong enough to either exonerate or condemn. The experts were asked to attempt a second analysis using more accurate methods, and from this obtained conclusive proof that the semen samples were not from Abbitt. Progress was especially slow in the case, which dragged on until 2nd September 2009, when Abbitt at last obtained a ruling that canceled his original verdict. By then, he had been imprisoned for fourteen years.[17]

---

[16] According to Professor Godsey the prosecution later found the actual perpetrator of the crime by searching a nation-wide digital DNA evidence archive, but since the victim did not want to be involved the prosecutor was not able to file any new proceedings. This case narrative is based on an account in the article headlined, 'Hello freedom', published in *The Columbus Dispatch*, 12 August 2008.

[17] An account of this case is found on the 'Know the Cases' section on the Innocence Project website www.innocenceproject.org/know.

The McCLendon and Abbitt cases both involved the charge of rape, as well as statements and identification of the accused by child victims. Because the victims in both cases knew their alleged perpetrators, their 'identification' was based more on perception and memory from before the crime and was not in fact perception or memory of the crime itself. One scholar in the USA has pointed out that a major factor leading to a wrongful conviction in the USA is a mis-identification of the accused by victims or eyewitnesses.[18] Among the 242 cases of wrongful conviction, which as mentioned before were discovered through DNA evidence analysis, mistaken identification occurred 75% of the time.[19] This is likely related to the type of case most often re-examined by The Innocence Project: many of them involve those who have been convicted of rape, and rape convictions very often take as their main evidence victim and eyewitness testimony.[20] Despite the fact that in one of these cases a verdict was issued by a judge and the other from a jury, in both cases the unreliable testimony of the victims became the major basis of the guilty verdict.

In both cases, the determination of wrongful conviction relied on the high-certainty analysis of DNA evidence. Given the problems of long-term management of material evidence, as well as the nature of the relation between semen traces and rape, DNA re-analysis, even after a long hiatus as in the cases of McClendon and Abbitt, cannot absolutely exclude that the claimants committed the crime. It does not necessarily establish a reasonable doubt that the claimant is not guilty, but it certainly meets the standard for preponderant evidence that the claimant is not guilty.

12.4 The Standard of Proof for Redressing Wrongful Convictions in UK

The legal systems of the UK and the USA are largely similar, in particular, their standards of proof required for the determination of a wrongful conviction; however, in the UK the process of rectifying a wrongful conviction in the UK is separated into several stages, each of them with different standards of proof. The claimants applying for rectification of a wrongful conviction must first undergo examination by the Criminal Cases Review Commission. The standard for whether the Review Commission will refer the case to the appeals court for re-trial is if there is "a true possibility of overturning the original verdict".[21]

---

[18] See Thompson (2008).

[19] This data comes from the website of the Innocence Project, on the column entitled "Eyewitness Identification Reform." www.innocenceproject.org/fix/Eyewitness-Identification.

[20] Because wrongful criminal conviction determination reveals slips in the system of identification, the American states are constantly improving the rules for identification, as in the establishment of "double blind" identification rules, meaning the person organizing the identification activity also does not know which person in the lineup is the suspect; also, the person making the identification is informed that the perpetrator of the crime may not be among those in the lineup.

[21] See McConville and Wilson (2003, pp. 464–467).

If the appeals court accepts the case sent up from the Review Commission, it will conduct a new trial. Although the relevant laws do not clearly state any standard for proving a wrongful conviction in the new trial, based on the decisions of the appeals court where original verdicts were successfully revoked ("The Guildford Four"—1990, "The Birmingham Six"—1991, Judith Ward—1992 and Carl Bridgewater—1997), we can affirm that the standard for determining a wrongful conviction is the introduction of new evidence or evidence of new discoveries sufficient to the establishment of reasonable doubt of the guilty verdict and to overturning the original conviction.[22]

The UK issues 'state compensation' to victims of wrongful conviction but the determination of wrongful conviction in an appeals court does not automatically guarantee compensation. The party involved must still apply to the courts for compensation, and if the finding is that compensation is merited, such compensation would be awarded through the Ministry of Justice. Otherwise, no compensation is awarded. The standard for proving that compensation is merited is higher than that required to determine a wrongful conviction. The British government's 2004 standard of proving that compensation is merited was that the applicant must be able to prove beyond a reasonable doubt that he is innocent. However, the UK Supreme Court recently lowered the standard for proving compensation merit.[23] It was the murder case of Raymond McCartney and Eamonn MacDermott that gave rise to this change in policy.

In 1977 the Royal Ulster Constabulary (RUC) detective constable Patrick McNulty was shot dead allegedly by members of the Irish Republican Army (IRA). A week later Jeffery Agate, Managing Director of the DuPont factory, was also shot dead, allegedly also by members of the IRA. Police identified Raymond McCartney and Eamonn MacDermott as suspects in the murders and used 'special interrogation methods' to elicit confessions from the two suspects. In 1979, McCartney and MacDermott were tried for murder in the Criminal Court of Northern Ireland, all the while maintaining their innocence, protesting that their confessions had been extorted. The defense brought forward other witnesses whose testimony related to their own experiences of torture at the hands of police, but the courts did not admit this to be used as evidence. McCartney and MacDermott were convicted of murdering of Patrick McNulty based largely on their confessions. McCartney was also convicted of murdering Jeffrey Agate. The two men were sentenced separately to life in prison. McCartney and MacDermott challenged the decisions and filed appeals, which were rejected by the Appeals Court of Northern Ireland in September 1982. MacDermott was released on parole after having served fifteen years in prison, after which he worked as a journalist. McCartney was released after serving seventeen years,

[22]Ibid, pp. 459–461.

[23]In October 2009, the Supreme Court of the United Kingdom was established, replacing the House of Lords Committee as Britain's final court of appeal and independent of both Parliament and other law enforcement agencies. The UK Supreme Court consisted of twelve judges. For civil suits, the Supreme Court accepts appeals from all regions within the United Kingdom; for criminal cases, it accepts cases from England, Wales, and Northern Ireland (but not Scotland). The conditions for accepting a case are generally controversial legal issues important to the public interest.

became a commander of the IRA and participated in a fifty-three-day hunger strike. Later, he became a member of *Sinn Fein*. The two men have steadfastly maintained their innocence and that their confessions had been false and illegally obtained. After their release, they continued to file appeals in an effort to clear their names. Eventually, they obtained new evidence to support their claims and in September 2006 the UK Criminal Cases Review Commission found the probability that the two claimants had been subject to torture to be high, and so referred the case to the appeals court for retrial. The appeals court finally issued a ruling in February 2007, canceling both guilty verdicts. The judges remarked that in light of the new evidence "doubts existed regarding the surety of the guilty verdicts". After the ruling was announced McCartney was quoted as saying: "When we talk about these matters, we must consider the interrogation methods used by the UAR, and we must see how the court just wanted to put IRA members in jail with oral testimony alone".[24]

After they had been exonerated McCartney and MacDermott applied for compensation. In 2008, the Court of Northern Ireland accepted their application but ruled that the evidence supplied failed to prove their innocence beyond a reasonable doubt, and so the two of them would not receive government compensation. They appealed to the Supreme Court, which on 11 May 2011 issued their ruling with a vote of five to four: McCartney and MacDermot would receive compensation. In their ruling, the Supreme Court also established a new standard for compensation, lowering it from "proving innocence beyond a reasonable doubt" to "new evidence sufficient to deny a guilty verdict." The judges pointed out: "If new or newly-discovered facts conclusively show that evidence used in charges against the defendant have been overturned, and to such an extent that a guilty verdict would not be forthcoming based on the evidence", then this indicates a wrongful conviction under the law, with compensation due. The Chief Justice of the Supreme Court, Lord Nicholas Phillips, added that although the new standard would not ensure that only the truly innocent would receive compensation, "it would, however, ensure that innocent defendants whose evidence of guilt had been overturned would not be denied compensation because they could not prove their own innocence beyond a reasonable doubt", meaning that the new standard "possessed practicality under realistic conditions". Justice Hope added: "In their case, we cannot say that these newly discovered facts conclusively show that they are innocent, but we can say that, based on these newly discovered facts, the evidence used to charge them has been overturned, and to such an extent that the evidence is now insufficient to return a guilty verdict again".[25]

[24] Based on 'Murder convictions ruled unsafe', *BBC News,* 15 February 2007.

[25] The Supreme Court examined the cases of McCartney and MacDermott and of another claimant, Andrew Adams at the same time, but unanimously rejected the request made by Adams, noting that a reasonable jury might still convict Adams even with the new evidence. Adams, who had been declared guilty in 1993 of murdering retired teacher Jack Royal, had by served fourteen years of his sentence by 2007, when an appeals court canceled his guilty verdict and declared him not guilty. He applied for government compensation. His application was rejected by a high court, but he appealed and the application was examined by the Supreme Court. See 'UK court sets new standard on compensation for wrongful convictions', *Associated Press*, 11 May 2011. See also 'Two men jailed for murder can seek compensation', *The Irish Times*, 12 May 2011.

After the ruling was announced, a spokesperson for the Ministry of Justice, who as previously noted pays out the compensation, announced: We welcome the ruling to reject Adams' request and affirm the rightness of the decision not to apply compensation. This was a lengthy and complex decision requiring some time to read thoroughly. Although the court has established new standards for wrongful conviction, we hope that compensation for wrongful conviction will still be applied only in the minimum number of cases.[26]

Public reaction to the new standards established by the ruling was also mixed. Some felt the new standards be too low, as the words above from the Ministry of Justice indicate. Some felt that the standards to be still not low enough. BBC reporter Danny Shaw, for example, pointed out that between 2009 and 2010 the number of wrongful conviction compensations was extremely low: on average, only one in thirty-seven claimants won compensation. This was because the standards for wrongful conviction compensation established by the Labour Party (proof beyond reasonable doubt) were too high. The Supreme Court's ruling effectively announced that the standards for proof were not appropriate, but it was thought by many that the newly established standards (that with new evidence a guilty verdict would not be forthcoming) were also high. An appeals court might, when canceling a guilty verdict, rule the present evidence insufficient for a retrial. Under such circumstances, the claimant must prove in the application for compensation that the present evidence could not possibly lead to a guilty verdict, which is an extremely difficult case to make. For example, Barry George, who was found guilty of murder in 2000, had his guilty verdict canceled in 2008 by the appeals, which then indicated that the evidence in the case merited retrial. Even if George were acquitted by a jury in the subsequent retrial, it would be difficult for him to win compensation. Thus, if the Supreme Court had opened the door to compensation, it was only by a small crack.[27]

In summary, the standards for proving wrongful conviction in the UK involve three levels: first the standard by which the Criminal Cases Review Commission refers the case to the appeals court, the 'real possibility for overturning the original verdict'. Second, the standard by which the appeals court will overturn the original verdict is that 'new evidence is sufficient to establish reasonable doubt of the guilty verdict'. And third, the standard for issuing state compensation for wrongful conviction is that 'the evidence [including any new evidence] cannot possibly lead once again to a guilty verdict'. Whether the enacting of these standards is reasonable is not a question the author will address here, but I do believe that the UK system of separating the standards into these different levels is one that we Chinese can learn from.

---

[26] See 'Supreme Court allows miscarriage of justice appeals', *BBC News*, 11 May 2011.

[27] Ibid.

12.5 The Standard of Proof for Redressing Wrongful Convictions in Germany

In Germany Karl Peters (1904–1998) well deserves recognition as the greatest champion of research into wrongful conviction. His book *Fehlerquellen im Strafprozess: Eine Untersuchung der Wiederaufnahmeverfahren in der Bundesrepublik Deutschland*, first published in the 1970s, is the most authoritative work on the subject.[28] It is divided into three volumes: *Introduction and Survey of Types of Cases*; *Sources of Error in the Judicial System: Research and Conclusions*; and *Sources of Error in the Judicial System: Retrial Procedure*. The objects of his research were 1150 cases of criminal wrongful conviction overturned in retrials in the German courts between 1951 and 1964. Among them, ninety-one were retrials ordered by the prosecution, and could be termed cases of "wrongful release" or "light punishment". The other 1059 cases were retrials upon application by the defendant, and could be termed cases of "wrongful conviction" or "heavy punishment". Professor Peters maintains that verdicts overturned were not necessarily wrongful, because there is a spectrum of uncertainty between definitely guilty and definitely not guilty. In other words, the defendant might be guilty and might not be guilty. Professor Peters delineates the verdict determinations of the retrial into five types: the original verdict is definitely wrongful; the original verdict might possibly be wrongful; the original verdict cannot be proven fully; the original verdict might be correct; and, the original verdict is most likely correct. According to Professor Peters, in the first three circumstances the judge presiding at the retrial should find the verdict wrongful, while in the last two cases, even though the judge cannot find with certainty that the verdict was wrongful, a ruling should be produced that is favorable to the defendant.[29]

Professor Peters' views are instructive to our study of problems relating to standards of proof in cases of wrongful conviction. For ease of discussion, we can use hypothetical to show the standards by which wrongful conviction is determined based on comprehensive review of the evidence. In cases of the first type, the rate of finding the conviction wrongful is 100%; among type two, the rate is 80%; among type three, 60%; among type four, 40%, and among type 5, 20%. Professor Peters advocates that the first three types should be determined as wrongful. That is to say, the lowest rate of determination should be 60%. The "standard for proving the conviction to be wrongful" in these circumstances refers to this lowest level for proving the decision had been erroneous. Professor Peters posited that in types four and five, even though a mistaken verdict cannot be determined, a ruling should be issued in favor of the defendant. This accords with the German criminal procedure principle of *in dubio pro reo*: if the court cannot issue a definite ruling on the facts of a case based the

---

[28] English translation of this book title is: *Sources of Errors in Criminal Proceedings: A Study of Cases of Successful Petitions of Revision in the Federal Republic of Germany*.

[29] In the summer of 2010, this author traveled to Germany to serve as a visiting scholar at the Max Planck Institute for Foreign and International Criminal Law. While there, I spoke with German scholars and judges to learn about the state of wrongful conviction cases in Germany. These texts were translated by Zhou Zunyou, a doctoral student then at the Max Planck Institute.

evidence *in toto*—in other words, if there be any doubt—the ruling must be in favor of the defendant. What follows is an example of this in Germany's recent history:

> Early in the morning on 29th April 1997, in Karlsruhe, a city in Baden-Württemberg, police officer Andrea Zacher was bound by the neck with a scarf and left in a position so that she was deprived of oxygen. Zacher survived but was brain-dead. Her father, who had found her, rang the police immediately.
>
> Investigators discovered no traces of forced entry but did collect two fingerprints from a pair of latex gloves, as well as a plastic bag containing a scarf, gloves and cigarettes. According to the victim's father, police focused on two suspects. First, Harry Wörz, Zacher's husband of three years and the father of her child. The couple was involved in divorce proceedings. The other suspect was Thomas Hein, a colleague and Zacher's lover. Hein was also married, and his wife testified that he had spent the entire evening with her and so could not have been at the scene of the crime. Based on this, police removed Hein from the list of suspects. DNA evaluation by crime-lab analysts determined that the fingerprints on the latex gloves belonged to Wörz. Additionally, police determined that the contents of the plastic bag belonged to him. On 16 January 1998 and after a trial, the Karlsruhe Regional Court sentenced Wörz to eleven years in prison for attempted murder. The defendant refused to accept the verdict and appealed. That August the Federal Appeals Court rejected the application and upheld the original decision.
>
> After the sentence had gone into effect, Worz's parents filed a civil suit for compensation. The Karlsruhe Regional Civil Court examined the case without influence from the criminal proceedings and on 5th April 2001, the judge ruled that the evidence was insufficient to prove without doubt that the Wörz was indeed guilty. The judge commented on the fact that the defendant had willingly submitted to a lie-detection test that had corroborated his claim of innocence. Wörz subsequently and successfully appealed to the Supreme Court for a retrial in the criminal court. On 6th October 2005 the Mannheim Criminal Court issued its ruling to cancel the original verdict on the grounds of insufficient evidence to prove guilt beyond a reasonable doubt. Worz was declared not guilty.
>
> The Mannheim prosecutor's office and the victim's family filed an appeal with the Federal Court, it was accepted, and on 16th October 2006, a ruling was issued to cancel the previous verdict on the basis of legal errors found in the determination. The case was sent for retrial once again. On 22nd October 2009, the judge of the Mannheim Regional Court once more declared the Wörz not guilty by reason of insufficient evidence.[30]

As mentioned in Chap. 2, German criminal procedure applies the principle of "free proof with intimate conviction", meaning that the law has no specific rules regarding the evaluation of evidence and the standards of proof, but rather a requirement that the judge determining guilt reaches a point of "intimate conviction". We may call this the 'intimate conviction' standard of proof. Correspondingly, whenever the judge is unable to come to a point of "intimate conviction" about the values of all the evidence, and then he or she must determine the original guilty verdict to have been wrongful. In other words, the German standard for proving a wrongful conviction can be expressed as an "overturning intimate conviction" standard. In the Wörz case, the Mannheim Regional Court's not-guilty verdict exemplifies this concept. Strictly speaking, the evidence in hand was far from sufficient to preclude any possibility that Wörz was the perpetrator. And regardless of the fact that the judge thought Hein should have remained a suspect, and thought also that his wife had given false

---

[30] See Zhou (2011).

testimony, there was still drastically insufficient evidence to prove Hein's guilt or innocence. Under these circumstances, since the court could not reach "intimate conviction" about the guilt of Wörz, it was required to cancel the original verdict, and declare Wörz not guilty. This shows that, even though the principle of 'free proof with intimate conviction' entrusts the judge with discretionary powers, the standard for proving wrongful conviction is clearly lower than that for proving guilt.

12.6 The Restatement of the Standard of Proof for Redressing Wrongful Convictions in China

In the course of determining wrongful conviction, both ambiguity and antagonism can be encountered; to overcome this, there should be a unified and clear standard of proof, else the determination would differ according to those involved, or to details of the event, the time or the place. Some wrongful convictions are determined with relative ease, unimpeded, while others are pushed forward step by painful step. Some people will use the excuse that the standard of proof is not clear, or else apply their own interpretation of the standard to obstruct the determination and rectification of a wrongful conviction, leading to endless appeals and petitions.

Determination of the true facts behind a case of wrongful conviction is not always a black-and-white process; sometimes there is a gray zone, meaning that there is no way to determine with accuracy whether the defendant is guilty or not. In other words, the line between good guys and bad guys is not clear-cut, but rather fuzzy, and vague. As a result, coming up with standards regarding the rectification of wrongful conviction becomes problematic. In what follows, I will discuss the standards for determining the facts leading to wrongful conviction cases. This discussion represents the level and degree of knowledge that law enforcement officials must bring to their roles within the judiciary.

Chinese law lacks clear-cut standards for proving wrongful conviction, but does stipulate the conditions for enacting a retrial. And since retrial is the first step towards redressing wrongful conviction, criteria for retrial and standards for proving wrongful conviction are closely connected. Article 242 of CPL states: "If a petition presented by a party or his legal representative or his near relative conforms to any of the following conditions, the people's court shall retry the case: (1) There is new evidence to prove that the confirmation of the facts in the original judgment or ruling is definitely wrong; (2) The evidence upon which the conviction was made and the punishment was meted out is unreliable or insufficient, or should be excluded according to law, or the major pieces of evidence for proving the facts in the case contradict each other; (3) The application of law in making the original judgment or ruling is definitely incorrect; or (4) The judges in trying the case committed acts of embezzlement, bribery, or malpractices for personal gain, or bent the law in making judgment."

Article 243 states: "If the president of a People's Court at any level finds some definite error in a legally effective judgment or ruling of his court as to the determination of facts or application of law, he shall refer the case to the trial committee for deliberation." Paragraphs two and three of this article also use the term 'definite error'. According to the rules stipulated here, standards for proving wrongful conviction have been interpreted to be standards of 'definite error'.

Before discussing these standards further, I first want to explain the method of proving wrongful conviction in China. Based on the different ways wrongful conviction is discovered and proved, we can classify the methods for proving wrongful conviction into two types: direct proof, and indirect proof.

The first method means using evidence to prove that the accused did not commit the criminal act for which they had been convicted. This situation is common to cases where the alleged victims have "come back from the dead", as in the case of She Xianglin and to instances where major evidence from the original trial has been re-examined and subsequently rejected, as with the American Innocence Project.

The second type (indirect) includes methods for counter-proof, meaning proof that another person has committed the crime thus indirectly proves the defendant from the original trial to be not guilty. This situation is common to cases where a suspect or defendant in another case confesses that he is the true perpetrator in the original case, as in the case of Nie Shubin, and when evidence prove the existence and guilt of true perpetrator, as in the case of Shi Dongyu.[31] It is also common to cases where new evidence comes to light and which indicates clearly an error in the original verdict, as in the case of Du Peiwu.[32] Such scenarios occur also in combination.

As stated earlier, in some cases proof of wrongful conviction may be ironclad, as with the case of She Xianglin. Not every case must achieve such a high standard. The "definite error" rule is sometimes interpreted to mean equal to the standard that demands "clear facts in the case, with full and reliable evidence" to issue a guilty verdict, with the result that the accused is often required to provide evidence full and reliable enough to prove their innocence, or else full and reliable enough to prove that another person is the true perpetrator. This interpretation is mistaken, or at least inappropriate.

First of all, "definite error" cannot be understood to mean that all the facts leading to a determination of guilt are incorrect, but rather that errors may exist in some of the facts. For example, in the case of Shi Dongyu the original verdict had been based on forensic testing of blood type to determine the traces of blood on the defendant's clothing to be that of the victim, Guan Chuansheng. Later a second test showed the original test results to have been erroneous, and that the defendant's clothing had no blood from the victim on it. This is a determination of "definite error". This standard neither demands full and reliable evidence that Shi Dongyu was not the murderer, nor did it require full and reliable evidence that Liang Baoyou was the murderer.

Second, Item (2) of Article 242, as stated above, stipulates that if: "The evidence upon which the conviction was made and the punishment was meted out is unreliable or insufficient, or should be excluded according to law, or the major pieces of evidence for proving the facts in the case contradict each other". The law certainly does not

[31] I introduced this case in Chap. 6.

[32] I mentioned this case in Chap. 1.

require reliable and sufficient evidence, but rather should be seen as holding to a standard of finding "evidence either unreliable or insufficient". This is similar to the "formation of a reasonable doubt" standard of the USA and the UK, and also to the German 'overturn the intimate conviction' standard.

Finally, when using counter-evidence to prove that the claimant is not guilty, proving that another person is the true culprit certainly goes hand-in-hand with proving the conviction to be wrongful. The two standards are not equivalent. Excluding the possibility that the suspects committed the crime together, the probability that one of the two suspects committed the crime may go up or down. For example, in the Nie Shubin case, if the probability that Wang Shujin committed the murder and rape was 20%, then the chance that Nie Shubin committed the crime would have been 80%. And if Wang's odds reached 80%, then there would have been only a 20% chance that Nie could have been the perpetrator.

In summary, the rules regarding the standard for proving wrongful conviction in Chinese law are not clear enough and need to be enhanced with interpretation by relevant judicial agencies. It may be beneficial to learn from and perhaps incorporate aspects of the UK method of 'setting out the standards in levels', separated accordingly to redress wrongful convictions. The first standard relates to calling for a retrial or registering a wrongful conviction case, somewhat similar to the 'definite error' standard explained above, and similar in scope to the UK Criminal Cases Review Commission standard for sending cases up to the Appeals Court: "possessing true potential to overturn the conviction". The second level is the standard determining wrongful conviction in retrial, which can be formulated as "preponderant evidence", meaning that the evidence proves the probability the claimant is not guilty to be greater than the probability of guilt. The third level is the standard for determining state compensation, which can be formulated as "evidence being reliable and sufficient", meaning that reliable evidence proves sufficiently that the claimant is indeed not guilty.

References

He, Jiahong. 2016. *Back from the Dead: Wrongful Convictions and Criminal Justice in China*. Honolulu: University of Hawai'I Press.

He, Jiahong. 2017. Rethinking on the Nie Shubin Case. *Theoretical Horizon* 2017(1): 42–47.

He, Jiahong, and Ran He. 2012. Empirical studies of Wrongful Convictions in Mainland China. *University of Cincinnati Law Review* 80 (4): 1277–1292.

Li, Xianfeng. 2013. Final verdict: Wang Shujin is not the true perpetrator in the Nie Shubin Case. *Jinghua Times*, Sept 28.

Liu, Pinxin (ed.). 2009. *Criminal Wrongful Conviction: Factors and Strategies*. Beijing: China Legal Publishing House.

McConville, Mike, and Geoffrey Wilson. 2003. *English Criminal Justice Process*. Translated by Yao Yongji and others. Beijing: Law Press.

Thompson, S.G. 2008. Beyond a Reasonable Doubt? Reconsidering Uncorroborated Eyewitness Identification Testimony. *UC Davis Law Review* 41: 1487–1545.

Zhang, Jian. 2013. The four groups of prosecution evidence prove that Wang Shujin is not the true perpetrator. *Jinghua Times*, July 11.
Zhao, Ling. 2007. A culprit with a conscience and court without: Nie Shubin's wrongful conviction. *Southern Weekend*, Nov 2.
Zhao, Ling. 2009. Uncertain prospects for overturning the Nie Shubin case. *Southern Weekend*, Nov 11.
Zhou, Xifeng. 2005. Wang Shujin, madman. *Xiaoxiang Morning News*, March 7.
Zhou, Zunyou. 2011. *'How Does Germany Rectify Wrongful Conviction?' Evidence Law Forum*, 16, 240–269. Beijing: Law Press.

Erratum to: Methodology of Judicial Proof and Presumption

Erratum to:
J. He, *Methodology of Judicial Proof and Presumption*, Masterpieces of Contemporary Jurisprudents in China, https://doi.org/10.1007/978-981-10-8025-8

In the original version of the book, the section numbering has been changed from Roman numerals (I, II, III, IV…) to Arabic numerals (1.1, 1.2, 1.3, 1.4…) in all the chapters. The erratum book has been updated with the change.

The updated online version of this book can be found at
https://doi.org/10.1007/978-981-10-8025-8

J. He, *Methodology of Judicial Proof and Presumption*,
Masterpieces of Contemporary Jurisprudents in China,
https://doi.org/10.1007/978-981-10-8025-8_13

Bibliography

Bartlett, Robert. 2007. *Trial by Fire and Water: The Medieval Judicial Ordeal*. Translated by Xin Xu, et al. Hangzhou: Zhejiang Rennin Publishing House.

Bian, Jianlin (ed.). 2000. *Evidence Law*. Beijing: China University of Political Science and Law Press.

Bian, Jianlin (ed.). 2004. *The Theory of Criminal Proof*. Beijing: China Renmin Public Security University Press.

Chen, Shengqing (ed.). 1982. *Legal History of Foreign Countries*. Beijing: Peking University Press.

Chen, Yiyun (ed.). 1991. *The Study of Evidence*. Beijing: China Renmin University Press.

Chen, Xingliang. 2001. *Criminal Jurisprudence In and Of Itself*. Beijing: The Commercial Press.

Chen, Weidong (ed.). 2002. *The Study of Countermeasures for Issues of Fact in Criminal Procedure*. Beijing: China Legal Publishing House.

Chen, Ruihua. 2010. *The Criminal Procedure of Chinese Mode*. Beijing: Law Press China.

Fan, Chongyi (ed.). 1999. *The Law of Criminal Procedure*. Beijing: China University of Political Science and Law Press.

Fan, Chongyi (ed.). 2001. *Evidence Law*. Beijing: Law Press China.

Guo, Xinyang. 2011. *Analysis of Misjudged Criminal Cases*. Beijing: China Renmin Public Security University Press.

He, Jiahong (ed.). 2014. *Late Justice—The Ten Wrongful Convictions Impacting China's Judiciary*. Beijing: China Legal Publishing House.

He, Jiahong, and Weiping Zhang (eds.). 2000. *Foreign Evidentiary Laws: Selected Translations*, vol. 1. Beijing: The Publishing House of People's Court.

Hochstedler, Steury Ellen, and Nancy Frank. 2002. *Criminal Court Process*. Translated by Weidong Chen & Meijun Xu. Beijing: China Renmin University Press, 2002.

Jon, Waltz. 1983. *Criminal Evidence*, 2nd ed. Chicago: Nelson-Hall Press.

Liang, Zhiping (ed.). 1994. *Cultural Explanations of Law*. Beijing: SDX Joint Publishing Company.

Lin, Shantian. 2004. *Criminal Procedure Law*. Taipei: Wunan Publishing House.

Liu, Jinyou (ed.). 2001. *Evidence Law*. Beijing: China University of Political Science and Law Press.

Liu, Pinxin (ed.). 2009. *Criminal Wrongful Conviction: Factors and Strategies*. Beijing: China Legal Publishing House.

McConville, Mike, and Geoffrey Wilson. 2003. *English Criminal Justice Process*. Translated by Yao Yongji et al. Beijing: Law Press China.

Noye, William Andrew. 1991. *Evidence: Its History and Policies*. Australia: Butterworths Pty Ltd.

Qi, Shujie (ed.). 2002. *British Law of Evidence*. Xiamen: Xiamen University Press.

Xia, Zhiqian. 1990. *Trial by the Gods*. Beijing: SDX Joint Publishing Company.

Yang, Fengkun (ed.). 1980. *Collected Cases of Justice Rectified*, original text by Song Ci of the Southern Song Dynasty (1127–1279). Beijing: Qunzhong Publishing House.

J. He, *Methodology of Judicial Proof and Presumption*,
Masterpieces of Contemporary Jurisprudents in China,
https://doi.org/10.1007/978-981-10-8025-8

Zhang, Hongsheng (ed.). 1983. *Western History of Law Thought*. Beijing: Peking University Press.

Zhang, Jinfan (ed.). 1985. *History of Chinese laws*. Beijing: Qunzhong Publishing House.

Zhang, Wen, et al. 1997. *Essentials of Criminal Liabilities*. Beijing: Peking University Press.

Zhang, Yuqing. 2004. *Criminal Proceedings: Theory and Practice*. Taipei: Wunan Publishing House.

Zhou, Lengjia. 1985. *The Four Strange Cases in the Late Qing Dynasty*. Beijing: Qunzhong Publishing House.

Zuo, Weimin. 2010. *The Prospect of Criminal Procedure in China*. Beijing: SDX Joint Publishing Company.

MIX
Papier aus verantwortungsvollen Quellen
Paper from responsible sources
FSC® C105338

If you have any concerns about our products,
you can contact us on
ProductSafety@springernature.com

In case Publisher is established outside the EU,
the EU authorized representative is:
Springer Nature Customer Service Center GmbH
Europaplatz 3, 69115 Heidelberg, Germany

Printed by Libri Plureos GmbH
in Hamburg, Germany